Understanding China

The series will provide you with in-depth information on China's social, cultural and economic aspects. It covers a broad variety of topics, from economics and history to law, philosophy, cultural geography and regional politics, and offers a wealth of materials for researchers, doctoral students, and experienced practitioners.

Ren Xiaolan

Patent Administrative Litigation

Rules and Review

Ren Xiaolan
Beijing, China

Translated by
Liu Li
University of International Business
and Economics
Beijing, China

Proofread by
Shi Yueru
Beijing Wiztech Co., Ltd.
Beijing, China

ISSN 2196-3134   ISSN 2196-3142   (electronic)
Understanding China
ISBN 978-981-97-1130-7   ISBN 978-981-97-1131-4   (eBook)
https://doi.org/10.1007/978-981-97-1131-4

Jointly published with Intellectual Property Publishing House
The print edition is not for sale in China (Mainland). Customers from China (Mainland) please order the print book from: Intellectual Property Publishing House.
ISBN of the Co-Publisher's edition: 978-751-30-4320-5

Translation from the Chinese language edition: "专利行政诉讼案件法律重述与评论" by Ren Xiaolan, © Intellectual Property Publishing House 2016. Published by Intellectual Property Publishing House. All Rights Reserved.

This work was sponsored by the Chinese Fund for the Humanities and Social Sciences (20WFXB006)
© Intellectual Property Publishing House 2024

This work is subject to copyright. All rights are solely and exclusively licensed by the Publisher, whether the whole or part of the material is concerned, specifically the rights of translation, reprinting, reuse of illustrations, recitation, broadcasting, reproduction on microfilms or in any other physical way, and transmission or information storage and retrieval, electronic adaptation, computer software, or by similar or dissimilar methodology now known or hereafter developed.
The use of general descriptive names, registered names, trademarks, service marks, etc. in this publication does not imply, even in the absence of a specific statement, that such names are exempt from the relevant protective laws and regulations and therefore free for general use.
The publishers, the authors, and the editors are safe to assume that the advice and information in this book are believed to be true and accurate at the date of publication. Neither the publishers nor the authors or the editors give a warranty, express or implied, with respect to the material contained herein or for any errors or omissions that may have been made. The publishers remain neutral with regard to jurisdictional claims in published maps and institutional affiliations.

This Springer imprint is published by the registered company Springer Nature Singapore Pte Ltd.
The registered company address is: 152 Beach Road, #21-01/04 Gateway East, Singapore 189721, Singapore

If disposing of this product, please recycle the paper.

Foreword

The Guiding Case system, serving as an effective complement to the application of statutory laws in China, is assuming an increasingly significant role in the administrative and judicial review of intellectual property cases. Specifically, in patent cases encompassing complex technology and intricate professional knowledge across diverse fields and employing relatively abstract and generalized review criteria, the utilization of typical cases as supplementary guidance in the handling of patent law applications aids in the establishment of unified review standards. This approach also ensures the fulfillment of reasonable expectations from the involved parties and the public, thereby facilitating a fair trial.

Xiaolan and I have enjoyed a long-standing acquaintance, originating from our prior collaboration at the Patent Reexamination Board. We have also had the privilege of engaging in insightful discussions, sharing a workspace, and serving on the same panel at the Intellectual Property Court of the Supreme People's Court. Xiaolan is an accomplished professional, a quick learner, a willing researcher, and also a diligent reviewer. Over a span of five years, she has diligently collected, organized, and contemplated numerous typical cases of patent administrative litigation, culminating in the completion of this remarkable book. It is a great honor for me to be one of the book's first readers and to contribute the foreword prior to its publication.

The author carefully selected 200 recent patent administrative retrial cases and cases removed for trial by the Supreme People's Court, including inventions, utility models, and designs protected by the *Patent Law* and involving both the requests for reexamination of rejected patent applications and requests for invalidation of patent rights. The book consists of two parts. Part I includes 14 chapters. Taking the internal logic of the patent law system as a general framework, the author discusses the following legal topics in detail, starting from the core of patent protection—the technical solution claimed by the claims, revolving around the examination of claim construction, patentable subject matter, practical applicability, sufficient disclosure, the definiteness of claims, the determination of the prior art disclosures, novelty, inventive step, whether the claims are supported by the description, whether the claims lack necessary technical features, whether the amendments go beyond the scope, procedural issues, and the related legal issues of designs. Each chapter focuses on several specific issues and presents to the readers the decisions of the Patent Reexamination Board and the courts of the first instance and the second instance and the final opinions of the Supreme People's Court in patent granting and patent confirmation cases through the restatement of the laws in concrete cases. Part II consists of the remaining seven chapters. After summarizing the cases in Part I, the author proposes her academic opinions and suggestions regarding current hot issues, difficulties, and controversies in patent law, such as the examination of claim construction, sufficient disclosure, the definiteness of the claims, whether the amendments go beyond the scope, and the *ex officio* review in the reexamination procedure and the invalidation procedure, based on her solid research and rich experience in examination practice. The author also cited many cases of the U.S. Court of Appeals for the Federal Circuit and the U.S. Supreme Court to compare and analyze for a full discussion on the definiteness of claims.

This book is published against the backdrop of both the administrative and judicial organs of intellectual property valuing the significance of guiding cases. Its timely and practical nature establishes it as a rare gem within the industry, serving as a reliable reference for professionals.

Beijing, China
April 2016

MA Hao
Deputy Director
Examination Management
Department of the Patent Office,
China National Intellectual Property
Administration

Translator's Preface

It is a great honor and pleasure to be the translator of the book *Legal Restatements and Comments on Patent: Administrative Litigation Cases*. The book provides a comprehensive and in-depth discussion of the legal principles governing patent litigation cases and an analysis of specific cases. The author, Ms. Xiaolan Ren, is a renowned expert in the field of patent law who has years of practice in patent administrative agencies and work experience at the Supreme People's Court. Her research and practice have had an extensive and profound influence on the development of China's *Patent Law*. Ms. Ren collected and summarized over 200 court judgments on patent administrative litigation cases (2009–2015) and conducted in-depth analysis and comments from a legal perspective, aiming to provide a reference for lawyers, judges, scholars, and other practitioners in the field of patent administrative litigation. Therefore, the English version of this book is meaningful for understanding the Chinese patent legal system and its practice. The translation of this book is sponsored by the Chinese Academic Translation Project of the National Social Science Fund, which aims to introduce Chinese academic works to the world and to promote exchanges and cooperation between Chinese and foreign intellectual circles.

The translation of this book is a complex and challenging task. It is especially true when translating patent law books from Chinese to English, which contain a vast amount of technical terminology and legal jargon that must be accurately rendered in the target language to ensure that the original text's meaning is preserved. One of the biggest challenges in translating this book is the need to accurately convey the technical terminology and legal jargon, which requires the translator to have not only a thorough understanding of the legal concepts and terminology in both languages but also a profound understanding of technology as the translation of patent claims requires a STEM background to understand the content thoroughly. In addition, due to the particularity of patent claims, some specific sentence structures and long sentences need to be employed to reflect the features of patent claims. Another challenge is the need to convey the cultural context and nuances accurately. The book often contains references to cultural concepts and practices that may not be easily understood by readers in the English language. Therefore, to ensure that the translation is faithful to the original text, the translator must have a thorough understanding of the cultural context and cultural nuances of both languages. Besides, the *Patent Law* in China has been amended after the completion of this book, so the translator needs to be aware of the recent changes, even including the changed structure of the patent administrative agencies, to keep the translated version of the book up to date.

By taking the time to understand and address these challenges, I tried my best to ensure that the translation was accurate and faithful to the original text. I also took a few measures to ensure the best possible results. First, I spent quite some time getting familiar with the *Patent Law* of China and that of other major countries in the world. Luckily, my academic background (master's in English and doctorate in Law) helped immensely in this aspect. Second, I added some translator's notes to correct certain harmless errors made by the author and to provide additional information regarding specific details to help the readers better understand the text. Moreover, I also relied on the help of a native legal professional in the translation team to review and proofread the translation to ensure that any errors were caught before the text was published. Despite all the efforts, some errors may still occur due to the limitation of my ability. All these errors remain the errors of mine.

At last, I would like to express my sincere gratitude to my editors, whose names may not be all listed here; however, the gratefulness is all the same: Mr. Huang Qingming, Ms. Liu Shuang, Ms. Shi Yueru, Mr. Wang Ruipu, and Ms. Fang Xi, without whose help and valuable advice this translation task would not have been accomplished so smoothly.

Beijing, China   Liu Li

Preface

In recent years, the intellectual property cases heard and concluded by the Intellectual Property Division of the Supreme People's Court have kept rising, among which patent administrative cases have increased significantly. For example, statistics show that 31 patent administrative cases were concluded in 2010, and the number peaked in 2015 to reach 62 cases.[1]

Since 2008, the Supreme People's Court has begun to publish typical cases with guiding opinions concluded that year in the form of an annual report. Although not necessarily binding in the same way as the Supreme Court opinions in common law countries, these cases serve as a powerful guide for lower courts and exert significant social influence. Therefore, in April 2015, the Supreme People's Court Intellectual Property Guiding Case Research Center (Beijing) was established in the Beijing Intellectual Property Court, aiming to "collect, compile, and edit guiding cases to summarize intellectual property trial rules and experience promptly, properly publish them, further standardize judicial conduct, enhance judicial openness, distill judicial wisdom to promote the unification of law application vividly and enhance judicial credibility."[2] Against this backdrop, it will be of great benefit to the prediction of case results by studying the judgments of the Supreme People's Court.

In addition to the cases selected in the annual report, the author found that the rules applied by the Supreme People's Court in some other cases were also a vital reference for the Patent Reexamination Board[3] and all sectors of society. In particular, if the same types of cases were put together, the evolution of the views held by the Supreme People's Court on this type of issue could be easily seen, which was also helpful for the research and analysis of the future development direction of the Supreme People's Court on such issues.

---

[1] The author collected 273 judgments in total, among which three were decided in 2009, 31 in 2010, 41 in 2011, 33 in 2012, 52 in 2013, 51 in 2014, and 62 in 2015.

[2] People's Court Daily, April 24, 2015.

[3] Translator's note: When the author finished the book, the Patent Reexamination Board was referred to as the Patent Reexamination Board of China Patent Office of State Intellectual Property Office (SIPO). In 2019, it was renamed the Patent Reexamination and Invalidation Department (PRD) of the Patent Office, China National Intellectual Property Administration (CNIPA).

Over the years, the author has been collecting and studying the Supreme People's Court's judgments and rulings through various channels. Whenever encountering referential judgments, the author habitually took notes and ruminated on them in her spare time. She had accumulated study notes of more than 100,000 words on about 200 judgments over the years without even noticing. After editing and sorting out these cases in a specific logical sequence, the author tried to restore and demonstrate the overall approach of the Supreme People's Court.

As a Chinese proverb says, "It is fun to listen to music oneself and even more fun to listen together." The author hopes that the study notes of these judgments can be enlightening to readers. Although the author hopes to be able to reproduce the opinions of the judgments as objectively as possible, trying to avoid bringing in her personal opinions by quoting the statements and opinions of the judgments in this book, it is very natural for people to interpret the same judgment differently due to differences in stances and understanding. Therefore, this book only represents the author's understanding and may not be consistent with the official interpretation of the Supreme People's Court. In addition, to facilitate readers' understanding of the gist of the cited judgments, the author also supplemented the background information about the cases when necessary. In principle, the author arranged the topics according to the logical order of patent examination. However, the index of the titles at all levels is only for the convenience of the readers to locate and read the text and does not strictly follow a logical order among them.

In addition to restating the relevant rules, the author offered commentary on certain subjects in her shallow understanding, either supporting or questioning the views of the Court, all representing the author's personal views.

Beijing, China   Ren Xiaolan

Contents

Part I Legal Restatements

1 Claim Construction 3
   1.1   The Broadest Reasonable Interpretation Principle 3
   1.2   Determination of the Scope of Protection by the Terms
          of the Claims 4
   1.3   Construction of Technical Features in the Claims Based
          on Disclosure Contained in the Description 6
   1.4   Common Understandings of a Person Skilled in the Art 12
   1.5   Construction of Product-by-Process Claims 13
   1.6   Construction of Features of Effect 14
   1.7   Limitation of Features of Drug Administration and Side
          Effects on Swiss-Type Claims 14
   1.8   Similarities and Differences in Claim Construction
          in Patent Granting, Patent Confirmation and Patent
          Infringement Procedures 17

2 Patentable Subject Matter 19
   2.1   Technical Problem, Technical Means and Technical Effect 19
   2.2   Patentability of Business Methods 22

3 Practical Applicability 23
   3.1   Violation of the Law of Conservation of Energy 23
   3.2   The Relationship Between Practical Applicability
          and Sufficient Disclosure 26

4 Sufficiency of Disclosure 29
   4.1   The Subject to Determine Sufficiency of Disclosure 29
   4.2   Steps to Determine Sufficiency of Disclosure 31
   4.3   Ambiguous Technical Means 32
   4.4   Claimed Technical Problems not Solved 33
   4.5   A Lack of Necessary Experimental Evidence to Confirm
          Technical Effects 34

	4.6	Post-filing Date Evidence to Prove Sufficiency of Disclosure	36
5	**Definiteness of Claims**		39
6	**Disclosure of Prior Art Documents**		41
	6.1	Determining the Disclosure of a Reference Document by Considering It as a Whole	41
	6.2	Does the Disclosure of a Reference Document Include the Disclosure of Its Cited Documents	43
	6.3	Implicit Disclosure in Reference Documents	45
	6.4	Shall the Practical Applicability of Relevant Contents Be Considered in Determining the Disclosure of Reference Documents	48
7	**Novelty**		49
8	**Inventive Step**		51
	8.1	Technical Field and the Closest Prior Art	51
	8.2	Comparison of Technical Features	53
	8.3	Technical Problems to Be Solved by the Invention and Technical Effect	56
	8.4	Teachings	61
	8.5	Auxiliary Standards to Determine an Inventive Step	65
	8.6	Inventive Step of Inventions and Utility Models	69
	8.7	The Inventive Step of Chemical Inventions	72
9	**Is a Claim Supported by the Description**		77
	9.1	A Claim Contains a Technical Solution that Obviously Cannot Achieve the Purpose of the Invention	77
	9.2	Solutions not Covered by the Embodiments Are not Supported (by the Description) Due to a Lack of Prior Art	78
	9.3	Numerical Range	80
	9.4	"Dead Pixels" in the Description	81
	9.5	Inconsistencies Between the Description and the Technical Solutions in the Claims	82
	9.6	Obvious Errors in Claims	85
	9.7	Determination of Whether a Dependent Claim is Supported by the Description	87
	9.8	Burden of Proof Regarding Whether a Claim is Supported by the Description in an Invalidation Procedure	88

10	**Claims Lacking Essential Technical Features**	91
	10.1 Basic Approaches for Determining Whether a Claim Lacks Essential Technical Features	92
	10.2 The Relationship Between Rule 21(2) of the *Implementing Regulations of the Patent Law* and Article 26(3)/26(4) of the *Patent Law*	94
	10.3 Will Features of Function Render a Claim Incompliant with Rule 21(2) of the *Implementing Regulations of the Patent Law*	96
11	**Amendments Beyond Scope**	99
	11.1 The Legislative Intent of Article 33 of the *Patent Law*	99
	11.2 Basic Criteria for Determining the Scope of Amendments	101
	11.3 Generalization by Generic Terms	102
	11.4 Amendments by Cancellation	103
	11.5 Amendments of Technical Features	104
	11.6 Closed Claims Amended to Open Claims	106
	11.7 The Relationship Between the Amendments Beyond Scope and the Points of Novelty	108
	11.8 The Relationship Between the Restriction to the Amendments of Patent Application Documents and the Scope of Patent Protection	109
	11.9 The Relationship Between the Restriction to the Amendments of Patent Application Documents and Estoppel	110
12	**Procedure Related Issues**	113
	12.1 Selective Application of the *Guidelines for Patent Examination*	113
	12.2 *Ex Officio* Examination in Reexamination Procedure	114
	12.3 Burden of Presenting Evidence of Common Knowledge by the Panel in the Reexamination Procedure	117
	12.4 *Ex officio* Examination and Examination upon Request in the Invalidation Procedure	118
	12.5 Burden of Proof on Common Knowledge in the Invalidation Procedure	124
	12.6 Amendments in the Invalidation Procedure	125
	12.7 Principle of Hearing	128
	12.8 Determination of the Authenticity of Evidence	129
	12.9 Determination of the Openness of Evidence	133
	12.10 New Evidence Submitted During Administrative Litigation	135
	12.11 Options for the Court to Overturn the Decision of the Patent Reexamination Board	137

13 Issues Related to Designs ... 139
- 13.1 A Normal Consumer ... 139
- 13.2 Determination of Identical or Similar Categories ... 142
- 13.3 Comparison Basis for Identical or Similar Categories ... 143
- 13.4 Design Space ... 144
- 13.5 The Right to Apply for a Trademark as a Prior Legitimate Right Afforded by Article 23 of the *Patent Law* ... 145

14 Conclusion ... 149

Part II Comments

15 Similarities and Differences of Claim Construction in Patent Granting, Patent Confirmation, and Patent Infringement Procedures ... 153
- 15.1 The Meaning of Claim Construction ... 153
- 15.2 Possible Differences Among the Claim Construction Rules in Patent Granting, Patent Confirmation, and Patent Infringement Procedures ... 155
- 15.3 Similarities and Differences of Claim Construction in Patent Granting, Patent Confirmation, and Patent Infringement Procedures ... 158

16 Patentable Subject Matter ... 165

17 Sufficiency of Disclosure ... 167
- 17.1 The Intendment of Article 26(3) of the *Patent Law* ... 167
- 17.2 Determination Elements and Methods Under Article 26(3) of the *Patent Law* ... 170
- 17.3 Disclosure of the Uses of Product Inventions in Chemical and Pharmaceutical Fields ... 171
- 17.4 Extent of Disclosure of the Uses of Product Inventions in the Chemical and Pharmaceutical Fields ... 174
- 17.5 Experimental Evidence Submitted After the Filing Date to Prove Sufficiency of Disclosure ... 178

18 Definiteness of Claims ... 181
- 18.1 Legislative Intent ... 182
- 18.2 The Standard for Determining the Definiteness of Claims ... 183
- 18.3 Determining the Definiteness of Claims ... 183
- 18.4 Circumstances in Which the Issue of Indefinite Claims Arises ... 192
- 18.5 Lessons from the American Rules for Determining the Definiteness of Claims for the State Intellectual Property Office of the People's Republic of China ... 199

19	**Amendments Beyond Scope**	203
	19.1 The Legislative Intent of Article 33 of the *Patent Law*	204
	19.2 How to Understand "The Scope of the Original Description and Claims"	205
	19.3 Distinction Between "Point of Novelty" Amendments and "Contents Other Than Point of Novelty" Amendments	208
	19.4 Post-grant Remedial Procedures for "Contents Other Than Point of Novelty" Amendments Errors	209
20	***Ex Officio* Examination in the Reexamination Procedure**	213
	20.1 Consensus and Conflicts Between the Patent Reexamination Board and the People's Court	213
	20.2 The Purpose of the Reexamination Procedure and the Necessity of the *Ex Officio* Examination in This Procedure	220
	20.3 Factors to Be Considered in the Determination of the Scope of the *Ex Officio* Examination in the Reexamination Procedure	221
	20.4 How to Determine Obvious Substantive Defects Triggering an *Ex Officio* Examination	223
	20.5 Is the Request for Reexamination Being Denied a Prerequisite for the *Ex Officio* Examination	227
21	***Ex Officio* Examination in the Invalidation Procedure**	231
	21.1 The Legal Nature of the Invalidation Procedure	232
	21.2 The Relationship Between the Principle of Examination Upon Request and the Principle of *Ex Officio* Examination Under Dual Nature and the Application of the Principle of *Ex Officio* Examination	236
	21.3 Application of Rule 72 of the *Implementing Regulations of the Patent Law*	239
	21.4 How to Better Exercise the Administrative Function of Correcting Improper Patent Granting Without Causing Social Dissatisfaction	241
Appendix		245

Part I
Legal Restatements

In this part, the author summarizes and concludes the legal principles elucidated in over 130 patent administrative litigation cases adjudicated by the Supreme People's Court between 2009 and 2015. The restatement of these principles follows the sequential order of patent examination.

Chapter 1
Claim Construction

Claim construction is the core of the *Patent Law*, a constant focus in patent examination and infringement judgments. Article 59(1) of the *Patent Law* provides that: "The extent of protection of the patent right for invention or utility model shall be determined by the terms of the claims. The description and the appended drawings may be used to interpret the content of the claims."

1.1 The Broadest Reasonable Interpretation Principle

The Supreme People's Court (hereinafter the "SPC") interpreted the purposes and fundamental principles of claim construction in the case *(2014) Xing Ti Zi. No. 17*[1]:

In patent granting and patent confirmation procedures, the purpose of claim construction is to determine whether the claims meet the granting conditions or how valid they are by clarifying the meaning and scope of protection of these claims. Therefore, in claim construction, it is necessary to take into account the requirements of the *Patent Law* which provides that the technical solutions of the invention shall be sufficiently disclosed in the description, the claims be supported by the description, and the amendment to the patent application document not go beyond the scope of the disclosure contained in the initial description and the claims.

In general, in patent granting and patent confirmation procedures, the interpretation of the technical features in patent claims shall follow the broadest reasonable interpretation principle which means if the description does not explicitly define the meaning of the disputed technical features in the claims, in principle, the ordinary

---

[1] Invention patent No. 03123304.X. The invalidation decision (No. WX14794) maintained the validity of the patent right. The first instance judgment (*(2010) Yi Zhong Zhi Xing Chu Zi No. 3093*) and the second instance judgment (*(2011) Gao Xing Zhong Zi No. 1106*) both upheld the invalidation decision. The invalidation petitioner filed for a retrial. The SPC ruled to bring the case up for trial, vacated the invalidation decision, and the first and second instance judgments.

meanings of such technical features as understood by a person skilled in the art after reading the claims, description, and drawings shall be adopted. Undue limitations on such technical features shall be avoided when referring to the description or examination documents to conclude clearly whether the claims meet the granting conditions and the validity of such claims, to encourage the applicant to amend and polish the patent application documents, and improve the quality of patent granting and patent confirmations.

The case related to a reflective Sagnac interferometer-type all-fiber optical current transformer. Claim 1 recites "An all-fiber optical current transformer comprising at least an opto-electronic unit connected with an optical fiber current induction unit," mentioning nothing about the technical feature "reflective coating" (this feature appears in claim 10 which is a dependent claim). The SPC held that "In the description, neither is the technical solution with the 'reflective coating' described in the background of the invention, nor is the technical feature 'reflective coating' used to specifically define the 'all-fiber optical current transformer' recited in claim 1…The invalidation decision erred in the application of the law by introducing the additional technical feature in the dependent claim and the description to define the 'all-fiber optical current transformer' in claim 1 in a restrictive way."

1.2 Determination of the Scope of Protection by the Terms of the Claims

Claim construction shall be conducted primarily by "the terms of the claims," which means claim construction shall be based on the technical features defined in the claims to avoid interpreting into claims content that is not defined in the claims but only described in the description, thereby improperly narrowing the scope of the claims.

In the case *(2012) Zhi Xing Zi No. 59*,[2] the patent at issue relates to a laminate flooring. Claim 1 has a distinguishing feature of "wear-resistant paper layer" compared with the reference document. The patentee believed that claim 1 clearly defined that the wear-resistant paper layer was made by spraying aluminum oxide on the base paper and then impregnating the base paper in liquid melamine resin. The second instance judgment erred in holding that "Claim 1 does not specifically describe the relevant materials." Regarding this issue, the SPC held that "Claim 1 of the patent at issue does not define specifically the material of the 'wear-resistant paper layer.' Therefore, the 'wear-resistant paper layer' in product claim 1 cannot be restrictively construed as that 'the wear-resistant paper layer in this patent is made

---

[2] Invention patent application No. 03112761.4. The invalidation decision (No. WX14220) declared that claims 9 and 10 were invalid, and maintained the validity of the patent right to the extent of claims 1–5. The first instance judgment (*(2010) Yi Zhong Xing Chu Zi No. 2023*) maintained the invalidation decision. The second instance judgment (*(2011) Gao Xing Zhong Zi No. 911*) vacated the invalidation decision and the first instance judgment. The patentee filed for a retrial and was rejected by the SPC.

1.2 Determination of the Scope of Protection by the Terms of the Claims 5

by impregnating the base paper in liquid melamine resin' based on the recitation of the process claims and the embodiments in the description."

The case *(2011) Zhi Xing Zi No. 29*[3] related to similar issues. The patent at issue claims a trackless electric retractable gate. Claim 1 defines that the retractable gate includes "a plurality of crossbars (2) connected to the main frames, and connecting pipes (3) connecting the main frames...." The patentee asserted that claim 1 should be construed as including the feature that "each crossbar is articulated with only one connecting pipe" to be distinguished from the background of the invention which recited that "each crossbar is articulated with two to four connecting pipes." The SPC held that, under Article 59[4] of the *Patent Law*, "The description and the appended drawings may be used to interpret the content of the claims. However, if, to distinguish the claim from the prior art, or through direct generalization of the specific embodiments in the description, unclaimed features are directly included in the scope of protection of the claim, such unclaimed features are not within the scope of claim construction. Since claim 1 does not claim the articulated connection relationship between each crossbar and the connecting pipes, nor is there any such related expression, 'each crossbar is connected with one connecting pipe' is not the construction of claim 1."

"By the terms of the claims" does not mean that claim construction is restricted solely to the wording in the claims as to exclude the terms or depiction in the description; instead, it means to avoid actual amendment to the claims by relying on the content of the description. In the case *(2011) Zhi Xing Zi No. 91*,[5] the SPC emphasized that: "When there are different understandings of the meaning of a technical term in the claims, the definition or description of the technical term in the description or drawings may be relied on to construe the claims. In claim construction, technical features not recited in the claims shall not be read into the claims to constitute an actual amendment to the claims and compromise the public notice function of the claims."

Claim 1 of the patent at issue "only defines that 'pores and/or cracks are provided in the surface layer of the ceramic tile,' but does not recite any features related to the manufacturing method of the pores and/or cracks. The second instance judgment, relying solely on the relevant manufacturing method recited in the description, interpreted the pores and/or cracks in claim 1 as 'after polishing, the ceramic tile

---

[3] Invention patent No. 01107559.7. The invalidation decision (No. WX13794) declared that claims 1, 3, 4 and 6 were invalid, and maintained the validity of the patent right to the extent of claims 2 and 5. The first instance judgment (*(2010) Yi Zhong Xing Chu Zi No. 485*) maintained the invalidation decision. The second instance judgment (*(2010) Gao Xing Zhong Zi No. 1234*) upheld the first instance judgment. The patentee filed for a retrial and was rejected by the SPC.

[4] Translator's note: It was a mistake by the author. Article 56 should be Article 59.

[5] Utility model patent application No. 200620154970.8. The invalidation decision (No. WX13991) declared the patent right invalid in whole. The first instance judgment (*(2010) Yi Zhong Xing Chu Zi No. 483*) maintained the invalidation decision. The second instance judgment (*(2010) Gao Xing Zhong Zi No. 918*) vacated the invalidation decision and the first instance judgment. The invalidation petitioner filed for a retrial and was rejected by the SPC.

shows large and small pores and/or cracks formed by adding a pore-forming agent and firing'. This judgment erred in both fact-finding and law application."

The SPC reiterated its view in the case *(2011) Xing Ti Zi No. 8.*[6] The patent at issue claims a compound preparation consisting of sulbactam and piperacillin or cefotaxime. Welman Pharmaceutical claimed that the compound preparation in claim 1 referred to a (lyophilized) powder for injection. Regarding this, the SPC held that "If all technical features in claim 1 are taken into consideration together, claim 1 only defines the mixing of sulbactam with piperacillin or cefotaxime in a specific ratio to make a compound preparation without limiting the specific dosage form of this compound preparation. Compound preparation is a generic term with a definite meaning in the field, covering various specific dosage forms including (lyophilized) powder for injection. Welman Pharmaceutical contends that the compound preparation in claim 1 can only be interpreted as a (lyophilized) powder for injection in accordance with the closed drafting method of claim 1 and the description of the patent at issue. This contention is essentially to limit a generic term with a certain meaning in the claim to a specific term only recited in the description, which is an actual amendment to the claim rather than claim construction." As a result, the SPC dismissed Welman Pharmaceutical's contention for a restrictive interpretation of claim 1.

1.3 Construction of Technical Features in the Claims Based on Disclosure Contained in the Description

The description and its drawings are the most important vehicles for claim construction. When the description and its drawings are relied on for claim construction, the description should serve as the basis so that the scope of protection of the claims is consistent with the scope of the contents disclosed in the description. The SPC emphasized this point in the case *(2012) Xing Ti Zi No. 29.*[7] The issue of this case was the meaning of "the cathode plate" in claim 1 of the patent at issue, i.e., whether the structure and making method of the cathode plate in the description could be used to interpret "the cathode plate." In response to this issue, the SPC explained that "Generally, the cathode plate of a battery refers to a plate used as the cathode

---

[6] Invention patent application No. 97108942.6. The invalidation decision (No. WX8113) declared the patent right invalid in whole. The first instance judgment (*(2006) Yi Zhong Xing Chu Zi No. 786*) maintained the invalidation decision. The second instance judgment (*(2007) Gao Xing Zhong Zi No. 146*) vacated the invalidation decision and the first instance judgment. The invalidation petitioner filed for a retrial. The SPC vacated the second instance judgment and upheld the invalidation decision.

[7] Utility model patent application No. 01234722.1. The invalidation decision (No. WX13560) declared the patent right invalid in whole. The first instance judgment (*(2009) Yi Zhong Xing Chu Zi No. 2300*) vacated the invalidation decision. The second instance judgment (*(2011) Gao Xing Zhong Zi No. 676*) upheld the first instance judgment. The invalidation petitioner filed for a retrial. The SPC vacated the first and second instance judgments and upheld the invalidation decision.

1.3 Construction of Technical Features in the Claims Based on Disclosure ...

of the battery, which includes not only a single-layer plate, but also a multilayer plate, a multilayer plate formed by electroplating and a multilayer plate formed by other means such as lamination. When the description and its drawings are relied on for claim construction, the description should serve as the basis so that the scope of protection of the claims is consistent with the scope of contents disclosed in the description."

To further explain the meaning of "the cathode plate," the SPC examined the patent description at issue. Firstly, it could be inferred from the background of the invention in the patent description that "The patent applicant failed to recognize the respective pros and cons of a laminated cathode plate and an electroplated cathode plate from the moment the invention was motivated until the patent application was filed. Rather, the applicant realized that the reason why mercury could prevent leakage was that it could form isolation between zinc and other materials or metals to prevent contact between them. Therefore, the applicant believed that the key to solving the problems in producing mercury-free button batteries lay in finding a material that could replace mercury, so that it could also form isolation between zinc and other materials or metals, but the applicant did not realize that specific improvements should be made to the structure of the cathode plate itself."

Secondly, according to the Summary of the Invention section of the patent description in this case, "The applicant of the patent at issue mainly explored which metal electroplated on the cathode plate could successfully control the contact between the cathode zinc paste and the cathode plate. No tentative exploration on the structural changes of the cathode plate itself was made." Furthermore, the "patent applicant believed that the invention had been completed by plating indium or tin on the cathode plate to prevent gas swelling caused by the contact between zinc and the cathode plate without realizing whether further improvement could be made to this invention, such as by making further improvements to the structure of the cathode plate itself and by putting in creative work to do so."

In the patent at issue, "The cathode plate may be either a bare metal plate before nickel or copper plating, or a final product after being plated with indium or tin. Therefore, the patent applicant did not think of distinguishing the concepts of cathode plates to embody the improvements made to the structure of the cathode plate when applying for the patent." Therefore, the patent at issue was not an improvement to the structure of the cathode plate. Newleader Battery Industry (Deqing) Co., Ltd. and Zhaoqing Xinlida Batteries Industry Co., Ltd.'s assertion that the cathode plate in claim 1 of the patent at issue specifically referred to an electroplating structure had no factual and legal basis.

When the description is relied on to interpret disputed terms or features in the claims, it is necessary to first examine whether there is a specific interpretation of the disputed terms or features in the claims and/or description. If the claims and/or description fail to specifically define such terms, the ordinary meaning in the field shall generally be adopted and then whether the entire content of the description supports such a meaning shall be examined.

For example, in the two cases *(2013) Zhi Xing Zi No. 103* and *(2013) Zhi Xing Zi No. 104*,[8] regarding the meaning of the disputed term "connected to a bus" in claim 1, the SPC held that the description did not provide further details on this term. A person skilled in the art would usually interpret "connected to a bus" as "directly connected." Figure 2 of the description also showed direct connections. Therefore, the term "connected to a bus" should be interpreted as "directly connected."

In the case *(2012) Zhi Xing Zi No. 57*,[9] claim 1 of the patent at issue claims a process for smelting ferronickel from nickel oxide ore free of crystal water in a blast furnace. The two parties disputed over what was meant by "nickel oxide ore." The SPC explained in its judgment that "The description of the patent at issue does not specifically define nickel oxide ore. Generally, an ore containing nickel oxide is called nickel oxide ore, which includes nickel oxide ores both with and without chromium oxide. It is mentioned in the description of the patent that 'however, because Cr_2O_3 as concomitant commonly exists in laterite nickel ore, extremely high melting point of its own can lead to large viscosity of molten iron water so that iron water containing nickel and chrome can't flow out successfully and cause severe results such as frozen furnace and damaged furnace,' and that 'In metallurgical method of ferronickel by smelting nickel and chrome iron ore provided by the present invention, the addition of fluorite can lower the influence of chrome on furnace temperature effectively and raise the fluidity of iron water, meanwhile, because the addition quantity of fluorite in metallurgical method provided by the present invention is strictly calculated, the accidents, such as burnout of the crucible, caused by too high addition quantity of fluorite, can be effectively avoided' However, the description of the patent at issue neither recites anything about the relationship among the quantity of the added fluorite, the content of chromium oxide, and the fluidity of molten iron, nor does it mention what creative work the retrial petitioner has conducted on the basis of the special properties of chromium oxide in solving the problem in the fluidity of molten iron.

When the description and its drawings are relied on for claim construction, the description should serve as the basis so that the scope of protection of the claims is consistent with the scope of the contents disclosed in the description. In this sense, it is improper to interpret the nickel oxide ore in claim 1 of the patent at issue as nickel

---

[8] Utility model patent applications No. 200620047703.0 and No. 200620047704.5. The invalidation decisions (No. WX13862 and No. WX13861) both maintained the validity of the patent right. The first instance judgments (*(2006) Yi Zhong Xing Chu Zi No. 1837* and *(2006) Yi Zhong Xing Chu Zi No. 1936*) both maintained the invalidation decisions. The second instance judgments (*(2011) Gao Xing Zhong Zi No. 842* and *(2011) Gao Xing Zhong Zi No. 840*) both upheld the first instance judgments. The invalidation petitioner filed for a retrial and was rejected by the SPC.

[9] Invention patent application No. 200510102984.5. The invalidation decision (No. WX12819) declared that claims 1 and 2 and the technical solutions of claims 4–7 depending on claim 1 were invalid, and maintained the validity of the patent right to the extent of claim 3 and the technical solutions of claims 4–7 depending on claim 3. The first instance judgment (*(2009) Yi Zhong Xing Chu Zi No. 1138*) maintained the invalidation decision. The second instance judgment (*(2010) Gao Xing Zhong Zi No. 364*) upheld the first instance judgment. The patentee filed for a retrial and was rejected by the SPC.

1.3 Construction of Technical Features in the Claims Based on Disclosure … 9

oxide ore containing chromium oxide only and the quantity of fluorite added as the quantity calculated based on the content of chromium oxide in nickel oxide ore only.

Viewing from these two aspects, the protection scope of claim 1 of the patent at issue includes a process for smelting ferronickel from nickel oxide ore containing no chromium oxide in a blast furnace, wherein the quantity of the added fluorite also includes the quantity of the added fluorite calculated based on other impurities. Therefore, the retrial petitioner's assertion that the quantity of the added fluorite in the patent at issue is calculated based on the content of chromium oxide in nickel oxide ore and that the patent at issue solves a long-felt but unsolved technical problem, overcomes a technical prejudice, and produces an unexpected technical effect has no factual and legal basis and cannot be sustained."

The description is an indispensable part of a patent application, and the thesaurus of the patent applicant or the patentee. In the interpretation of the meaning of a disputed term or feature of the claims, all parts of the description shall be examined as a whole.

In the case *(2012) Zhi Xing Zi No. 23*,[10] the issue was whether, as claimed by the patentee, the "multi-SIM bidirectional transmit-receive" mobile phone in the claims of the patent at issue could be interpreted as a "multi-SIM simultaneous bidirectional transmit-receive" mobile phone. The SPC explained in the judgment: "Firstly, the claims of the patent only define 'a multi-SIM bidirectional transmit-receive' mobile phone, but do not explicitly define 'a multi-SIM simultaneous bidirectional transmit-receive' mobile phone. Secondly, the problem existing in the prior art disclosed by the patent description is that one mobile phone can only be equipped with one SIM card. People who need more than two numbers have to carry multiple mobile phones. The prior art fails to address the technical problem that 'when one of the SIM cards works, the other one stops.' In order to solve the technical problem recited in the description, the present invention provides a mobile phone with a bidirectional transmit-receive function and capable of holding multiple SIM cards. There are four paragraphs in Detailed Description of Specific Embodiments, where the first and second paragraphs recite the basic hardware structure of this patent without mentioning anything about the structure that can support the mobile phone's 'simultaneous' bidirectional transmit-receive function. The third paragraph relates to the operation of one SIM card in the mobile phone when a call comes in. The fourth paragraph relates to the operation of making a call on a specific SIM card. None of the above paragraphs relates to the 'simultaneous' bidirectional transmit-receive operations between a particular SIM card and other SIM cards. The second instance judgment held that the claims of this patent only defined 'multi-SIM bidirectional transmit-receive,' but did not specify whether the multiple SIMs worked in a 'simultaneous' transmit-receive manner or a 'non-simultaneous' bidirectional transmit-receive manner. The description of the patent at issue only mentioned 'multi-SIM

---

[10] Utility model patent application No. 200320102652.3. The invalidation decision (No. WX14276) declared the patent right invalid in whole. The first instance judgment (*(2010) Yi Zhong Xing Chu Zi No. 1168*) vacated the invalidation decision. The second instance judgment (*(2010) Gao Xing Zhong Zi No. 1422*) vacated the first instance judgment. The patentee filed for a retrial and was rejected by the SPC.

bidirectional transmit-receive,' but did not disclose any specific technical solutions for the multi-SIM simultaneous bidirectional transmit-receive function. Therefore, it is not improper for the second instance judgment to find that claim 1 of this patent lacked novelty...".

The Background Art, as part of the description, may also be a basis for claim construction. In the case *(2015) Zhi Xing Zi No. 7*,[11] the comparison between the patent at issue and the reference document involved the interpretation of the term "bell-shaped wheel hub" in claim 1. The SPC held that a bell-shaped structure was introduced in the Background Art section of the description of the patent. Although this introduction was "provided in the Background Art section, a technology described in the Background Art section in a description is not necessarily a technology that has been disclosed and shall not be assumed as forming part of the prior art, and there is no corresponding evidence to prove that the bell-shaped hub is prior art in this case. Moreover, in this case, as far as the bell-shaped wheel hub is concerned, the patent does not make any further changes based on the shape of the wheel hub disclosed in the background art. That is, the patent description shows that the bell-shaped wheel hub introduced in the Background Art section is adopted by this patent. Therefore, the content recited in the Background Art section of this patent description may be used for claim construction... The technical feature 'bell-shaped wheel hub' may be interpreted as all hubs with a nearly bell-shaped structure."

Claim construction is to clarify the inherent meanings of the terms or features in the claims. The objects of the invention and the technical effects recited in the description may be used to interpret the meanings of the disputed terms or features. The interpretation of the technical features or terms shall be consistent with the objects of the invention and shall not be contradictory to the common knowledge in the art.

There are several cases of the SPC involving interpretation in line with the objects of the invention, including *(2013) Zhi Xing Zi No. 109* and *(2013) Zhi Xing Zi No. 110*.[12] The issues in these two cases both related to a component, the "upper driven wheel." Claim 1 defines: "upper driven wheels (9) provided on the left and right rolling wheel frames (T) to contact with the upper sides of the endless belts

---

[11] Utility model patent No. 200820139377.5. The invalidation decision (No. WX20200) maintained the validity of the patent right. The first instance judgment (*(2013) Yi Zhong Xing Chu Zi No. 2289*) vacated the invalidation decision. The second instance judgment (*(2014) Gao Xing Zhong Zi No. 1126*) upheld the first instance judgment. The patentee filed for a retrial and was rejected by the SPC.

[12] The case *(2013) Zhi Xing Zi No. 109* involved the invention patent application No. 99110929.5. The invalidation decision (No. WX16929) maintained the validity of the patent right. The first instance judgment (*(2012) Yi Zhong Xing Chu Zi No. 272*) maintained the invalidation decision. The second instance judgment (*(2012) Gao Xing Zhong Zi No. 1076*) upheld the first instance judgment. The invalidation petitioner filed for a retrial and was rejected by the SPC. The case *(2013) Zhi Xing Zi No. 110* involved the same invention patent, and the invalidation decision (No. WX13733) declared the patent right invalid in whole. The first instance judgment (*(2009) Yi Zhong Xing Chu Zi No. 2684*) maintained the invalidation decision. The second instance judgment (*(2010) Gao Xing Zhong Zi No. 383*) vacated the first instance judgment and the invalidation decision. The invalidation petitioner filed for a retrial and was rejected by the SPC.

1.3 Construction of Technical Features in the Claims Based on Disclosure ...

(11) to limit sagging of the endless belts (11) ...and the diameter of the upper driven wheel (9) is set such that from the side view, the lower side of the outer periphery of the upper driven wheel stretches out more downward than the bottom of the rolling wheel frame (T)." The issue was whether the lower side of the upper driven wheel was in contact with the endless belt.

The SPC held that based on the recitation of claim 1, logically the upper driven wheel could stretch downward until it was in contact with the endless belt. However, it could be seen from the purpose of setting the upper driven wheels and its technical effects that, if the upper and lower sides of the upper driven wheel were in contact with the endless belt at the same time, "obviously there is no space for receiving a protrusion when there is one, which does not conform to the object of the invention and cannot solve the technical problem or produce the intended technical effect of the invention. The second instance judgment is correct in holding that 'it cannot be concluded that the lower side of the upper driven wheel is also in contact with the endless belt based on the claims, description, and drawings of this patent.' This finding is not to read the technical features that is only reflected in the description and its drawings into patent claims to limit the scope of protection of the patent right, or to directly define the meaning of the corresponding technical feature in the claims by the specific structure that is only reflected in the drawings of the description, rather, it is to construe the claims in accordance with the description and its drawings, which complies with the law."

Another case is *(2013) Xing Ti Zi No. 17*,[13] in which the SPC emphasized that: "For technical features with ambiguous literal meanings, claim construction regarding such technical features shall be conducted relying on the description and its drawings. The interpretation of the technical features shall conform to the object of the invention at issue, and shall not be contradictory to the common knowledge in the art." One of the issues in this case was how to understand the meaning of the feature in claim 1 which recited that "the keyboard, the mouse, the display, the network card, and the power supply are connected through an integrated power socket and an integrated plug." The invalidation decision held that the power supply was the object to which the keyboard, the mouse, the display, and the network card were connected, i.e., the keyboard, the mouse, the display, and the network card were connected to the power supply through an integrated power plug and an integrated socket. The patentee asserted that the power supply was parallel with the keyboard, the mouse, the display, and the network card and they were all connected to an integrated power socket through an integrated plug.

Regarding this issue, the SPC found that the literal meaning of the expression "and...connected...and..." in the disputed technical feature was ambiguous, which was subject to at least two interpretations as were manifested in the invalidation decision and the assertion of the patentee. However, according to the relevant object

---

[13] Invention patent No. 01106125.1. The invalidation decision (No. WX13610) declared the patent right invalid in whole. The first instance judgment (*(2009) Yi Zhong Xing Chu Zi No. 2215*) and the second instance judgment (*(2012) Gao Xing Zhong Zi No. 293*) both upheld the invalidation decision. The patentee filed for a retrial. The SPC ruled to bring the case up for trial and vacated the invalidation decision and the first and second instance judgments.

of the invention and technical effects recited in the description, the improvement made by the present invention and the common knowledge in the art, it was more proper to understand this technical feature as "the power supply is parallel with keyboard, mouse, display, and the network card and they are all connected to an integrated power socket through an integrated plug." If this feature were interpreted in the same way as the invalidation decision which held that the keyboard, mouse, monitor, network card and power supply were connected through the connection of an integrated plug and an integrated power socket, it would be impossible to realize the object of one-through plug/unplug operation of this invention and was also contrary to the common knowledge in the art.

1.4 Common Understandings of a Person Skilled in the Art

A person skilled in the art is the subject of claim construction. When the patent as a whole does not specifically define the disputed terms or features, the interpretation of such disputed terms or features shall be conducted based on the common understanding of the claims by a person skilled in the art after reading the patent description and drawings. The SPC clarified this rule in the case *(2010) Zhi Xing Zi No. 9*.[14] The issue of this case was how to understand the word "bottom" in the additional technical feature of claim 3, which recited "for the wood board with color printing veneer, a layer of plastic film suitable for color printing or hot stamping is adhered to the bottom of the wood base board."

In its ruling, the SPC held that: "This patent does not explicitly define the word 'bottom,' nor does it specifically explain it in the drawings and embodiments. Therefore, the interpretation of this term shall be based on the common understandings of a person skilled in the art after reading the patent description and drawings. Claims 2 and 3 define, respectively, that a layer of veneer suitable for color printing is adhered to the surface and to the bottom of the wood base board. According to the common understanding of a person skilled in the art, for the object of the invention (including aesthetics, etc.), claims 2 and 3 define, respectively, that a layer of veneer suitable for color printing is adhered to the outer surface and to the inner surface of the wooden box. Therefore, the 'surface' in claim 2 refers to the outer surface of the wooden box; the 'bottom' in claim 3 refers to the other side corresponding to the surface in claim 2, i.e., the inner surface of the wooden box. OUYANG Xuan emphasized that the 'bottom' in claim 3 referred to the outer surface of the wooden box and there were two layers of veneer suitable for color printing when claim 3 was dependent on claim 2. This interpretation does not conform to the common understanding of a person skilled in the art. After reading this patent, a person skilled in the art cannot

---

[14] Utility model patent application No. 200420015152.0. The invalidation decision (No. WX12310) declared the patent right invalid in whole. The first instance judgment (*(2009) Yi Zhong Xing Chu Zi No. 487*) maintained the invalidation decision. The second instance judgment (*(2009) Gao Xing Zhong Zi No. 1114*) upheld the first instance judgment and the invalidation decision. The patentee filed for a retrial and was rejected by the SPC.

clearly understand that claim 3 intends to define that there are two layers of veneer suitable for color printing on the outer surface of the wooden box.

1.5 Construction of Product-by-Process Claims

Claims can be classified into product claims and process claims in terms of the types of claimed subject matter. Part II, Chapter 2, §3.1.1 of the *Guidelines for Patent Examination* provides that "in the determination of the extent of patent protection of a claim, generally all the features in the claim shall be taken into account; however, the actual definite effect of each feature shall finally be reflected on the subject matter of the claim."

In the case *(2012) Xing Ti Zi No. 24*,[15] the SPC made it clear that "For product claims, even if one or more technical features are defined by features of process, the protection scope of the claim is still determined by examining whether these features of process ultimately lead to a certain structure and/or composition of the product. When comparing the technical solution of a product claim which contains features of process with the prior art, the final form of the claimed product shall be compared with the prior art. If the product has a specific structure and/or composition that is different from the prior art due to the introduction of the features of process, it is necessary to consider the limitation of the features of process. If the introduction of the features of process fails to distinguish the structure and/or composition of the product from the prior art, there is no need to consider the limitation of the features of process e."

In this case, the difference between claim 2 and reference document 2 is that in reference document 2, a protrusion (23) is formed by stamping, while in claim 2, a spacer is formed by folding. Claim 2 and reference document 2 are different in terms of shape and forming methods. The SPC held that, "The function of the spacer in claim 2 in the final product is only to separate the heatsink plates by a predetermined angle. The function of the protrusion in the final product in reference document 2 is also to separate the heatsink plates by a predetermined angle. The spacer and the protrusion have the same function." Therefore, the difference in the forming methods did not lead to a substantial difference between the two. It was not improper for the invalidation decision and the first instance judgment to hold that the two methods were customary means in the art.

---

[15] Invention patent application No. 02800004.8. The invalidation decision (No. WX14314) declared the patent right invalid in whole. The first instance judgment (*(2010) Yi Zhong Xing Chu Zi No. 1283*) maintained the invalidation decision. The second instance judgment (*(2011) Gao Xing Zhong Zi No. 784*) vacated the first instance judgment and the invalidation decision. The invalidation petitioner filed for a retrial. The SPC ruled to bring the case up for trial, vacated the second instance judgment and upheld the first instance judgment and the invalidation decision.

1.6 Construction of Features of Effect

The so-called feature of effect refers to a feature which characterizes a technical content by the technical effect that can be produced by a technical solution rather than the structure, composition, method, etc.

In the case *(2013) Zhi Xing Zi No. 31*,[16] claim 1 of the patent at issue defines that "the efficacy against at least one weed is 70% to 100%." The SPC held that: "This feature is a feature of effect to be produced by the present invention, the technical effect generated by applying the technical solution defined in the patent to solve the technical problem. In the examination of inventive step, the feature of effect shall be considered together with other technical features that lead to the effects. All features shall be viewed collectively rather than individually. The invention cannot be simply concluded as involving an inventive step on the basis that the end values of the efficacy are not completely disclosed. Arysta LifeScience North America, LLC's assertion that claim 1 of this patent has an inventive step because of the limiting effect of the technical feature 'efficacy' is not sustained."

1.7 Limitation of Features of Drug Administration and Side Effects on Swiss-Type Claims

In China, Article 25 of the *Patent Law* provides that no patent right shall be granted for methods for the diagnosis or for the treatment of diseases. Therefore, inventions the point of novelty of which is the discovery of new uses of drugs may only be protected as "Swiss-type" claims. Some known substances which have been found to be useful for a certain medical purpose cannot be used in practice due to reasons such as excessive side effects, etc. If an inventor after research finds that certain side effects of the substance can be controlled by adopting specific methods of administration, dosage, etc., do the features of the method of administration, dosage, or non-toxic and side effects have a limiting effect on Swiss-type claims?

The SPC expounded its view on this issue in the case *(2012) Zhi Xing Zi No. 75*.[17] First, if the essence of the invention and its improvement to the prior art lie in the medical use of a substance, the claims shall be drafted as Swiss-type claims when a patent application is filed, and the scope of protection of the claims shall

---

[16] Invention patent application No. 99811707.2. The reexamination decision (No. FS11964) maintained the decision of rejection. The first instance judgment (*(2008) Yi Zhong Xing Chu Zi No. 628*) maintained the invalidation decision. The second instance judgment (*(2009) Gao Xing Zhong Zi No. 719*) upheld the first instance judgment and the invalidation decision. The patent applicant filed for a retrial and was rejected by the SPC.

[17] Invention patent application No. 99812498.2. The invalidation decision (No. WX13188) declared the patent right invalid in whole. The first instance judgment (*(2009) Yi Zhong Xing Chu Zi No. 1847*) maintained the invalidation decision. The second instance judgment (*(2010) Gao Xing Zhong Zi No. 547*) upheld the first instance judgment and the invalidation decision. The patentee filed for a retrial and was rejected by the SPC.

1.7 Limitation of Features of Drug Administration and Side Effects ...

be limited by the technical features related to pharmaceutical use. Second, if the feature of not producing specific toxic and side effects in the claims does not change the known treatment objects or indications, nor new properties of the drug have been discovered to distinguish it from the known uses, such a feature does not have a limiting effect on the invention of medical use claimed in the claims. Third, the impact of the feature of administration process on the drug preparation process requires case-by-case determination and analysis. The features that are only reflected in the administration process but are not technical features of pharmaceutical use do not have a limiting effect on the pharmaceutical method itself in Swiss-type claims.

The case related to a medical use of daptomycin. It is known in the prior art that daptomycin is a known antibiotic that can be used to treat and prevent bacterial infections. Daptomycin would produce skeletal muscle toxicity if used in high doses. However, the inventor of the patent at issue discovered that daptomycin would "not produce skeletal muscle toxicity" in an actual application by the specific administration method and dosage of the patent at issue, making daptomycin a really safe and industrially applicable drug for the treatment of serious gram-positive bacterial infections. Therefore, the inventor filed for a patent application which defined the Swiss-type claims with the feature of administration method and the feature of toxic and side effects of the drug.

Claim 1 of the patent at issue recites the: "Use of daptomycin for the manufacture of a medicament for treating a bacterial infection in a human patient in need thereof that minimizes skeletal muscle toxicity, wherein a dose for said treating is 3 to 75 mg/kg of daptomycin, wherein said dose is repeatedly administered in a dosage interval of once every 24 hours to once every 48 hours..." The patentee believed that, on the one hand, "minimizes skeletal muscle toxicity" was the critical function and feature of effect of the present patent which distinguished this patent substantially from the prior art; on the other hand, the dosage and dosage interval were the features reflected in the drug package inserts in the pharmaceutical process and had a limiting effect on the Swiss-type claims.

Regarding whether the feature of "minimizes skeletal muscle toxicity" had a limiting effect, the SPC explained in the ruling: "'Minimizes skeletal muscle toxicity' is not a symptom that a patient presents before the administration of daptomycin, but the result of changes of certain indicators in the body after the administration of daptomycin by the patient and reflects whether the drug itself has toxic and side effects. The patent in this case that 'minimizes skeletal muscle toxicity' only alleviates the adverse reaction of daptomycin, and reduces skeletal muscle toxicity. Neither the treatment objects nor indications of daptomycin are changed by the patent, nor new properties of the drug have been discovered. The indications for daptomycin are for the treatment of bacterial infections, regardless of whether skeletal muscle toxicity is produced. As far as the use of daptomycin is concerned, there is no difference in terms of indications. The limitation of 'minimizes skeletal muscle toxicity' in this patent does not distinguish the patent from the known uses disclosed in the prior art. Such a limitation has no limiting effect on the medical use of the drug or the claims of this patent."

Regarding whether the feature of the administration method has a limiting effect, the SPC explained in the ruling: "In practice, administration objects, administration methods, dosage, and dosage intervals, etc. are common features in Swiss-type claims. It is the key to determining the novelty of a claimed technical solution compared with the prior art by analyzing whether each technical feature embodies behaviors in pharmaceutical manufacturing or drug administration, and whether the new use is substantially different from the known use. As Swiss-type claims limit the manufacturing behavior of pharmaceutical companies of a drug for a certain purpose, the technical features shall still be analyzed from the perspective of process claims. Usually, the raw materials, preparation steps and process conditions, final drug products or composition and equipment are direct limitations on process claims.

The pharmaceutical manufacturing process in the sense of *Patent Law* usually refers to the act of preparing a specific drug with specific steps, processes, conditions, raw materials, etc., and does not include the drafting of drug package inserts, labels, and packaging as well as other procedures before factory packaging of the drug. For features that only relate to how to use the drug, such as the dosage of the drug, the time interval, etc., if there is no direct correlation between these features and the pharmaceutical manufacturing method, essentially such features are specific administration methods upon the human body after the drug is obtained by implementing the pharmaceutical manufacturing method and not directly and necessarily related to the specific pharmaceutical manufacturing method. Such features that are only reflected in the administration of the drug are not technical features of pharmaceutical use and do not have a limiting effect on Swiss-type claims.

Unit dose and dosage are different concepts: unit dose usually refers to the amount of drug contained in each drug unit and depends on the amount of drug added in the preparation process; dosage refers to the amount of drug taken each time or daily. Dosage is the amount of the drug used and can be determined by the drug user, such as twice a day or three times a day. Dosage means how to use a drug. In clinical practice, if a unit dose of the drug is less than the dosage, multiple unit doses of the drug may be taken. If a unit dose of the drug is greater than the dosage, then the drug is taken in an amount lesser than the unit dose.

Claim 1 of the patent at issue recites that the dose for said treating is 3 to 75 mg/kg of daptomycin, without specifying whether it is a unit dose or an administered dose. The patent description does not specify any impact this dose will have on the pharmaceutical manufacturing process and pharmaceutical uses. For a person skilled in the art, the common understanding of the dose for said treating of 3 to 75 mg/kg described in claim 1 of the patent is that the active ingredient per kilogram is 3 to 75 mg. It limits the dosage of administration. It is a treatment of a disease with a drug in the medication process to modify the administration method and dosage to cater to individual patients in order to achieve the best therapeutic effect of the drug. The change in the dosage does not necessarily affect the preparation process to cause a change in the content of the drug. Similarly, the dosing plan formed with time intervals of the patent is a feature of process of how to use the drug in the medication process. The dosing plan is a medical practice reflected in the medication process but not the pharmaceutical manufacturing stage. This feature of the medication process is neither necessarily related to the manufacturing of the drug nor does it change the preparation method of daptomycin to affect the drug itself. Such a process does not have a limiting effect on the manufacturing process and is not enough to make the Swiss-type claim novel."

1.8 Similarities and Differences in Claim Construction in Patent Granting, Patent Confirmation and Patent Infringement Procedures

Although the patent granting, patent confirmation and patent infringement procedures all involve the cognition of the content of claims and the interpretation of the scope of claims, due to the respective different positioning and functions of the three procedures, the methods of claim construction in these procedures are in a large extent similar but also slightly different.

In the case *(2010) Zhi Xing Zi No. 53-1*,[18] the SPC first analyzed the similarities of the methods of claim construction in patent granting, patent confirmation and patent infringement procedures. The similarities are "reflected in at least the following two aspects: first, claim construction is a type of text interpretation and must follow the general rules of text interpretation regardless of whether it is in a patent granting, patent confirmation or patent infringement procedure; second, claim construction must also follow the general rules for claim construction regardless of whether it is in a patent granting, patent confirmation or patent infringement procedure."

Then, based on the different purposes of claim construction in different procedures, the SPC believed that there were certain differences in the interpretation methods in particular circumstances: "In patent granting and patent confirmation procedures, the purpose of claim construction is to determine whether the claims meet the granting conditions or how valid they are by clarifying the meaning and scope of protection of these claims For this purpose, when interpreting the meaning of the terms of a claim, the requirements of the *Patent Law* shall be taken into account, such as the description sufficiently disclosing the technical solutions of the invention, claims being supported by the description and the amendment to the application documents not going beyond the scope of the disclosure contained in the initial description and claims. If the description does not explicitly define the meaning of the term, in principle, the ordinary meaning of the term that can be understood by a person skilled in the art after reading the claims, description and drawings shall be adopted. Improper limitation on a term shall be avoided when the description or examination documents are relied on in order to reach clear conclusions on whether

---

[18] Invention patent No. 00131800.4. The invalidation decision (No. WX11291) declared the patent right invalid in whole. The first instance judgment (*(2008) Yi Zhong Xing Chu Zi No. 1030*) maintained the invalidation decision. The second instance judgment (*(2009) Gao Xing Zhong Zi No. 327*) vacated the first instance judgment and the invalidation decision. The patentee filed for a retrial and was rejected by the SPC.

the claims meet the granting conditions as well as validity issues, so as to encourage applicants to amend and improve patent application documents and improve the quality of patent granting and patent confirmation procedures.

In patent infringement procedures, claim construction aims to determine whether the alleged infringing technical solution falls within the scope of protection of the patent by clarifying the meaning and protection scope of the claims. If the literal meaning of the claimed scope of the patent is defined too broadly that the claims cannot be supported by the description, the prior art is included, or the patent examination documents have made a restrictive interpretation of the meaning of the term to make it possible to apply the estoppel principle, etc. the scope of protection may be restricted by relying on the description, examination documents, etc., so as to reach an objective and fair conclusion on whether the alleged infringing technical solution falls within the scope of protection."

Finally, the SPC held that the difference in the interpretation methods in patent granting, patent confirmation and patent infringement procedures was "prominently manifested in the function of the observations of the parties. Such a function shall be subject to certain limitations of the *Patent Law* in specific circumstances when claims are interpreted in patent granting and patent confirmation procedures. For example, the *Patent Law* provides that the description shall recite the invention clearly and completely, that claims shall be supported by the description and that the amendment to the patent application document shall not go beyond the scope of the disclosure contained in the initial description and claims. The description or the initial description and claims shall be the basis for determining whether a certain patent or patent application meets the above-mentioned requirements. The parties' observations may not and shall not play a decisive role. On the contrary, if the parties' observations are relied on decisively to determine whether a patent or patent application meets the above-mentioned statutory requirements, the patent applicant will not be encouraged to cover relevant content in the description as much as possible and the above-mentioned statutory requirements of the *Patent Law* will not be fulfilled either.

Therefore, in patent granting and patent confirmation procedures, the applicant's observations in the examination documents may only be used as a reference rather than a decisive basis to understand the meaning of the description and the claims under usual circumstances. Whereas in patent infringement procedures, when interpreting the scope of protection of the claims, as long as the party concerned abandons a certain technical solution through observations in the patent application or granting procedure, generally the scope of protection shall be interpreted narrowly based on the observations of the party."

Chapter 2
Patentable Subject Matter

Article 2(2) of the *Patent Law* provides the basic definitions of inventions and utility models. Under this provision, an invention means any new technical solution relating to a product, a process, or improvement thereof; a utility model means any new technical solution relating to the shape, the structure, or their combination, of a product, which is fit for practical use. For an invention-creation to be patentable, either as an invention or as a utility model, the precondition is that it must be a technical solution. As provided in Part One, Chapter 2, §6.3 and Part Two, Chapter 1, §2 of the *Guidelines for Patent Examination*, a technical solution is an aggregation of technical means applying the laws of nature to solve a technical problem. Usually, technical means are embodied as technical features.

2.1 Technical Problem, Technical Means and Technical Effect

In practice, one of the focal issues of patent cases usually involves determining whether the subject matter of a patent is a technical solution. The SPC pointed out in the case *(2013) Zhi Xing Zi No. 67*[1] that: "Article 2(2) of the *Implementing Regulations of the Patent Law* (i.e., Article 2(1) of the current *Patent Law*[2]) laid down the principles for patentable subject matters. If the claimed solution does not utilize technical means or natural laws, nor does it solve the technical problem or produce

---

[1] Invention patent application No. 200610061959.1. The reexamination decision (No. FS40583) maintained the rejection decision for incompliance with Article 2(2) of the *Patent Law*. The first instance judgment (*(2012) Yi Zhong Zhi Xing Chu Zi No. 3315*) and the second instance judgment (*(2013) Gao Xing Zhong Zi No. 998*) both upheld the reexamination decision. The patent applicant filed for a retrial and was rejected by the SPC.

[2] Translator's note: Here, the current *Patent Law* refers to the *Patent Law* as amended in 2008 and effective on October 1, 2009.

the technical effect, the solution does not constitute a technical solution, and is not a patentable subject matter."

In this case, claim 1 claims "a game graphics composition and a composition method thereof for a Path to Success Game consisting of the graphics of the game setting simulating real-life human society, chess pieces representing players, dice determining the moves a player makes, and items such as a bachelor's certificate, a master's certificate, a doctoral certificate, a patent certificate, a medal certificate, and an award certificate, etc., characterized in that the graphics of the game setting simulating real-life human society consists of an essential life journey from the infant stage, elementary school stage, middle school stage, university stage, work stage, entrepreneurial stage to the destination-new starting point to success as the main game area and real social forms as auxiliary game areas, including a hospital representing the medical system, a reward and punishment center representing the reward and punishment system, a court representing the judicial system, and a training colleges representing the adult education system."

The SPC believed that the problem that the solution of claim 1 aimed to solve was "to play a game in an artificially designed game setting consisting of social forms and an essential life journey, and is not a technical problem. The means adopted is to divide the chessboard into different areas and to move the chess pieces or graphics in the game area depending on dice rolling according to artificial rules which are made as a result of pure human brain activities, hence not a technical means. The effect achieved is to mainly conduct civic ideological and moral education, and does not constitute a technical effect." Therefore, the solution claimed in claim 1 was not a technical solution and not a patentable subject matter.

In the case *(2011) Zhi Xing Zi No. 68*,[3] the SPC analyzed whether the solution was a technical solution from three dimensions: technical problem, technical means, and technical effect, and concluded that the patent application at issue did not comply with Article 2(2) of the *Patent Law*. The patent application at issue relates to a mobile phone payment service system consisting of a paying party, a mobile network operator, a charging party, and a bank, characterized in that the four-parties: the mobile network operator, the charging party, the paying party, and the bank cooperate with each other, wherein the mobile network operator opens a charging party account, manages the mobile phone user's mobile phone card account, and at the same time opens a mobile network operator account in the bank; the mobile phone user deposits in the mobile network operator account in exchange for the prepayment in the mobile phone card account, and when an expense incurs on the part of the mobile phone user, he/she applies to the mobile network operator for a payment, i.e., the prepayment in the user's mobile phone card account is transferred to the charging party, after which the mobile network operator notifies the bank to transfer the corresponding amount from the mobile network operator's account to the charging party's account and

---

[3] Invention patent application No. 200710120845.4. The reexamination decision (No. FS22835) maintained the rejection decision for incompliance with Article 2(2) of the *Patent Law*. The first instance judgment (*(2010) Yi Zhong Zhi Xing Chu Zi No. 2703*) and the second instance judgment (*(2011) Gao Xing Zhong Zi No. 473*) both upheld the reexamination decision. The patent applicant filed for a retrial and was rejected by the SPC.

2.1 Technical Problem, Technical Means and Technical Effect

the charging party receives the notice of payment transfer from the mobile network operator through a mobile signal-receiving device or other similar devices; when the mobile phone user needs to deposit or withdraw cash or pay the fees of the mobile phone, he/she does so by interacting with an ATM through wireless communication.

The SPC believed that "the solution essentially carries out the transfer rules agreed upon by the mobile network operator, the charging party, the paying party, and the bank in advance by integrating the commonly known computer equipment and networks through the existing mobile communication network technology. The four parties transfer money among accounts in an agreed-upon way to provide mobile phone users with a channel for consumption or depositing and withdrawing money. In this process, there is no technical transformation of the internal performance or structure of the existing equipment and network. The problem solved and the effect achieved are the commercial cooperation of the four parties. As the solution does not use a technical means to solve a technical problem and achieve a technical effect that conforms to the laws of nature, it is not a technical solution in the sense of the patent law and not a patentable subject matter."

In the case *(2014) Zhi Xing Zi No. 73*,[4] the SPC reiterated that if the claimed technical solution only set artificial rules on existing commonly known equipment, "but does not adopt a technical means to solve the technical problem and achieve a technical effect that conforms to the laws of nature, it is not a technical solution in the sense of the patent law and not a patentable subject matter."

The patent at issue relates to an electronic deposit and payment system consisting of a computer center of a bank, coin cards, cash registers, recharge machines, and a computer center of coin cards, wherein the data of the change in transactions are stored in the coin cards and then are transmitted through the network between the cashiers and the computer center of the coin cards, to deposit the change in cash transactions in the coin cards as a payment made to the user; and the user transfers the change deposited in the coin card through a recharge machine to a payment to be made to others so that it will not be inconvenient or unhygienic for the user to carry the change around if the change is provided to the user. The SPC held that the recitation of claim 1 showed that the technical solution aimed to "deposit the change in cash transactions in the coin cards through which the user can make a payment or withdraw cash to avoid the inconvenience and hygiene problems caused to the user by receiving the change. This solution is an artificially set payment rule on cash transactions, not a technical means utilizing natural laws, and therefore does not constitute a technical problem," and did not meet the requirements of Article 2(2) of the *Patent Law*.

---

[4] Invention patent application No. 200410027344.8. The reexamination decision (No. FS40616) maintained the rejection decision for incompliance with Article 2(2) of the *Patent Law*. The first instance judgment (*(2012) Yi Zhong Zhi Xing Chu Zi No. 2341*) and the second instance judgment (*(2013) Gao Xing Zhong Zi No. 671*) both upheld the reexamination decision. The patent applicant filed for a retrial and was rejected by the SPC.

2.2 Patentability of Business Methods

A common characteristic of business method patent applications is: computers and network technologies are used as technical means; business models or methods adopted in business activities are the subject matter; and the purpose of such applications is to exclude or prohibit others without legitimate rights or reasons from implementing the claimed solution or concepts of the patent application. In the patent examination practice in China, Article 2 of the *Patent Law* has always been applied in the examination of business methods and a business method may be refused to be granted a patent for not being a technical solution. Article 25 of the *Patent Law* may also be relied on to deny a business method the patent right because the claimed business method is "rules and methods for mental activities."

In the *(2015) Zhi Xing Zi No. 21*[5] ruling, the SPC held that the patent application for "an e-commerce logistics and distribution management method for retail fresh produce using the Internet and transit facilities" was not a patentable subject matter under Article 2(2) of the *Patent Law*. The reason was that, "the recitation in claim 1 of the patent at issue that a registered consumer may enjoy distribution logistics and returned logistics between the distribution center and the destination of fresh produce through one-stop transit by determining the location of the transit facilities is a management method or an implementation plan for a specific business activity system." Firstly, "although it is inevitable to obey or be subject to the laws of nature to formulate or implement the solution, and necessary to operate corresponding technical equipment and set certain restrictions on the furnishment or use of the technical equipment, yet the plan mainly reflects the subjective requirements of humans on participants and other relevant elements of business activities and is an artificially made rule of business activities." Secondly, "the problem to be solved by the solution of the patent at issue is to overcome the defects in business operation of the original management model, such as scattered orders, inconvenient loading and unloading, low distribution efficiency, and high operating costs to achieve the business effects of reduced cost and improved efficiency." Furthermore, "although the solution also relates to software and hardware equipment and information and data processing processes, yet they are all subject to and at service of the overall operation plan in the sense of business management, and are specific means and measures for the implementation of the business plan. These equipment and information and data processing have not been technologically improved in terms of structure, performance, etc., as a result of being applied in this business plan. Therefore, the essential attributes of the patent application at issue as a business management plan have not been changed."

---

[5] Invention patent application No. 201110024602.7. The reexamination decision (No. FS58291) maintained the rejection decision for incompliance with Article 2(2) of the *Patent Law*. The first instance judgment *((2014) Yi Zhong Zhi Xing Chu Zi No. 450)* and the second instance judgment *((2014) Gao Xing Zhong Zi No. 1227)* both upheld the reexamination decision. The patent applicant filed for a retrial and was rejected by the SPC.

Chapter 3
Practical Applicability

Practical applicability means that the product or method of a patent application for invention or utility model must be one which can be made or used in an industry and can solve technical problems. Part Two, Chapter 5, §3.2 of the *Guidelines for Patent Examination* provides that "can be made or used" means that it is possible for the technical solution of an invention or utility model to be made or used industrially. Lack of practical applicability is owing to the inherent defect of the technical solution.

3.1 Violation of the Law of Conservation of Energy

If a technical solution cannot be carried out in the industry because it violates the laws of nature, this technical solution will not be patented for lack of practical applicability. In the case *(2010) Zhi Xing Zi No. 10*,[1] the SPC affirmed the Patent Reexamination Board's[2] determination that claim 1 lacked practical applicability. The case related to an "energy-free self-pressing water suction device." The SPC held that "according to the technical solution recited in the patent application, once the self-pressing water suction device starts to work, it can continuously pump water from a low level to a high level, i.e., do work without any energy input from other energy sources. Apparently, this technical solution violates the law of conservation of energy and is not practically applicable."

---

[1] Invention patent application No. 02100209.6. The reexamination decision (No. FS10155) maintained the rejection decision for incompliance with Article 22(4) of the *Patent Law*. The first instance judgment (*(2007) Yi Zhong Zhi Xing Chu Zi No. 705*) and the second instance judgment (*(2007) Gao Xing Zhong Zi No. 519*) both upheld the reexamination decision. The patent applicant filed for a retrial and was rejected by the SPC.

[2] Translator's note: The Patent Reexamination Board was renamed the Reexamination and Invalidation Department of the Patent Office, CNIPA, in 2019.

In the case *(2015) Zhi Xing Zi No. 48*,[3] the SPC held that the water buoyancy converter, as claimed in claim 1, did not satisfy the requirement of Article 22(4) of the *Patent Law*. The specific reasons were: in the technical solution of claim 1, "the round soft pipe conveyor floats in the water, in which case the buoyancy and gravity of the conveyor are balanced, and in the absence of any other external forces, there is no displacement of the round soft pipe conveyor, as a result of which the water buoyancy acting on the round soft pipe conveyor will not do work, and the buoyant potential energy of the round soft pipe conveyor will not change, and cannot be converted into continuous kinetic energy and transmitted to the driving wheels." Even if, as asserted by the patent applicant, "the round soft pipe conveyor can rotate, as there is no overall displacement of the round soft pipe conveyor, both the buoyant potential energy and the gravitational potential energy of the conveyor remain constant, which means no energy output will be generated. In the absence of external energy input, the round soft pipe conveyor will stop moving due to the drag in the water, the friction drag of the double blocking wheels, etc., and it will not produce continuous energy output." Therefore, this solution obviously violates the law of conservation of energy.

In practice, the cases involving magnetoelectric energy conversion technology are most likely to cause disputes over practical applicability. A general rule to follow in this type of cases is, "if the claimed invention or utility model violates the commonly accepted and practice-proven law of conservation of energy, and is unable to be made or used, the invention or utility model cannot be patented under Article 22 of the *Patent Law*." This was the view the SPC emphasized in the case *(2015) Zhi Xing Zi No. 53*.[4] The patent at issue claims a magnetic power machine which is characterized in that a cylinder cover of a piston transmission mechanism is provided with an electromagnet, and the corresponding piston is provided with a permanent magnet; the electromagnet is started by a battery, and the N and the S poles of the electromagnet are alternated by a current commutator; the permanent magnet on the piston has fixed polarities, and the reciprocating motion of the piston is realized by using the principle that like poles repel each other but opposite ones attract each other; the power output of the piston can be connected to a generator for power generation. The SPC held that "the above-mentioned magnetic power machine has no external energy input after it is started by the battery, but it can continuously output extra energy to the outside world, which violates the law of conservation of energy. The invention cannot be made or used and does not comply with the practical applicability requirement under Article 22(4) of the *Patent Law*.

---

[3] Invention patent application No. 200910147641.9. The reexamination decision (No. FS42529) maintained the rejection decision for incompliance with Article 22(4) of the *Patent Law*. The first instance judgment (*(2012) Yi Zhong Zhi Xing Chu Zi No. 3061*) and the second instance judgment (*(2013) Gao Xing Zhong Zi No. 53*) both upheld the reexamination decision. The patent applicant filed for a retrial and was rejected by the SPC.

[4] Invention patent application No. 201110056234.4. The reexamination decision (No. FS66342) maintained the rejection decision for incompliance with Article 22(4) of the *Patent Law*. The first instance judgment (*(2014) Yi Zhong Zhi Xing Chu Zi No. 6105*) and the second instance judgment (*(2014) Gao Xing Zhong Zi No. 3328*) both upheld the reexamination decision. The patent applicant filed for a retrial and was rejected by the SPC.

3.1 Violation of the Law of Conservation of Energy

In the case *(2010) Zhi Xing Zi No. 11*[5] which related to a natural power generation patent, the SPC also held that "the essence of the technical solution claimed by claim 1 is to continuously generate electricity like a generator in the prior art by relying only on the 'natural power of magnets' without any other forms of energy input. However, according to the law of conservation of energy, it is impossible to continuously output electric energy by relying only on the limited 'natural power of magnets' without any other forms of energy input or repeated magnetization of the magnet by other external energy. Therefore, the first instance and second instance judgments are correct in holding that the patent application in this case did not satisfy the requirements of Article 22(4) of the *Patent Law*."

In addition, the case *(2015) Zhi Xing Zi No. 90*[6] also related to a magnetoelectric conversion technology. In this case, the SPC held that "those skilled in the art of electric machines can usually recognize that a generator converts kinetic energy into electric energy through the magnetic circuit of the generator while an electromotor converts electric energy into kinetic energy through the magnetic circuit of the electromotor and the function of the magnetic circuit is to convert energy only." The technical solution of the patent application at issue, i.e., a generator-electromotor linked power device, which "provides surplus electric energy for other equipment without continuous external energy input, obviously violates the law of conservation of energy and lacks practical applicability."

The whole content of the patent application documents submitted on the filing date shall be the basis to determine whether an invention or utility model violates the laws of nature. The issue of the case *(2013) Zhi Xing Zi No. 44*[7] was to determine whether the technical solution of the patent application complied with the law of conservation of energy. The claims in this case related to a method for improving the output efficiency of a transmission line. The Patent Reexamination Board believed that "when the input energy of the transmission line is constant, the number of parallel filaments on the load side needs to be continuously increased to raise the output power in order to improve the output efficiency of the transmission line. If the parallel filaments are to work at their rated power, the output energy of the transmission line in this application will inevitably increase. The present patent application recites that the

---

[5] Invention patent application No. 97118378.3. The reexamination decision (No. FS10945) maintained the rejection decision for incompliance with Article 22(4) of the *Patent Law*. The first instance judgment (*(2007) Yi Zhong Zhi Xing Chu Zi No. 1371*) and the second instance judgment (*(2008) Gao Xing Zhong Zi No. 140*) both upheld the reexamination decision. The patent applicant filed for a retrial and was rejected by the SPC.

[6] Invention patent application No. 200610137229.5. The reexamination decision (No. FS36836) maintained the rejection decision for incompliance with Article 22(4) of the *Patent Law*. The first instance judgment (*(2012) Yi Zhong Zhi Xing Chu Zi No. 1300*) and the second instance judgment (*(2013) Gao Xing Zhong Zi No. 271*) both upheld the reexamination decision. The patent applicant filed for a retrial and was rejected by the SPC.

[7] Invention patent application No. 200510064778.X. The reexamination decision (No. FS21594) maintained the rejection decision for incompliance with Article 22(4) of the *Patent Law*. The first instance judgment (*(2010) Yi Zhong Zhi Xing Chu Zi No. 1425*) and the second instance judgment (*(2011) Gao Xing Zhong Zi No. 67*) both vacated the reexamination decision. The Patent Reexamination Board filed for a retrial and was rejected by the SPC.

output power can be increased by 11 times while the input power is constant and that the output energy can be greater than the input energy.... which obviously violates the law of conservation of energy." Therefore, the rejection decision was maintained for lack of practical applicability. The SPC did not sustain this determination and explained in the ruling that: "according to the law of conservation of energy, the general energy for matter movement can neither be created nor destroyed and can only be transformed from one form to another. Energy does not perish and originates on its own, and the total energy in the universe remains constant."

The Patent Reexamination Board asserted that the technical solution of this application did not comply with the law of conservation of energy mainly based on the recitation in the description that the output power P2 in Figure 2 was increased by 11 times relative to the output power P2 in Figure 1. This comparison made sense only when the input powers P1 in both Figures were the same. However, the presumption that the input power P1 in Figure 1 was the same as that in Figure 2 lacked factual support. The SPC concurred with the Patent Reexamination Board that "practical applicability shall be determined based on the whole content of the description and claims submitted on the filing date as well as the applicant's design ideas rather than only on the drawings of the description."

However, in this case, the Patent Reexamination Board "violated this very principle. The whole content of the description and claims shows that the patent applicant intends to illustrate the energy-saving effect of the present invention by comparing the ratio of the input power and output power of the prior art with the ratio of the input power and output power of the present invention, different from the understanding of the Patent Reexamination Board that the output power of the prior art is compared with that of the present invention to illustrate the energy-saving effect of the present invention by assuming that the input power of both the prior art and the present invention is the same."

3.2 The Relationship Between Practical Applicability and Sufficient Disclosure

Under the *Guidelines for Patent Examination*, "an invention or utility model can be made or used" means that it is possible for the technical solution of an invention or utility model to be made or used industrially and that it is irrelevant how the invention or utility model was created or whether it has been implemented. "Can produce effective results" means that, on the date of filling the application, the economic, technical, or social effects produced by the invention or utility model can be expected by a person skilled in the art. These effects shall be positive and advantageous. A technical solution that satisfies the requirement of practical applicability shall not violate the laws of nature and shall be reproducible.

Lack of practical applicability because of inability to be made or used is owing to the inherent defect of the technical solution and is irrelevant to the extent of disclosure of the description. In the case *(2011) Xing Ti Zi No. 4*,[8] the patent at issue claimed a coal-, oil-, and gas-firing boiler with double-layer fire grates. The invalidation petitioner asserted that the patent failed to satisfy the requirement of practical applicability because the patent description had not disclosed the technical solution to carry out this three-fuel boiler. Regarding this assertion, the SPC held that: first, "it is not impossible to make and use this three-fuel boiler relying on the disclosure of this patent description"; second, "it is possible to achieve effective results by realizing the interchange of multiple fuels without major alterations or changes to the boiler body"; third, the invalidation petitioner explicitly admitted in the retrial that there was no evidence to show that the patent could not achieve the interchange of the three fuels. Therefore, this patent complies with the practical applicability requirement of Article 22(4) of the *Patent Law*. As to whether the description discloses the technical solution definitely and sufficiently for carrying out this three-fuel boiler, it is a question to be addressed by the examination of sufficient disclosure of the description, rather than that of practical applicability.

---

[8] Invention patent No. 99219875.5. The invalidation decision (No. WX3974) maintained the validity of the patent. The first instance judgment (*(2001) Yi Zhong Zhi Chu Zi No. 309*) maintained the invalidation decision. The second instance judgment (*(2002) Gao Min Zhong Zi No. 202*) vacated the first instance judgment. The Patent Reexamination Board filed for a retrial. The SPC ruled to bring the case up for trial, vacated the second instance judgment and upheld the invalidation decision.

Chapter 4
Sufficiency of Disclosure

According to the provisions of Article 26(3) of the *Patent Law*, the description shall set forth the claimed invention or utility model in a manner sufficiently clear and complete so as to enable a person skilled in the relevant art to carry out the invention or utility model based on what is recited in the description to solve the technical problems and produce the expected technical effects.

4.1 The Subject to Determine Sufficiency of Disclosure

To determine whether the description discloses the claimed technical solution in a manner sufficiently clear and complete so that those skilled in the art can carry it out, the knowledge level and cognitive ability of those skilled in the art shall be considered. In the case *(2014) Zhi Xing Zi No. 119*,[1] the SPC stressed that "a person skilled in the art shall not only read the patent application documents carefully, but also possess a good technical background that those skilled in the art should possess so that he or she may contribute supplementary information to the patent application documents based on common general knowledge. For those skilled in the art with the above-mentioned knowledge level and cognitive abilities, if the description, drawings and claims as a whole specifically and clearly disclose the technical contents necessary to carry out the invention, enabling those skilled in the art to carry out the technical solution of the invention without the need of exercising creative or undue efforts to solve the technical problems of the invention and produce the expected technical effects, the requirements of Article 26(3) of the *Patent Law* shall be deemed as met."

---

[1] Invention patent No. 200510100795.4. The invalidation decision (No. WX19287) maintained the validity of the patent right. Both the first instance judgment (*(2013) Yi Zhong Zhi Xing Chu Zi No. 2209*) and the second instance judgment (*(2013) Gao Xing Zhong Zi No. 2257*) upheld the invalidation decision. The invalidation petitioner filed for a retrial. The SPC ruled that the application for retrial was rejected.

© Intellectual Property Publishing House 2024
R. Xiaolan, *Patent Administrative Litigation*, Understanding China,
https://doi.org/10.1007/978-981-97-1131-4_4

This case related to a bridge type shield construction method for a box girder bridge, comprising seven steps of: (1) carrying out foundation pit excavations at a road section where the box girder bridge is to be built based on a designed height of the box girder bridge; (2) fabricating sliding plates based on the length of the bridge; (3) prefabricating the box girder bridge based on design requirements; (4) manufacturing a shield based on the height and width of the box girder bridge, and installing the shield; (5) reinforcing a pipeline as needed; (6) carrying out cycled box bridge jacking operations in an order of sub-shield tunneling, center soil excavation and transportation, axis measurement, box girder bridge jacking, jacking rectification, and line maintenance; and (7) restoring normal operation of the line and removing the shield when the box girder bridge has been jacked to reach a target position. Among these steps, it was further defined in claim 1 that "a shield climbing rectification plate is mounted under a first beam in the front; a sub-shield box is mounted on a front end of a main beam of the shield, and a rear end of the top of each sub-shield is connected to a thin iron drag-reducing plate having the same width as that of the sub-shield."

The issue in this case was whether the technology of "shield climbing rectification plate" in claim 1 was sufficiently disclosed in the description. The invalidation petitioner filed for a retrial and claimed that as of the filing date, a person skilled in the art would have been unable to understand or implement the feature based on their cognitive and comprehensive abilities. The patentee's statement regarding the feature was a post-filing statement, thus preventing those skilled in the art from directly and unambiguously determining the feature based on all relevant contents of the patent description. Therefore, the patentee's statement should not be admitted by the invalidation decision. Regarding this, the SPC held that first, the patent description specified the position of the "shield climbing rectification plate" and its connection with other components; second, evidence 1–4 submitted in the invalidation procedure showed that jacking rectification was a common process in shield construction methods; furthermore, after reading the technical information recited in the description, those skilled in the art should have been able to supplement their own common general knowledge to shield jacking rectification with ease, and should be able to understand that the term "climbing rectification" in the phrase "shield climbing rectification plate" referred to upward rectification measures taken in the elevation direction to prevent land subsidence as well as to prevent cantilever sagging of the shield. As a result, the shield climbing rectification plate was necessarily inclined upward at a certain angle. Thus, those skilled in the art should be able to clearly understand the meaning of the phrase "shield climbing rectification plate," and carry out the technical solution provided by the present invention to solve any corresponding technical problems, and achieve the invention's technical effects. The disputed technical solution thus complied with the provisions of Article 26(3) of the *Patent Law*.

4.2 Steps to Determine Sufficiency of Disclosure

According to the provisions of Article 26(3) of the *Patent Law*, two requirements must be met to determine whether a description sufficiently disclosed the claimed invention or utility model: the description shall set forth the invention or utility model "in a manner sufficiently clear and complete" and "enable a person skilled in the art to carry it out." These two requirements apply to all claimed inventions or utility models. Therefore, when making a judgment for a particular case, one shall firstly identify the subject matter of the invention or utility model, then ascertain whether the explanation of the invention or utility model is complete and clear in the description, and finally, confirm whether those skilled in the art could carry out the invention or utility model based on the contents of the description. This was the view explicitly held by the SPC in its judgment *(2014) Xing Ti Zi No. 8*.[2] The subject matter claimed in this case was "crystalline Form I atorvastatin hydrate containing 1 to 8 moles of water." In addition to limiting the water content of the crystalline Form I atorvastatin hydrate to be 1 to 8 moles of water, claim 1 also defined the microstructure of the hydrate using XPRD data. However, the description did not provide evidence showing that all crystals with water content, regardless of the ratio, could exhibit the XPRD pattern defined in claim 1.

The invalidation decision held that the claimed product was not sufficiently disclosed in the description. The second instance court vacated the invalidation decision and held that "to determine whether an invention is sufficiently disclosed, the technical problem solved by the invention must also be determined… The technical problem to be solved by this invention is to obtain a crystalline form of atorvastatin, in particular crystalline Form I atorvastatin, so as to address the technical problem that amorphous atorvastatin is not suitable for filtration and drying in large-scale production." The invalidation decision concluded that the patent description did not meet the requirements for sufficient disclosure. However, "[when] the technical problem to be solved by the present invention is not determined, and it is unclear which chemical and physical property parameters are related to the technical problem to be solved, it is obviously inappropriate to determine that the invention was not sufficiently disclosed without considering the technical problem the present invention is intended to solve as a whole."

The SPC corrected the error made by the second instance court and held that "in determining whether the description meets the requirements of Article 26(3) of the *Patent Law*, it is necessary to consider the technical problems to be solved by the invention. If the description provides the technical means, but those skilled in the art cannot solve the problem via the same means, the description does not comply with

---

[2] Invention patent No. 96195564.3. The invalidation decision (No. WX13582) declared the patent right invalid in whole. The first instance judgment (*(2009) Yi Zhong Xing Chu Zi No. 2710*) maintained the invalidation decision. The second instance judgment (*(2010) Gao Xing Zhong Zi No. 1489*) vacated the first instance judgment and the invalidation decision. The Patent Reexamination Board and the invalidation petitioner filed for a retrial. The SPC reviewed the case, vacated the second instance judgment and upheld the first instance judgment and the invalidation decision.

the provisions of Article 26(3) of the *Patent Law*. However, this does not mean that the technical problem to be solved by the invention must be considered first. If the technical solution of an invention cannot be carried out, it obviously does not meet the requirements of Article 26(3) of the *Patent Law*, and it is no longer meaningful to consider the technical problem to be solved by the invention. Therefore, there is a sequential logical relationship between the reproduction of the technical solution and the evaluation of whether the technical problem is solved and the technical effect is achieved. It is necessary to first determine whether those skilled in the art can carry out the technical solution based on the contents disclosed in the description, and then determine whether the technical problem is solved and the technical effects are achieved. When it is uncertain whether the technical solution itself can be carried out, it is meaningless to discuss whether it can solve the corresponding technical problem and achieve beneficial technical effect compared to prior art. In this case, the second instance court did not actually consider the enablement of the technical solution defined by the claims of the patent; rather, it first considered the technical problem to be solved by the invention, and then evaluated the chemical and physical property parameters related to the technical problem to be solved. Such reasoning was improper and must be corrected."

4.3 Ambiguous Technical Means

If the technical means recited in the description are too ambiguous for those skilled in the art to carry out the invention, the disclosure of the invention in the description does not satisfy the requirements of Article 26(3) of the *Patent Law*. One of the issues in the case *(2011) Zhi Xing Zi No. 71*[3] was whether the technical information disclosed in the patent description was sufficient to allow those skilled in the art to carry out the invention. In this case, the patent discloses a dynamic decompression purification process for carbon dioxide, mainly comprising the following steps: subjecting raw gas to two-stage gas–water separation, compressing and cooling, performing two-stage gas–water separation, and then passing through a high-efficiency impurity removal system, high-efficiency purifiers, coarse and fine filters, a liquefier, and a dynamic decompression purification system, thereby obtaining the resulting gas product. According to the description, the problem to be solved by this patent is to increase the purity of carbon dioxide product from 99.95 to 99.999%, while also significantly reduce energy consumption. The SPC held that "although this patent description specifies the process flow, each step in the process is not sufficiently clear and complete to enable those skilled in the art to implement the process by following the description, nor can they understand the means used to achieve the effect of

---

[3] Invention patent No. 00126685.3. The invalidation decision (No. WX12482) declared the patent right invalid in whole. Both the first instance judgment (*(2009) Yi Zhong Xing Chu Zi No. 687*) and the second instance judgment (*(2010) Gao Xing Zhong Zi No. 785*) upheld the invalidation decision. The patentee filed for a retrial. The SPC ruled that the application for retrial was rejected.

improving the purity of the carbon dioxide product and reducing the amount of energy consumed during the process. Specifically, the two-stage gas-water separation is performed on the raw gas twice before and after compression and cooling. After the two separations are performed, the 'high-efficiency' impurity removal system and the 'high-efficiency' purifiers can still further remove moisture in the raw gas, and the impurity removal system and the purifiers are also similar in removing organic impurities. Considering that this patent aims to solve the technical problem of improving gas purity, it is apparent that the multiple steps, which remove both moisture and organic impurities, are included in the process flow to improve the purity. However, the description does not specify what impurity removal system and purifiers should be used in these steps to continuously remove moisture and organic impurities so as to improve the purity, nor does it clarify how the so-called 'high-efficiency' impurity removal system and the 'high-efficiency' purifiers differ from common devices in terms of their structure and effects. Further, the description does not provide specific embodiments regarding the coarse filter, the fine filter, and the dynamic decompression purification system related to improving the purity of the final gas product. Moreover, the energy consumption of the entire process obviously increases if additional means such as filtering steps and devices are adopted to improve the purity of the final product. However, this patent reduces energy consumption while improving purity, which necessitates a clarification of the specific technical means required to achieve the particular technical effect provided in the description. Thus, although the technical means are provided in the description, they are ambiguous and cannot be implemented by those skilled in the art."

Despite Kaimeite's (hereafter referred to as "KMT") claim that the various steps, tools, and devices entailed in the process outlined in this case were conventional techniques adopted by those skilled in the art in certain circumstances, or were mentioned in 'No. 111 European Patent as the prior art, the SPC held that "first, KMT did not provide evidence to show that the steps in the process or the tools and devices used are conventional technical means. Second, even if these means are indeed conventional technical means, KMT failed to clarify how to modify or combine these conventional technical means to achieve the effect of improving product purity while reducing energy consumption. The technical solutions and effects disclosed in 'No. 111 European Patent differ from those of this patent, and patent documents are not textbooks, technical manuals, or other technical documents that are generally regarded as accurate by the public, thus making it difficult to prove the enablement of this patent's technical solution."

4.4 Claimed Technical Problems not Solved

If a specific technical solution is recited in the description, but a person skilled in the art could not anticipate that the technical solution could solve the claimed technical problem according to prior art and no experimental evidence is recited therein, the disclosure of the technical solution in the description does not satisfy the requirements of Article 26(3) of the *Patent Law*. In the case *(2011) Zhi Xing Zi No. 23*,[4] the SPC held that "one of the technical problems to be solved by this application is to use an insulin sensitivity enhancer in combination with a biguanide to achieve a significant synergistic effect compared with the administration of either drug alone for the prevention and treatment of diabetes. However, those skilled in the art cannot predict whether the combined use of an insulin sensitivity enhancer and a biguanide can achieve the significant synergistic effect recited in this application. Under the *Patent Law* and the *Guidelines for Patent Examination*, this application's description should recite relevant experimental data. Although in the description, Example 1 recites that pioglitazone as an insulin sensitivity enhancer has a synergistic effect when used in combination with voglibose, which is a preferred example of an α-glucokinase inhibitor, the mechanism of enzyme inhibitors is to inhibit digestive enzymes, while the mechanism of biguanides includes inhibition. In the absence of sufficient evidence to prove that both α-glucokinase inhibitors and biguanides achieve the above inhibitory effects in the exact same way, it is not conclusive whether α-glucokinase inhibitors work in the same way as biguanides solely based on the recitation of the description. Therefore, the second instance court ruled that the description of this application did not comply with Article 26(3) of the *Patent Law* because those skilled in the art could not predict whether the combined use of an insulin sensitivity enhancer and a biguanide could achieve the significant synergistic effect described in this application. This ruling is not improper."

4.5 A Lack of Necessary Experimental Evidence to Confirm Technical Effects

If a specific technical solution is recited in the description but without any experimental evidence, and those skilled in the art must rely on such experimental results to predict the technical effects of the technical solution, the description does not meet the enablement requirements and does not comply with Article 26(3) of the *Patent Law*.

In the case *(2014) Zhi Xing Zi No. 123*,[5] the patent at issue claimed a background interference method for the fine structure of elementary particles. The China National Intellectual Property Administration rejected the application for a lack of practical

---

[4] Invention patent No. 02149132.1. The reexamination decision (No. FS15379) maintained the rejection decision. Both the first instance judgment (*(2009) Yi Zhong Zhi Xing Chu Zi No. 1096*) and the second instance judgment (*(2010) Gao Xing Zhong Zi No. 857*) maintained the invalidation decision. The patent applicant filed for a retrial. The SPC ruled that the application for retrial was rejected.

[5] Invention patent No. 200610075959.7. The reexamination decision (No. FS57456) maintained the rejection decision. Both the first instance judgment (*(2013) Yi Zhong Xing Chu Zi No. 3711*) and the second instance judgment (*(2014) Gao Xing Zhong Zi No. 1112*) upheld the invalidation decision. The patent applicant filed for a retrial. The SPC ruled that the application for retrial was rejected.

4.5 A Lack of Necessary Experimental Evidence to Confirm Technical Effects

applicability. The Patent Reexamination Board maintained the rejection decision on the grounds that the patent application at issue did not comply with Article 26(3) of the *Patent Law*. The reexamination decision stated that the technical solution was not based on any existing scientific theory, but on an ultimate segmentation theory developed by the petitioner itself. The description failed to provide any experimental results to verify that an artificial magnetic field could indeed interfere with the background magnetic field of the working space, thereby interfering with neutron decay. Therefore, those skilled in the art could not predict and confirm that, by carrying out the technical solution claimed in this application, the technical effect of interfering with the background magnetic field of the working space with an artificial magnetic field, thereby interfering with the neutron decay, could be achieved. The SPCt upheld this decision and noted in its judgment that "the description does not provide any data obtained from scientific experiments from which those skilled in the art could be convinced that the technical solution claimed by the patent application in the case can achieve the technical effect disclosed in the description." In addition, the description does not disclose "the natural laws and technical means it adopted. The three pieces of experimental evidence submitted by the patent applicant cannot be admitted to prove that the description at issue sufficiently disclose the technical solution." Therefore, the invalidation decision, the first instance judgment, and the second instance judgment were correct regarding insufficient disclosure.

It is most common in chemical and pharmaceutical fields that experimental evidence is required to verify the effect of the technical solution, including the invention of a new product and a new use of a known product. In the cases *(2015) Zhi Xing Zi No. 340*[6] and *(2015) Zhi Xing Zi No. 342*,[7] the issue was whether the expression in the description "compounds of the present invention have IC_{50} from less than 1 nM to 50 mM" to describe the effect of the compound, complied with Article 26(3) of the *Patent Law*. Regarding this issue, the SPC pointed out that "when a person skilled in the art, based on prior art, cannot predict that at least a part of the claimed compounds can achieve the use or effect described in the patent application document, he or she will have reasonable doubts about the authenticity of the use and effect. Therefore, the corresponding experimental data shall be recited in the description to prove that the inventor has conducted experiments to confirm that at least one specific analytical compound among those that claimed protection has the use or effect recited in the application document before the filing date, and to enable those skilled in the art to verify the authenticity of the experiment. Otherwise, the patent application document does not meet the requirements of Article 26(3) of the *Patent Law* for sufficient disclosure of the description."

---

[6] Invention patent No. 200480026458.9. The reexamination decision (No. FS45152) maintained the rejection decision. Both the first instance judgment (*(2013) Yi Zhong Xing Chu Zi No. 751*) and the second instance judgment (*(2013) Gao Xing Zhong Zi No. 1602*) upheld the invalidation decision. The patent applicant filed for a retrial. The SPC ruled that the application for retrial was rejected.

[7] Invention patent No. 200580043628.9. The reexamination decision (No. FS45016) maintained the rejection decision. Both the first instance judgment (*(2013) Yi Zhong Xing Chu Zi No. 604*) and the second instance judgment (*(2013) Gao Xing Zhong Zi No. 1604*) upheld the invalidation decision. The patent applicant filed for a retrial. The SPC ruled that the application for retrial was rejected.

The patent application in the case of *(2015) Zhi Xing Zi No. 340* claimed a compound represented by a general formula. The efficacy experiment in the description recites the method and steps of the EGFR/ErbB2 enzyme assays, and states that "compounds of the present invention have IC_{50} from less than 1 nM to 50 mM" without indicating the specific compounds used in the experiment. The patent applicant argued that the term "compounds of the present invention" used in this application included the compounds prepared in the examples as well as their equivalents represented by the general formula, that "compounds of the present invention have IC_{50} from less than 1 nM to 50 mM" recited in the biological assay examples must be from the compounds prepared in the examples, and that, following the assay procedures disclosed in the description, it required nothing more than simple and routine experimentation for a person skilled in the art to confirm that the activity values of these compounds were indeed within the above numerical range. The SPC did not agree with this and held that, first of all, the description did not clearly recite "which specific compound or compounds were used in the experiment. Those skilled in the art could not know the experimental results were obtained from which compound or compounds, and therefore could not confirm that the claimed compound has the use or effect claimed by the applicant." Secondly, "the compounds of the present invention are expressed by the general formula and cover numerous compounds which are structurally different. The IC50 values provided in the experimental results also cover a wide range. Based on the existing information, those skilled in the art cannot be convinced of the assay results, which, therefore, cannot be used to prove that the compound in this application has the claimed activity." In view of the fact that those skilled in the art cannot predict the use or effect of the compounds of the present invention based on the prior art, the invalidation decision was appropriate to hold that the description of this application failed to sufficiently disclose the technical solutions claimed in claims 1–3.

4.6 Post-filing Date Evidence to Prove Sufficiency of Disclosure

Article 26(3) of the *Patent Law* is about the vehicle that expresses the claimed technical solution, which requires that the contents disclosed in the description should be sufficient enough to enable those skilled in the art to carry out the invention. In principle, sufficiency of disclosure of the description shall be determined according to the ability and cognition level of those skilled in the art as of the filing date, mainly based on the contents of the description and claims. Since the experimental evidence submitted after the filing date shows that the description meets the above requirements generally by means of ex post facto verification, the *Guidelines for Patent Examination* provides in Part Two, Chapter 10, §3.4 that sufficiency of disclosure of the description is judged on the basis of the disclosure contained in the initial

4.6 Post-filing Date Evidence to Prove Sufficiency of Disclosure

description and claims and that any embodiment and experimental data submitted after the date of filling shall not be taken into consideration.

The SPC modified this provision in the case *(2014) Xing Ti Zi No. 8*[8] and held that "if it can be proved that the invention can be carried out based on the contents disclosed in the description and the knowledge level and cognitive ability of a person skilled in the art before the filing date, the experimental evidence to prove that the disclosure in the description is sufficient, even submitted after the filing date, shall be considered. Such experimental evidence shall not be rejected only because it is submitted after the filing date. Timing and subject shall be strictly reviewed when considering whether to admit experimental evidence. First of all, the experimental conditions and methods involved in the experimental evidence shall be directly obtained or easily thought of by those skilled in the art by reading the description before the filing date or the priority date. Second, the knowledge level and cognitive ability of those skilled in the art shall be the standard for evaluating such evidence."

In this case, both parties submitted experimental evidence in the proceedings. Among the experimental evidence submitted by the patentee, the experimental conditions and methods were inconsistent with those in the description, especially in terms of the heating time and cooling mode, and such different experimental conditions and methods could not been readily thought of by a person skilled in the art by reading the description before the priority date of this patent. In addition, the case also involved the common general knowledge evidence submitted after the filing date. The SPC held that "this court will consider evidence that can prove the common general knowledge in the art before the priority date of this patent."

---

[8] Invention patent No. 96195564.3. The invalidation decision (No. WX13582) declared the patent right invalid in whole. The first instance judgment (*(2009) Yi Zhong Xing Chu Zi No. 2710*) maintained the invalidation decision. The second instance judgment (*(2010) Gao Xing Zhong Zi No. 1489*) vacated the first instance judgment and the invalidation decision. The Patent Reexamination Board and the invalidation petitioner filed for a retrial. The SPC vacated the second instance judgment and upheld the first instance judgment and the invalidation decision.

Chapter 5
Definiteness of Claims

A fundamental requirement for patent protection is that the scope of protection is expressed and defined clearly. In terms of the definiteness of claims, the most common issue in practice is whether the meaning of the words in a claim is definite.

The scope of protection of a claim shall be construed according to the meaning of the words used in the claim. Generally, the words used in a claim shall be understood as having the meaning that they normally have in the relevant art. In particular circumstances, where the description explicitly gives a certain word a special meaning and, by virtue of the definition of the word in the description, the scope of protection of the claim using the word is defined sufficiently clearly, such a case is allowed.

In the case *(2012) Zhi Xing Zi No. 81*,[1] a gas guiding means was the essential equipment of the patent at issue. Claim 1 of the patent at issue described the structure of the gas guiding means as: "a gas guiding means (3), which extends along the circumference of the tank (1) and is adapted to guide the gas flow closest to the wall of the tank towards the interior of the tank essentially perpendicular to the main gas flow direction (P), is arranged between the levels in at least one pair of juxtaposed nozzle levels (L1-L2, L2-L3), the guiding means (3) extending into the tank (1) to a distance from the wall thereof, which over the major part of the circumference of the wall at each point is 10-90% of the distance between the nozzle (2) positioned closest to the respective point and the wall."

The SPC held that "the key to determining the structure of the gas guiding means is to determine the distance of extending into the tank from the wall thereof, which is divided into two parts: one is 'which over the major part of the circumference of the wall at each point is 10%-90% of the distance between the nozzle (2) positioned closest to the respective point and the wall'; the other is the distance of extending into the tank from the wall thereof, corresponding to other points of the circumference of

---

[1] Invention patent No. 98802322.9. The invalidation decision (No. WX13177) declared that all patent rights were invalid. The first instance judgment (*(2009) Yi Zhong Xing Chu Zi No. 2001*) and the second instance judgment (*(2010) Gao Xing Zhong Zi No. 642*) both upheld the invalidation decision. The patentee filed for a retrial and was rejected by the SPC.

© Intellectual Property Publishing House 2024
R. Xiaolan, *Patent Administrative Litigation*, Understanding China,
https://doi.org/10.1007/978-981-97-1131-4_5

the wall than the above-mentioned 'the major part of the circumference of the wall at each point.' However, it is difficult to determine the distance from the description of claim 1. First, 'the major part of the circumference of the wall at each point' is an indefinite description with no recognized meaning in the field of the patent at issue and there is no explanation or illustration in the description. As a result, those skilled in the art cannot determine definitely and reliably, according to the teaching of the description or the recognized meaning in the technical field, which points on the circumference of the tank wall are 'the major part of the circumference of the wall at each point,' or which points are excluded from 'the major part of the circumference of the wall at each point,' so as to determine the distance of 'the major part of the circumference of the wall at each point' extending into the tank. Second, it is impossible to know from claim 1 what points are other points of the circumference of the wall than 'the major part of the circumference of the wall at each point' or how the distance into the tank is determined. Therefore, those skilled in the art are unable to determine the structure of the gas guiding means according to claim 1. Claim 1 does not comply with Article 20(1) of the *Implementing Regulations of the Patent Law* (i.e., Article 26(4) of the current *Patent Law*)."

The SPC summarized in the case *(2015) Zhi Xing Zi No. 223*[2] that "the definiteness of the term in a claim shall be determined based on the recitation of the claim, the description, and its drawings. If the only correct and reasonable interpretation of the technical feature recited in the claim can be concluded from the description and its drawings, the technical feature, and the scope of protection of the claim shall be considered definite."

In this case, claim 1 claims a sewing machine comprising a thread-cutting mechanism, and a cam mechanism having a first cam that transforms a rotating drive force of a drive motor into a driving force for the thread-cutting mechanism, and a second cam that transforms the rotating drive force of the drive motor into the drive force for a presser foot lifting mechanism, etc. The invalidation petitioner argued that terms such as "the drive cam mechanism," "first cam," "second cam," and "cam mechanism" were used in claim 1. However, as the meaning of "the drive cam mechanism" was unclear, the concept of "idle section" in claim 1 was indefinite. Regarding this, the SPC held that "it could be determined unambiguously based on the logical relationship among these terms in claim 1, the recitation of the description and the illustration of the drawings that the "drive cam mechanism" in claim 1 refers to the cam mechanism formed by the "first cam" and the "second cam" ... The 'idle section' refers to the operating state of the sewing machine during a certain period of time... The meanings of these terms are clear. A person of ordinary skill in the art can determine the scope of protection of the claim based on the description and its drawings."

---

[2] Invention patent No. 03103421.7. The invalidation decision (No. WX20220) maintained the validity of the patent. The first instance judgment (*(2013) Yi Zhong Xing Chu Zi No. 2268*) and the second instance judgment (*(2014) Gao Xing Zhong Zi No. 1584*) both upheld the invalidation decision. The invalidation petitioner filed for a retrial and was rejected by the SPC.

Chapter 6
Disclosure of Prior Art Documents

Statistics show that over 80% of patent examination cases relate to the examination of novelty and inventive step. Determination of what has been disclosed in the prior art documents is the focus of the evaluation of novelty and inventive step. If determining what is claimed in the patent at issue is mostly a matter of claim construction, determining what is disclosed in the prior art documents is purely a matter of fact-finding.

6.1 Determining the Disclosure of a Reference Document by Considering It as a Whole

Reference documents in patent examination are various, including formal publications such as patent documents, periodical articles, books, etc., and informal printed materials such as product samples, product manuals, etc. Moreover, the ways of expressing technical information vary in different publications. Therefore, to identify published technical information in a reference document, it is necessary to treat all parts of it as a whole to avoid partial and inaccurate interpretation.

The issue in the case *(2012) Zhi Xing Zi No. 13*[1] was whether Evidence 8 disclosed the technical feature in claim 26 of the patent at issue that "the end sealing plates are wrapped in the inner wall of the ends of the hollow pipe." Claim 26 in this case claims a hollow reinforced concrete pipe, comprising a hollow pipe body and end sealing plates, wherein the end sealing plates enclose the hollow pipe to form a sealed cavity.

---

[1] Invention patent No. 02122558.3. The invalidation decision (No. WX14143) declared that claims 1–25, claim 31, claims 57–72, claims 74–82, claim 84 and claim 85 were invalid and the patent rights were valid to the extent of claims 26–30 and claims 32–55. The first instance judgment (*(2010) Yi Zhong Xing Chu Zi No. 1404*) vacated the invalidation decision. The second instance judgment (*(2010) Gao Xing Zhong Zi No. 1172*) reversed the first instance judgment and maintained the invalidation decision. The invalidation petitioner filed for a retrial and was rejected by the SPC.

Claim 26 defines that "a longitudinal cemented seam is formed by joining two edges of the slurry green body of the pipe wall, and the end sealing plates are wrapped in the inner wall of the ends of the hollow pipe." The invalidation petitioner argued that claim 26 lacked novelty because the product obtained according to the production method of Embodiment 1 of Evidence 8 must be the product of claim 26 of the patent at issue. However, it could be ascertained from the relevant words in Embodiment 1 of Evidence 8 that the method of Embodiment 1 of Evidence 8 only disclosed that "two end caps 1 are rotated onto the two ends, respectively, of the cement slurry body 3 containing additional material," without specifying whether the "end cap" was inside or outside the rolled hollow pipe. The SPC held that "in the event that the preceding words are unclear, other illustrations and words in the description (Evidence 8) that specifically describe the technical solution in Embodiment 1 of Evidence 8 may be relied on to interpret Embodiment 1. Figure 2 in Evidence 8 illustrates step c in Embodiment 1…Figure 2 directly and accurately shows that the end caps 1 are rotated onto the outer mold 2, rather than the cement slurry body 3, i.e., not at the ends of the hollow pipe. Therefore, taking Figure 2 and step c of Embodiment 1 into consideration, it can be determined that Embodiment 1 in Evidence 8 does not disclose the technical feature of claim 26 that 'the end sealing plates are wrapped in the inner wall of the ends of the hollow pipe.'".

In addition, the identification of disclosure of a reference document shall be made from the perspective of a person skilled in the art. The disclosure of such reference document shall be determined based on the overall understanding of a person skilled in the art after reading it. In the case *(2012) Zhi Xing Zi No. 15*,[2] the patent at issue relates to an underground maintenance-free rotary compensator. Claim 1 defines "annular steps" on the outer wall of the inner pipe and the inner wall of the outer casing. The invalidation petitioner claimed that the stop of the maintenance-free rotary compensator in Annex 2 was equivalent to the "annular steps" in the patent at issue. It was found that Fig. 2 of the description of Annex 2 disclosed a "⌐"-shaped projected component on the right side of a steel ball 9 and a stop on the left side of it but did not specify how the stop was set. The Patent Reexamination Board found that the literal meaning of a "stop" meant that the stop should be a movable component rather than fixed on the outer wall of the inner pipe or the inner wall of the outer casing.

The SPC did not sustain this finding on the grounds that: "the working principle of a rotary compensator shows that the role of the steel ball 9 in Annex 2 is to reduce interfacial friction when the rotary compensator is working; and one function of setting a stop is to define the relevant position of the steel ball together with the '⌐'-shaped projected component to limit the axial movement between the inner and outer pipes. Therefore, although Annex 2 does not describe how the stop is set, nor does it define the connecting relationship between the stop and the '⌐'-shaped

---

[2] Utility model patent No. 200720033902.0. The invalidation decision (No. WX13158) maintained the validity of the patent. The first instance judgment (*(2009) Yi Zhong Xing Chu Zi No. 1681*) vacated the invalidation decision. The second instance judgment (*(2010) Gao Xing Zhong Zi No. 407*) affirmed the first instance judgment. The patentee filed for a retrial and was rejected by the SPC.

projected component and the inner and outer pipe walls, a person skilled in the art from the setting of the stop and the 'Ј'-shaped projected component and the function and position of the steel ball in Annex 2, can easily realize that the stop and the 'Ј'-shaped projected component are fixedly connected to the inner and outer pipe walls respectively to obtain the 'annular step' technical feature of claim 1 of this patent. The Patent Reexamination Board erred in determining that the reference document did not disclose the annular step technical feature in claim 1 of this patent."

6.2 Does the Disclosure of a Reference Document Include the Disclosure of Its Cited Documents

When a reference document cites other prior art documents, whether the disclosure of these prior art documents can be automatically considered as the disclosure of the reference document is a matter to be determined on a case-by-case basis.

The SPC pointed out in the case *(2013) Zhi Xing Zi No. 57*[3] that: "For other prior art documents cited in a reference document, it depends on the function of a cited document to determine whether this document can be relied on as a reference document for assessing the patent at issue or is treated merely as a reference document. In reality, prior art documents may be enumerated in the "Background Art" section of the patent description or cited in the "Summary" or "Detailed Description" sections of the description for various purposes, such as for explaining the defects in the prior art, or for simplicity of description of the technical solution of this patent. Therefore, there is not a one-size-fits-all solution to a prior art cited in a reference document." In this case, Reference Document 1, which was relied on to evaluate the inventive step of the patent at issue, cited Reference Document 1A in the Detailed Description, i.e., "the over-temperature protection device shown in Figure 8B is an improvement of the 3A, 3B, 3C devices described in GB-A-2194099."

The SPC held that "Reference Document 1 cited Reference Document 1A to explain the basis for improving the embodiments and thus described part of the embodiments concisely. It is reasonable that a complete understanding of the original technical solution can be obtained only after the citation of Reference Document 1A. In addition, the applicants for Reference Document 1A and Reference Document 1 are both 'OTTER CONTROLS LIMITED.' From the perspective of restoring the process of invention-creation, it is likely that the same company made further improvements to this heating vessel. When applying for a patent, the company cited its previous patent to avoid repetition."

---

[3] Invention patent No. 95194418.5. The invalidation decision (No. WX16325) declared that claim 1 and claim 18 were invalid and the patent rights were valid to the extent of claims 2–17 and claims 19–34. The first instance judgment (*(2011) Yi Zhong Xing Chu Zi No. 2028*) maintained the invalidation decision. The second instance judgment (*(2012) Gao Xing Zhong Zi No. 1215*) affirmed the first instance judgment and the invalidation decision. The patentee filed for a retrial and was rejected by the SPC.

Apart from this issue, another issue in the case was whether Reference Document 1 disclosed the feature of the patent at issue that "a heating element is provided on the side wall." STRIX Limited argued that Reference Document 1A cited in Reference Document 1 disclosed this feature.

The SPC did not sustain this claim, holding that the disclosure of Reference Document 1A on which STRIX based its claim "is in the first paragraph of the 'Background Art' section of the patent description of Reference Document 1A. The description of the invention patent usually includes the following five parts: Technical Field, Background Art, Summary, Brief Description of the Drawings and Detailed Description. Among them, the 'Background Art,' as the name suggests, describes the background technology that is useful for understanding, searching, and examining the invention and cites some documents that reflect these background technologies if possible; and the 'Summary' discloses to the public the technical problem to be solved by this patent and the technical solution adopted to solve the technical problem. The recitation that "the head is at or in the vicinity of the hole in the wall" in Reference Document 1A does not describe the technical solution of Reference Document 1A; rather, it reflects the content of GB-A-1401954 cited in the Background Art and thus did not constitute the disclosure to the public of the technical problem to be solved by the invention and the technical solution to solve the technical problem by Reference Document 1A. Therefore, it is inappropriate to regard the documents cited in the Background Art section of Reference Document 1A as part of the invention disclosed in Reference Document 1A."

The SPC further clarified this issue in the case *(2015) Zhi Xing Zi No. 67*[4]: "the content disclosed in the Background Art helps understand the technical solution of the invention or utility model but is not necessarily included in the technical solution to carry out the invention or utility model. When the technical content disclosed in the Background Art in the patent document is not clearly defined or cannot be determined directly and undoubtedly by a person skilled in the art from the patent document, adding such content to the patent document to make it a part of the embodiment of the invention or utility model will undoubtedly modify the objective disclosure of the technical content in a patent document."

In this case, Reference Document 2 is a prior art document cited in the Background Art section of Reference Document 1. Reference Document 1 is an "improved electroplating device" designed based on Reference Document 2. The invalidation petitioner claimed that in Reference Document 1, the difference between Reference Document 1 and Reference Document 2 was recited in the charactering portion, and the improvements made based on Reference Document 2 were illustrated with words and drawings in the description, omitting what did not need to be improved in Reference Document 2. Therefore, the part omitted in Reference Document 2 should

---

[4] Utility model patent No. 200920059107.8. The invalidation decision (No. WX19614) maintained the validity of the patent. The first instance judgment (*(2013) Yi Zhong Xing Chu Zi No. 1702*) and the second instance judgment (*(2014) Gao Xing Zhong Zi No. 2243*) both affirmed the invalidation decision. The invalidation petitioner filed for a retrial and was rejected by the SPC.

be added to Reference Document 1 as the technical solution disclosed in Reference Document 1 to evaluate the novelty of the patent application at issue.

Regarding this, the SPC held that: "The Background Art in the description aims to facilitate the understanding, search, and patentability examination of the invention or utility model. The *Guidelines for Patent Examination* also requires citations of documents that reflect such background art as much as possible, particularly prior art documents that contain the technical features of the preamble portion of independent claims in the claims of an invention or utility model. In this case, Reference Document 1 cited Reference Document 2 in the Background Art of the description, and its drafting complied with the requirements of the *Guidelines for Patent Examination*. However, Reference Document 1 defined the improvement made based on Reference Document 2 in the charactering portion without explaining in the description whether other technical features of Reference Document 2 were retained or whether the improvement made was limited to only the technical features in claim 1… (Since) the background art cited in Reference Document 1 is not necessarily technical features to carry out Reference Document 1, it cannot be concluded that the omitted, i.e., unimproved, technical content in Reference Document 2 belongs to the preamble portion of Reference Document 1 and is included in the disclosure of Reference Document 1."

6.3 Implicit Disclosure in Reference Documents

The disclosed technical content in a reference document includes what is explicitly recited in the reference document and what is implicit but can be determined by a person skilled in the art directly and unambiguously. However, the content of a reference document shall not be extended or narrowed down at will. The issue in the case *(2012) Zhi Xing Zi No. 3*[5] was whether Evidence 1 disclosed the technical feature in claim 1 that "a unidirectional flow limiting device is provided along the circumference of the piston." The patent at issue relates to a fast-in slow-out type elastic damper buffer, wherein a unidirectional flow limiting device (check valve) functions to adjust the flow rate of the elastic damper filling the inner cavity of the buffer. During the compression stroke (positive stroke), as the check valve opens, the flow rate of the damper increases, and the damping force decreases; during the return stroke (reverse stroke), as the check valve closes, the flow rate of the damper decreases, and the damping force increases. The adjustment function of the check valve makes the drive head advance fast and retreat slowly, protecting the equipment and reducing the noise.

---

[5] Utility model patent No. 01274761.0. The invalidation decision (No. WX14603) declared that the patent rights were invalid. The first instance judgment (*(2010) Yi Zhong Xing Chu Zi No. 2005*) vacated the invalidation decision. The second instance judgment (*(2011) Gao Xing Zhong Zi No. 213*) affirmed the first instance judgment. The Patent Reexamination Board filed for a retrial and was rejected by the SPC.

Evidence 1 disclosed an elastic cement buffer with a check valve. As can be seen from the description of Fig. 1(a) in the Description, although Fig. 1(a) does not disclose the specific shape and position of the check valve, it shows a solution with a check valve that functions to return the compressed piston rod to the original position. Therefore, the SPC held that the function of the check valve in Evidence 1 was different from the unidirectional flow limiting device in claim 1 of the patent at issue. Evidence 1 could not be regarded as implicitly disclosing the technical feature that "a unidirectional flow limiting device is provided along the circumference of the piston" in claim 1 of the patent at issue.

The content implicitly disclosed in a reference document includes not only what can be implied from the words of the reference document but also what can be directly and ambiguously determined from the drawings of the reference document. Therefore, contents inferred from the drawings or merely dimensions and their relationships measured from the drawings without verbal description shall not be considered disclosed contents of the reference document.

In the case of *(2014) Zhi Xing Zi No. 89*,[6] the patent at issue includes a feature that "the axial tooth pitch of the worm is 5–6 mm." The issue of this case was whether Evidence 3–5 submitted by the invalidation petitioner in the invalidation procedure disclosed this feature. The invalidation petitioner claimed that based on the scale and the relative positions of the adjusting worm and the positioning brake disclosed in the description and drawings of Evidence 3–5 and the recitation in the description that "the width of the positioning brake should be 1.5 thread pitches of the adjusting worm" and "the positioning brake is arranged in the center line of the length of the adjusting worm," and that "the unit of measurement is millimeters" in Evidence 5, etc., it can be directly and undoubtedly determined that the axial tooth pitch of the worm is 5–6 mm, without using any measuring tools to measure or infer the dimensions of relevant components from the drawings. Therefore, Evidence 3–5 disclosed this feature of the patent at issue. Regarding this, the Patent Reexamination Board determined that "when the wrench shown in the drawings of Evidence 3-5 has clearly marked the scale range, a person skilled in the art can directly and undoubtedly determine the axial distance between two adjacent threads of the worm gear shaft to be roughly 5-6 mm, which is not inferred from the drawings but a technical feature explicitly disclosed in the prior art."

The SPC did not uphold this determination. It held in its ruling that "the function of the drawings is to supplement the verbal expression in the description with figures so that each technical feature and the overall technical solution of the utility model can be directly and visually understood. Only the technical features that can be directly and unambiguously determined from the drawings are the disclosed contents. Contents inferred from the drawings or dimensions and their relationships measured from the drawings without verbal description shall not be considered as disclosed contents."

---

[6] Invention patent No. 200420090400.8. The invalidation decision (No. WX18323) declared that claims 1–5 were invalid. The first instance judgment (*(2012) Yi Zhong Xing Chu Zi No. 2252*) maintained the invalidation decision. The second instance judgment (*(2013) Gao Xing Zhong Zi No. 1744*) reversed the first instance judgment and the invalidation decision. The invalidation petitioner filed for a retrial and was rejected by the SPC.

6.3 Implicit Disclosure in Reference Documents

In this case, "the scale in Evidence 3-5 indicates the jaw capacity of the adjustable wrench. There are no words to explicitly define the sizes of the positioning brake and the worm or the ratio between the jaw and the brake. A person skilled in the art cannot directly and undoubtedly determine the size of the positioning brake from the size of the jaw unless directly measuring the drawings or guesswork. Therefore, for a person skilled in the art, a 5-6 mm axial tooth pitch of the worm is not a technical feature that can be directly and undoubtedly determined from the drawings."

A design patent document can be used as a reference document to evaluate the patentability of an invention or utility model. In determining the technical contents disclosed by a design patent, the three-dimensional structure of the product shall be identified from various views and the perspective of a person skilled in the art. When there is a defect in some views of a design patent, "if ordinary consumers can clearly overcome this defect to obtain a definite structure of the product, through the common sense knowledge of design or common design techniques of the same or similar types of products before the filing date and by a comprehensive analysis from each view, the design patent shall be considered as having disclosed the product structure that ordinary consumers can ascertain, unless the defect is so severe that ordinary consumers cannot determine the structure of the product in combination with all the views and his common-sense knowledge of relevant products." This is the gist of the SPC's ruling in the case *(2011) Zhi Xing Zi No. 29*.[7]

The patent in this case claims a trackless electric retractable gate. One of the issues was whether the design patent in Evidence 1–2 disclosed the "subframe" in claim 1 of the patent at issue. The SPC held that "although there are drawing flaws at intersections of the components in some views in Evidence 1-2, for example, the upper part of component 5 in the bottom view cannot be blocked by the connecting pipe component 3 considering both the front view and the right view, so it is defective to draw the component 5 as blocked by the component 3. However, ordinary consumers can further determine that component 5 is an arched frame structure based on the six views of Evidence 1-2 and the common-sense knowledge of a retractable gate before the filing date of the patent at issue. Therefore, Evidence 1-2 has disclosed the subframe in claim 1."

---

[7] Invention patent No. 01107559.7. The invalidation decision (No. WX13794) declared that claim 1, claim 3, claim 4, and claim 6 were invalid, and the patent rights were valid on the basis of claim 2 and claim 5. The first instance judgment (*(2010) Yi Zhong Xing Chu Zi No. 485*) maintained the invalidation decision. The second instance judgment (*(2010) Gao Xing Zhong Zi No. 1234*) affirmed the first instance judgment. The patentee filed for a retrial and was rejected by the SPC.

6.4 Shall the Practical Applicability of Relevant Contents Be Considered in Determining the Disclosure of Reference Documents

The novelty and inventive step of a patent application must be evaluated based on specific reference documents. Is it necessary that a prior art document have practical applicability in examining whether the prior art document can be used as a reference document to evaluate the novelty and inventive step of an invention-creation? The SPC answered this question in the case *(2015) Zhi Xing Zi No. 75*.[8] The patent application in this case related to a potentiometric creepage protection plug. During the reexamination procedure, citing Reference Document 3 and Reference Document 4, the Patent Reexamination Board determined that claims 1–8 lacked an inventive step. The patent applicant argued in the retrial petition that Reference Document 3 lacked practical applicability and thus should not be considered as the prior art of the patent application at issue because the TRIAC in Reference Document 3 could not be triggered, and the relay could not work.

The SPC held that "novelty, inventive step, and practical applicability are different legal issues. Practical applicability is not required in the identification of prior art. A patent document known to the public before the filing date of the patent at issue constitutes part of the prior art of the patent at issue and can be used to evaluate the novelty or inventive step of this patent application." In this case, "the publication dates of both Reference Documents 3 and 4 were before the filing date of the patent at issue; thus Reference Documents 3 and 4 constitute part of the prior art of the patent application at issue. In the event that Reference Document 3 discloses the relevant technical feature of claim 1, whether Reference Document 3 has practical applicability, how the TRIAC acts in it, and whether the indicator light is real and effective is irrelevant to the evaluation of the novelty or inventive step of the patent application at issue."

---

[8] Invention patent application No. 200710112701.4. The reexamination decision (No. FS44817) maintained the rejection decision. The first instance judgment (*(2012) Yi Zhong Xing Chu Zi No. 3654*) and the second instance judgment (*(2013) Gao Xing Zhong Zi No. 1557*) both affirmed the reexamination decision. The patent applicant filed for a retrial and was rejected by the SPC.

Chapter 7
Novelty

The novelty requirement for an invention or utility model to be granted a patent right means that it shall differ not only from the prior art but also from a patent application filed before and published after the filing date of the patent at issue. Under the provisions of Part II Chapter 3 of the *Guidelines for Patent Examination*, if compared with the disclosed content in the reference document, the technical solution defined in the claims of a patent application is substantially the same as the technical solution disclosed in the reference document, and if a person skilled in the art can determine from both technical solutions that these two technical solutions can be applied to the same technical field, solve the same technical problem, and have the same expected effect, the patent at issue and the reference document are considered to be the same invention or utility model.

The SPC pointed out in the ruling of the case *(2015) Zhi Xing Zi No. 158*[1] that "the determination of the novelty of a claim shall be based on whether the prior art discloses the same or substantially the same technical solution as the claim. Regarding the technical fields, technical problems, and expected effects of the patent at issue and the prior art, since the description of these aspects in the patent at issue generally is the patent applicant's subjective description of the patent at issue based on his own understanding, it is not strictly required that the prior art disclose the same technical field, technical problems, and expected effects as the patent at issue. However, where the patent at issue and the prior art are in the same technical field, if a person skilled in the art can reasonably determine that the prior art can also solve the technical problem claimed to be solved by the patent at issue and achieve the same expected effect, the claim shall be deemed to lack novelty."

---

[1] Utility model patent No. 200720142844.5. The invalidation decision (No. WX21304) declared that all patent rights were invalid. The first instance judgment (*(2013) Yi Zhong Zhi Xing Chu Zi No. 3305*) vacated the invalidation decision. The second instance judgment (*(2014) Gao Xing Zhong Zi No. 1198*) reversed the first instance judgment and upheld the invalidation decision. The patentee filed for a retrial and was rejected by the SPC.

In this case, the patent at issue relates to a conductor pattern structure of a capacitive touch panel. One of the issues of this case was whether claims 5–7 were novel relative to the reference documents. The patentee argued in the retrial petition that although the patent at issue and the reference document were directed to capacitive touch panels, the technical problems to be solved, technical solutions, and expected technical effects were not substantially the same. Therefore, they were different invention-creations.

The SPC did not support this argument. In the ruling, the court first analyzed the technical fields of the patent at issue and the reference document and concluded that both were capacitive conductor pattern structures; thus, the technical fields were the same; next, it analyzed the disclosed content in the reference document and held that the reference document had disclosed all the technical features of claim 5 of the patent at issue and thus disclosed a technical solution substantially the same as that of claim 5. Then the court analyzed the technical problems to be solved and the expected technical effects of the reference document and the patent at issue and believed that the technical problem recited in the "purpose of invention" and the technical effect recited in the "beneficial effects" in the description of the patent at issue had been disclosed in the reference documents. On this basis, the court concluded that claim 5 was not novel.

Chapter 8
Inventive Step

An inventive step is an essential indicator for evaluating whether patent rights can be granted for a patent application for an invention or utility model. Under the provisions of Article 22(3) of the *Patent Law,* the inventive step of an invention or utility model means that the technical solution of this invention or utility model is nonobvious relative to the prior art and can produce beneficial effects.

The "three-step method" is the most commonly used method for determining whether an invention or utility model is obvious relative to the prior art, which usually includes: (1) determining the closest prior art; (2) determining the distinguishing features of an invention or utility model and its actual technical solution of it; and (3) determining whether the claimed invention or utility model is obvious to a person skilled in the relevant art.

8.1 Technical Field and the Closest Prior Art

An inventive step is an essential characteristic of an invention-creation, a requirement of the level of inventiveness relative to the prior art. In determining the inventive step of an invention-creation, not only the technical solution itself shall be considered, but also the pertaining technical field, the technical problems to be solved, and the technical effects to be produced shall be considered as a whole, i.e., the technical principles, technical ideas, and technical effects of the invention-creation shall be determined comprehensively.

In the case *(2012) Xing Ti Zi No. 7*,[1] Cao Zhongquan argued that the patent's international classification number differed from that of Annex 5-1 and that they were neither in the same technical field nor in similar or related technical fields. Therefore, Annex 5-1 could not be used as a reference for determining the inventive step of the patent at issue.

The SPC did not sustain this argument. It held that "The technical field refers to the specific area of technology to which the claimed invention or utility model pertains or is applied. It is neither an upper nor adjacent technical field, nor is the invention or utility model itself. Determining the technical field of an invention or utility model shall be based on the content defined in the claims, taking into account the subject matter of the patent along with the technical functions and uses achieved by the technical solution. Annex 5-1 discloses the technology relating to the lubrication of a coil winding machine lubrication system. The technical solution of this patent aims to solve the problem of oil retention and lubrication of the helical gear set of a cutting machine. While the coil winding machine falls under the category of textile machinery and the cutting machine is considered garment machinery, both devices operate in distinct environments. However, both the patented technical solution and that of the reference document involve lubricating the mechanical system, placing them within the same technical field. As a result, it was appropriate for the Patent Reexamination Board to consider Annex 5-1 as a reference when evaluating the inventive step of this patent."

The technical field shall be the specific area of technology to which the claimed invention or utility model pertains or is applied. It is neither an upper or adjacent technical field, nor is the invention or utility model itself. In the case *(2011) Zhi Xing Zi No. 19*,[2] the SPC held that "the patent at issue is a utility model patent named 'hand dynamometer.' In determining whether it has an inventive step, the technical field of the hand dynamometer and related and similar technical fields should be determined first. Determining the technical field shall be based on the content defined in the claims, taking into account the subject matter of the patent along with the technical functions and uses achieved by the technical solution. The lowest position of a patent in the International Patent Classification can be a reference for determining its technical field. Similar technical fields generally refer to fields similar in the functions and specific uses of the utility model patent. Related technical fields generally refer to functional fields in which the distinguishing technical features of the utility model patent relative to the closest prior art are applied." The technical

---

[1] Utility model patent No. 200520014575.5. The invalidation decision (No. WX13216) declared all patent rights invalid. The first instance judgment (*(2009) Yi Zhong Xing Chu Zi No. 1326*) and the second instance judgment (*(2010) Gao Xing Zhong Zi No. 634*) both upheld the invalidation decision. The patentee filed for a retrial. The SPC brought the case up for trial and vacated the invalidation decision and first and second instance judgments.

[2] Utility model patent No. 97216613.0. The invalidation decision (WX12613) declared all the patent rights were invalid. The first instance judgment (*(2009) Yi Zhong Xing Chu Zi No. 466*) maintained the invalidation decision; the second instance judgment (*(2010) Gao Xing Zhong Zi No. 811*) vacated the first instance judgment and invalidation decision. The Patent Reexamination Board filed for a retrial and was rejected by the SPC.

function of the patent at issue was a force-measuring device, the specific use of which was to measure the gripping power of a human hand.

The closest prior art is the basis for accurately determining an inventive step. The technical solution in the prior art is most closely related to the claimed invention. In the case *(2014) Zhi Xing Zi No. 84*,[3] the SPC made it clear that "When determining whether a piece of the prior art can be used as the closest reference document, it is necessary to make this judgment from multiple perspectives, including the technical field it belongs to, its technical problem to be solved, technical effects, or use, whether it is capable of performing the function of the claimed invention, and how many technical features of the claimed invention does it disclose. If an existing technology is in the same technical field as the claimed invention and discloses the greatest number of technical features of the claimed invention, or although it is in a technical field different from that of the claimed invention, it can achieve the function of the claimed invention and disclose the greatest number of technical features of the claimed invention, then this technology can be used as the closest prior art to evaluate the inventive step of the claimed invention. The technical field shall be determined by the content defined in the claims, generally based on the subject matter of the patent in combination with the technical functions and uses realized by the technical solution." In this case, the patent at issue claimed a lead-free solder alloy and Evidence 1 disclosed an alloy connecting material for semiconductors, both of which belonged to the field of soft solder alloys. They are in the same technical field. Moreover, Evidence 1 disclosed the technical features of claim 1, i.e., the composition of the lead-free solder alloy, the content of Cu, and the balance being Sn. Therefore, Evidence 1 can be used as the closest reference to determine the inventive step of the patent at issue.

8.2 Comparison of Technical Features

The determination of the inventive step of the technical solution of an invention or utility model usually starts with dividing the claimed technical solution of this patent into several technical features, followed by determining which technical features are disclosed in the closest prior art, which technical features in the closest prior art are equivalent to the corresponding ones in the patent at issue and which technical features are distinguishing technical features.

1. Based on All the Technical Features of the Claim

All the technical features recited in the claims shall be considered in the determination of an inventive step in the technical solution of an invention or utility model.

---

[3] Utility model patent No. 99800339.5. The invalidation decision (WX15158) declared all the patent rights invalid. The first instance judgment (*(2011) Yi Zhong Xing Chu Zi No. 1113*) maintained the invalidation decision; the second instance judgment (*(2012) Gao Xing Zhong Zi No. 528*) upheld the first instance judgment and invalidation decision. The patentee filed for a retrial and was rejected by the SPCSPC.

In the case *(2010) Zhi Xing Zi No. 13*,[4] the patent at issue was a full-screen segmented light display timing traffic light, consisting of a light pole, a main signal light and a supplementary (auxiliary) signal light, wherein claim 1 not only defined the features of the light display part and the light control part, but also the features of the fixing parts in installation of each component. The invalidation petitioner claimed in the retrial application that the patent at issue should be regarded as a "whole" to determine the inventive step of the claim, i.e., the technical solution, the technical problem to be solved and the technical effect produced in the patent at issue should be considered as a whole. Since a light display and control part of the "reflector and control circuit" part in claim 1 was the feature that solved the technical problem of "serving as both a traffic command signal and a command signal countdown display" and produced the technical effect of "full-screen segmented light display timing", the eight distinguishing features in claim 1 of the patent relative to Annex 1 determined in the invalidation decision could not solve this problem. Therefore, only the features that could solve the technical problem should be considered in the determination of an inventive step.

Regarding this argument, the SPC emphasized that "it actually splits the technical solution of the patent at issue rather than consider the patent as an integrated technical solution to compare only the light display and control parts of claim 1 with Annex 1 and ignore the distinguishing features in this patent of the fixing part in installation different from Annex 1. Such practice does not comply with the provisions of the *Guidelines for Patent Examination* on the determination of an inventive step."

2. Focusing on Technical Features and Their Functions, Principles, and Uses

In the comparison of technical features, not only the technical features shall be focused on, but also the functions, principles, and effects of the relevant technical features shall be analyzed where the technical features are the same.

In the case *(2014) Zhi Xing Zi No. 43*,[5] the patent at issue was a closing device. When examining whether the patent had an inventive step, the SPC pointed out that "an invention is an integrated whole. The technical features in the technical solution are not isolated from each other. The relationship among technical features should not be split, nor should the role that these features play in the overall technical solution be overlooked. In particular, when the inventions-creations are related to the field of the structure of mechanism, components that seem similar in terms of the structure or the position may play a completely different role in the entire technical solution due to the difference in technical ideas, operating modes, and technical effects in the two

---

[4] Utility model patent No. 99214371.3. The invalidation decision (No. WX8034) maintained the validity of the patent right. The second instance judgment (*(2007) Gao Xing Zhong Zi No. 183*) upheld the invalidation decision. The invalidation petitioner filed for a retrial and was rejected by the SPC.

[5] Invention patent No. 96194851.5. The invalidation decision (No. WX16394) declared all the patent rights invalid. The first instance judgment (*(2011) Yi Zhong Zhi Xing Chu Zi No. 2961*) maintained the invalidation decision; the second instance judgment (*(2013) Gao Xing Zhong Zi No. 1759*) vacated the first instance judgment and the invalidation decision. The invalidation petitioner filed for a retrial and was rejected by the SPC.

8.2 Comparison of Technical Features

technical solutions. Therefore, when determining whether a certain technical feature in the prior art is equivalent to the corresponding technical feature of the patent at issue, it is necessary to consider whether they play the same role in the respective technical solutions."

In this case, "the engagement surface and the extension section defined in claim 1 are both set on a free end of the lever 11. When in use, the extension section cooperates with the second part to provide initial closing leverage; and the engagement surface contacts the second part to provide final closing leverage." That is, "both the extension section and the engagement surface in claim 1 are provided at one end of the lever that can move freely away from the second part. This limitation... determines the working mode and function of the extension section and the engagement surface. In comparison with this, the end of the lever 11A with the notch 24A and the extension part extending beyond the notch 24A in Evidence 1...cannot be separated from the second part, and its motion trail is fixed." In other words, the positional relationship of the notch 24A and the extension part extending beyond the notch 24A relative to other components in Evidence 1 was obviously different from the positional relationship between the engagement surface and the extension section and other components in this patent. The technical problems to be solved and the technical effects to be achieved were also different. The invalidation petitioner's claim that the two technical features were equivalent was not sustained.

In the case of *(2015) Xing Ti Zi No. 12*,[6] the SPC also analyzed the difference between the patent at issue and the closest reference from the perspectives of the technical features and their functions and uses. The patent at issue relates to a replaceable baffle curtain for the seed box of the precision dibbler. Claim 1 defined in the preamble portion that it included a seed box of a precision dibbler and defined in the features part the structures of and the relationship between the seeding window and the baffle curtain of the seed box. The invalidation decision held that the distinguishing feature 1 between claim 1 and supplementary Evidence 1 (the side of the seeding window was installed with a rubber curtain pressed by a pressure plate) was disclosed by supplementary Evidence 3. This decision was overturned by the SPC. The reason was that, structurally, "the seeding window in claim 1 refers to the place where the seed picking wheel is installed on the seed box, a window to allow seeds to reach the seeding compartment from the seed chamber, a channel that connects the seed chamber to the seeding compartment."

In supplementary Evidence 3, the seed hole itself was set on the seeding wheel, which was actually equivalent to the seed picking compartment on the seed picking wheel of this patent, and its outer opening was not equivalent to the seeding window of this patent; at the same time, in supplementary Evidence 3, the outer opening of the seed hole and the soft elastic material were in contact with the entire outer opening

---

[6] Utility model patent No. 200720183183.0. The invalidation decision (No. WX17922) declared all the patent rights invalid. The first instance judgment (*(2012) Yi Zhong Zhi Xing Chu Zi No. 1191*) vacated the invalidation decision; the second instance judgment (*(2012) Gao Xing Zhong Zi No. 1455*) vacated the first instance judgment and maintained the invalidation decision. The patentee filed for a retrial. The SPC ruled to bring the case up for trial and vacated the invalidation decision and second instance judgment.

while in this patent, the rubber curtain was only covered on one side of the seeding window. Functionally, the distinguishing feature 1 of this patent was to prevent excessive seeding or missing seeding during seeding and ensure easy replacement and maintenance of the rubber curtains, solving the problem that the conventional sealed compartment device, which is undetachable from the seeding box, is difficult to repair once damaged. The technical means in supplementary Evidence 3 functions to prevent the seeds that do not fall into the seed holes from being discharged to solve the problem of excessive or missing seeding. The two functions are not the same. The invalidation decision erred in the determination of distinguishing feature 1.

8.3 Technical Problems to Be Solved by the Invention and Technical Effect

1. Determination of the Technical Problem by the Technical Effects Achieved by Distinguishing Features

The technical problem solved by an invention shall be determined according to the technical effect that the distinguishing feature can achieve. In principle, all the technical effects that can be concluded by a person skilled in the art from the content recited in the description of the patent application can serve as the basis to determine the actual technical problem to be solved by the invention.

The case *(2014) Zhi Xing Zi No. 8*[7] relates to a pipe coupling. Compared with reference 1, claim 1 is different in three aspects: (1) in claim 1, the two clamping members define generally a U-shaped cross-section while the shank in reference 1 corresponding to the clamping members of the patent at issue has a circular cross-section; (2) in claim 1, the pipe coupling acts on the housing through the nut threaded on the clamping screw, while the pipe coupling in reference 1 does not have a nut, and the screw on the pipe coupling is tightened with an internally threaded transverse hole of one of the shank members so that the shell fastens; (3) the clamping screw passes with clearance through the shape formed by the two clamping members of claim 1; while a shank of reference 1 cannot hold a screw with clearance because it has an internally threaded transverse hole. The Patent Reexamination Board argued that the replacement of all the above-mentioned distinguishing feature structures was a conventional technical means in the field, and moreover, the bending stress was a technical defect inevitably brought about by the original structure of a clamp-type pipe coupling connecting the pipe ends, i.e., reference 1. However, this defect could be expected by a person skilled in the art based on their common knowledge and

---

[7] Invention patent No. 93100162.5 The invalidation decision (No. WX17265) declared that all patent rights were invalid. The first instance judgment (*(2012) Yi Zhong Zhi Xing Chu Zi No. 1171*) maintained the invalidation decision. The second instance judgment (*(2013) Gao Xing Zhong Zi No. 1465*) vacated the first instance judgment and the invalidation decision. The Patent Reexamination Board filed for a retrial and was rejected by the SPC.

8.3 Technical Problems to Be Solved by the Invention and Technical Effect

through logical analysis and limited experiments. Improvements made on this basis did not have prominent substantive features and notable progress.

The SPC did not sustain this argument. Firstly, regarding the determination of the technical problem solved by distinguishing features, the SPC held that "through the reading and comprehension of the patent's description at issue, one can determine that, compared with the pipe coupling disclosed in reference 1, the technical problem to be solved by this patent is to prevent the clamping screw from being affected by bending stress and to keep the clamping force basically only acting on the peripheral direction of the housing. In the analysis of the distinguishing features and the technical problems to be solved, the invalidation decision failed to recognize the technical problem solved by this patent to prevent the clamping screw from being affected by bending stress and to keep the clamping force basically only acting on the peripheral direction of the housing. In the absence of sufficient evidence and reasons, the invalidation decision's determination of the technical problem to be solved on the basis of distinguishing features of the patent at issue is unconvincing. Secondly, regarding the argument of the Patent Reexamination Board that "the bending stress is a technical defect caused by the original structure of the clamp-type pipe coupling connecting the pipe ends, i.e., reference 1", the SPC held that "a technical defect is generally discovered by a person skilled in the art through the use of the product, or obtained by them with an analysis of the prior art. There is not a necessary causal relationship between whether the defects of prior art can be expected and whether the improvement thereof has prominent substantive features and notable progress." Accordingly, the invalidation decision of the Patent Reexamination Board was vacated.

2. Unexpected Technical Effect

The technical effect of an invention is an important factor in determining the inventive step. If the technical effect of an invention changes significantly in quality or quantity compared with the prior art, beyond the reasonable expectations of a person skilled in the art, the invention has unexpected technical effect.

In the case *(2013) Zhi Xing Zi No. 77*,[8] the SPC reiterated that, "when determining whether there is an unexpected technical effect, factors such as the characteristics of the technical field to which the invention belongs, especially the expectation of the technical effect, the technical teachings of the prior art, etc. shall be considered comprehensively. Generally, the clearer the technical teachings given in the prior art, the more expected the technical effect." Claim 1 of the patent at issue claims a pharmaceutical composition for the treatment of mammary gland hyperplasia. In addition to limiting the components of the bulk drug of the composition, claim 1 also defines its preparation method, i.e., water extraction, alcohol extraction, and concentration to make granules. Compared with Evidence 1 submitted by the invalidation petitioner,

---

[8] Invention patent No. 200510000429.1. The invalidation decision (No. WX15409) declared that all patent rights were invalid. The first instance judgment (*(2011) Yi Zhong Zhi Xing Chu Zi No. 675*) vacated the invalidation decision. The second instance judgment (*(2011) Gao Xing Zhong Zi No. 1704*) vacated the first instance judgment and upheld the invalidation decision. The patentee filed for a retrial and was rejected by the SPC.

the components and proportions of the two are the same except that the patent at issue omits the step of vacuum drying, and the dosage form of the patent at issue is granules, while the dosage form of Evidence 1 is tablets. The patentee claimed that the patented product at issue was prepared by the method defined in claim 1. Compared with Evidence 1, the content of the active ingredient salvianolic acid B changed significantly, causing significant improvement in the efficacy of the final product. Therefore, the patented product at issue and Evidence 1 were different not just because of changes in the preparation method and dosage form, but the significant change in product composition, thus bringing about a significant improvement in clinical efficacy.

Regarding this, the SPC in its ruling first examined the issue of whether the content of salvianolic acid B constituted the distinguishing feature between the patent at issue and Evidence 1. It held that neither the claims nor the description of the patent at issue recited the technical content of salvianolic acid B such as functions, effects, etc. After reading the claims and description of the patent at issue, a person skilled in the art could neither know that the claimed technical solution was to increase the content of the extract of salvianolic acid B, nor that the content was related to the technical problem to be solved by the patent at issue. Therefore, the content of salvianolic acid B was not the distinguishing feature between the patent at issue and Evidence 1.

Then the SPC pointed out that "tablets and granules are both common dosage forms in the field of traditional Chinese medicine. There has been relatively ample research on the preparation methods and the expectation of the technical effects brought by them in this field. Where there is a reasonable expectation of the technical effect, when facing the technical problem of changing the dosage form to be solved by this patent, a person skilled in the art can easily think of using the conventional preparation method for preparing granules from traditional Chinese medicine extracts disclosed in the Pharmacopoeia of Evidence 3... Since neither of the two specific conventional granule preparation methods contains a vacuum drying step, a person skilled in the art can easily expect that the conventional granule preparation method adopted in the patent at issue helps to maintain the activity of the drug and achieve easier disintegration, better drug dissolution and bioavailability, and a better efficacy of the drug is also within reasonable expectations. Therefore, the expectation of the technical effect is brought about by the technical solution which combines the prescription of Evidence 1 with the conventional granule preparation method. Under the circumstance where there is a clear technical teaching in the prior art as a whole, the technical effect inevitably produced by the preparation method does not exceed the reasonable expectations of a person skilled in the art."

3. Technical Effect Evidence Submitted After the Filing Date

As the patent system provides protection in exchange for disclosure, the protection of the patent right shall be commensurate with the technical contribution made by the inventor compared with the prior art before the filing date. The technical contribution shall be fully disclosed and recited in the original description. Technical contributions that are not recited in the original description shall not be used as a basis for claiming patent protection.

8.3 Technical Problems to Be Solved by the Invention and Technical Effect

In the case *(2013) Zhi Xing Zi No. 77*,[9] the SPC emphasized that "the patent application document submitted on the filing date is the basis for determining whether the patent can be granted. Technical documents submitted by the patentee after the filing date to prove the technical content not recited in the patent description generally are not the basis to determine whether the patent can be granted if the technical content does not belong to the common knowledge before the date of the patent application, or is not used to prove the knowledge level and cognitive ability of a person skilled in the art." In this case, the patentee submitted Counterevidence 3 in the invalidation procedure to prove that the invention had achieved unexpected technical effects. The SPC held that "Counterevidence 3 is a paper published after the filing date of this patent, which used salvianolic acid B as an index to compare the difference in content of the extracts of Rukuaixiao tablets prepared by vacuum drying and spray drying and concluded that the content of salvianolic acid B in Rukuaixiao tablets prepared by spray drying was relatively higher. In this case, Counterevidence 3 explains the relationship between the preparation process and the content of salvianolic acid B to a certain extent, but it is a technical document published after the filing date of this patent, and the technical content is not within the knowledge level and cognitive ability possessed by a person skilled in the field before the filing date of the patent. Therefore, the content recited in Counterevidence 3 should not be used as the basis for determining the technical effect of this patent. As the patent description does not recite the increase of salvianolic acid B content and its effect, Counterevidence 3 should not be used as comparative experimental data."

In another case, *(2012) Zhi Xing Zi No. 41*,[10] the SPC emphasized again that "the technical content disclosed in the patent description submitted by the patent applicant in the application is the basis for the patent administration department of the State Council to examine the patent, for the applicant to amend the application documents, and also for the public to understand, disseminate and utilize patented technologies. A description shall fully disclose an invention or utility model. The field of chemistry belongs to experimental science, in which the factors affecting the result of an invention are multi-faceted, intersecting, and intricate. A description shall be drafted in a way that a person skilled in the art can implement the invention. When a person skilled in the art cannot predict on the basis of the prior art that the claimed technical solution can achieve the claimed purpose and technical effect, the description should recite clearly and fully corresponding experimental data, so that

---

[9] Invention patent No. 200510000429.1. The invalidation decision (No. WX15409) declared that all patent rights were invalid. The first instance judgment (*(2011) Yi Zhong Zhi Xing Chu Zi No. 675*) vacated the invalidation decision. The second instance judgment (*(2011) Gao Xing Zhong Zi No. 1704*) vacated the first instance judgment and upheld the invalidation decision. The patentee filed for a retrial and was rejected by the SPC.

[10] Invention patent No. 96111063.5. The invalidation decision (No. WX12712) declared that part of the patent rights were invalid. The first instance judgment (*(2009) Yi Zhong Zhi Xing Chu Zi No. 1371*) maintained the invalidation decision. The second instance judgment (*(2010) Gao Xing Zhong Zi No. 566*) affirmed the first instance judgment. The patentee filed for a retrial and was rejected by the SPC.

a person skilled in the art can implement the technical solution, solve its technical problems, and produce the expected technical effect.

What a person skilled in the art cannot directly and exclusively obtain from the prior art shall be recited in the description. If a person skilled in the art cannot expect the claimed therapeutic effect of the technical solution based on the prior art, the description should also provide sufficient experimental data to prove that the technical solution can produce the claimed effect. Technical solutions, technical effects, etc. that are not disclosed in the patent description generally should not be used as the basis for evaluating whether the patent right meets the statutory patent-granting and post-grant review standards. The experimental data submitted after the filing date are not content recited and disclosed in the original patent application document, and cannot be accessed by the public. If these experimental data are not the prior art of the application, and cannot be obtained by a person skilled in the art before the filing date, it will be contrary to the first-to-file principle and the nature of the patent system to provide protection in exchange for disclosure if such data are relied on to determine that the technical solution can achieve the claimed technical effect. It is unfair to the public if patent rights are granted on this basis. When a patent applicant or patentee intends to submit comparative test data to prove that the claimed technical solution has an inventive step relative to the prior art, the premise of admitting the data is that the data must correspond to the technical effects clearly recited in the original application documents."

In this case, the patentee Takeda Pharmaceutical Co., Ltd. submitted Counterevidence 7 in the invalidation procedure to prove that the combination drug therapy of pioglitazone and glimepiride achieved unexpected blood glucose lowering effect compared with the single drug therapy and other combination drug therapies. However, "the patent description only uses the experimental results of the combination of pioglitazone and voglibose, as well as the combination of pioglitazone and glimepiride to prove that the combination of an insulin sensitivity enhancer and an insulin secretion enhancer has better effect than that in one of the drugs alone in terms of lowering blood glucose, but does not mention the pros and cons of the effects of different drug combination therapies. The technical effect which Takeda Pharmaceutical Co., Ltd. submitted the experimental data to prove is not recited in the original application documents, nor is it verified. Such experimental data cannot serve as the basis to determine the inventive step of an invention."

In addition, a precondition for the technical effect evidence submitted after the filing date to be admitted and considered in the determination of an inventive step is that it is recited in the original description or relevant to the technical effects that have been mentioned in the original description.

In the case *(2011) Zhi Xing Zi No. 86*,[11] in the invalidation procedure, Boehringer Ingelheim Pharma GmbH and Co KG submitted Counterevidence 1, intending to

---

[11] Invention patent No. 01817143.5. The invalidation decision (No. WX12206) declared that all patent rights were invalid. The first instance judgment (*(2009) Yi Zhong Zhi Xing Chu Zi No. 83*) maintained the invalidation decision. The second instance judgment (*(2010) Gao Xing Zhong Zi No. 751*) affirmed the first instance judgment. The patentee filed for a retrial and was rejected by the SPC.

prove that the monohydrate claimed by the patent at issue was superior to the anhydrate of Evidence 1 in terms of "particle size stability." Regarding this issue, the SPC held that "Boehringer admits in this Court's inquiry that 'particle size stability' in Counterevidence 1 refers to the physical stability of particle size. However, the last paragraph on page 1 of the description only refers generally to 'the activity stability of the starting material under various environmental conditions, the stability in the pharmaceutical preparation manufacturing process and the stability of the final pharmaceutical composition'; paragraph 5 on page 2 of the description further describes the aforementioned 'the stability in the pharmaceutical preparation manufacturing process,' i.e. 'another problem that can arise in the milling process for the manufacturing of the desired pharmaceutical preparation is the energy input caused in the process and the stress on the crystal surface, which can lead to changes in polymorphism, amorphous formation, or crystal lattice.' It can be seen that the recitation of physical stability in the description mentions only the crystal form and crystal lattice, not the 'particle size' mentioned in Counterevidence 1, nor does it give any relevant technical teachings and inspirations. Moreover, according to the provisions of the Pharmacopoeia (2000 edition), during the 'accelerated test', it is necessary to conduct the test according to the key test items of stability. The test item 'inhalation (powder) aerosols' listed in the attached table of the Pharmacopoeia does not include the 'particle size' mentioned in Counterevidence 1. Therefore, a person skilled in the art after reading the description and the provisions of the *Pharmacopoeia (2000)* on the 'accelerated test', cannot conclude that the technical effect of 'particle size stabilization' described in Counterevidence 1 has been recited in the description. The technical effect described in Counterevidence 1 should not be considered in the evaluation of the inventive step of claim 1."

8.4 Teachings

The core of the evaluation of an inventive step lies in whether there are any technical teachings in the prior art as a whole to motivate a person skilled in the art, when facing a technical problem to be solved by the invention, to introduce the technical means expressed by the distinguishing features to improve the closest prior art.

1. A Distinctive Feature Formed by Common Knowledge or a Customary Method to Solve the Same Technical Problem in the Art

If the distinguishing feature between a claim and a reference is common knowledge or a customary method in the art to solve the same technical problem, there are technical teachings in the prior art as a whole to introduce the said distinguishing feature. In the case *(2011) Xing Ti Zi No. 8*,[12] claim 1 claims an anti-β-lactamase antibiotic

---

[12] Invention patent No. 97108942.6. The invalidation decision (No. WX8113) declared that all patent rights were invalid. The first instance judgment (*(2006) Yi Zhong Zhi Xing Chu Zi No. 786*) maintained the invalidation decision. The second instance judgment (*(2007) Gao Xing Zhong Zi*

complex which is a compound preparation prepared by mixing sulbactam and penicillin or cefotaxime. The reference disclosed that sulbactam could be used clinically in combination with piperacillin or cefotaxime in particular proportions to overcome the problem of antibiotic resistance and expand the antibacterial spectrum; however, it did not disclose a compound preparation prepared from the complex consisting of sulbactam, penicillin, and cefotaxime. The issue of this case was whether there were any technical teachings from the combination of the two drugs to the compound preparation of them.

The SPC first examined the relationship between the clinical combination of the drugs and the compound preparation, i.e., "although the combination of the two drugs and the compound preparation of them belong to different technical fields and are in different properties, they are also very closely related." The Court concluded that "clinical medical practice, including drug combination, is an important basis and source for the development and verification of β-lactamase inhibitor antibiotic compound preparations; the preparation of multiple drugs in the combination into a compound preparation is a specific way to realize the combination of β-lactamase inhibitors and antibiotics. The close relationship between the two represents precisely the saying 'medicine and pharmacy are two beans in a pod' in this technical field. In the case where sufficient technical information is disclosed for clinical combination drug use, a person skilled in the art can obtain corresponding technical teachings from it."

The Court then examined the disclosed content of the reference and held that the reference had disclosed the information on the combination use of the two drugs amply and accurately. "A person skilled in the art can obtain enough teachings and motivation to think of adopting conventional processes to prepare sulbactam and piperacillin or cefotaxime into a compound preparation for the convenience of combination use. The nature of sulbactam, piperacillin, and cefotaxime shows that no prior art teaches away or is an obvious obstacle to making a compound preparation of them."

Therefore, the Court finally concluded that the second-instance judgment one-sidedly emphasized the difference between the combination drug and the compound preparation and ignored the close relationship between the two; failed to determine and consider the technical content disclosed in the reference comprehensively and accurately, as the result of which the second instance judgment found that claim 1 had an inventive step compared to the reference. The second instance judgment erred in both the facts-finding and the application of the law.

In the case *(2015) Zhi Xing Zi No. 156*,[13] the patent application at issue relates to a thermometer for measuring the temperature of edible oil. The distinguishing

---

No. 146) vacated the first instance judgment and the invalidation decision. The invalidation petitioner filed for a retrial. The SPC ruled to bring the case up for trial, vacated the second instance judgment and upheld the invalidation decision.

[13] Invention patent No. 200710006408.X. The reexamination decision (No. FS41041) maintained the decision of refusal. The first instance judgment (*(2012) Yi Zhong Zhi Xing Chu Zi No. 2947*) and the second instance judgment (*(2013) Gao Xing Zhong Zi No. 37*) both upheld the reexamination decision. The patentee filed for a retrial and was rejected by the SPC.

8.4 Teachings

feature between claim 1 and reference 1 was that reference 1 used different color-changing printing ink to indicate temperature range during cooking, while the patent application at issue adopted the percentage of the temperate range of the edible oil in cooking[14] to indicate the cooking temperature.

The issue between the two parties was whether the above-mentioned distinguishing feature brought about an inventive step to the claim. The SPC held that the technical effect to be achieved in reference 1 and claim 1 "is the same, i.e., to indicate more visually the temperature of the edible oil during cooking. Therefore, for those of ordinary skill in the art, since reference 1 has taught a method other than the ordinary temperature scale to indicate the oil temperature, and it has been commonly known to those of ordinary skill in the art that the percentage of the highest oil temperature can be used to indicate the temperature of edible oil during cooking when faced with the technical problem of how to indicate the temperature of edible oil more visually, those of ordinary skill in the art will easily think of using the percentage of the highest oil temperature to indicate the temperature of the edible oil. This method of indicating the oil temperature does not produce any unexpected technical effect to the application." Therefore, the patent application at issue did not meet the inventive step requirement.

2. A Distinctive Feature Disclosed in Another Reference and with the Same Function

If the distinguishing feature between a claim and the prior art has been disclosed in another reference, and it plays the same role in the patent at issue as in the reference, there is a teaching in the prior art that cites the said distinguishing feature.

In the case *(2014) Zhi Xing Zi No. 29*,[15] the patent at issue relates to a traditional Chinese medicine preparation for the treatment of oral inflammation. The difference between claim 1 and Annex 1 is that one of the components in claim 1 is *Lonicerae Flos*, while in Annex 1 it is *Lonicerae Japonicae Flos*. The issue of this case was whether the said substitution would bring about an inventive step to the patent at issue. The SPC, after examining the contents of Annexes 3 and 4 submitted by the invalidation petitioner about the functions and indications of Lonicerae Japonicae Flos and Lonicerae Flos, held that "both have the functions of clearing away heat and removing toxicity, cooling and dispelling wind-heat, and both can be used for the treatment of carbuncle, swelling and hard furuncle, pharyngitis, erysipelas, pyrotoxic dysentery, common cold with wind-heat syndrome, and damp-heat diseases. For a person skilled in the art, oral inflammation is a particular disease within the scope of carbuncle, swelling and hard furuncle treatment. Therefore, since the nature, flavor, channel tropism, and main indications of the Lonicerae Flos and Lonicerae Japonicae

---

[14] Translator's note: The patent description recites that the oil temperature range (− 10–210 °C) is divided into 11 equal intervals, each covering a range of 20 °C, with − 10–10 °C as zero percent done, 10–30 °C as 10% done…and 190–210 °C as 100% done.

[15] Invention patent No. 200710151989.6. The invalidation decision (*No. WX18566*) declared that all patent rights were invalid. The first instance judgment (*(2012) Yi Zhong Zhi Xing Chu Zi No. 3190*) and the second instance judgment (*(2013) Gao Xing Zhong Zi No. 640*) both upheld the invalidation decision. The patentee filed for a retrial and was rejected by the SPC.

Flos are the same, and the main efficacy of the Lonicerae Flos for the treatment of carbuncle, swelling and hard furuncle is also very similar to the use of Lonicerae Japonicae Flos in the treatment of oral inflammation in Annex 1, a person skilled in the art can easily think of combining Annexes 1, 3 and 4 and replacing the Lonicerae Japonicae Flos in Annex 1 with the Lonicerae Flos, which is very obvious."

3. Invention by Replacing Elements and Invention by Omitting Elements

An invention by replacing elements refers to an invention formed by replacing one element of a known product or method with another known element; an invention by omitting elements refers to an invention that omits one or more elements of a known product or method. If the replacement of a certain element in a product or method results in the omission of other elements related to it, such an invention is not an invention by omitting elements. The inventive step of this invention shall be determined as an invention by replacing elements.

In the case *(2015) Zhi Xing Zi No. 362*[16] the patent at issue relates to a vehicle-mounted ice-storage air conditioner for electric vehicles. One of the differences between claim 1 and reference 1 is claim 1 utilizes supercooled water for cooling, wherein the supercooled water at the bottom of the vehicle-mounted ice-storage tank flows through a water inlet pipe, a frequency converter speed adjusting pump, a heat exchanger, and a water outlet pipe back to the bottom of the vehicle-mounted ice-storage tank; while reference 1 uses ice-cooled ethylene glycol enclosed in the circulation pipeline as the coolant. The patentee argued that the patent application at issue did not contain the expansion water tank, the three-way valve, the expansion water pipe, and the heat pipe in the ice-storage tank in reference 1. The patent application at issue omitted many parts of reference 1 and at the same time produced unexpected technical effect difficult to predict in advance by a person skilled in the art. Therefore, under the relevant provisions of the *Guidelines for Patent Examination* on "the invention by omitting elements", the patent application at issue had an inventive step.

Regarding this, the SPC held that "compared with reference 1, the fundamental reason why this application lacks the corresponding components is that the different refrigerants used in the two cause the difference in the structures of the corresponding ice-storage air conditioners. The refrigerant used in the former is supercooled water, which is pumped into the ice-storage tank by the water inlet pipe and then returns through the water outlet pipe to the ice-storage tank. Since the supercooled water is non-corrosive and does not need to be isolated from the ice in the ice-storage tank, an open circulation system is used. The refrigerant used in the latter is ethylene glycol solution which is corrosive and is not suitable for use in an open system. Therefore, the ethylene glycol solution as a refrigerant is isolated from the ice in the ice-storage tank, and a closed circulation system is used. When the temperature of

---

[16] Invention patent application No. 201010167896.4. The reexamination decision (No. FS72420) maintained the decision of refusal. The first instance judgment (*(2015) Jing Zhi Xing Chu Zi No. 7*) and the second instance judgment (*(2015) Gao Xing Zhi Zhong Zi No. 1989*) both upheld the reexamination decision. The patentee filed for a retrial and was rejected by the SPC.

8.5 Auxiliary Standards to Determine an Inventive Step

the refrigerant changes, a closed circulation system will undergo thermal expansion, which will cause the pressure in the circulation pipeline to change. Therefore, an expansion tank, an expansion pipe and a three-way valve are added to the latter to supplement water and stabilize the pressure, so as to overcome the above defects in the closed circulation system. It can be seen that the technical solutions of the present application and reference 1 are not a simple element omission, but essentially the replacement of the corresponding ice-storage air conditioner structure due to different choices of refrigerants. Therefore, Jinjian's claim that the technical solution of the patent application at issue was an invention by omitting elements on the basis of the technical solution disclosed in reference 1 is not sustained by this Court."

8.5 Auxiliary Standards to Determine an Inventive Step

In addition to the three-step method for the determination of the inventive step of an invention-creation, the *Guidelines for Patent Examination* also provides auxiliary judgment standards in five situations, such as inventions that solve a long-felt but unsolved technical problem, inventions that overcome technical prejudices, and inventions that are commercially successful, etc.

1. Technical Prejudice

Overcoming a technical prejudice in the prior art is an important auxiliary examination standard for judging the inventive step of an invention. The so-called "technical prejudice" refers to pervasive perception that deviates from objective facts among a person skilled in the art regarding a certain technical problem within a certain period of time and in a certain technical field, which leads people to ignore other possibilities and hinders research and development in the field of the art.

In the case *(2013) Zhi Xing Zi No. 31*,[17] the SPC held that "if an invention is made by overcoming a technical prejudice and adopting a technical means that was abandoned due to the prejudice, and hereby has solved a technical problem, the invention has prominent substantive features and represents notable progress, and thus has an inventive step. Whether there is a technical prejudice in the prior art should be judged in light of the overall content of the prior art."

The case relates to the use of a compound of formula (I) for the selective control of at least one weed in crops of cereals. The patentee contended that, based on the content of reference 2, the patent application at issue overcomes the technical prejudice. The contention was not sustained by the SPC. The Court explained in its ruling: "Although the data in Table A-2 of reference 2 show that the effect of using the sodium salt (I - 2, Na salt) of the compound of formula (I) identical to the

---

[17] Invention patent No. 99811707.2. The reexamination decision (No. FS11964) maintained the decision of refusal. The first instance judgment (*(2008) Yi Zhong Xing Chu Zi No. 628*) and the second instance judgment (*(2009) Gao Xing Zhong Zi No. 719*) both upheld the reexamination decision. The patentee filed for a retrial and was rejected by the SPC.

present patent application alone is poorer compared with the synergistic effect of its combined use with metribuzin, reference 2 does not disclose that the sodium salt (I - 2, Na salt) of the compound of formula (I) cannot be used for crop range and herbicidal range described in reference 2. Instead, the data in Table A-2 of reference 2 show that the use of the sodium salt (I-2, Na salt) of the compound of formula (I) alone has an efficacy of 60% against windgrass and 90% against Setaria viridis respectively. Arysta LifeScience North America, LLC claims that patent application at issue overcomes a technical prejudice and has an inventive step. A precondition for this claim to be sustained is that Arysta can prove such technical prejudice is objective. Since the evidence Arysta submits fails to prove that the use of a compound of formula (I) (I-2, Na salt) alone as the selective control of weeds in crops of cereals is a technical solution abandoned by a person skilled in the art, its claim that the application overcomes a technical prejudice is not sustained by this Court."

In the case *(2012) Zhi Xing Zi No. 41*,[18] the patent at issue claims a pharmaceutical composition for preventing or treating diabetes, etc., consisting of pioglitazone or a pharmacologically acceptable salt thereof, and sulfonylurea, wherein pioglitazone or its salt is used as an insulin sensitivity enhancer and sulfonylurea is used as an insulin secretion enhancer. Evidence 1 submitted by the invalidation petitioner discloses that for diabetic conditions, sulfonylureas can be administered alone, or combined with insulin sensitivity enhancers together, wherein insulin sensitivity enhancers can be pioglitazone, troglitazone, etc. The patentee, Takeda Pharmaceutical Co., Ltd., contended that in the prior art, there was a technical prejudice which favored troglitazone over pioglitazone or ciglitazone as an insulin sensitivity enhancer.

The SPC held that "technical prejudice refers to the understanding of persons skilled in the art of a certain technical problem in a technical field during a certain period of time that departs from objective facts, leads a person skilled in the art to believe that there is no other possibility and hinders the research and development in that technical field." In this case, "no (evidence) discloses that troglitazone is superior to pioglitazone and therefore there is a tendency not to choose pioglitazone in the treatment of diabetes. Moreover, science and technology are in constant development and change with twists and turns sometimes, which means the state of art after the priority date is not necessarily consistent with the previous state of art. The fact that pioglitazone has not been selected as an insulin-sensitivity enhancer like others in some literature does not suggest that pioglitazone has side effects that make it unsuitable for use as a human drug." Some evidence does not involve studies of pioglitazone, which "does not suggest that pioglitazone cannot be used as an insulin sensitivity enhancer, nor does it mean that pioglitazone has not been studied in the prior art. The above content is far from forming a general understanding that pioglitazone is not suitable as a human drug, nor can it hinder the research and development in related technical fields. Takeda Pharmaceutical Co., Ltd.'s contention

---

[18] Invention patent No. 96111063.5. The invalidation decision (No. WX12712) declared that part of the patent rights were invalid. The first instance judgment (*(2009) Yi Zhong Zhi Xing Chu Zi No. 1371*) maintained the invalidation decision. The second instance judgment (*(2010) Gao Xing Zhong Zi No. 566*) affirmed the first instance judgment. The patentee filed for a retrial and was rejected by the SPC.

8.5 Auxiliary Standards to Determine an Inventive Step

that the patent at issue has an inventive step because it overcomes the technical prejudice in the field is not sustained."

2. Commercial Success

Commercial success of an invention is another auxiliary factor for determining an inventive step. The preconditions for applying this auxiliary factor are: first, the invention has indeed achieved commercial success; second, the commercial success of the invention is the direct result of the technical features of the invention instead of other factors.

The SPC explained this matter in the case *(2012) Xing Ti Zi No. 8*.[19] The case relates to a B-Mode ultrasonic monitoring instrument for induced abortion. The invalidation decision and the first-instance judgment both held that claim 1 in this case did not have an inventive step compared to the combination of Annexes 2 and 4. The patentee submitted new evidence during the second-instance trial of the case. The second-instance judgment held that "the new Evidence 1 and 3 can prove that the patent at issue and the obstetrics and gynecology surgical instrument with B-ultrasonography monitoring produced in accordance with the technical solution of this patent solve the problem of how to improve the success rate of induced abortion in the prior art, reduce the occurrence of surgical complications, and solve the problem of conducting an operation by obstetrics and gynecologists under blindsight. The new Evidence 2 and 3 can prove that obstetrics and gynecology surgical instrument with B-ultrasonography monitoring produced in accordance with the technical solution of this patent has been widely promoted throughout the country and has a certain market share through government procurement. The above evidence can prove that this patent has achieved commercial success which is directly caused by the technical features of this utility model patent." The invalidation decision was vacated accordingly.

The Patent Reexamination Board was not satisfied with the second-instance judgment and petitioned the SPC, arguing that the second instance judgment erred in fact-finding and law application regarding the "commercial success" of the patent at issue. To be specific, "first, the second instance judgment erred in fact-finding because the judgment directly determined the commercial success of the product based on a government procurement contract and a published compact disc, without taking into account that the publication of the compact disc was a conduct 'similar to unilateral advertising' or whether the conclusion of the sales contract was based on technical factors. Second, in the judgment of an inventive step, 'commercial success' refers to the examination and evaluation of whether an invention can obtain a corresponding monopolistic position from the perspective of its stimulating effect

---

[19] Invention patent No. 200420012332.3. The invalidation decision (No. WX12728) declared that all patent rights were invalid. The first instance judgment (*(2009) Yi Zhong Xing Chu Zi No. 911*) maintained the invalidation decision. The second instance judgment (*(2011) Gao Xing Zhong Zi No. 1441*) vacated the first instance judgment and the invalidation decision. The Patent Reexamination Board filed for a retrial. The SPC ruled to bring the case up for trial and vacated the second instance judgment. (Translator note: The author made a mistake here by indicating that the second instance judgment was (2009) Gao Xing Zhong Zi No. 1441 and that the SPC upheld the second instance judgment.)

on the social economy, which shall come into play only when it is difficult to draw a clear conclusion by the three-step method or when only a negative conclusion can be reached. The application of this judgment method should be followed that: (1) commercial success must be caused by a certain feature distinguished from the prior art, rather than an existing technical solution in the prior art; (2) commercial success must be caused by this distinguishing feature, rather than factors such as sales strategies, sales methods, etc.; (3) 'commercial success' requires not only that the product corresponding to a certain technical solution be sold, but also that the product be significantly superior to existing ones commercially due to the improvement of the prior art made by the technical solution at issued. The second instance judgment erred in the application of law because it generally concluded that 'the patent has achieved commercial success' without examining whether there was a distinguishing feature between the patent at issue and the prior art or whether the sales contract in new Evidence 3 was brought about by the distinguishing feature and because it directly determined that the 'government procurement' and 'sales contract' were 'commercial success' under the *Patent Law* without taking into account the various factors that government procurement was subject to and the particularity of medical device sales in our country."

The SPC agreed with the argument of the Patent Reexamination Board. The SPC pointed out in its judgment that "the evaluation of the inventive step of a technical solution generally starts from the perspective of its contribution to the prior art, following the relatively objective 'three-step method' to determine whether the claimed technical solution constitutes a substantial 'contribution' to the prior art, so as to decide whether a patent right shall be granted. When it is difficult to determine the inventive step of a technical solution, or when a technical solution lacks an inventive step by relying on the 'three-step method', commercial success will be factored into the inventive step judgment to encourage social-economic development. When the product of a technical solution is commercially successful, if this success is directly caused by its technical features, which on the one hand reflects the beneficial effect of the technical solution, and on the other hand also shows that it is not obvious, the technical solution has an inventive step. However, if the commercial success is due to other reasons, such as the improvement of sales techniques or advertising, then commercial success is not a basis for determining an inventive step.

Therefore, when a technical solution is not distinctive enough from the prior art to be granted a patent, if there is evidence showing that the distinguishing technical feature has achieved success in the market, commercial success is recognized from the perspective of promoting economy. Commercial success is an auxiliary factor for the judgment of an inventive step. Compared with the relatively objective 'three-step method', a relatively strict standard shall be followed in the determination of whether the commercial success has indeed resulted in the technical solution being granted a patent right. When an applicant or patentee claims his invention or utility model has achieved commercial success, the following shall be examined: (1) whether the technical solution of the invention or utility model has truly achieved commercial success; (2) whether the commercial success is caused by the technical feature improved by the technical solution of the invention or utility model relative to the prior art, not by factors other than the technical feature.

Commercial success reflects the degree to which an invention or utility model is recognized by the society. In theory, commercial success should be determined by the market share occupied by the technology or product represented by the invention or utility model compared with other similar technologies or products in the same industry. Mere product sales cannot represent commercial success. The direct reasons for the commercial success of an invention or utility model should be the focus of inventive step judgment. What leads to commercial success must be the technical feature of the technical solution of the invention or utility model that has been improved compared with the prior art, rather than factors other than the technical feature. Therefore, the reasons for the commercial success must be analyzed in detail, so as to exclude the influence of the factors other than the technical feature on the commercial success.

In this case, in the invalidation procedure, the patentee did not assert that the patent was commercially successful, nor did he submit any evidence of the commercial success of the patent. Therefore, it was not improper for the Patent Reexamination Board not to take into account the factor of commercial success when determining the inventive step of this patent. The patentee submitted evidence in the second instance to prove the commercial success of the patented product. New Evidence 1 is the testimony of doctors in 11 hospitals, which records the effect of the 'induced abortion with transvaginal ultrasound' technology in these hospitals. New Evidence 2 is the government procurement contracts entered into between the Population and Family Planning Committees of Hubei, Henan and Heilongjiang Provinces and Wuxi Belson Imaging Technology Co., Ltd. respectively concerning Belson-700A, Belson-700D, Belson-700C products.

New Evidence 3 is the certificate issued by Chinese Medical Multimedia Press on the publication of the 'induced abortion with transvaginal ultrasound technique' DVD-ROM. The above evidence shows that the Population and Family Planning Committees of Hubei, Henan and Heilongjiang Provinces purchased 116 sets of the patented product, which however is not enough to show that the patented product has achieved commercial success in view of the sales volume of it. Therefore, the second instance judgment which held that 'the patent has achieved commercial successes based on new Evidence 2 and 3 lacks sufficient evidence and is not sustained by this Court."

8.6 Inventive Step of Inventions and Utility Models

The legislative intent of the *Patent Law* is to protect the legitimate rights and interests of patentees, encourage invention and innovation, promote the application of inventions-creations, improve innovation capabilities, and promote scientific and technological progress and economic and social development. It can be seen that the patent system not only protects the legitimate rights and interests of patentees, but also that of the public in order to achieve a balance between the two. It is necessary to set reasonable patent granting standards to achieve this balance. For invention or utility model patents, it is necessary to establish a reasonable inventive step judgment standard. If the inventive step standard is set too low, it will make it easier for patent applications with a low degree of innovation to be granted or difficult to be declared invalid, which will inevitably limit the dissemination and utilization of technology, hinder scientific and technological progress and social development, and harm the interests of the public. If the inventive step standard is set too high, it will be much more difficult for patent applications to be granted, which will undermine the incentive effect of the *Patent Law* on technological innovation.[20]

For this reason, Article 22(3) of the *Patent Law* sets forth different standards for determining the inventive step for invention and utility model patents, i.e., the inventive step standard for invention patents should be higher than those for utility model patents. For an invention patent to have an inventive step, it must have prominent substantive features and notable progress compared with the prior art, while for a utility model patent to have an inventive step, it only needs to have substantive features and progress compared with the prior art.

Under the provisions of Chapter VI of Part IV of the *Guidelines for Patent Examination*, the difference between the standards for determining the inventive step for inventions and utility models mainly lies in whether there are technical teachings in the prior art. To be specific, one is the field of the prior art, and the other is the quantity of the prior art.

1. Technical Field of the Prior Art

The SPC clarified the difference between the inventive step evaluation standard of inventions and that of utility models compared with the prior art in the case *(2011) Zhi Xing Zi No. 19*[21] that "as the inventive step evaluation standards of invention patents and utility model patents are different, the technical fields to be considered in the technical comparison should also be different, which is an important aspect that reflects the difference between the inventive step evaluation standard of invention patents and that of utility model patents." Since "the evaluation standard of the inventive step of a utility model patent is relatively lower, the scope of the field of prior art to be considered when evaluating the inventive step should also be narrower, and the comparison should generally focus on the prior art in the technical field to which the utility model patent belongs. However, where the prior art has given clear technical teachings to motive a person skilled in the art to search for relevant technical means in similar or related technical fields, the prior art in similar or related technical fields may also be considered. The so-called clear technical teachings refer

---

[20] *(2011) Zhi Xing Zi No. 19*. For detailed information, see next note.

[21] Utility model patent No. 97216613.0. The invalidation decision (No. WX12613) declared that all patent rights were invalid. The first instance judgment (*(2009) Yi Zhong Xing Chu Zi No. 466*) maintained the invalidation decision. The second instance judgment (*(2010) Gao Xing Zhong Zi No. 811*) vacated the first instance judgment and the invalidation decision. The Patent Reexamination Board filed for a retrial and was rejected by the SPC.

to technical teachings clearly documented in the prior art or that a person skilled in the art can directly and undoubtedly determine from the prior art." In other words, if a prior art belongs to a similar or related technical field, the prior art can be used to evaluate the inventive step of a utility model patent only when the prior art gives clear technical teaching.

In this case, claim 1 of the utility model patent at issue claims a handgrip dynamometer, which differs from the closest prior art Evidence 7 in terms of force sensors. The invalidation decision held that claim 1 did not have an inventive step relative to the combination of Evidence 7 and 2. The SPC ruled that Evidence 2 disclosed a portable digital display electronic scale for measuring gravity. "Although a handgrip dynamometer and an electronic scale are both force measuring devices, they have different specific uses. Gravity and the grip strength of a human hand are applied to different objects and in different directions. Gravity is purely downward, while the grip strength of a human hand is not simply downward but from the surrounding to the center, so the two forces do not belong to the same technical field. However, the patent at issue and the portable digital display electronic scale have the same functions and similar uses. The force measurement principles of the two load cells are basically the same, therefore the portable digital display electronic scale can be regarded as a similar technical field of the patent at issue." However, since the prior art has not provided any clear technical teachings, the invalidation decision erred in the application of law by considering the load cell of the portable electronic scale when evaluating the inventive step of the patent at issue.

2. Quantity of Prior Arts

Regarding the difference in the evaluation standards for the inventive step of an invention and a utility model in terms of the quantity of prior arts, the SPC pointed out in the case *(2012) Zhi Xing Zi No. 15*[22] that "an inventive step is the essential characteristic of an invention-creation, and is the required degree of innovation of an invention-creation compared to prior art. Although the current *Patent Law* and its implementing regulations have not provided explicitly the number of references to be used to evaluate the inventive step of utility model patents, the relevant provisions of the *Guidelines for Patent Examination* may be applied by the people's courts as a reference.

The *Guidelines for Patent Examination* provides in the section on the examination of the inventive step of a utility model patent that, for a utility model patent, generally one or two prior arts can be cited to evaluate its inventive step. For a utility model patent that is formed by 'simple superposition' of prior arts, multiple prior arts can be cited to evaluate its inventive step according to the situation. The so-called simple superposition means that the claimed technology is only a combination or connection of some known products, each working in its conventional way, and the

---

[22] Utility model patent No. 200720033902.0. The invalidation decision (No. WX13158) maintained the validity of the patent rights. The first instance judgment (*(2009) Yi Zhong Xing Chu Zi No. 1681*) and the second instance judgment (*(2010) Gao Xing Zhong Zi No. 407*) both vacated the invalidation decision. The patentee filed for a retrial and was rejected by the SPC.

overall technical effect is the sum of the effects of the combined parts, and there is no functional interaction among the technical features after the combination. Simple superposition is not innovation. If only one or two prior arts are allowed to be used to evaluate the inventive step of a utility model formed by simple superposition, the granting standard for utility model patents will be lowered. Therefore, the *Guidelines for Patent Examination* provides that multiple prior arts can be cited to evaluate the inventive step."

The case relates to a ground-buried maintenance-free rotary compensator. The first- and second-instance judgments cited a combination of three prior arts and two pieces of common knowledge and determined that the utility model patent claims did not have an inventive step and vacated the invalidation decision of the Patent Reexamination Board accordingly. The Patent Reexamination Board filed for a retrial claiming that the second-instance judgment which cited the combination of three prior arts and two pieces of common knowledge to judge the inventive step of the utility model patent did not comply with the provisions of the *Guidelines for Patent Examination* on the evaluation of inventive step of utility model patents.

The SPC responded to this issue that in this case, "it is obvious to a person skilled in the art that the technical solution of claim 1 of the patent at issue can be obtained by combining the technical solutions in Annexes 2-4. The overall technical function is only the sum of the functions of each part, and no new technical effect has been achieved. The technical solution of claim 1 of the patent at issue is essentially a mere mixture of the technical solutions disclosed in Annexes 2-4. Therefore, it is not improper that the first and second instance courts evaluated the inventive step of this patent at issue based on multiple prior arts."

8.7 The Inventive Step of Chemical Inventions

Inventions in the field of chemistry have certain particularities. In addition to general provisions, the *Guidelines for Patent Examination* also sets forth special provisions in Part Two, Chapter 10 for the examination of inventions in the field of chemistry.

1. Inventive Step of Chemical Process Inventions

In the field of chemistry, in addition to preparation methods and uses of substances, method inventions also include methods of use, processing methods, and treatment methods of substances. The claims of such inventions are usually defined by features such as processing methods, steps, conditions, etc. In practice, there are three difficulties in judging the inventive step of chemical process inventions: the determination of distinguishing features; the determination of technical effects; and the determination of whether there is are technical teachings.

8.7 The Inventive Step of Chemical Inventions

The case *(2013) Zhi Xing Zi No. 115*[23] reviewed by the SPC claims a method for producing thiourea by using the acid waste gas discharged from an oil refinery, which is characterized by the direct use of the acid waste gas discharged from the oil refinery to react with calcium cyanamide to produce thiourea. The process flow is to first use calcium cyanamide and water or scrubbing solution to generate calcium hydroxide suspension, and then react with acid waste gas to generate calcium hydrosulfide to reach the reaction end point. Then according to the amount of calcium hydrosulfide, calcium cyanamide is added proportionally to generate thiourea. The production process of claim 1 can be divided into three steps with a two-step reaction process. In contrast, Evidence 2 discloses a process of producing thiourea based on the principle of using lime nitrogen (i.e., calcium cyanamide) solution to directly absorb hydrogen sulfide to generate thiourea. The process flow is that lime nitrogen and water (reflux stock solution or scrubbing solution) are mixed uniformly in a synthesis reaction kettle, and hydrogen sulfide gas is introduced into the synthesis reaction while stirring to form a thiourea solution. Therefore, the production process of Evidence 2 is a one-step reaction, which is the major difference between claim 1 and Evidence 2.

Regarding whether this difference brings about an inventive step to the technical solution of claim 1, the SPC held that, "it is well known to a person skilled in the art that lime nitrogen reacts with water to form calcium hydroxide. Therefore, in fact, in Evidence 2, lime nitrogen and water must also react to generate calcium hydroxide when they are mixed and stirred." Namely, Evidence 2 is also a two-step reaction. "In addition, Evidence 2 also discloses in its 'conventional process for thiourea production' section that calcium hydroxide and hydrogen sulfide are first used to generate calcium hydrosulfide, and then calcium hydrosulfide and lime nitrogen are used for to generate thiourea. This two-step reaction is the same as the calcium hydrosulfide process and the thiourea synthesis process in claim 1 of the patent at issue. Therefore, Evidence 2 provides the technical teaching that there are two steps of using lime nitrogen to absorb hydrogen sulfide, i.e., lime nitrogen is added twice… It is not inappropriate for the invalidation decision and the first-instance judgment to hold that the production process of claim 1 of this patent can be technically taught by Evidence 2."

In addition, with regard to whether the patent had achieved unexpected technical effects, the SPC held that "the description of the patent at issue recites that the thiourea produced by the production process of the patent at issue enables the benefits of comprehensive utilization of the three wastes to increase by dozens of times, and that the thiourea product has reached the national standard, but there is no corresponding evidence to prove it. Moreover, Evidence 2 has recited that its technical solution has the effects of good product quality and low cost. In the retrial petition, Wantong claimed that its production scale, output and quality of thiourea ranked first in the

---

[23] Invention patent No. 03112085.7. The invalidation decision (No. WX16411) declared that all patent rights were invalid. The first instance judgment (*(2011) Yi Zhong Xing Chu Zi No. 2552*) and the second instance judgment (*(2012) Gao Xing Zhong Zi No. 744*) both upheld the invalidation decision. The patentee filed for a retrial and was rejected by the SPC.

same industry in the country, but there was no evidence to prove such claims. The inventive step of this patent cannot be evaluated on this basis."

2. Inventive Step of Compound Crystals

Compound crystal inventions are subordinate inventions formed on the basis of compound inventions. Compared with parent compounds, compound crystal inventions exhibit certain characteristics in microstructure, which may affect the use effect of compounds. Regarding the judgment of the inventive step of a compound crystal, a controversy in the industry is whether the rules of Chapter 10 of Part II of the *Guidelines for Patent Examination* are applicable. In particular, is the claimed crystal compared with the known crystals or amorphisms of the compound "similar in structure"?

The SPC answered this question in the case *(2011) Zhi Xing Zi No. 86*.[24] The patent at issue claims a monohydrate of a certain compound. Evidence 1 discloses the anhydrous crystal of the compound, and Evidence 5a discloses the X hydrate of the compound. One of the issues of this case was whether the monohydrate crystal of this patent and the anhydrous crystal disclosed in Evidence 1 and the X hydrate disclosed in Evidence 5a were "compounds similar in structure" as stipulated in the *Guidelines for Patent Examination*. Regarding this, the SPC held that "although the physicochemical parameters of crystalline compounds may be different based on different molecular arrangements, crystalline compounds still belong to the category of compounds, so the provisions of the *Guidelines for Patent Examination* on the inventive step of compounds can be applied to the determination of the inventive step of new crystalline compounds.

When applying for a retrial, Boehringer Ingelheim Pharma GmbH and Co KG claimed that the term 'similar in structure' referred to in the *Guidelines for Patent Examination* included not only the same chemical structure, but also the similarity of microscopic crystal structures. If the microscopic crystal structures are not similar, even if the chemical structures are the same, the two compounds still should be determined to be structurally dissimilar."

The SPC held that "crystalline compounds have various microscopic crystal structures. A compound in the solid state may produce different solid crystal forms due to two or more different molecular arrangements. Not all microscopic crystal structure changes will inevitably lead to prominent substantive features and notable progress, so it cannot be determined that two compound crystals are not similar in structure simply because the microscopic crystal structures of them are not similar. That is, "the 'compound similar in structure' referred to in the *Guidelines for Patent Examination* only means that the compounds have the identical basic core structure or basic rings, without comparing the microscopic crystal structures. In the inventive step judgment of a crystal, the microscopic crystal structure must be considered together with whether it brings unexpected technical effects.

---

[24] Invention patent No. 01817143.5. The invalidation decision (No. WX12206) declared that all patent rights were invalid. The first instance judgment (*(2009) Yi Zhong Xing Chu Zi No. 83*) and the second instance judgment (*(2010) Gao Xing Zhong Zi No. 751*) both upheld the invalidation decision. The patentee filed for a retrial and was rejected by the SPC.

8.7 The Inventive Step of Chemical Inventions

In this case, claim 1 claims a tiotropium bromide monohydrate crystal, Evidence 5a discloses a tiotropium bromide X hydrate and Evidence 1 discloses a tiotropium bromide crystal. The above three substances may be different in the microscopic crystal structures, but because the basic core parts are all tiotropium bromide which makes them have the same activity, the three substances are compounds similar in structures for a person skilled in the art. Therefore, the three substances are 'compounds similar in structure' as referred to by the *Guidelines for Patent Examination*. Boehringer's ground for retrial that the microcrystals were structurally different to constitute compounds not similar in structure was not sustained."

3. Inventive Step of Derivatives of Known Compounds

It is a common method in the process of pharmaceutical research and development to make pharmaceutically acceptable salts, esters and other derivatives from known compounds. Compared with the known compound, the inventive step of its derivative depends on whether there is a technical teaching in the prior art on the corresponding derivatization method for the compound and whether there is evidence to show that the derivative can achieve unexpected technical effects. In the case *(2015) Zhi Xing Zi No. 353*,[25] the patent at issue claims a dabigatran etexilate mesylate. The SPC held that although Annex 2 did not disclose the form of the dabigatran mesylate, it did disclose that the compounds of formula I including dabigatran etexilate mesylate could be converted into pharmacologically acceptable salts. Moreover, example 84 of Annex 2 disclosed a hydrochloride of dabigatran etexilate analogues. Since "methanesulfonic acid is a type of strong acid and mesylate is a common pharmaceutical salt in the art which is widely used in marketed drugs, it is easy for a person skilled in the art to think of using dabigatran and methanesulfonic acid to generate dabigatran etexilate mesylate on the basis of Annex 2." Claim 19 did not have an inventive step relative to Annex 2.

4. Inventive Step of Product Inventions and Product Preparation Methods

It is most common in the field of chemistry that a product and the preparation method thereof are both claimed in a patent. Generally speaking, if a product is novel and has an inventive step, the method for preparing the product should also be novel and have an inventive step. However, if the method for preparing the product is novel and has an inventive step, it does not necessarily mean that the product is also novel and has an inventive step.

In the cases *(2015) Zhi Xing Zi No. 261 and No. 262*,[26] the SPC upheld the Patent Reexamination Board's decision that the preparation method had an inventive

---

[25] Invention patent No. 03805473.6. The invalidation decision (No. WX20640) declared that all patent rights were invalid. The first instance judgment (*(2014) Yi Zhong Xing Chu Zi No. 885*) and the second instance judgment (*(2014) Gao Xing Zhong Zi No. 1661*) both upheld the invalidation decision. The patentee filed for a retrial and was rejected by the SPC.

[26] The two cases related to invention patents No. 20060000601.8 and No. 20060000200.2, respectively. The invalidation decisions (No. WX19578) and (No. WX17576) both declared that part of the patent rights were invalid. The first instance judgments (*(2013) Yi Zhong Xing Chu Zi No. 989*) and (*(2012) Yi Zhong Xing Chu Zi No. 1327*) and the second instance judgments (*(2014) Gao Xing*

step but the product did not. The patents in the two cases both claimed high-purity ulinastatin and the preparation method thereof, wherein, claims 1 and 8 of case No. 261 were products and claims 2–7 were the preparation methods thereof. Claim 1 and reference 2 differed in that the parametric features of claim 1 were not recited in reference 2. The SPC held that "although the specific activity disclosed in reference 2 is lower than the specific activity defined in this patent, reference 2 has provided a technical teaching for purifying ulinastatin. When reference 2 has suggested that kallikrein is used as the target of impurity control, in order to further improve purity, a person skilled in the art can easily think of using the purification method mastered by them to achieve this purpose." Meanwhile, the patentee did not submit evidence to prove that "the further purification of ulinastatin products requires overcoming specific technical difficulties, which are beyond the ability of a person skilled in the art who master only conventional purification methods." In the petition for retrial, the patentee argued that the inventor's contribution to the ulinastatin product with higher purity should be considered when determining the inventive step of the claims of the patent at issue.

Regarding this, the SPC held that the patentee's argument "is based on the technical solution defined in this patent. In the invalidation examination of claims 2-7 of the method, the invalidation decision has determined that the method had an inventive step in comparison with the combination of references 2 and 3 and common knowledge." The SPC further pointed out that "claim 1 of this patent is not a product defined by claims 2-7. In the absence of evidence to prove the product of claim 1 can only be obtained by the method of claims 2-7, and higher-purity ulinastatin products can be obtained by other methods, if it is determined that the ulinastatin product of claim 1 of this patent has an inventive step, it will lead high-purity ulinastatin products obtained by other methods to fall within the scope of the protection claimed in claim 1 of this patent, which does not match the technical contribution made by the inventor of this patent to claim 1. Since claims 1 and 8 of this patent are not defined by the specific purification methods of claims 2 to 7, the invalidation decision determined that the purification methods of claims 2 to 7 of this patent had an inventive step, which is not inconsistent with the decision that the products of claims 1 and 8 do not have an inventive step." Accordingly, the invalidation decision was upheld.

Zhong Zi No. 1454) and (*(2013) Gao Xing Zhong Zi No. 191*) both upheld the invalidation decision. The patentee filed for a retrial and was rejected by the SPC.

Chapter 9
Is a Claim Supported by the Description

A claim shall be supported by the description, which means that the technical solution in a claim shall be one that a person skilled in the art can conclude or generalize from the sufficiently disclosed content of the description, and shall not exceed the scope disclosed in the description. The reason why it is required by the *Patent Law* that claims be supported by the description is that the protection an applicant receives should commensurate with his or her contribution to the society, i.e., the protection scope of claims shall be the same as the scope disclosed in the description, neither overly broad to exceed the scope disclosed in the description, nor overly narrow to hurt the entitled rights and interests of the applicant for disclosing his or her invention. If the protection scope of a claim is overly broad to include prior art or an invention that (the applicant) has not completed yet but may be accomplished by other inventors in the future, the public's interests may be harmed. On the contrary, if the protection scope of a claim is overly narrow to amount to donation of part of the invention by the applicant to all mankind, it may be unfair for the applicant.

9.1 A Claim Contains a Technical Solution that Obviously Cannot Achieve the Purpose of the Invention

Claims are vehicles through which a patent applicant or a patent agent writes to delineate the scope of protection that the applicant seeks to claim on the basis of the description. In the process of expressing abstract inventive contemplation in words, due to the drafter's verbal expression or subjective understanding, there could be technical solutions in claims that obviously cannot achieve the purpose of the invention. Will this situation result in the claims unsupported by the description and incompliance with Article 26(4) of the *Patent Law*?

The case *(2013) Zhi Xing Zi No. 102*[1] related to this problem. The patent at issue is directed to a filter. Normally filters are divided into high-pass, low-pass, band-pass, band stop, etc. filters in the field. The applicant and the invalidation petitioner both admitted that high-pass filters could not perform the functions recited in the embodiment of the description. The issue in this case was whether the claims violated para. 4 of Article 26 of the *Patent Law* because the claims included a subordinate concept which a person skilled in the art would consider obviously unable to achieve the purpose of the invention. Regarding this issue, the SPC expounded, "Technically speaking, claims shall be drafted on the basis of the description to delineate the claimed scope of the patent. When drafting claims, a patent applicant shall exclude a subordinate concept if it obviously cannot achieve the effect of the invention. However, whether claims are supported by the description shall be decided by a person skilled in the art, who is supposed to thoroughly and comprehensively read the technical solution defined in the patent document to correct some obvious errors and interpret properly relevant technical features. If those skilled in the art generally and unequivocally conclude that the subordinate concept cannot achieve the purpose of the invention, it is not required to hold the patent at issue to be in violation of para. 4 of Article 26 of the *Patent Law* on the grounds that the subordinate concept fails to support the claims. In this case, by reading the description, a person skilled in the art is perfectly capable of understanding the filter's functions in the technical solution. Though the claims and the description do not recite specific limitations of the filter, a person skilled in the art knows clearly the filter's installation, structure and functions. Therefore, the claims are supported by the description and are in compliance with para. 4 of Article 26 of the *Patent Law*."

9.2 Solutions not Covered by the Embodiments Are not Supported (by the Description) Due to a Lack of Prior Art

Whether a claim is supported by the description or not shall be determined by a person skilled in the art based on his or her expertise in prior art and common knowledge in the field. If a prior art lacks predictable teachings for the technical solution, and the embodiment(s) in the description fail(s) to extend the protection scope as covered by the claim, the claim is not supported by the description.

In the case *(2013) Zhi Xing Zi No. 3*,[2] the patent at issue is directed to a method for production of a target substance, L-amino acids using a microorganism, comprising

---

[1] Utility model patent No. 200620046588.5. The invalidation decision (No. WX13813) maintained the validity of the patent. The first instance judgment (*(2010) Yi Zhong Xing Chu Zi No. 1933*) and the second instance judgment (*(2011) Gao Xing Zhong Zi No. 833*) both upheld the invalidation decision. The invalidation petitioner filed for a retrial and was rejected by the SPC.

[2] Invention patent No. 94194707.6. The invalidation decision (No. WX13841) declared that all the patent rights were invalid. The first instance judgment (*(2010) Yi Zhong Xing Chu Zi No. 535*) and

the steps of: cultivating a microorganism in a culture medium, to allow a target substance to be produced and accumulated in an increased amount in said culture medium; and collecting said target substance from said culture medium, wherein the said microorganism is a microorganism belonging to the genus Escherichia or a Coryneform bacterium.

The invalidation decision found that the examples of the patent at issue recited only the *Escherichia coli* (*E. coli*) AJ12929 strain, *E. coli* AJ12872 strain and *E. coli* AJ12930 strain, all of which were introduced with plasmids carrying transhydrogenase genes, and verified the amino-acid-producing ability of only the *E. coli* B-3996 strain, Brevibacterium lactofermentum AJ3990 strain and *E. coli* AJ12604 strain prepared by using the method of the patent at issue. However, claim 1 generally referred to the said microorganisms as the genus Escherichia or a Coryneform bacterium, both of which included various species, and each species had various strains. Species, even strains of the same species differ from each other in their properties. Though the patent at issue managed to obtain strains with the above-mentioned functions by a transgenic method, not all strains belonging to Escherichia or Coryneform bacterium, transformed with the method of the patent at issue, can achieve the expected technical effects of the invention. Moreover, there was no record in prior art that all the above-mentioned microorganisms could acquire the above-mentioned functions through transgenic methods. Hence, the claim was not supported by the description.

The SPC upheld the decision of the Patent Reexamination Board, and explained in the ruling that, first, "Escherichia cannot be narrowly construed as Escherichia coli, nor can Coryneform bacterium be narrowly construed as Corynebacterium glutamicum. Escherichia and Coryneform bacterium include various species, and each species has various strains. Although the strains used in the examples of the description of the patent at issue, possess the function of 'enhancing the productivity of the microorganism for reduced nicotinamide adenine dinucleotide phosphate (NADPH) by increasing an enzyme activity of nicotinamide nucleotide transhydrogenase (NNT) in cell of the microorganism,' as recited in the background art of the description, 'a physiological function of the enzyme is still almost unknown'. The examples of the description of the patent at issue only verify certain strains. Based on the description and prior art, a person skilled in the art cannot predict and reasonably infer that all the strains belonging to the genus Escherichia or Coryneform bacterium can enhance the productivity of L-amino acids by improving the activity of NNT in the cell of the said microorganism. Thus, the retrial petition of the Ajinomoto Co. Inc. on the grounds that claim 1 of the patent at issue is supported by the description is not granted."

---

the second instance judgment (*(2010) Gao Xing Zhong Zi No. 1506*) both upheld the invalidation decision. The patentee filed for a retrial and was rejected by the SPC.

9.3 Numerical Range

The *Guidelines for Patent Examination* requires that if a claim is a numerical range improved on the basis of background art, the description include embodiments close to (preferably at) both ends of the range and if the numerical range is rather wide, the description include at least one embodiment of intermediate value. In the case *(2012) Zhi Xing Zi No. 4*,[3] the SPC held that if the technical solution of an invention "is directed to improving a numerical range, the public expect to obtain embodiments that at least contain values of the two ends. However, it does not mean that the description must include embodiments of all the numerical endpoints recited in the claims, nor does it mean that a certain numerical range in a claim is not supported by the description for merely one embodiment. As long as a person skilled in the art can determine undoubtedly that the numerical range in a claim can achieve the purpose of the invention through the embodiments recited in the description, the claim is supported by the description."

Claim 1 of the patent at issue claims a pharmaceutical composition comprising candesartan cilexetil and oxyalkylene polymer with a melting point in the range of 20–90 °C. Claim 3 claims a tablet composition comprising candesartan cilexetil and polyethylene glycol (PEG) with a molecular weight of 1000–10,000. The patent description recited six examples, wherein example 5 related to oily compounds other than oxyalkylene polymer and was irrelevant to the technical solutions of claims 1 and 3; examples 1–4 and 6 all used PEG 6000 as the example to prove this substance could achieve the purpose of the invention.

The SPC held that "oxyalkylene is an extremely broad concept encompassing varieties differing in molecular weights, the number of oxygen atoms and the number of carbon bonds. The physicochemical properties of different substances belonging to oxyalkylene vary considerably from one another, while depending on the form and degree of polymerization, the physicochemical properties of polymers of the same substance also vary considerably from one another. Thus, the range of substances formed by the composition of 'oxyalkylene' with diverse quantities and properties and complex forms of 'polymer' will necessarily include more complex forms of 'oxyalkylene polymers'. The limit set on the range of melting point of the 'oxyalkylene polymers' in claim 1 does not negate the fact that the physicochemical properties of oxyalkylene polymers vary considerably. The description recites that the commonality of the said '20-90 °C oxyalkylene polymers' is that they are all 'low-melting-point oily compounds'. However, a person skilled in the art cannot determine whether all the said 'oxyalkylene polymers' of different types are 'oily compounds'; even if they are 'oily compounds,' since the physicochemical properties of polymers

---

[3] Invention patent No. 93100008.4. The invalidation decision (No. WX11016) declared that part of the patent rights were invalid. The first instance judgment (*(2008) Yi Zhong Xing Chu Zi No. 440*) maintained the invalidation decision. The second instance judgment (*(2009) Gao Xing Zhong Zi No. 647*) vacated the first instance judgment and the invalidation decision. The patentee filed for a retrial and was rejected by the SPC.

differ significantly, a person skilled in the art cannot ascertain undoubtedly that the technical solution of claim 1 can still achieve the purpose of the invention."

As to claim 3, the SPC held that "although they are all PEGs, there are significant differences between PEG 1000 and PEG 10000 in terms of physical form, solubility, hygroscopicity, freezing point, viscosity and dissolution after being mixed with drug to make preparations. Despite of the commonality of 'oily substances,' a person skilled in the art still cannot ascertain undoubtedly that the technical solution of claim 3 can achieve the purpose of the invention." Furthermore, "since chemistry and medicine are experimental disciplines, in most cases it is difficult to predict whether a chemical or pharmaceutical invention can be implemented or achieve the purpose of the invention, and experimental results are often necessary for verification. Thus, a claim shall contain a technical solution generalized from a multitude of experimental data. If the generalization of a claim contains speculation of the patentee and the effect is hard to determine and evaluate in advance, such generalization exceeds the scope disclosed in the description. The description of the patent at issue does not recite sufficient experimental data to prove that apart from PEG 6000, an oxyalkylene polymer with a melting point between 20-90 °C or PEG with a molecular weight of 1000-10000, is equally capable of achieving the purpose of the invention."

Finally, the SPC reiterated that "for a patent to be granted, the patent applicant shall first clearly and convincingly demonstrate to the opposite party to the patent right, i.e., the public, that the scope of protection of the claims is based on and supported by the description. If the description of the patent fails to provide corresponding evidence to prove that the claims are supported by the description, the burden of proof shall not be unreasonably shifted to the public."

9.4 "Dead Pixels"[4] in the Description

The description, as the most important vehicle for proving the scope of claims, is convincing evidence for determining whether claims are supported by the description. If embodiments in the description are within the scope of claims, but the effect obtained is contrary to the effect intended by the applicant, such a dead pixel works against the extension of the protection scope of claims.

Claim 1 of the case *(2009) Zhi Xing Zi No. 3*[5] claims a method for preparation of β-isomer-enriched difluorinated nucleoside, wherein the product is β-isomer-enriched difluorinated nucleoside of formula I; the raw material and the amount thereof are at

---

[4] Translator's note: A "dead pixel", also referred to as a "defective pixel", is a pixel on a liquid crystal display (LCD) that is not functioning properly. In this context, the author uses "dead pixel" to indicate defects in a description.

[5] Invention patent No. 93109045.8. The invalidation decision (No. WX9525) declared that all the patent rights were invalid. The first instance judgment *((2007) Yi Zhong Xing Chu Zi No. 922)* vacated the invalidation decision. The second instance judgment *((2008) Gao Xing Zhong Zi No. 451)* vacated the first instance judgment, and upheld the invalidation decision. The patentee filed for a retrial and was rejected by the SPC.

least one mole equivalent of protected nucleobase (R″) with sulfonyloxy at position 1, protected α-isomer-enriched sugar of formula II at positions 3 and 5; the reaction step is performing SN2 nucleophilic substitution to the sulfonyloxy group in the α-isomer-enriched sugar with nucleobase R″, followed by deprotection; the solvent can be any suitable solvent of choice and the temperature is from about 170° to negative 120°. In the tabular example of the description, the patentee cited a total of 104 sets of data, among which 11 sets showed that the β-isomer-enriched difluorinated nucleosides could not be obtained.

The SPC ultimately upheld the decision of the Patent Reexamination Board to invalidate the claims for lack of support by the description. The SPC held that "the technical solution claimed shall be one that a person skilled in the art can conclude or generalize from the sufficiently disclosed content of the description, and shall not exceed the scope disclosed in the description. A claim shall be deemed as not supported by the description, if the generalization of the claim gives a person skilled in the art reason to suspect, that one or more subordinate concepts or alternatives included in that superior generalization or parallel generalization cannot solve the technical problem to be solved by the invention and achieve the same technical effects."

In this case, "the description recites that the said stereoselective method is affected by a number of factors, including not only the leaving group of the raw sugar, the raw sugar configuration and the amount of nucleobase but also the choice of temperature and solvent. The range of factors in the preparation methods generalized in claim 1, i.e., the leaving group, the nucleobase type, the nucleobase equivalent, the reaction temperature, the reaction solvent, etc., is very broad. A person skilled in the art has reasonable grounds to believe that, in addition to the 11 unworkable cases, the generalization of claim 1 contains numerous other technical solutions that cannot solve the technical problem to be solved by the invention, and that it is difficult to arrive at a technical solution that can solve the technical problem by conventional experimentation or reasonable speculation from the various permutation and combination of reaction conditions, rather, a great amount of repeated experimentation or undue labor would be required to determine the scope of claim 1." Therefore, it was not improper for the invalidation decision and the second instance judgment to conclude that claim 1 of the patent at issue was not supported by the description on this basis.

9.5 Inconsistencies Between the Description and the Technical Solutions in the Claims

The technical solutions claimed by each claim shall be one that a person skilled in the art can conclude or generalize from the sufficiently disclosed content of the description, and shall not exceed the scope disclosed in the description.

A claim is not supported by the description if the technical solution cannot be concluded or generalized from the content disclosed in the description. The case

9.5 Inconsistencies Between the Description and the Technical Solutions ...

(2014) Xing Ti Zi No. 32[6] is directed to a soft starter for brushless auto-controlled motor.

Claim 1 defines that the starter comprises a static electrode (1) and a moving electrode (2), wherein an elastic resistance device is placed between the two electrodes to prevent the moving electrode (2) from moving towards the static electrode (1), and the resistance of the said elastic resistance device is inversely proportional to the distance between the two electrodes. The original claim 3 defined that the said elastic resistance device was a tension spring installed on the moving electrode and the side wall of the inner ring of the concave cavity; the original claim 4 defined that the said elastic resistance device was a compression spring installed between the moving electrode and the static electrode.

During the examination, the patentee deleted the original claim 4 in order to overcome the defect pointed out by the examiner that claim 4 was not supported by the description. The invalidation decision found that claim 1 was not supported by the description on the grounds that the description did not recite any component set between the moving electrode (2) and the static electrode (1), and such a conclusion could not be inferred from the drawings either. The characterizing part in dependent claims 2–5 did not overcome the defect of lacking support from the description and therefore dependent claims 2–5 were not supported by the description either.

During the retrial, the patentee claimed that the word "between" in claim 1 should be perceived as a relationship of resistance rather than of position; the description had clearly recited the function of the elastic resistance device, and the solution recited in the embodiment that a tension spring set on the moving electrode and the side wall of the inner ring of the concave cavity was the elastic resistance device satisfied the requirements of the elastic resistance device in claim 1.

As to this, the SPC held that firstly, "as a product patent, the claims of the patent at issue should clearly describe the structure and components of the product as well as the relationship between the structure and the components. As is recited in claim 1 of this patent… the above content is clear and definite. It limits not only the inverse relationship between the resistance of the elastic resistance device and the distance between the moving and static electrodes, but also the specific positional relationship. The positional relationships between the elastic resistance device, as a specific separate component, and the moving electrode, the static electrode and the guide rod are clearly defined in claim 1, and the resistance generated by the resistance device should come from this structure of the device." Thus, the word "between" in claim 1 should be considered to "define a specific positional relationship between the said device and the moving and static electrodes instead of a relationship of resistance."

---

[6] Invention patent No. 03112809.2. The invalidation decision (No. WX15243) declared that all the patent rights were invalid. The first instance judgment (*(2010) Yi Zhong Zhi Xing Zi No. 5*) vacated the invalidation decision. The second instance judgment (*(2012) Gao Xing Zhong Zi No. 1836*) vacated the first instance judgment and upheld the invalidation decision. The patentee file for a retrial. The SPC reviewed the case and vacated the invalidation decision, the first and second instance judgments.

Based on this, the SPC held that "the embodiments in the description disclose only the 'beyond' situations. The technical solution of installing a compression spring 'between' the moving electrode and the static electrode is not recited in the description or in the drawings. Moreover, the length of the compression spring cannot be compressed to zero, while the description recites that the implementation of this patent requires the moving electrode and the static electrode stick together, and the resistance value between the two electrodes be zero so as to complete the start-up process. If certain difficulties or defects need to be overcome in the technical solution of installing the compression spring, and the description does not recite any relevant teachings or guidance, a person skilled in the art cannot determine the exact methods to implement the patent." Thus, claim 1 was not supported by the description.

If the technical solution claimed by the claim is inconsistent with the technical solution disclosed in the description, the said claim is not supported by the description. Claim 1 of the case *(2010) Zhi Xing Zi No. 23*[7] is directed to a kind of fully-sealed automatic multifunctional electric cooker, which uses a "⊏" shaped structure to make lid [5], gasket [6], and cooker body [7] compressed and sealed; the said "⊏" shaped structure, lid [5], gasket [6], cooker body [7], electric heating plate [8] and flash switch [13] form the automatic pressure control mechanism of the said electric cooker, wherein the said "⊏" shaped structure can be a "⊏" shaped structure, a "square" shaped structure or a "cylinder" shaped structure.

The Patent Reexamination Board believed that the technical solution of claim 1, which recited that the "⊏" shaped structure was a "cylinder" structure, was not supported by the description. This is also the issue of the case. In the end, the SPC upheld the decision of the Patent Examination Board in terms of this issue. The SPC held that, "based on drawing 2 and paragraph 2 of column 9 on page 6 of the description, the working state of the technical solution of the 'cylinder' structure is: the rigid arm/lid, the gasket, the cooker body and the electric heating plate altogether are pressed between the inner edge at the top of the upright cylinder and the flexible arm, so as to make them compressed and sealed. The working state of the technical solution of the '⊏' shaped structure in drawing 1 is: the lid, the gasket, the cooker body and the electric heating plate are pressed between the rigid arm and the flexible arm, so as to make them compressed and sealed. Since the above two structures differ in their ways of connecting the rigid arm to the upright cylinder and the lid, it is impossible to generalize from the two embodiments above, that in the technical solution of the '⊏' shaped structure, the lid, the gasket, the cooker body and the electric heating plate are pressed between the rigid arm and the flexible arm in the '⊏' shaped structure. In other words, the technical solution of the '⊏' shaped structure in claim 1 merely recites the '⊏' shaped structure and the double '⊏' shaped structure which is also called a 'square' shape structure… the technical solution of the 'cylinder' structure does not correspond to the relevant part recited in the description and the technical solution in

---

[7] Invention patent No. 91100026.7. The invalidation decision (No. WX8713) declared that part of the patent rights were invalid. The first instance judgment (*(2007) Yi Zhong Zhi Xing Zi No. 190*) and the second instance judgment (*(2009) Gao Xing Zhong Zi No. 623*) both upheld the invalidation decision. The patentee filed for a retrial and was rejected by the SPC.

drawing 2. Thus, the technical solution of claim 1 concerning the 'cylinder' structure cannot be concluded or generalized from the disclosed content of the description, so the claim is not supported by the description."

9.6 Obvious Errors in Claims

Claims are a summary and generalization by the patent applicant of the essence and core of the invention-creation recited in the description. In the process of expressing abstract inventive contemplation in words, due to the limitation of language and the drafting level of the agent, there are inevitably defects in the claims such as sloppy wording or inaccurate expression. Drafting errors can be classified into obvious errors and unobvious errors according to the nature and degree of defects. An "obvious error" means that by using his or her ordinary technical knowledge, a person skilled in the art can identify an error in a technical feature immediately after reading the claim, and at the same time determine the only correct answer with his or her common technical knowledge after reading relevant content in the description and the drawings.

Will an obvious error in a claim render the claim unsupported by the description? In the ruling of the case *(2011) Xing Ti Zi No. 13*,[8] the SPC, first from the perspectives of the functions of claims, the relationship between claims and the description and the specific meaning of basing claims on the description, expounded the legislative purpose of para. 4 of Article 26 of the *Patent Law*, i.e., "the scope generalized from the claims shall be the same as the scope disclosed in the description, neither overly broad to exceed the scope disclosed in the invention, nor overly narrow to hurt the entitled rights and interests of the applicant for disclosing his or her invention."

Then, from the perspectives of the inevitability of drafting errors in claims, the classification of drafting errors the delineation role of claims, the SPC analyzed and discussed that drafting errors in claims would not necessarily result in the claims not complying with para. 4 of Article 26 of the *Patent Law*. Finally, the SPC concluded, "Under the basic principle of protecting the patent right to invention-creations and encouraging invention-creations, on one hand, a patentee shall be allowed to provide the correct interpretation of an obvious error in the claims of a granted patent; on the other hand, a patentee shall also be prevented from abusing the right to interpretation. Obvious errors shall be defined precisely so as to properly protect the interests of the patentee and safeguard the interests of the public to achieve the legislative purpose of the *Patent Law* which is to promote technological progress and innovation." "If after obvious errors have been correctly interpreted, the claimed technical solution can be concluded or generalized from the sufficiently disclosed content of the description

---

[8] Invention patent No. 200720128801.1. The invalidation decision (No. 13091) declared that the patent rights were invalid. The first instance judgment (*(2009) Yi Zhong Zhi Xing Zi No. 1356*) and the second instance judgment (*(2010) Gao Xing Zhong Zi No. 500*) both upheld the invalidation decision. The patentee filed for a retrial. The SPC reviewed the case and vacated the invalidation decision, the first and the second instance judgments.

without exceeding the scope disclosed in the description, the claim shall be considered as supported by the description and in conformity with para. 4 of Article 26 of the *Patent Law*."

The patent at issue claims a rotary compensator with a torque device for a heating network. The background art recites that the axial thrust and displacement of the heating network is absorbed by the rotation of the inner and outer sleeves of the rotary compensator. The rotary compensator, as a pressure piping component, must meet the inspection requirements including a weld inspection, a pressure test and an air tightness test. That is, the outer sleeve and the extension tube defined in claim 1 must be seamlessly connected and shall not lead to any leakage of the transmission medium. However, according to the recitation of claim 1 that "the other end of the said outer sleeve is connected to the extension tube with a gap between the two", it could be interpreted that there is a gap between the "outer sleeve" and the "extension tube."

The issue in this case was what the "two" in "with a gap between the two" actually referred to in the feature recited in claim 1. Judged from the structure and the operating principle of the compensator claimed by claim 1, it comprises an outer sleeve, an inner sleeve, a compact flange, an extension tube and sealing materials, wherein one end of the outer sleeve is connected to the inner sleeve via the flange and the other end is connected to the extension tube and the rotary compensator absorbs the axial thrust and displacement of the heating network through the rotation of the inner and outer sleeves. Therefore, it is impossible for the inner sleeve and the outer sleeve, or the outer sleeve and the extension tube, to be both connected and separated with a gap between them. The "two" in "with a gap between the two" in claim 1 cannot refer to the outer sleeve and the extension tube, but only the inner sleeve and the extension tube. This interpretation is also consistent with the disclosed content in the description of the patent. Based on this, the SPC concluded, "A person skilled in the art, relying on his or her common technical knowledge, knows that there is a drafting error in claim 1, and by reading the description and the drawings can determine directly and undoubtedly that the 'two' in 'with a gap between the two' should refer to the extension tube and the inner sleeve, instead of mistaking it for a gap between the outer sleeve and the extension tube. 'Between the two' is an obvious error... As a person skilled in the art can come up with only one definite and correct interpretation, i.e., 'with a gap between the two' means there is a gap between the inner sleeve and the extension tube, which is consistent with the content disclosed in the description, the technical solution claimed by claim 1 of this patent at issue can be concluded from the disclosed content of the description, and it is supported by the description and complies with para. 4 of Article 26 of the *Patent Law*."

In the case *(2015) Zhi Xing Zi No. 171*,[9] following the above-mentioned line of thought and principle, the SPC held that there was an obvious error in the drafting

---

[9] Invention patent No. 200780001269.X. The invalidation decision (No. WX174921) declared that the patent rights were invalid. The first instance judgment (*(2012) Yi Zhong Zhi Xing Zi No. 953*) and the second instance judgment (*(2013) Gao Xing Zhong Zi No. 123*) both vacated the invalidation decision. The invalidation petitioner filed for a retrial and was rejected by the SPC.

of claim 1 of the patent at issue. The patent in this case claims a juicer, and the SPC held, "the drafting format and the language of claim 1 would make readers believe that 'forming vertically on the inner surface of the said mesh cylinder to insert into the said aligning arms' is 'describing the wall knives,' i.e., multiple wall knives are inserted into the said aligning arms."

However, taking into consideration the common technical knowledge of a person skilled in the art, the description and the drawings together, it can be concluded that "as components for alignment and fixation, the aligning arms which actually work with the bottom rings of the mesh cylinder fix and limit the movement of the mesh cylinder, so the wall knives do not function to work by inserting into the aligning arms... The method of inserting the wall knives into the said aligning arms can be easily excluded by a person skilled in the art after reading the description and the drawings... The obvious error in claim 1 was not serious enough to prevent a person skilled in the art from following the description to carry out the technical solution of the juicer." Thus, since claim 1 "although with a drafting defect, can be understood by a person skilled in the art..., and the technical solution has been sufficiently disclosed in the description, the technical solution claimed by the claim which was correctly interpreted of an obvious error, can be concluded from the sufficiently disclosed description without exceeding the scope of disclosure in the description and thus shall be deemed to comply with para. 4 of Article 26 of the *Patent Law*."

9.7 Determination of Whether a Dependent Claim is Supported by the Description

Claims can be divided into independent claims and dependent claims according to drafting formats. Independent claims are claims that illustrate technical solutions of the invention or utility model as a whole; dependent claims are claims that by referring to the prior claims further recite additional technical features on the basis of the claims referred to. For claims that include both independent and dependent claims, it is necessary to determine whether each claim is supported by the description. The fact that an independent claim is supported by the description does not necessarily mean that its dependent claims are also supported by the description.

In the case *(2014) Xing Ti Zi No. 32*,[10] the SPC reiterated, "For a claim that is dependent on another claim in form but in fact replaces certain technical features, the protection scope shall be determined in accordance with the substance of the technical solution it limits, and whether this claim is supported by the description shall then be determined on this basis. It cannot be directly concluded that a claim

---

[10] Invention patent No. 03112809.2. The invalidation decision (No. WX15243) declared that all the patent rights were invalid. The first instance judgment (*(2010) Yi Zhong Zhi Xing Zi No. 5*) vacated the invalidation decision. The second instance judgment (*(2012) Gao Xing Zhong Zi No. 1836*) vacated the first instance judgment and upheld the invalidation decision. The patentee filed for a retrial. The SPC reviewed the case and vacated the invalidation decision, the first and second instance judgments.

that is a dependent one in form is not supported by the description simply because the claim it depends on is not supported by the description. Instead, it is a conclusion to be reached by considering specific circumstance of the patent at issue."

This case related to a soft starter for brushless auto-controlled motor. Claim 1 defines that the starter comprises a static electrode (1) and a moving electrode (2), wherein an elastic resistance device is placed between the two electrodes to prevent the moving electrode (2) from moving towards the static electrode (1); dependent claim 3 defined that the said elastic resistance device was a tension spring installed on the moving electrode and the side wall of the inner ring of the concave cavity.

The SPC held that the elastic resistance device in claim 1 was set "between" the moving electrode and the static electrode, but dependent claim 3 defined that one end of the tension spring was fixed to the moving electrode and the other end was fixed to the side wall of inner ring of the concave cavity, which was contradictory to the relevant position feature in claim 1 that it referred to. Therefore, claim 3 was "a claim that is dependent on another claim in form but in fact replaces certain technical features, so the protection scope shall be determined in accordance with the substance of the technical solution it limits, and whether this claim is supported by the description shall then be determined on this basis." Since embodiments are recited in the description for the technical solution defined by claim 3, claim 3 is supported by the description.

9.8 Burden of Proof Regarding Whether a Claim is Supported by the Description in an Invalidation Procedure

Under relevant provisions of the *Guidelines for Patent Examination*, if the generalization of a claim gives a person skilled in the art reason to suspect that one or more subordinate concepts or alternatives included in the superordinate generalization or parallel generalization cannot solve the technical problem to be solved by the invention or utility model and achieve the same technical effect, the claim is not supported by the description.

In the case *(2014) Zhi Xing Zi No. 34*,[11] the SPC expressed its opinion on the allocation of burden of proof under para. 4 of Article 26 of the *Patent Law* argued by the requester in the invalidation procedure. The case related to a method of producing conductor track structures placed on an electrically non-conductive supporting material. The Patent Re-examination Board declared that all the patent rights were invalid on the grounds that the claims of the patent at issue were not supported by the description, and this determination was upheld by the courts of first and second instance.

---

[11] Invention patent No. 02812609.2. The invalidation decision (No. WX18680) declared that all the patent rights were invalid. The first instance judgment (*(2012) Yi Zhong Zhi Xing Zi No. 3286*) and the second instance judgment (*(2013) Gao Xing Zhong Zi No. 577*) both upheld the invalidation decision. The patentee filed for a retrial and was rejected by the SPC.

9.8 Burden of Proof Regarding Whether a Claim is Supported …

The patentee filed for a retrial, arguing that if the invalidation requester wanted to have the decision that claims of the granted patent were supported by the description reversed, he should have provided relevant evidence to prove it instead of mere subjective speculation and suspicion. In this case, the invalidation requester did not submit any relevant evidence.

The argument of the patentee was not supported by the SPC on the grounds that "First, in an invalidation procedure, the invalidation requester has the responsibility to fully explain the reasons for claiming that the relevant claims do not comply with the provisions of Para. 4 of Article 26 of the *Patent Law*, and at the same time…may decide on a case-by-case basis whether to provide relevant evidence…In the examination of whether a patent complies with the provisions of Para. 4 of Article 26 of the *Patent Law*, the invalidation requester is not required to provide evidence to show that the generalized claims contain a technical problem that cannot be solved by the invention, but sufficiently explain or provide relevant evidence to show that a person skilled in the art has reason to suspect that the superordinate generalization contains a solution that does not solve the technical problem to be solved by the invention and achieves the same technical effect. Second, the decision of the Patent Reexamination Board was based on reasonable inference by a person skilled in the art rather than groundless speculation. As previously stated, based on the disclosed content of the patent description, a person skilled in the art could not reasonably ascertain whether the materials with the structure of the spinel or similar to the spinel structures defined by claims 1 and 3 both could isolate nuclei of heavy metals and thereby solve the technical problem to be solved by the invention and achieve the same technical effect."

Chapter 10
Claims Lacking Essential Technical Features

In drafting an application document, it is required that the essential technical features of solving the technical problems be recited in independent claims. Under the provisions of the *Guidelines for Patent Examination*, the essential technical features are technical features indispensable for an invention or utility model to solve the technical problems, the aggregation of which is sufficient to constitute the technical solution of the invention or utility model, distinguishing it from other technical solutions recited in the Background Art.

Although the *Guidelines for Patent Examination* provides that the recitation of essential technical features is applicable in an independent claim, not directly applicable in a dependent claim, this provision applies only in substantive examination and reexamination procedures. The SPC expounded its view in the three cases *(2014) Xing Ti Zi Nos. 11–13*[1] that "in an invalidation procedure, if the invalidation petitioner asserts that both an independent claim and a dependent claim lack essential technical features, and when the independent claim is found to be inconsistent with Rule 21(2) of the *Implementing Regulations of the Patent Law* of the People's Republic of China (hereinafter *Implementing Regulations of the Patent Law*), it is not improper for the Patent Reexamination Board to continue to examine whether the dependent claim complies with Rule 21(2) of the *Implementing Regulations of the Patent Law*." The SPC explained in the judgment that under Article 47 of the *Patent Law*, any patent right which had been declared invalid should be deemed to be non-existent from the beginning, and therefore, "if an independent claim is declared invalid, it shall be deemed to be non-existent from the beginning, and a dependent claim directly dependent on the independent claim shall become a new independent claim, which

---

[1] Invention patent No. 02803734.0. The invalidation decisions (No. WX14538, No. WX14542, No. WX14543) all declared that part of the patent rights were invalid. The first instance judgments (*(2010) Yi Zhong Zhi Xing Zi No. 2636, No. 2637, No. 2635*) and the second instance judgments (*(2011) Gao Xing Zhong Zi No. 522, No. 401, No. 531*) all upheld the invalidation decision. The patentee filed for a retrial. The SPC ruled to review the case and vacated the invalidation decision, the first and the second instance judgments.

shall also recite the essential technical features of solving the technical problems to comply with Rule 21(2) of the *Implementing Regulations of the Patent Law*."

10.1 Basic Approaches for Determining Whether a Claim Lacks Essential Technical Features

The determination of whether a technical feature is an essential technical feature, shall be based on the technical problems to be solved by the invention while considering the overall contents of the description.

A proper determination of the technical problems under Rule 21(2) of the *Implementing Regulations of the Patent Law* sets the basis for determining whether an independent claim lacks any essential technical features. This was the first issue addressed by the SPC in the three cases *(2014) Xing Ti Zi Nos. 11–13*. The SPC held that Article 21(2) of the *Implementing Regulations of the Patent Law* "aims to further regulate the correspondence between the description and the independent claims, which are claims with the broadest scope of protection in the claims, so that the technical solution defined by the independent claims can conform to the contents of the description, especially to the background art, the technical problems and the beneficial effects, etc. Therefore, the 'technical problems' in Rule 21(2) of the *Implementing Regulations of the Patent Law* refers to technical problems that the patent aims to solve in the description, and the patent applicant, based on subjective understanding of the background art, subjectively claims to solve in the description. The background art, the technical problems and the beneficial effects in the description interrelate with and corroborate each other, explaining the technical problems to be solved by the patent from different perspectives. Therefore, the determination of technical problems to be solved by the patent shall be based on the technical problems recited in the description, and consider comprehensively the background art and its technical defects in the description, the beneficial effects of the patent at issue as compared with the background art, etc. The technical features recited in the independent claims are not, by themselves, the basis for determining the technical problems to be solved by the patent." In this case, it is incorrect for the invalidation petitioner to claim that the technical problems solved by the claims were "self-propelled" and "realizing the four functions of the supporting means (supporting, centering, immobilizing and lifting)," based on the technical features recited in claim 1.

The technical problems under Rule 21(2) of the *Implementing Regulations of the Patent Law* differ from those technical problems actually solved by the patent which are redetermined according to the distinguishing technical features in the determination of the inventive step of the claims. This is the second issue addressed by the SPC in the three cases *(2014) Xing Ti Zi Nos. 11–13*. The SPC held that in the determination of inventive step, "the purpose of redetermining the technical problems is to regulate the exercise of discretion, so that the determination of whether or not there exists a technical motivation in the prior art and the determination of

10.1 Basic Approaches for Determining Whether a Claim Lacks Essential …

whether or not the patent involves an inventive step can both be more objective. This purpose is fundamentally different from the legislative purpose of Article 21(2) of the *Implementing Regulations of the Patent Law*." Moreover, in the determination of inventive step, "as the closest prior art for comparison with the claims differs, the determined distinguishing technical features will often change, and so will the redetermined technical problems. Thus, the redetermined technical problems are dynamic, relative, and usually different from those the patent is aimed to solve as recited in the description. Therefore, the redetermined technical problems cannot be the basis for determining whether a claim lacks any essential technical features."

Where a patent can solve multiple technical problems which are independent of each other, and the technical features for solving each technical problem are also independent of each other, an independent claim complies with Rule 21(2) of the *Implementing Regulations of the Patent Law* as long as it recites essential technical features that can solve one or part of the technical problem, and it is not required that this independent claim recite all the technical features that solve every technical problem. However, if the description expressly recites that the technical solutions are capable of solving multiple technical problems at the same time, the independent claim shall recite all the essential technical features that can solve all the technical problems in the technical solution at the same time.

This is the third issue addressed by the SPC in the three cases *(2014) Xing Ti Zi Nos. 11–13*. The SPC held that if a technical solution solved multiple technical problems by innovations from different angles and aspects as compared with multiple background art references, such a patented technology should be properly protected and encouraged. If the technical problems were independent of each other, and the technical features for solving these technical problems were also independent of each other, requiring recitation in the claim all the technical features for solving these technical problems "will result in too many technical features being recited in the independent claim and the scope of protection being unduly limited, which is not commensurate with the extent of its innovation and deviates from the legislative purpose of the *Patent Law* to 'encourage inventions-creations'."

On the contrary, if the patent applicant had made it clear that the technical solution of the patent required simultaneous technical improvements in multiple aspects, the ability to solve multiple technical problems at the same time would itself "constitute an important effect of the technical solution of the patent, which will have a substantial impact on the grant, patent confirmation and post-grant protection of the patent," and requiring recitation of all the technical features that solve these technical problems would be commensurate with the contribution to society. In this case, the description lists eleven prior art references, none of which "satisfactorily solves all of the problems relating to the following aspects…" Considering the technical problems, the background art and the beneficial effects recited in the description of the patent at issue, it can be concluded that "in order for the patent at issue to simultaneously solve the technical problems in the aspects of reliable transmission, transmission speed, space reduction and cost reduction, the independent claim 1 should contain essential technical features that can simultaneously solve the technical problems of the above four aspects." The invalidation decision and the second instance judgment erred in both the finding of the facts and the application of the law for failing to determine the technical problems to be solved by the patent at issue based on the recitation in the description of the patent at issue, but instead on the technical features recited in claim 1.

10.2 The Relationship Between Rule 21(2) of the *Implementing Regulations of the Patent Law* and Article 26(3)/26(4) of the *Patent Law*

Article 26(4) of the *Patent Law* and Rule 21(2) of the *Implementing Regulations of the Patent Law* both relate to the correspondence between the claims and the description. In the three cases *(2014) Xing Ti Zi Nos. 11–13*, the SPC reiterated, "Article 26(4) of the *Patent Law* with its broad scope of application, is applicable not only to independent claims but also to dependent claims, not only to circumstances where technical features (such as technical features of function) recited in the claims are too broad for the technology itself to be supported by the description, but also to circumstances where the independent or dependent claims lack technical features such that technical solutions defined in the claims cannot solve the technical problems to be solved by the patent, and the claims as a whole are not supported by the description. Therefore, if an independent claim does not comply with Rule 21(2) of the Implem*enting Regulations of the Patent Law* for lack of essential technical features, normally it will not be supported by the description and thus incompliant with Article 26(4) of the *Patent Law*."

In the three cases, the invalidation decision, on the one hand, held that claim 1 did not describe in detail the structure of the supporting means and how to simultaneously support, position, stop moving and lift a motor vehicle with the supporting means, and therefore lacked essential technical features; on the other hand, it held that although claim 1 used technical features defined by function, a person skilled in the art, based on the description, the drawings and common knowledge of the art, could determine the appropriate ways of carrying out the invention, and accordingly it found claim 4 to be in compliance with Article 26(4) of the *Patent Law*. These two conclusions were contradictory, and the application of the law was incorrect.

In the case *(2015) Zhi Xing Zi No. 56*,[2] the SPC, while examining whether the patent at issue complied with Rule 21(2) of the *Implementing Regulations of the Patent Law*, noted that "the basic function of the description is to disclose technical solutions, whereas the basic function of the claims is to delineate the protection scope of the patent right. The examination of the lack of essential technical features shall

---

[2] Utility model patent No. 200720120561.0. The invalidation decision (No. WX20022) declared that part of the patent rights were invalid. The first instance judgment (*(2013) Yi Zhong Zhi Xing Zi No. 1442*) upheld the invalidation decision, and the second instance judgment (*(2013) Gao Xing Zhong Zi No. 2041*) vacated the invalidation decision and the first instance judgment. The patentee filed for a retrial and was rejected by the SPC.

10.2 The Relationship Between Rule 21(2) of the *Implementing Regulations* ...

focus on independent claims to determine whether the independent claims recite the essential technical features to solve the relevant technical problems. Therefore, the determination of whether an independent claim lacks essential technical features is not affected by how sufficiently the description discloses the technical solutions. In other words, even if the description has sufficiently disclosed the technical solutions, as long as the independent claim does not recite all the essential technical features, the claim will still be invalidated for lacking essential technical features."

The issue in this case was whether the automatic roll changing device in claim 2 lacked any essential technical features. The invalidation petitioner argued that the patent at issue related to large machinery, so it was impossible for a person skilled in the art to carry out the technical solution by merely knowing the names of the components. As a new and creative technical solution, the positions, movements and connections between the components in claim 2 were the essential technical features to achieve the technical effects and solve the technical problems. Regarding this, the patentee believed that claim 2 aimed to solve the problems of high labor cost and low production efficiency caused by manual roll-changing, and in order to solve these problems, an automatic roll changing device was provided on the basis of claim 1, which consisted of a cylinder, a winding shaft hook connected to the cylinder and a winding shaft fixed to the winding shaft hook. A person skilled in the art, based on his or her common knowledge and customary means, could understand the functions of the components, furthermore, the working order or process of these components itself had a certain logical relationship, so the working principle, positional relationship, connection relationship and action relationship in motion needed no proof for verification. Therefore, claim 2 did not lack any essential technical features.

After reviewing the case, the SPC found that "The technical problem to be solved by claim 2 of this patent is to provide an automatic roll changing device to improve safety performance and production efficiency. However, the claim only recites the components and their connection relationship, but not the positional relationship or the action relationship; moreover, among the components recited in the claim, there is no component that moves the new winding shaft 24 to the position of the original winding shaft 14... To rotate the new winding shaft to the position of the original winding shaft is the core step of the automatic roll changing... Without such a component to move the new winding shaft 24 to the position of the original winding shaft 14, it cannot be ascertained that the new winding shaft 24 would move to the position of the original winding shaft 14 so as to complete the roll changing automatically." Therefore, the Court of Second Instance did not err in determining that claim 2 lacked essential technical features.

10.3 Will Features of Function Render a Claim Incompliant with Rule 21(2) of the *Implementing Regulations of the Patent Law*

Part II, Chapter 2 of the *Guidelines for Patent Examination* provides that, when a technical feature cannot be defined by a feature of structure, or when it is more appropriate to define the technical feature by a feature of function or effect than by a feature of structure, and the function or effect can be verified directly and positively by experiments, operations or customary means in the art as recited in the description, the invention can be defined by features of function or effect. In the three cases *(2014) Xing Ti Zi Nos. 11–13*,[3] the SPC pointed out that "although the use of features of function is strictly limited, yet it is not completely prohibited by laws and regulations."

The invalidation decision and the second instance judgment both held that claim 1 "does not describe in detail the structure of the supporting means and how to simultaneously support, position, stop moving and lift a motor vehicle with the supporting means… A person skilled in the art cannot figure out how a centering action can be performed by means of a horizontal motion of wheels through the supporting means and thus claim 1 lacks essential technical features." Following this logic, all the independent claims with functional features can be held as lacking essential technical features for failing to describe in detail the specific structure or specific way of realizing the function, which would lead to the complete exclusion of using technical features of function in independent claims. Therefore, the invalidation decision and the second instance judgment both erred in the application of the law.

If an independent claim defines the essential technical features for solving technical problems with features of function, it complies with Rule 21(2) of the *Implementing Regulations of the Patent Law*, and it is inappropriate to hold the independent claim lacking essential technical features on the grounds that it does not recite the specific structure or specific way of realizing the function. The compliance with Article 26(4) of the *Patent Law* shall be examined to determine whether the features of function are properly generalized. This is another important issue discussed in the three cases *(2014) Xing Ti Zi Nos. 11–13*. The SPC held that "a patentee may generalize the technical features in the embodiments in claim drafting, such as a superordinate generalization or a functional generalization, so as to obtain a broader scope of protection than that of the embodiments." A patentee defines the scope of protection of an independent claim with features of function if he makes a functional generalization. If "the generalization of the features of function is held as inappropriate and unsupported by the description and it is necessary to further define in the

---

[3] Invention patent No. 02803734.0. The invalidation decisions (No. WX14538, No. WX14542, No. WX14543) all declared that part of the patent rights were invalid. The first instance judgments (*(2010) Yi Zhong Zhi Xing Zi No. 2636, No. 2637, No. 2635*) and the second instance judgments (*(2011) Gao Xing Zhong Zi No. 522, No. 401, No. 531*) all upheld the invalidation decision. The patentee filed for a retrial. The SPC ruled to review the case and vacated the invalidation decision, the first and the second instance judgments.

independent claim the specific structure or specific way of realizing the function, the examination shall be conducted separately in accordance with Article 26(4) of the *Patent Law*," and the claim shall not be held lacking essential technical features on this ground. The reason is that whether the claim lacks essential technical features is a matter of the existence of features, while the appropriateness of the generalization of essential technical features is a matter of whether they can be supported by the description.

Chapter 11
Amendments Beyond Scope

Since 2011, the SPC has expressed its opinions on Article 33 of the *Patent Law* in a number of cases about the legislative intent, meaning, and understanding of this article.

11.1 The Legislative Intent of Article 33 of the *Patent Law*

The legislative intent of Article 33 of the *Patent Law* was clarified by the SPC in the cases *(2010) Zhi Xing Zi No. 53*[1] and *(2013) Xing Ti Zi No. 21*.[2] "the meaning of Article 33 of the *Patent Law* is two folds, one is to allow the applicant to amend the patent application documents, and the other is to restrict the amendments of the patent application documents." In the case *(2010) Zhi Xing Zi No. 53*,[3] the SPC explained that "the main reasons why the applicant is allowed to amend the patent

---

[1] Invention patent No. 00131800.4. The invalidation decision (No. WX11291) declared that all the patent rights were invalid. The first instance judgment (*(2008) Yi Zhong Zhi Xing Zi No. 1030*) upheld the invalidation decision. The second instance judgment (*(2009) Gao Xing Zhong Zi No. 327*) vacated the first instance judgment and the invalidation decision. The invalidation petitioner filed for a retrial and was rejected by the SPC.

[2] Invention patent No. 02127848.2. The invalidation decision (No. WX15307) declared that all the patent rights were invalid. The first instance judgment (*(2011) Yi Zhong Zhi Xing Zi No. 1139*) upheld the invalidation decision. The second instance judgment (*(2011) Gao Xing Zhong Zi No. 1577*) upheld the first instance judgment and the invalidation decision. The patentee filed for a retrial. The SPC ruled to review the case and vacated the invalidation decision, the first and second instance judgments.

[3] Invention patent No. 00131800.4. The invalidation decision (No. WX11291) declared that all the patent rights were invalid. The first instance judgment (*(2008) Yi Zhong Zhi Xing Zi No. 1030*) upheld the invalidation decision. The second instance judgment (*(2009) Gao Xing Zhong Zi No. 327*) vacated the first instance judgment and the invalidation decision. The invalidation petitioner filed for a retrial and was rejected by the SPC.

© Intellectual Property Publishing House 2024
R. Xiaolan, *Patent Administrative Litigation*, Understanding China,
https://doi.org/10.1007/978-981-97-1131-4_11

application documents are that: first, there are limitations on the applicant's expression and cognitive ability. In the process of expressing abstract inventive concepts in words, and generalizing them into specific technical solutions, due to the limitation of language, there are inevitably defects of sloppy wording or inaccurate expression. Moreover, when drafting the patent application documents, the applicant may misunderstand the invention-creation because of his or her limited knowledge of prior art and the invention-creation. In the process of patent application, as the understanding of prior art and invention-creation deepens, especially after the examiner issues the Office Action, the applicant often needs to amend the claims and the description based on his or her new understanding of the invention-creation and prior art.

Second, amendments are allowed to meet the requirement of improving the quality of patent application documents. Since patent application documents are important vehicles for delivering patent information to the public, in order to facilitate the public's understanding and use of inventions-creations and to promote the application and dissemination of inventions-creations, it is objectively necessary to improve the accuracy of patent application documents through amendments. While allowing the applicant to amend the patent application documents, Article 33 of the *Patent Law* also limits the amendments of patent application documents, i.e., the amendments of patent application documents for inventions and utility models may not go beyond the scope of disclosure contained in the initial description and claims.

Reasons for this restriction are firstly, to limit the amendments within the scope of disclosure contained in the initial description and claims, it can encourage the applicant to disclose the invention sufficiently at the application stage so that the granting procedure can be carried out smoothly. Secondly, the restriction prevents the applicant from obtaining the rights and interests of first-to-file improperly by subsequently adding to the patent application documents the content that was not completed at the date of filing, ensuring that the first-to-file principle is followed out. Thirdly, the restriction safeguards the public's reliance on patent information to avoid unnecessary damage to third parties who rely on the initial application documents to take actions accordingly. It can be seen that the legislative intent of Article 33 of the *Patent Law* is to strike a balance between the rights and interests of the patent applicant and that of the public, so that on the one hand, the applicant has the opportunity to make amendments and rectification to the patent application documents to make sure truly inventive inventions-creations can be granted and protected; on the other hand, it can also prevent the applicant from gaining unlawful rights and interests from the content of the invention that was not disclosed at the date of filing, which would undermine the public's reliance on the initial patent application documents. The interpretation of the meaning of Article 33 of the *Patent Law* must be consistent with this legislative intent."

11.2 Basic Criteria for Determining the Scope of Amendments

The SPC has embraced two different views over time on the criteria for determining whether or not the amendments go beyond the scope, namely the "theory of determination" and the "theory of support." In the case *(2013) Xing Ti Zi No. 21*,[4] the SPC adopted the "theory of determination." It held that the term "the scope of disclosure contained in the original description and claims" in Article 33 of the *Patent Law* "should be interpreted as all the information of the invention-creation disclosed in the initial description and claims, a fixture of all the information of the invention-creation... The scope of disclosure contained in the initial description and claims can be embodied specifically as: what is directly recited in words and figures in the initial description, drawings and claims, as well as what can be determined by a person skilled in the art based on the initial description, drawings and claims."

However, in the case *(2010) Zhi Xing Zi No. 53*,[5] the SPC adopted the "theory of support", i.e., "the scope of disclosure contained in the initial description and claims" in Article 33 of the *Patent Law* "should be determined from the perspective of a person skilled in the art based on the technical contents disclosed in the initial description and claims. All the technical contents disclosed in the initial description and claims shall be interpreted as belonging to the scope of the disclosure in the initial description and claims. It shall be prevented that the interpretation of the recited scope is so overly broad that it covers the technical contents not disclosed by the applicant in the initial description and claims, or so overly narrow that any technical contents disclosed by the applicant in the initial description and claims are ignored. From this perspective, the scope of disclosure contained in the initial description and claims should include the following: first, the contents clearly expressed in words or figures in the initial description, drawings and claims; second, the contents that can be directly and undoubtedly deduced by a person skilled in the art by considering all together the initial description, drawings and claims. As long as the deduced contents are obvious to a person skilled in the art, the contents can be determined as belonging to the scope of disclosure contained in the initial description and claims. Therefore, if the amended patent application documents introduce no new technical contents as compared with the above-mentioned contents, the amendments to the

---

[4] Invention patent No. 02127848.2. The invalidation decision (No. WX15307) declared that all the patent rights were invalid. The first instance judgment (*(2011) Yi Zhong Zhi Xing Zi No. 1139*) upheld the invalidation decision. The second instance judgment (*(2011) Gao Xing Zhong Zi No. 1577*) upheld the first instance judgment and the invalidation decision. The patentee filed for a retrial. The SPC ruled to review the case and vacated the invalidation decision, the first and second instance judgments.

[5] Invention patent No. 00131800.4. The invalidation decision (No. WX11291) declared that all the patent rights were invalid. The first instance judgment (*(2008) Yi Zhong Zhi Xing Zi No. 1030*) upheld the invalidation decision. The second instance judgment (*(2009) Gao Xing Zhong Zi No. 327*) vacated the first instance judgment and the invalidation decision. The invalidation petitioner filed for a retrial and was rejected by the SPC.

patent application documents are within the scope of disclosure contained in the initial description and claims."

Based on this, the SPC reiterated that, in determining whether or not the amendments to the patent application documents go beyond the scope of disclosure contained in the initial description and claims, "consideration should be given not only to the contents of the initial description, drawings, and claims expressed in words or figures but also to the contents that would be obvious to a person skilled in the art after combining the above-mentioned contents. In this process, the focus shall not be put solely on the former, reaching a conclusion simply by making a literal comparison of the text before and after the amendments, nor can the latter be understood rigidly, regarding the contents deduced directly and undoubtedly by a person skilled in the art as the sole content that can be determined following mathematical logics."

11.3 Generalization by Generic Terms

The so-called generalization by generic terms refers to amending a specific embodiment or a specific term disclosed in the initial application document by a generic term. In the case *(2013) Xing Ti Zi No. 21*,[6] the SPC upheld the decision of the Patent Reexamination Board that amending a specific term to a generic term was not in compliance with the provisions of Article 33 of the *Patent Law*. In the substantive examination, the patentee amended the "round bolt holes" in claims 1 and 2 to "round holes", "substantially round holes" in claim 6 to specifically the holes for the connecting bolts to pass through, and "compression moulding" to "pressing." The Patent Reexamination Board invalidated all the claims on the ground that said amendments were beyond the scope of the patent.

The SPC brought the case up for trial and held in the judgment that, based on the legislative intent of Article 33 of the *Patent Law* (to strike a balance between the rights and interests of the patent applicant and the public in the first-to-file system: on the one hand, the patent applicant is allowed to make amendments and corrections to the patent application documents so that truly inventive inventions-creations can be granted; on the other hand, the patent applicant's right to make amendments is limited to the technical information disclosed at the date of filing, so as to safeguard the public's reliance interest on the initial patent application documents), the term "the scope of the disclosure contained in the initial description and claims" in Article 33 of the *Patent Law* "shall be interpreted as all the information of the invention-creation disclosed in the initial description and claims, a fixture of all the information of the

---

[6] Invention patent No. 02127848.2. The invalidation decision (No. WX15307) declared that all the patent rights were invalid. The first instance judgment (*(2011) Yi Zhong Zhi Xing Zi No. 1139*) upheld the invalidation decision. The second instance judgment (*(2011) Gao Xing Zhong Zi No. 1577*) upheld the first instance judgment and the invalidation decision. The patentee filed for a retrial. The SPC ruled to review the case and vacated the invalidation decision, the first and second instance judgments.

invention-creation. This is not only the cornerstone of the first-to-file system, but also the objective basis for the subsequent stages of the patent application. The scope of the disclosure in the initial description and claims can be embodied specifically as: what is directly recited in words and figures in the initial description, drawings, and claims, as well as what can be determined by a person skilled in the art based on the initial description, drawings, and claims."

On this basis, the SPC first analyzed the meanings of "round holes" and "round bolt holes" in this case and concluded that they had different technical meanings, and the amendment of "round bolt holes" to "round holes" went beyond the scope of the disclosure in the initial application documents; then it examined the relationship between "compression moulding" and "pressing", and found that in the field of machinery, compression moulding referred to a process of pressure processing with the use of moulds or mould-like tools, while pressing referred to a process of manufacturing by the means of pressing, which did not necessarily involve the use of moulds, but might also involve other technical means such as forging, stamping, etc. For a person skilled in the art, "pressing" was a generic term of "compression moulding," and the two terms had different technical meanings. Thus, amending "compression moulding" to "pressing" was not what could be determined from the initial application documents. Although the SPC eventually vacated the decision of the Patent Reexamination Board on the ground that the specific limitation of "substantially round holes" in claim 6 to "holes for the connecting bolts to pass through" was recited in the initial application documents, the criteria for determining whether or not the amendments go beyond the scope in its judgment was the same as that of the Patent Reexamination Board.

11.4 Amendments by Cancellation

Broadly speaking, an amendment by cancellation refers to the deletion of part of the technical information recited in the initial application documents. A complete deletion of one or more claims does not raise the issue of amendments beyond the scope. The issue in practice is whether the cancellation of part of the technical features from the technical solution of a claim or the description will cause an amendment beyond the scope. The case *(2012) Zhi Xing Zi No. 94*[7] relates to this problem. The patent at issue is directed to a traditional Chinese medicine formula for treating fractures. During the substantive examination, the applicant deleted the expressions "a little" or "a tiny bit" which described the dosage of the medicinal primer on page 2 of the initial description. The Patent Reexamination Board found that this amendment did not comply with Article 33 of the *Patent Law*. The issue in this case

---

[7] Invention patent application No. 200610145533.4. The reexamination decision (No. FS31558) maintained the rejection decision. The first instance judgment (*(2011) Yi Zhong Zhi Xing Zi No. 2304*) and the second instance judgment (*(2012) Gao Xing Zhong Zi No. 117*) both upheld the reexamination decision. The patentee filed for a retrial. The SPC ruled that the court of second instance should retry the case.

was whether "a little" had a limiting effect on the "medicinal primer" as claimed by the patent applicant, and whether the deletion of the said limitation would result in the amendment going beyond the scope of the disclosure in the initial description and claims.

The SPC explained in its ruling rejecting the retrial petition: "If it is known to a person skilled in the art from the efficacy and the description that the presence or absence of a medicinal primer does not affect the curative effect of the drug, then the description is allowed not to recite the exact dosage of the medicinal primer. It is already known to a person skilled in the art that the effect of Crinis Carbonisatus (carbonized human hair) is to astringe and stop bleeding, resolve blood stasis, and promote diuresis. According to the description and the applicant's observations on the use of Crinis Carbonisatus, Crinis Carbonisatus not only acts as a guiding medicine but also influences the efficacy of the entire formula by its effects of astringing and stopping bleeding and resolving blood stasis for treating fractures. Moreover, the dosage of Crinis Carbonisatus differs for different types of fractures, and it needs to be prepared together with other medicines, therefore, Crinis Carbonisatus should not be simply regarded as an optional ingredient in this case, but its exact dosage or proportion should be recited. In the initial application documents, the applicant defined the amount of the 'medicinal primer' as 'a little,' a sort of limitation to the dosage of the drug, though not an expression of the exact amount, it still serves as a limitation to the dosage of the medicine. The cancellation of this limitation by the applicant broadened the scope of the initial description and claims, as the result of which a person skilled in the art would find different information from that in the initial application documents, and the information could not be directly and undoubtedly determined based on the initial description and claims, making the amendment exceed the scope of the initial claims and description, thus the first and the second instance judgments regarding this matter are not improper."

11.5 Amendments of Technical Features

If the amendment of one feature in the technical solution to another feature leads to the information obtained by a person skilled in the art different from the initial information, the amendment does not comply with Article 33 of the *Patent Law*; if the amendment of the technical feature does not change the substance of the technical information, the amendment complies with Article 33 of the *Patent Law*. In the case *(2011) Zhi Xing Zi No. 54*,[8] the SPC held that *"when examining whether the patent applicant's amendments to the patent application documents exceed the scope of the disclosure in the initial description and claims, full consideration should be given

---

[8] Invention patent application No. 00113917.7. The reexamination decision (No. FS20574) maintained the rejection decision. The first instance judgment (*(2010) Yi Zhong Zhi Xing Zi No. 1329*) and the second instance judgment (*(2010) Gao Xing Zhong Zi No. 1117*) both upheld the reexamination decision. The patentee filed for a retrial. The SPC ruled that the court of second instance should retry the case.

11.5 Amendments of Technical Features

to the characteristics of the technical field that the patent application belongs to, and the examination shall not be divorced from the knowledge of a person skilled in the art." The case relates to an ancient formula of traditional Chinese medicine. The examiner pointed out in the substantive examination that the dosage unit of the medicines in the formula was "Liang", which was not a unit used internationally. The patent applicant amended "Liang" to "gram" based on the conversion relationship of "one Liang" equaling "30 grams." The Patent Reexamination Board maintained the rejection decision of the substantive examination department on the ground that the amendment went beyond the scope. In the retrial, the SPC reversed the decision of the Patent Reexamination Board.

In the ruling, the SPC first analyzed the relationship between "Liang" and "gram", i.e., "in general, although it is true that there are differences between the old and new systems of converting 'Liang' to 'gram,' the relevant facts found by the Court show that in the field of traditional Chinese medicine formulas, especially in ancient formulas, the old system of 'one Jin = sixteen Liang' is followed in the conversion of 'Liang' to 'gram'. According to what is recited in the description of the patent at issue, the patent application is an improvement on the basis of the ancient formula Sanxian Dan, therefore, although it is not clearly stated in the description which conversion relationship is used for converting 'Liang' to 'gram,' a person skilled in the art, taking into account the Background Art and Summary of the patent at issue and the common knowledge in the art, can determine that the conversion of 'Liang' to 'gram' in the patent application should follow the old system rather than the new system of 'one Jin = ten Liang.'".

The SPC then examined a series of evidence submitted by the party concerned: "According to The Endorsement of the State Council on the Request Report of the Bureau of Standards and Metrology and Other Entities for Reforming the Units of Measurement in Prescriptions of Traditional Chinese Medicine, in the conversion of 'Qian' to 'gram,' 'one Qian' is equal to 'three grams' in the old system. Therefore, based on 'one Liang = ten Qian' in the old system, when converting by the old system, one Liang in the old system should obviously be converted to 30 grams. Judging from the relevant contents in textbooks and technical manuals such as *Chinese Materia Medica*, *Mineral Materia Medica*, and *Pharmacy of Chinese Materia Medica*, the conversion relationship of 'one Liang = 30 grams' is adopted in all of them. Therefore, as to the statement in *Prescriptions of Chinese Materia Medica* that 'the mantissa can be rounded off when converting,' a person skilled in the art is supposed to understand that said mantissa refers to the '1.25' in '31.25g,' i.e., the conversion relationship of 'one Liang = 30 grams' is adopted. Although the Patent Reexamination Board claims that there are other ways of rounding off the mantissa in practice, it failed to provide evidence to prove it, thus, the Patent Reexamination Board's claim is not sustained."

Finally, the SPC pointed out that "even if there are cases where the mantissa is rounded off in other ways or not rounded off at all in the conversion by the old system, it should be recognized that multiple ways of rounding-off the mantissa result from the technical characteristics of formulas of traditional Chinese medicine. There are only minor differences between different ways of rounding off the mantissa, which will not lead to substantial changes in the technical solutions. In practice, a person skilled in the art can choose a certain way of rounding-off the mantissa according to specific circumstances and requirements, and once a certain way is chosen, the person skilled in the art applies it consistently throughout the formula of traditional Chinese medicine, so there will not be and should not be a situation where different ways of rounding-off are applied in the same formula.

Therefore, choosing different ways of rounding-off the mantissa on the basis of the old system belongs to the contents that can be directly and undoubtedly determined by a person skilled in the art, and it does not introduce new technical content that undermines the rights and interests of the public; nor will there be a situation that 'may substantially change the technical solution of the invention and turn an unworkable technical solution into a workable one' as feared by the Patent Reexamination Board. In fact, in the substantive examination of the patent at issue, China National Intellectual Property Administration gave clear instructions on how to amend the patent application documents in the Second Office Action and Sixth Office Action for the patent at issue. The Second Office Action pointed out that 'eight Liang of mercury' did not use an international standard unit of measurement in the art and explicitly requested Zeng Guansheng to amend the unit of measurement 'Liang'; the Sixth Office Action expressly recognized the conversion relationship of 'one Liang = 30 grams' adopted by Zeng Guansheng.

The decision (No. 20574) and the first and second instance judgments failed to take into full consideration the technical characteristics of the art of the patent application at issue, the knowledge that a person skilled in the art should possess, as well as the reasons for Zeng Guansheng to make said amendments to the patent application at issue and the fact that said amendments had been recognized by China National Intellectual Property Administration, and since there is no obvious impropriety in the relevant office actions, the determination that Zeng Guansheng's amendments to the application documents of the patent at issue exceeded the scope of the disclosure in the initial description and claims erred in both the determination of the facts and the application of the law."

11.6 Closed Claims Amended to Open Claims

Closed claims and open claims are two ways of drafting a composition claim. An open claim means that the composition does not exclude components not recited in the claim, while a closed claim means that the composition includes only the recited components and excludes all other components. In the case *(2010) Zhi Xing Zi No. 18*,[9] the SPC expounded on how to determine whether the amendment of an open claim to a closed claim went beyond the scope. The patent in this case relates to

---

[9] Invention patent No. 96117491.9. The invalidation decision (No. WX9600) declared that all the patent rights were invalid. The second instance judgment (*(2008) Gao Xing Zhong Zi No. 308*) upheld the invalidation decision. The patentee filed for a retrial and was rejected by the SPC.

11.6 Closed Claims Amended to Open Claims

a saccharifying agent for a liquor-making process. The liquor flavoring and high-yielding agent products involved in the technical solutions of the initial claims and description as well as the embodiments are all made by combining an alcohol-active dry yeast, an aroma-producing active dry yeast, and a solid saccharifying enzyme. In the substantive examination, the patent applicant amended the claim to that the liquor flavoring and high-yielding agent containing "an alcohol active dry yeast, an aroma-producing (ester) active dry yeast and a solid saccharifying enzyme." The Patent Reexamination Board declared all the patent rights invalid on the ground that said amendment went beyond the scope. The SPC upheld the decision of the Patent Reexamination Board. In the ruling, the SPC held that "the technical solution of the liquor flavoring and high-yielding agent recited in the initial claims and description of the patent is expressed in a typical closed mode, in which it contains only three components, i.e., 'an alcohol dry yeast, an aroma-producing dry yeast and a solid saccharifying enzyme,' which themselves are three preparations comprising not only the active substances but also other substances used in the preparation process, such as the raw materials of the culture medium and other substances normally included in products of such preparations, in other words, the three components are not pure substances of yeast cells or saccharifying enzyme.

Although the technical solution on page 2 of the initial description recites 'each 1000 grams of the product is produced by combining … grams of the alcohol dry yeast and … grams of the aroma-producing (ester) dry yeast both containing more than … viable cells per gram, and … $\times 10^7$ units of the solid saccharifying enzyme' and 'each gram of the product contains … $\times 10^4$ enzyme activity units and over … $\times 10^8$ viable cells of the two yeasts.' yet, the term 'contains' refers to the number of viable cells and the amount of enzyme activity units per gram of the three components, namely the alcohol active dry yeast, the aroma-producing active dry yeast and the solid saccharifying enzyme, rather than indicating that the liquor flavoring and high-yielding agent may contain other components or preparations in addition to the above three components. Claim 1 in the announcement of granting the patent at issue is drafted in an open mode, and the high-yielding agent may contain, in addition to the three components 'an alcohol dry yeast, an aroma-producing dry yeast, and a solid saccharifying enzyme,' other components or any preparations containing other viable cells or enzymes, in other words, the amended claim contains a variety of indefinite components not recited in the initial description and claims, and the resulting technical solution is not recited in the initial claims and description and cannot be directly and undoubtedly determined from the information disclosed in the initial claims and description, therefore, the amendment does not comply with Article 33 of the *Patent Law*."

11.7 The Relationship Between the Amendments Beyond Scope and the Points of Novelty

Generally speaking, a technical solution contains several technical features, among which the technical feature that embodies the invention-creation's contribution to the prior art is usually referred to as the "point of novelty." The "point of novelty" endows the invention-creation with novelty and inventive step in relation to the prior art and is the basis and fundamental reason for the invention-creation to be granted a patent right. In the case *(2013) Xing Ti Zi No. 21*,[10] the SPC pointed out: "in patent granting and patent confirmation procedures, there are indeed cases where inventive inventions-creations are not granted because the amendments of technical features other than the 'points of novelty' go beyond the scope of the disclosure in the initial description and claims. Article 33 of the *Patent Law* does not adopt different standards for the amendments of patent application documents to distinguish between the 'points of novelty' and contents other than the 'points of novelty'. However, one of the legislative intents of this article is to ensure, as much as possible, that patent rights are granted for truly inventive inventions-creations and that the rights granted to the patent applicant are commensurate with his or her technical contribution. If the contribution of the entire invention-creation to the prior art is disregarded simply because the amendments to contents other than the 'points of novelty' go beyond the scope of the disclosure in the initial description and claims, consequently making it difficult for truly inventive inventions-creations to be patented, and the rights and interests obtained by the patent applicant incommensurate with his or her contribution to society, it not only harms substantive fairness, but also contradicts the legislative intent of Article 33 of the *Patent Law*, and is not conducive to encourage innovation and scientific and technical development as well.

Therefore, under the current legal framework and institutional system, relative departments should actively seek corresponding solutions and remedies to prevent patent applicants from obtaining illegitimate first-to-file rights and interests while actively rescuing inventions-creations with technical innovation value.

For example, attempts may be made to procedural measures such as setting up a corresponding response procedure in the administrative examination of patent granting and patent confirmation procedures, in which the patent applicant and the patentee are allowed to abandon amendments that do not comply with Article 33 of the *Patent Law* to restore the patent application and granted documents to the initial status at the date of filing, so as to prevent truly inventive inventions-creations from losing the entitled patent rights commensurate with their contribution to the prior art due to amendments to the contents other than the 'points of novelty' going beyond

---

[10] Invention patent No. 02127848.2. The invalidation decision (No. WX15307) declared that all the patent rights were invalid. The first instance judgment (*(2011) Yi Zhong Zhi Xing Zi No. 1139*) upheld the invalidation decision. The second instance judgment (*(2011) Gao Xing Zhong Zi No. 1577*) upheld the first instance judgment and the invalidation decision. The patentee filed for a retrial. The SPC ruled to bring the case up for trial and vacated the invalidation decision, the first and second instance judgments.

the scope of the disclosure in the initial description and claims, to promote scientific and technological progress and innovation, and to maximize the capability of science and technology to support and lead economic and social development."

11.8 The Relationship Between the Restriction to the Amendments of Patent Application Documents and the Scope of Patent Protection

Under Rules 51, 61 and 68 of the *Implementing Regulations of the Patent Law* and Article 59(1) of the *Patent Law*, the restriction to the amendments of patent application documents and the scope of patent protection are related to some degree and also differ significantly. In the case *(2010) Zhi Xing Zi No. 53*,[11] the SPC analyzed the relationship between the two and held that "the main difference between the two is that the amendments of patent application documents are limited by the scope of the disclosure in the initial description and claims, and the wider the scope recited and the more technical contents disclosed, the larger the scope of amendment is allowed, whereas the protection scope of an invention or utility model patent is determined by the contents of its claims, and the description and its drawings can be used for claim construction. The more technical features the claims recite, the narrower its protection scope becomes. At the same time, for amendments made by the patent applicant on his own initiative according to Rule 51 of the *Implementing Regulations of the Patent Law*, the patent applicant may, when amending the initial claims, either expand or narrow the claimed scope as long as the amendments do not go beyond the scope of the initial description and claims. The connection between the restriction to the amendments of patent application documents and the scope of patent protection lies in the fact that under Rule 68 of the *Implementing Regulations of the Patent Law*, in the examination of an invalidation request, the amendments of the claims by the patentee of an invention or utility model shall be limited by the protection scope of the initial patent and not go beyond the protection scope of the initial patent.

In this case, Seiko Epson Corporation made the amendment of the 'semiconductor storage device' in the initial claims at the time of filing the divisional application, not in the examination of the invalidation request, and there was no correlation between the legality of the amendment and the scope of protection claimed in the initial patent application documents. The retrial petitioner' assertion that the patent should be invalidated on the ground that the amendment goes beyond the scope of protection is not sustained."

---

[11] Invention patent No. 00131800.4. The invalidation decision (No. WX11291) declared that all the patent rights were invalid. The first instance judgment (*(2008) Yi Zhong Zhi Xing Zi No. 1030*) upheld the invalidation decision. The second instance judgment (*(2009) Gao Xing Zhong Zi No. 327*) vacated the first instance judgment and the invalidation decision. The invalidation petitioner filed for a retrial and was rejected by the SPC.

11.9 The Relationship Between the Restriction to the Amendments of Patent Application Documents and Estoppel

The SPC also analyzed the relationship between the restriction to the amendments of patent application documents and estoppel in the case *(2010) Zhi Xing Zi No. 53*.[12] First of all, the SPC held that "in the patent granting and patent confirmation procedures, the patent applicant needs to follow the good-faith principle, keep promises, be honest and not deceive, and should not go back on his or her word to undermine the reliance of third parties on his or her acts.

As an embodiment and requirement of the good faith principle, the doctrine of estoppel shall be applied in patent granting and patent confirmation procedures. However, the doctrine of estoppel in patent granting and patent confirmation procedures is not applied unconditionally, but rather limited by its own applicable conditions and other principles or legal provisions related to it. The application of the doctrine of estoppel presupposes that the patent applicant's reneging behavior undermines the third party's reliance on and expectation of his or her behavior. At the same time, the application of the doctrine of estoppel is also limited by explicit legal provisions and other equally important principles. These factors shall be considered comprehensively in the application of the doctrine of estoppel in patent granting and patent confirmation procedures."

"Under Article 33 of the *Patent Law* and Rule 68 of the *Implementing Regulations of the Patent Law*, in the patent granting procedure, the applicant may amend the patent application documents, but the amendments to the patent application documents for inventions and utility models shall not exceed the scope of the disclosure in the initial description and claims; in the patent confirmation procedure, the applicant may amend the claims, but shall not expand the scope of protection of the initial patent. Therefore, relevant law has given the applicant the right to amend the patent application documents in the patent granting procedure, as long as such amendments do not exceed the scope of the disclosure in the initial description and claims. Under Article 33 of the *Patent Law*, the public should be able to anticipate that the applicant may amend the patent application documents, and they should rely on the scope of the disclosure in the initial description and claims, i.e., the contents directly recited in words and figures in the initial description, drawings, and claims, as well as the contents that can be determined by a person skilled in the art based on the initial description, drawings, and claims, rather than solely on the scope of protection recited in the initial claims. Therefore, if the applicant's amendments to the patent application documents comply with Article 33 of the *Patent Law*, the doctrine of estoppel shall be inapplicable to the scope of such amendments."

---

[12] Invention patent No. 00131800.4. The invalidation decision (No. WX11291) declared that all the patent rights were invalid. The first instance judgment (*(2008) Yi Zhong Zhi Xing Zi No. 1030*) upheld the invalidation decision. The second instance judgment (*(2009) Gao Xing Zhong Zi No. 327*) vacated the first instance judgment and the invalidation decision. The invalidation petitioner filed for a retrial and was rejected by the SPC.

11.9 The Relationship Between the Restriction to the Amendments of Patent …

In this case, "since a person skilled in the art can deduce from the disclosed description, drawings and claims of the initial patent application documents that the technical solution of said patent application can also be applied to ink cartridges with a non-semiconductor storage device, the amendment made by Seiko Epson Corporation on its own initiative from the 'semiconductor storage device' in the initial claims to 'storage device' at the time of filing the divisional application does not go beyond the scope of the disclosure in the initial description and the claims, and such an amendment is foreseeable to the public. Moreover, this amendment will not undermine the reliance and interests of the public. Thus, the doctrine of estoppel is inapplicable to the amendment made by Seiko Epson Corporation concerning the 'storage device' in this case.

The Patent Reexamination Board claimed that in the process of applying for a patent, Seiko Epson Corporation actually considered that 'semi-conductor storage device' and 'storage device' had different meanings, while in the invalidation procedure, Seiko Epson Corporation declared that they had the same meaning. The process of amendment reflected its denial of its own words, thus the amendment from 'semiconductor storage device' to 'storage device' should be considered as denying its own words, which should be prohibited. This claim confuses the relationship between Article 33 of the *Patent Law* and the doctrine of estoppel… and the above claim of the Patent Reexamination Board is actually based on the applicant's explanation in the invalidation procedure after the amendment has been completed to determine whether the amendment of the patent application documents was beyond the scope, which in essence, is replacing Article 33 of the *Patent Law* with the doctrine of estoppel. The claim is not sustained."

Chapter 12
Procedure Related Issues

The Patent Reexamination Board, as the administrative organ responsible for examination on both the cases of request for reexamination and invalidation, shall make administrative decisions in accordance with prescribed procedures. In practice, controversial issues generally rise in the areas of reexamination procedure, scope of *ex officio* examination of the Patent Reexamination Board in the invalidation procedure, application of the principle of hearing, amendments in the invalidation procedure, presenting evidence of common knowledge, and application of the *Guidelines for Patent Examination*.

12.1 Selective Application of the *Guidelines for Patent Examination*

Along with the three revisions of the *Patent Law* and the *Implementing Regulations of the Patent Law* (hereinafter referred to as the *Implementing Regulations*), the *Guidelines for Patent Examination* also has been revised for five times. Except for the current version, all other versions of the *Guidelines for Patent Examination* adopted the wording like "the *Guidelines for Patent Examination* promulgated on … shall be repealed at the same time" in the *Explanatory Notes on the Amendment*. Each revision of the *Guidelines for Patent Examination* has made changes to some provisions, more or less. Therefore, in the specific examination process of cases, especially those in the fields of medicine and chemistry involving supplementary experimental data, which version of the *Guidelines for Patent Examination* shall apply is often a disputed issue, which has recently been discussed a lot. The prevailing view of the SPC seems to be that the version of the *Guidelines for Patent Examination* legally effective on the date of filing of the patent application shall apply. In the case *(2012) Xing Ti Zi No. 20*,[1] the SPC held that "With the filing date of July 5, 2002 and the grant date of January 9, 2008, the examination on this patent shall be governed by the 2001 Edition of the *Guidelines for Patent Examination*."

In the case *(2012) Zhi Xing Zi No. 59*,[2] the SPC explained: "The *Guidelines for Patent examination (2006)* entered into force from July 1, 2006, so it was the *Guidelines for Patent examination (2001)* that applied for the invalidation decision No. 8184 issued on March 15, 2006. According to the provisions of the *Guidelines for Patent Examination (2001)*, the composition features shall not be taken into account in the examination of inventive step for a utility model. However, this case involves the examination of inventive step for an invention, and the two versions of the *Guidelines for Patent Examination* mentioned above both require consideration of composition features. Therefore, the judgment criteria of the two are not completely consistent. In the determination of inventive step of claim 1 of this patent, as the parties concerned have a dispute over 'wear-resistant paper layer' which is a composition feature, it is inappropriate to regard the invalidation decision No. 8184 as the ground to make the determination that claim 1 of this patent does not involve an inventive step. The second instance judgment made inappropriate arguments on this issue, but it did not substantially affect the correctness of the judgment."

12.2 *Ex Officio* Examination in Reexamination Procedure

According to the provisions of the *Guidelines for Patent Examination*, the reexamination procedure has dual natures: on the one hand, it is a special "administrative reconsideration" procedure for the Patent Reexamination Board to resolve the dispute between the patent applicant and the previous examination department on the appropriateness of a decision of rejection; on the other hand, it is a continuation of the patent examination and approval proceedings. Based on its dual natures, the Patent Reexamination Board generally only examines whether a decision of rejection is appropriate in the reexamination procedure, and does not undertake the obligation to perform comprehensive examination. However, if a patent application has, for example, defects that have been notified to the parties concerned before the decision of rejection is made and sufficient to come to a conclusion to uphold the decision of

---

[1] Invention patent No. 02123866.9. The invalidation decision (No. WX13327) upheld the validity of the patent. The first instance judgment (*(2010) Yi Zhong Zhi Xing Zi No. 1729*), and the second instance judgment (*(2011) Gao Xing Zhong Zi No. 76*) both upheld the invalidation decision. The patentee filed for a retrial. The SPC brought the case up for trial, and ruled to uphold the invalidation decision, and the first and second instance judgments.

[2] Invention patent No. 03112761.4. The invalidation decision (No. WX14220) declared partial invalidation of the patent right. The first instance judgment (*(2010) Yi Zhong Zhi Xing Zi No. 2023*) upheld the invalidation decision; the second instance judgment (*(2011) Gao Xing Zhong Zi No. 911*) overturned the first instance judgment and the invalidation decision. The patentee filed for a retrial and was rejected by the SPC.

12.2 Ex Officio Examination in Reexamination Procedure

rejection, or defects of the same nature as those indicated in the decision of rejection, or obvious substantive defects, the Patent Reexamination Board may examine these defects *ex officio* and make a reexamination decision upholding the decision of rejection on that ground.

In recent years, there has been a lot of controversies around the scale of the *ex officio* examination by the Patent Reexamination Board in the reexamination procedure. In the case *(2014) Zhi Xing Zi No. 2*,[3] the SPC clarified its view on the examination criteria of the Patent Reexamination Board in the reexamination procedure. In this case, in the substantive examination, the examiner only assessed the novelty of the claims. In the reexamination procedure, the applicant amended the claims, and the Patent Reexamination Board issued a Notification of Reexamination, providing the opinion that the amended claims did not possess novelty or involve any inventive step, and finally upheld the decision of rejection on the ground that the claim did not involve an inventive step. The patent applicant believed that the assessment of inventive step was not for "obvious substantive defects" stipulated in the *Guidelines for Patent Examination*, and did not fall within the scope of the Patent Reexamination Board's *ex officio* examination. This also became a dispute in the case. In its request for a retrial, the Patent Reexamination Board held that, first of all, according to the provisions of the *Guidelines for Patent Examination*, in the reexamination procedure, although the panel generally only examined the grounds and evidence on which the decision of rejection was based, it did not prohibit the examination on the grounds other than the grounds for rejection, and also the Patent Reexamination Board had notified the applicant before making the decision of the grounds for not involving an inventive step, which was in line with the principles of conducting examination *ex officio* and hearing; secondly, those skilled in the art could come to a conclusion without in-depth investigation on whether the patent application involved an inventive step, so it was an "obvious substantial defect."

In response to the above point of view, the SPC pointed out: "The Patent Reexamination Board generally only examines the grounds and evidence on which the decision of rejection is based, and may also conduct examination *ex officio* without being limited by the scope of the party's request and the grounds and evidence presented." According to the provisions of the *Guidelines for Patent Examination*, "The Patent Reexamination Board examines patent applications *ex officio* is an exception, and the examination shall be carried out in strict accordance with the relevant provisions of laws, regulations, and rules." In this case, first of all, the assessment of inventive step does not fall within the scope of "obvious substantive defects", because "The *Guidelines for Patent Examination* lists various circumstances of "obvious substantive defects" in the chapter 'Preliminary Examination of Patent Applications for Invention,' including whether it is a complete technical solution, whether it is contrary to the laws or social morality, etc., all of which can be determined by those skilled in

---

[3] Invention patent application No. 200410047791X. Reexamination decision (No. FS30895). The first instance judgment (*(2011) Yi Zhong Xing Chu Zi No. 2876*), and the second instance judgment (*(2012) Gao Xing Zhong Zi No. 1486*) both decided against the Patent Reexamination Board. The Patent Reexamination Board filed for a retrial and was rejected by the SPC.

the art without in-depth investigation and verification or technical comparison, but the assessment of inventive step of an invention-creation is not included. The *Guidelines for Patent Examination* does not make specific provisions about the 'obvious substantive defects' in the chapters of 'Substantive Examination' and 'Examination of Requests for Reexamination and for Invalidation'. Although the scopes of preliminary examination, substantive examination, and examination for reexamination and invalidation shall not be exactly identical, the nature of 'obvious substantive defects' in the three should be the same. Therefore, the examination of 'obvious substantive defects' in 'Substantive Examination' and 'Examination of Requests for Reexamination and for Invalidation' shall be carried out on the basis of particular circumstances of individual cases in accordance with the nature of the circumstances enumerated in the chapter Preliminary Examination of the *Guidelines for Patent Examination*. Of course, the 'obvious substantive defects' in the preliminary examination listed in the *Guidelines for Patent Examination* are also the 'obvious substantive defects' in the 'Substantive Examination' and 'Examination of Requests for Reexamination and for Invalidation.' For those skilled in the art, the inventive step of an invention-creation means that it is non-obvious as compared with the prior art, and whether or not it involves an inventive step is an essential condition for granting a patent right to the invention-creation. In assessment of inventive step, not only shall the technical solution itself of the invention-creation be considered, but also the technical field to which the invention-creation belongs, the technical problems solved, and the technical effects produced should be considered. Therefore, it is inappropriate to expand the interpretation of the 'obvious substantive defects' listed in the *Guidelines for Patent Examination* to the determination of an inventive step. Secondly, the assessment of inventive step of the patent application at issue was not involved in the previous decision of rejection ... Therefore, this case is obviously not a circumstance that the Patent Reexamination Board shall conduct examination *ex officio*."

Contrary to the case *(2014) Zhi Xing Zi No. 2*,[4] the SPC supported the scope of the Patent Reexamination Board's *ex officio* examination in the case *(2014) Zhi Xing Zi No. 123*[5] concluded in 2015. In this case, the previous examination department made a decision of rejection on the ground that the patent application at issue was lack of practical applicability, and the Patent Reexamination Board introduced the Article 26(3) of the *Patent Law ex officio* in the reexamination procedure, and upheld the decision of rejection on that ground. The SPC held that, "Even if the petitioner for reexamination has overcome the problems pointed out in the previous decision of rejection or the Notification of Reexamination, if the Patent Reexamination Board believes that the application concerned has obvious substantive defects, it may reject

---

[4] Invention patent application No. 200410047791X. Reexamination decision (No. FS30895). The first instance judgment (*(2011) Yi Zhong Xing Chu Zi No. 2876*), and the second instance judgment (*(2012) Gao Xing Zhong Zi No. 1486*) both decided against the Patent Reexamination Board. The Patent Reexamination Board filed for a retrial and was rejected by the SPC.

[5] Invention patent application No. 200610075959.7. The reexamination decision (No. FS57456) upheld the decision of rejection. The first instance judgment (*(2013) Yi Zhong Xing Chu Zi No. 3711*), and the second instance judgment (*(2014) Gao Xing Zhong Zi No. 1112*) both upheld the invalidation decision. The patent applicant filed for a retrial, and was rejected by the SPC.

the request for reexamination on the grounds different from that of the previous rejection decision." In this case, "the insufficient disclosure of the description is an obvious substantive defect, and the Patent Reexamination Board has pointed out this defect to the petitioner for reexamination during the reexamination procedure and gave the petitioner an opportunity to made observations. Under the circumstance that the petitioner did not eliminate such defect, the reexamination decision made by the Patent Reexamination Board on the grounds that the application concerned did not comply with the Article 26(3) of the *Patent Law*, did not fail to follow the statutory procedures."

12.3 Burden of Presenting Evidence of Common Knowledge by the Panel in the Reexamination Procedure

According to the provisions of the *Guidelines for Patent Examination*, the Patent Reexamination Board may determine common knowledge *ex officio* during the examination on the cases of request for reexamination.

Regarding whether the Patent Reexamination Board needs to provide evidence when determining common knowledge *ex officio*, the SPC clarified in the case *(2014) Zhi Xing Zi No. 1*,[6] "According to Article 32 of the *Administrative Procedure Law* of the People's Republic of China, the Patent Reexamination Board shall bear the burden of proof on whether the decision it has made for the request for reexamination is legal, and the assumption of such burden of proof is not premised on whether the people's court requires it." In the reexamination procedure of this case, the Patent Reexamination Board found that claim 1 had three distinctive features as compared with Reference Document 3. Among them, the distinctive feature 1 was common knowledge. The court of second instance held that the Patent Reexamination Board did not present sufficient evidence in determination of common knowledge, and therefore overturned the reexamination decision. On this dispute, the SPC held that "While the Patent Reexamination Board considered that it was a conventional technical means in the field to use a microprocessor to centrally control various internal components and external devices for corresponding functions, but the patent applicant had objection to this, the Patent Reexamination Board had the burden of proof for the common knowledge introduced by it. As the Patent Reexamination Board did not provide corresponding evidence in the second instance, the determination of insufficient evidence made by the court of second instance was not inappropriate."

---

[6] Invention patent application No. 200610006562.2. Reexamination decision (No. FS31646). The first instance judgment *((2012) Yi Zhong Xing Chu Zi No. 868)* upheld the decision of the Patent Reexamination Board. The second instance judgment *((2012) Gao Xing Zhong Zi No. 1316)* overturned the first instance judgment. The Patent Reexamination Board filed for a retrial and was rejected by the SPC.

However, in the case *(2015) Zhi Xing Zi No. 173*,[7] the SPC seems to have come to a different conclusion on similar issues. In this case, the Patent Reexamination Board held in its reexamination decision that the use of an atomizing nozzle in atomization of water is a conventional technical means in the field, but no evidence was presented to support it. The SPC held that "The patent examination department shall conduct the examination of inventive step for a patent application based on the knowledge and ability of those skilled in the art. Those skilled in the art shall be aware of all the common technical knowledge and have access to all the technologies existing before the date of filing in the technical field to which the invention pertains." In this case, the determination of the Patent Reexamination Board was based on the knowledge and ability of those skilled in the field, and this was fully explained in the invalidation decision. Therefore, it was not inappropriate for the first and second instance judgments to not require the Patent Reexamination Board to present evidence.

12.4 *Ex officio* Examination and Examination upon Request in the Invalidation Procedure

With the third revision of the *Patent Law*, the debate on the nature of the invalid procedure has gradually subsided. The prevailing view for some time is that the invalidation procedure is an administrative review procedure in which the Patent Reexamination Board corrects improper grants by means of requests made by petitioners for invalidation. However, with the advancement of the fourth revision of the *Patent Law*, the controversy on the nature of the invalid procedure starts again.

In the case *(2014) Zhi Xing Zi No. 52*,[8] the SPC clarified the purpose and significance of the patent invalidation procedure: "According to the provisions of the *Patent Law*, the State Intellectual Property Office exercises its functions according to law for examination of novelty, inventive step, practical applicability, and other conditions for granting a patent right, but does not and cannot bear the burden of ensuring that the patent right is correctly granted. To this end, the *Patent Law* has set up a patent invalidation system, with the purpose of making full use of the power of the public to challenge granted patents of invention-creations that do not meet the conditions for granting a patent right, and to discover and correct improper patent granting decisions of the patent administration department for invention-creations that do not meet the conditions for granting a patent right, so as to improve the quality of patents

---

[7] Invention patent application No. 200710148482.5. Reexamination decision (No. FS47465). The first instance judgment (*(2013) Yi Zhong Xing Chu Zi No. 610*) upheld the decision of the Patent Reexamination Board. The second instance judgment (*(2013) Gao Xing Zhong Zi No. 1756*) upheld the first instance judgment. The patent applicant filed for a retrial and was rejected by the SPC.

[8] Invention patent No. 200610069781.5. The invalidation decision (No. WX17452) declared the patent right invalid in whole. The first instance judgment (*(2012) Yi Zhong Xing Chu Zi No. 761*), and the second instance judgment (*(2012) Gao Xing Zhong Zi No. 1377*) both upheld the invalidation decision. The patentee filed for a retrial and was rejected by the SPC.

granted and safeguard the interests of the public. If an invention patent right that has undergone substantive examination is not allowed to be invalidated through the invalidation procedure, the patent invalidation system will be meaningless."

1. Application of the Rule 72 of the *Implementing Regulations of the Patent Law*

In the invalidation procedure, on the one hand, due to the nature of the invalidation procedure, the Patent Reexamination Board generally only examines the grounds, scope and evidence for the invalidation request made by the petitioner, and is not obliged to undertake comprehensive examination on the validity of the patent; on the other hand, based on the requirement of correcting improper grants, the Patent Reexamination Board may, within a certain scope, introduce *ex officio* other grounds and evidence for invalidation than those mentioned by the petitioner without being limited by the grounds and evidence for invalidation proposed by the petitioner. At the same time, according to the Rule 72(2) of the *Implementing Regulations of the Patent Law*, if the Patent Reexamination Board finds based on the examination it has done that a decision invalidating the patent right in whole or in part can be made, even if the petitioner requests to withdraw his request for invalidation, the Patent Reexamination Board may not terminate the examination procedure.

In the case *(2013) Zhi Xing Zi No. 92*,[9] the grounds on which the petitioner requested for invalidation were that the patent at issue did not involve any inventive step as compared with a combination of Reference Document 2 and common knowledge, and a combination of Reference Document 3 and common knowledge. In the oral proceedings, the petitioner renounced the combination of Reference Document 3 and common knowledge as the ground for assessing the inventive step. The Patent Reexamination Board assessed the inventive step of the patent at issue using the combinations of Reference Documents 3, Reference Documents 2, and common knowledge, and declared the patent right invalid. One of the disputes in this case is the application of the Rule 72(2) of the *Implementing Regulations of the Patent Law*. In response to this dispute, the Patent Reexamination Board held that the Rule 72(2) of the *Implementing Regulations of the Patent Law* stipulated that the Patent Reexamination Board may conduct examination *ex officio* on the petitioner's request which is withdrawn or deemed withdrawn. To renounce part of the grounds for invalidation is of course to withdraw part of the request for invalidation. This provision shall be applicable to the circumstance where the petitioner renounces part of the grounds and evidence of the request for invalidation, otherwise there will be an unreasonable logic that the *ex officio* examination may be conducted for cases of entire renouncement but not for cases of partial renouncement. In the ruling, the SPC rejected this view of the Patent Reexamination Board. The SPC held that "The Rule 72(2) of the *Implementing Regulations of the Patent Law* … applies to the circumstance where

---

[9] Utility model patent No. 200620074801.3. The invalidation decision (No. WX18967) declared the patent right invalid in whole. The first instance judgment (*(2012) Yi Zhong Xing Chu Zi No. 3616*), and the second instance judgment (*(2013) Gao Xing Zhong Zi No. 530*) both overturned the invalidation decision. The Patent Reexamination Board filed for a retrial and was rejected by the SPC.

the petitioner for invalidation withdraws his request or the request for invalidation is deemed to be withdrawn. In this case, Foton Lovol did not withdraw the request for invalidation, and the circumstances of being deemed to have been withdrawn were also not applicable. Even if this stipulation, as alleged by the Patent Reexamination Board, is applicable to the circumstance where the petitioner renounced on his own initiative part of the grounds and evidence for invalidation… Foton Lovol had never raised the grounds for invalidation, and there was no fact of renouncing." Therefore, it is inappropriate for the Patent Reexamination Board to use Reference Document 3 renounced by the petitioner for invalidation and combine it with Reference Document 2 and common knowledge to assess the inventive step of the patent at issue.

2. Understanding of the Scope of *Ex Officio* Examination Listed in the *Guidelines for Patent Examination*

Regarding the circumstances where the Patent Reexamination Board shall conduct examination *ex officio* on the grounds and evidence not mentioned by the petitioner for invalidation, the *Guidelines for Patent Examination (2006)* listed three circumstances in Part IV, Chapter III, Section 4.1,[10] while the *Guidelines for Patent Examination* revised in 2010 expanded to seven,[11] The dispute in practice is whether these circumstances listed in the *Guidelines for Patent Examination* define an exhaustive

---

[10] The Patent Reexamination Board may conduct examination *ex officio* in the following circumstances: (1) where the grounds raised by the petitioner are obviously inappropriate to the evidence submitted, the Patent Reexamination Board may inform the petitioner of the meanings of the relevant provisions, and allow him to change the grounds to suitable ones; (2) where a patent is found to have such a defect not indicated by the petitioner as to inhibit further examination on the grounds raised by the petitioner, the Patent Reexamination Board may introduce *ex officio* a corresponding ground to the defect into the grounds for invalidation, and perform examination on the ground; and (3) the Patent Reexamination Board may determine *ex officio* whether a technical means belongs to common knowledge of the art, and may introduce such common knowledge evidence as those in a technical dictionary, technical manual, or textbook.

[11] The Patent Reexamination Board may conduct examination *ex officio* in the following circumstances: (1) where the grounds raised by the petitioner are obviously inappropriate to the evidence submitted, the Patent Reexamination Board may inform the petitioner of the meanings of the relevant provisions, and allow him to change the grounds to suitable ones; (2) where a patent is found to have the defect that obviously falls within the subject matters excluded from patent protection and the defect is not indicated by the petitioner, the Patent Reexamination Board may introduce a corresponding ground into the invalidation, and perform examination in that regard; (3) where a patent is found to have such a defect not indicated by the petitioner as to inhibit further examination on the grounds raised by the petitioner, the Patent Reexamination Board may introduce *ex officio* a corresponding ground to the defect into the grounds for invalidation, and perform examination on the ground; (4) where the petitioner requests for invalidating some of the claims which have reference relationship among them, does not request for invalidating the other claims on the same ground, and the examination conclusion will be unreasonable if the Patent Reexamination Board dose not introduce such ground, the Patent Reexamination Board may *ex officio* introduce such ground and perform examination on the other claims in that regard; (5) where the petitioner requests for invalidating some of the claims which have reference relationship among them on the ground that they have some defects, and does not indicate that the other claims have defects of the same nature, the Patent Reexamination Board may introduce a corresponding ground to the defect into the invalidation and examine the other claims in that regard; (6) where the petitioner requests for invalidating a patent on the ground that it is not in conformity with the Article 33 of the *Patent Law*

12.4 *Ex officio* Examination and Examination upon Request ...

or exemplified scope of *ex officio* examination by the Patent Reexamination Board in the invalidation procedure?

In the case *(2013) Zhi Xing Zi No. 92*,[12] the second dispute concerned this issue, namely the understanding of the three circumstances of *ex officio* examination provided in the *Guidelines for Patent Examination (2006)*. In response to this dispute, the Patent Reexamination Board held that, according to the *Guidelines for Patent Examination (2006)* about the principle of disposal by the party concerned, "For the scope, grounds or evidence renounced by the petitioner, usually the Patent Reexamination Board will not investigate or examine them any more." The term "usually" is a general description, and does not mean "absolutely." The three common circumstances where the *ex officio* examination "may be" conducted provided in the *Guidelines for Patent Examination (2006)* should be understood as merely a list of circumstances of *ex officio* examination, but not a limitation of *ex officio* examination. The SPC did not support this view. The SPC held that "The invalidation procedure was initiated upon the petitioner's request. As the basic principle of the invalidation procedure, the principle of examination upon request not only requires that the invalidation procedure must be initiated by the petitioner, but also that in the invalidation procedure, the Patent Reexamination Board generally only examines the grounds, scope, and evidence of the request for invalidation made by the petitioner, and is not obliged to undertake comprehensive examination on the validity of the patent. The principle of examination upon request also means that the petitioner has the right to dispose his own request, and is allowed to renounce all or parts of the grounds and evidence of the request for invalidation. For the grounds and evidence for invalidation renounced by the petitioner, usually the Patent Reexamination Board will not investigate or examine them any more without legal basis. The *Guidelines for Patent Examination (2006)* stipulates the principle of conducting examination *ex officio*, and lists the specific circumstances where the Patent Reexamination Board may conduct examination *ex officio*. These circumstances are exceptions to the principle of examination upon request: on the one hand, it gives the Patent Reexamination Board the authority to conduct examination *ex officio* in specific circumstances, and gives the public expectations; on the other hand, it also limits the scope that by the Patent Reexamination Board may conduct examination *ex officio*. There is no legal basis for the allegation of the Patent Reexamination Board that the *Guidelines for Patent Examination (2006)* merely provides 'a list of circumstances of *ex*

---

or the Rule 43(1) of the *Implementing Regulations of the Patent Law* and makes a specific analysis and description of the fact that the amendment goes beyond the scope of the original disclosure, but fails to submit the original application document, the Patent Reexamination Board may introduce the original application document of the patent as the evidence; and (7) the Patent Reexamination Board may determine *ex officio* whether a technical means belongs to common knowledge of the art, and may introduce such common knowledge evidence as those in a technical dictionary, technical manual, or textbook.

[12] Utility model patent No. 200620074801.3. The invalidation decision (No. WX18967) declared the patent right invalid in whole. The first instance judgment (*(2012) Yi Zhong Xing Chu Zi No. 3616*), and the second instance judgment (*(2013) Gao Xing Zhong Zi No. 530*) both overturned the invalidation decision. The Patent Reexamination Board filed for a retrial and was rejected by the SPC.

officio examination, but not a limitation of *ex officio* examination'. In this case, Foton Lovol did not indicate the grounds for invalidation that the patent did not involve an inventive step as compared with the combinations of Reference Document 3, Reference Document 2, and common knowledge, and it explicitly renounced in the oral proceedings the combination of Reference Document 3 and common knowledge as the ground for invalidation for assessing the inventive step of this patent. Where the petitioner did not indicate and clearly renounced Reference Document 3, the Patent Reexamination Board's introduction on its own initiative of the evidence renounced by the petitioner as well as the combination of evidence not mentioned by the petitioner, was not within the scope of *ex officio* examination under the *Guidelines for Patent Examination (2006)*. There is no legal basis for the Patent Reexamination Board to introduce the grounds for invalidation for examination on its own initiative and declare the patent invalid. As for the principle of hearing, it is a procedural requirement second to the principle of examination upon request or the principle of conducting examination *ex officio*, and to give an opportunity to the party concerned to make his observations does not mean that the examination on initiative without legal basis becomes legalized."

3. Scope of *Ex Officio* Examination

In the case *(2012) Zhi Xing Zi No. 50*,[13] the SPC affirmed the legitimacy of the Patent Reexamination Board to introduce common knowledge *ex officio*. In the oral proceedings of this case, the petitioner alleged that claims 1, 2, 5, and 7 did not possess novelty as compared to Reference Document 6, and expressly alleged that "setting 0-2 times (of focal length) is readily conceivable." With regard to the inventive step of claim 1, the petitioner's opinion was "the same as the observations on novelty." When the panel queried the patentee "whether there was any objection to the imaging law of 0-2 times of focal length for a convex lens as common knowledge", Gerui expressed its objection. In the invalidation decision, the Patent Reexamination Board analyzed the law that a change of the object distance between the convex lens and the light source causes a change of the beam convergence effect as common knowledge, and then concluded that claim 1 did not involve an inventive step as compared with a combination of Reference Document 6 and common knowledge. One of the disputes in this case was that whether the Patent Reexamination Board's use of the combination of Reference Document 6 and common knowledge in assessment of inventive step of the patent at issue violated the principle of examination upon request. In response to this issue, the SPC held that "the *Guidelines for Patent Examination (2006)* stipulates in Part IV, Chapter III, Section 4, Subsection 4.1(3) that the Patent Reexamination Board may determine *ex officio* whether a technical means belongs to common knowledge of the art, and may introduce such common knowledge evidence as those in a technical dictionary, a technical manual, or a textbook. Therefore, it is not inappropriate for the Patent Reexamination Board to take the

---

[13] Invention patent No. 200610035815.9. The invalidation decision (No. WX14933) declared the patent right invalid in whole. The first instance judgment (*(2010) Yi Zhong Xing Chu Zi No. 3027*), and the second instance judgment (*(2011) Gao Xing Zhong Zi No. 667*) both upheld the invalidation decision. The patentee filed for a retrial, and was rejected by the SPC.

initiative to introduce common knowledge when assessing the inventive step of this patent; and the panel has explicitly queried Gerui whether there was any objection to the imaging law of 0-2 times of focal length for a convex lens as common knowledge in the oral proceedings. Although Gerui has an objection to such common knowledge, if those skilled in the art, after considering the observations made by Gerui, still believe that the common knowledge is valid, the Patent Reexamination Board may determine on this ground after having given Gerui an opportunity to make its observations… The reason of the request for a retrial made by Gerui for violation of the principle of examination upon request by the Patent Reexamination Board … cannot be established."

In the case *(2014) Zhi Xing Zi No. 82*,[14] the SPC affirmed the legitimacy of changing the closest prior art in the invalidation procedure. The petitioner for invalidation alleged in the request for invalidation that Evidence 1 was the closest prior art, which was to be combined with Evidence 2 or Evidence 2 and Evidence 3 for assessing the inventive step of claim 1; while in the oral proceedings, the petitioner alleged that Evidence 3 was the closet prior art, which was to be combined with Evidence 2 or Evidence 2 and Evidence 1 for assessing the inventive step of claim 1. The invalidation decision declared claim 1 of the patent invalid based on the combination of Evidence 3 and Evidence 1. When the patentee filed for a retrial, he believed that the invalidation decision violated the statutory procedures by accepting such ground and declaring claim 1 on that ground. The Patent Reexamination Board argued that the combinations of Evidence 1, Evidence 2, and Evidence 3 had been included in the request for invalidation and the features had been compared, so accepting said ground did not violate the statutory procedures. The SPC held that the patentee "has fully stated his observations on the changed combinations, and his substantial rights and interests have not been affected." Moreover, the observations showed that the patentee had made a statement on the combination of Evidence 3 with any other reference document. Therefore, the invalidation decision, which only used the combination of Evidence 3 and Evidence 1 in assessment of inventive step of claim 1, did not affect the substantial rights and interests of the patentee and did not violate the principle of examination upon request.

---

[14] Invention patent No. 98800051.2. The invalidation decision (No. WX14219) declared claim 1 invalid. The first instance judgment (*(2010) Yi Zhong Zhi Xing Chu Zi No. 1885*), and the second instance judgment (*(2011) Gao Xing Zhong Zi No. 1505*) both upheld the invalidation decision. The patentee filed for a retrial, and was rejected by the SPC.

12.5 Burden of Proof on Common Knowledge in the Invalidation Procedure

In the case *(2009) Xing Ti Zi No. 4*,[15] regarding the issue whether common knowledge is well-known facts and whether it needs to be proved by evidence, the SPC first explained that "The Article 68, Paragraph 1(1) of the Provisions of the SPC on Several Issues Concerning Evidence in Administrative Litigation issued on July 24, 2002 and the Article 9, Paragraph 1(1) of the Several Provisions of the SPC on Evidence in Civil Litigation issued on December 21, 2001 both provide that the party concerned does not need to provide evidence to prove a well-known fact, unless the party concerned has sufficient counterevidence to overturn it. The 'well-known facts' referred to in the above judicial interpretations are relative in time and region, and generally shall meet the following three conditions. First, well-known facts shall be universal, that is, known to ordinary members of society within a specific time and space. Second, well-known facts shall be distinctive, that is, not only known to ordinary members of society within a specific time and space, but also to a judge who hears the case. Although the judge's knowledge and experience is supposed to be not less than the knowledge and experience of ordinary people in a specific time and space, if the judge handling the case does not know a well-known fact stated by one of the parties concerned, the fact shall of course not be an exempt fact. Third, well-known facts shall be definite, that is, they shall be undoubted facts and cannot be reasonably challenged. If a fact can be reasonably challenged or there is sufficient counterevidence to overturn it, the party alleging the fact still needs to provide evidence."

In this case, the dispute between the parties was whether the technical feature "a burner interface is provided on one side of the preheating chamber" in claim 1 was common knowledge. The second instance judgment held that "Before the utility model 'coal-, oil-, and gas-fired atmospheric hot water boiler' was granted, there were already three-use boilers using coal, oil, and gas as fuel. The technical solution of setting a burner interface on one side of the boiler door is commonly used among three-use boilers, which should be known to those skilled in the art and could be regarded as common technical knowledge in the art. The above-mentioned three-use boiler includes an atmospheric hot water boiler." The Patent Reexamination Board held that the determination of the second instance judgment lacked factual basis.

Regarding this dispute, the SPC held that: "First, it is necessary to accurately define the scope of the technical solution claimed by this patent. In the technical field involved in this case, the boiler, the back-firing boiler, the normal-firing boiler, the double-layer grate back-firing boiler, and the double-layer wave-grate back-firing

---

[15] Invention patent No. 92106401.2. Invalidation decision (No. WX3974) upheld the validity of the patent. The first instance judgment (*(2001) Yi Zhong Zhi Xing Chu Zi No. 309*) upheld the invalidation decision. The second instance judgment (*(2002) Gao Xing Zhong Zi No. 202*) overturned the first instance judgment and the invalidation decision. The Patent Reexamination Board filed for a retrial, and the SPC brought the case up for trial, and ruled to overturn the second instance judgment and upheld the first instance judgment and the invalidation decision.

boiler are generic and specific concepts in sequence, and the technical solutions defined by them are different but have subordinate relationships there between in turn. As mentioned above, claim 1 of the patent claims a double-layer grate back-firing boiler adaptive to the three uses of coal, oil and gas, rather than an ordinary boiler adaptive to the three uses of coal, oil and gas. Claim 4 of this patent further defines said boiler as a double-layer wave-grate back-firing boiler. On this basis, with the combination of the facts found in the previous trial and the trial of this court, as well as the allegations and expressions of the parties concerned in the various procedures of this case, there is no definite evidence to prove or the parties concerned have not unanimously recognized that there is a double-layer grate back-firing boiler adaptive to the three uses of coal, oil and gas that has been existing before the filing date of patent, not to mention that this three-use double-layer grate back-firing boiler already has the technical means of setting a burner interface on one side of the boiler door. Therefore, the determination of the second instance judgment was inaccurate or even incorrect. In addition, the second instance judgment also made a mistake in taking "before the patent right is granted" rather than the filing date of the patent application as the time point for examination and assessment of the patentability. Secondly, it cannot be proved in this case that the disputed technical feature "a burner interface is provided on one side of the preheating chamber" is common knowledge. In this case, the parties concerned had a dispute over whether the disputed feature is common knowledge, but the petitioner for invalidation failed to present evidence to prove it, and the Patent Reexamination Board also did not consider it to be common knowledge. In the absence of sufficient evidence or justified reasons, the judge examining the case shall not come to the conclusion that the disputed feature is common knowledge, nor shall he identify the disputed feature as a well-known fact in the context of procedural law, and exempt the party concerned from the burden of proof. By combining the specific contents of the grounds for invalidation in this case, it may be inadequately determined that the petitioner for invalidation has put forward the allegation of common knowledge in the procedure of the Patent Reexamination Board. However, the petitioner for invalidation failed to produce evidence not only in the procedure of the Patent Reexamination Board, but also in the procedures of first and second instance and even in the retrial procedure of this court, while the explanations were also insufficient and unconvincing. The allegation is not acknowledged by both the Patent Reexamination Board and the patentee, and the objective basis for the determination of the court of second instance cannot be found from the expression of the second instance judgment. Therefore, the determination of the court of second instance lacks factual basis."

12.6 Amendments in the Invalidation Procedure

With regard to the amendment to the claims in the invalidation procedure, the *Guidelines for Patent Examination* further refines the provisions of the *Implementing Regulations*, and makes provisions from the two aspects, i.e., the principles and manners of amendments. In recent years, the industry has raised many different voices on the limitation of amendments to the claims in the invalidation procedure.

In the case *(2011) Zhi Xing Zi No. 17*,[16] it involved the understanding of the provisions of the *Guidelines for Patent Examination* on the principles and manners of amendments to the claims in the invalidation procedure. Said case relates to a pharmaceutical composition consisting of amlodipine and irbesartan. It is recorded in the original text that the ratio of the two components in the composition is in the range of 1:(10-50). During the substantive examination, the patent applicant amended it to 1:(10-30), and was granted the patent right. In the invalidation procedure, the patent applicant further amended this ratio to 1:30. The Patent Reexamination Board held that the amendment went beyond the scope of the initial application document, which did not comply with the provisions of the Article 33 of the *Patent Law*, and such amendment was also not allowed in the invalidation procedure. Finally, on the basis of the text of the original granted patent document, the patent at issue was declared invalid in whole on the ground of not complying with the Article 26(4) of the *Patent Law*. The SPC did not support this conclusion of the Patent Reexamination Board.

In the ruling, the SPC firstly made a determination on whether the amendment was in conformity with the provisions of the Article 33 of the *Patent Law*, holding that "The *Guidelines for Patent Examination*[17] stipulates that the amendment to the claims in the invalidation procedure shall not go beyond the scope of disclosure contained in the initial description and claims... The issues involved in (this case) are all about whether the ratio of 1:30 is recorded in the initial description, and whether such amendment goes beyond the scope of the initial description and claims. According to the ascertained facts, the description of this patent has explicitly disclosed the combination of amlodipine 1 mg and irbesartan 30 mg, as well as the optimal dose ratio of amlodipine 1 mg/kg and irbesartan 30 mg/kg, while in the tablet preparation examples, there is also a combination corresponding to the ratio of 1:30. Therefore, the ratio of 1:30 has been disclosed in the description. For claims defining ratio relations, the specific embodiments in the description can only state specific numerical values, but cannot disclose an abstract ratio relation. Besides, the description of the patent discloses the results from experiments on rats. The description of the patent clearly states that the applicable dosage range is 2-10 mg of amlodipine and 50-300 mg of irbesartan. If it is determined that the optimal formula disclosed is only the specific dosages of 1 mg:30 mg rather than a ratio, then the optimal formula is not included in the above applicable range at all, obviously not in line with the common sense. For those of ordinary skill in the art, 1 mg/kg and 30 mg/kg indicate a ratio

---

[16] Invention patent No. 03150996.7. The invalidation decision (No. WX14275) declared the patent right invalid in whole. The first instance judgment (*(2010) Yi Zhong Zhi Xing Chu Zi No. 1364*) upheld the invalidation decision. The second instance judgment (*(2010) Gao Xing Zhong Zi No. 1022*) overturned the first instance judgment and the invalidation decision. The Patent Reexamination Board filed for a retrial and was rejected by the SPC.

[17] The *Guidelines* herein shall refer to the *Guidelines* applicable at the filing date of the case, i.e. the *Guidelines for Patent Examination (2001)*, in accordance with the opinion of the SPC in other cases. Similarly hereinafter.

of the two components rather than fixed dosages. Therefore, in this case, the ratio of 1:30 shall be taken as having been recorded in the description. The amendment does not go beyond the scope of the initial description and claims. In addition, the issue whether all the technical solutions meeting the ratio relation can achieve the purpose of the present invention falls within the scope whether the claims can be supported by the description, corresponding to the Article 26(4) of the *Patent Law*, and it is not appropriate to determine whether the amendment goes beyond the scope on that ground."

Then, the SPC discussed the manners of amendments to the claims in the invalidation procedure. The SPC clarified that "The *Guidelines for Patent Examination* provides that the specific manners of amendments are generally limited to deletion of a claim, combination of claims, and deletion of a technical solution in the invalidation procedure. The Patent Reexamination Board believed that even if it was determined that the amendment to the claims in this case complied with the above-mentioned principles of amendments, it still could not be accepted because it did not comply with the requirements on the manners of amendments in the *Guidelines for Patent Examination*. In this case, although the technical solutions of 1:(10-30) in the initial claims are not typical parallel technical solutions, in view of the fact that the specific ratio of 1:30 is explicitly disclosed in the initial description and is the recommended optimal dosage ratio thereof, those of ordinary skill in the art would be able to draw the conclusion that this patent contains the technical solution of 1:30 after reading the initial description. Further, this variable is the only one variable in the claims of the patent, and such amendment makes the scope of protection of the patent clearer, and does not cause other adverse effects, such as ambiguity in the scope of protection that may be caused by the amendment in the case of several variables. Therefore, allowing the amendment to be made is fairer. The *Implementing Regulations* and the *Guidelines for Patent Examination* restrict the amendments to the claims in the invalidation procedure for the purposes of, on the one hand, maintaining the stability of the scope of patent protection and ensuring the publicity of the claims, and on the other hand, preventing the patentee from preempting an earlier filing date for a later invention by incorporating into the claims of the patent a technical solution that has not been found by the filing date, at least not reflected in the description, by means of a later amendment. It is obvious that this case does not fall within the circumstances mentioned above. The ratio of 1:30 is the optimal dosage ratio explicitly recommended by the patentee in the initial description, and amending the claim to 1:30 neither goes beyond the scope of disclosure contained in the initial description and claims, nor expands the scope of protection of the initial patent, which is not the case to be avoided by the relevant laws restricting amendments. If, in accordance with the opinion of the Patent Reexamination Board, such amendment is not allowed only because it does not comply with the requirements on the manners of amendments, then the restriction on the amendment in this case is purely a punishment for improper drafting of the patentee's claims, which lacks rationality. Moreover, the *Guidelines for Patent Examination* provides that, on the premise of satisfying the principles of amendments, the manners of amendments are generally limited to the above three types, but other manners of amendments are not absolutely excluded.

For this reason, this court believes that, in this case, the second instance judgment's determination that the amendment complies with the provisions of the *Guidelines for Patent Examination* is not inappropriate, and the Patent Reexamination Board has interpreted the requirements in the *Guidelines for Patent Examination* on amendments in the invalidation procedure too strictly, and its reasons for appeal are not supported."

12.7 Principle of Hearing

The principle of hearing is a basic principle in patent examination, which means that before a reexamination or invalidation decision is made, the Patent Reexamination Board shall give at least one opportunity to the party adversely affected to make amendments or observations on the grounds and evidence on which the examination decision is based.

In the case *(2013) Xing Ti Zi No. 20*,[18] the SPC explained the principle of hearing and its application: "Although the *Patent Law*, the *Implementing Regulations of the Patent Law*, and the *Guidelines for Patent Examination (2006)* do not provide specific rigid provisions on how many Notifications of Reexamination an examiner shall issue during reexamination, the *Guidelines for Patent Examination (2006)* specifies, in Part IV, Chapter 2, Section 4.3, the circumstances in which a Notification of Reexamination shall be issued, and specifies, in Part II, Chapter 8, Section 6.1.1, the circumstances in which an Office Action shall be issued in substantive examination. Whether a Notification of Reexamination shall be issued and how many Notifications of Reexamination shall be issued fall within the ambit of the examiner's discretion, which shall be decided by the examiner in accordance with relevant laws and regulations and in accordance with specific circumstances."

In this case, in the reexamination procedure, the panel issued a Notification of Reexamination indicating that the amendment that the pharmaceutical composition contains "Iris lactea seed coat alcohol extract", "ricin toxin agglutinin", and "Rumex madaio tannin extract" is not in conformity with the Article 33 of the *Patent Law*. In response to the Notification of Reexamination, the petitioner for reexamination submitted the amended text, which overcome the defect of beyond-the-scope indicated in the Notification of Reexamination, but added new contents about the technical effects of the invention in the description. The panel directly made a reexamination decision to uphold the decision of rejection on the basis that the above contents were not in conformity with the Article 33 of the *Patent Law*. The petitioner filed

---

[18] Invention patent application No. 03123169.1. The reexamination Decision (No. FS15603) upheld the decision of rejection on the ground of not complying with the Article 33 of *the Patent Law*. The first instance judgment (*(2009) Yi Zhong Zhi Xing Chu Zi No. 937*) upheld the reexamination decision. The second instance judgment (*(2009) Gao Xing Zhong Zi No. 1395*) upheld the first instance judgment and the invalidation decision. The patent applicant filed for a retrial. The SPC brought the case up for trial, and ruled to overturn the invalidation decision, and the first and second instance judgments.

for a retrial, alleging that the Patent Reexamination Board did not give Lian Yaolin an opportunity to make observations and amend the documents for the new defects, which violated the statutory procedures.

The SPC held that, the *Guidelines for Patent Examination* (2006) provided, in Part IV, Chapter 2, Section 4.3, on the manners of examination that "for a request for reexamination, the panel may conduct examination in written form, by oral proceedings, or in both ways", and the Rule 62 of the *Implementing Regulations of the Patent Law* specified four circumstances in which a Notification of Reexamination shall be issued. According to the fourth circumstance, "as the Patent Reexamination Board rejects Lian Yaolin's request for reexamination on the grounds of the two new amendments beyond the scope, it shall reissue another Notification of Reexamination and give Lian Yaolin another opportunity to make amendments or observations. Accordingly, the Patent Reexamination Board's decision of rejection made without issuing another Notification of Reexamination violates the statutory procedures and should be corrected." In addition, the SPC also pointed out that "Regardless of whether the application concerned has the prospect of granting, if the Patent Reexamination Board rejects the applicant's request for reexamination on different grounds that are newly introduced, the applicant shall be given at least one opportunity to make observations or amendments, otherwise, it goes against the principle of hearing in reexamination and causes unfairness…Therefore, whether the application concerned has the prospect of granting cannot serve as the ground and basis for the Patent Reexamination Board to reject the application concerned."

12.8 Determination of the Authenticity of Evidence

The determination of the authenticity of evidence is the foundation for the examination of patent review cases. The court shall examine the evidence that has been cross-examined in court and evidence that does not need to be cross-examined one by one, and conduct comprehensive, objective and fair analysis and judgment on all the evidence in combination based on logical reasoning and life experience following the professional ethics of judges to clarify the probative relationship between the evidence and the facts of the case and rule out the evidence items without relevance, thereby accurately identifying the facts of the case.

In the case *(2013) Xing Ti Zi No. 18*,[19] the SPC emphasized that the authenticity of evidence shall be examined in accordance with the Article 56 of the Provisions of the SPC on Several Issues Concerning Evidence in Administrative Litigation, i.e. "The court shall take into account the specific circumstance of the case and examine the

---

[19] Design patent No. 200430067996.5. The invalidation decision (No. WX15790) declared the patent right invalid in whole. The first instance judgment *((2011) Yi Zhong Xing Chu Zi No. 831)* upheld the invalidation decision. The second instance judgment *((2011) Gao Xing Zhong Zi No. 1624)* upheld the first instance judgment and the invalidation decision. The patentee filed for a retrial. The SPC brought the case up for trial, and ruled to overturn the invalidation decision, and the first and second instance judgments.

authenticity of evidence from the following aspects: (1) causes in the formation of the evidence; (2) objective environment where the evidence is collected; (3) whether the evidence is an original; whether a photocopy or duplicate matches the original; (4) whether the provider of the evidence has interests in the party concerned; (5) other factors which may affect the authenticity of the evidence." The dispute in this case lied in whether the authenticity of the Zamboanga Star on February 20, 2004 in Evidence 1 was recognized. In response to this issue, the SPC held that "The Zamboanga Star on February 20, 2004 in Evidence 1 has no signs of tampering, alteration, soiling, or damage. The first page of the certification document has the stamp and seal of the Department of Foreign Affairs of the Republic of Philippines, the red silk ribbon fixed by the stamp connects all the materials for notarial certification together, and the subsequent attached certificate of notarial authorization and notarial documents are stamped with the steel seal of the Department of Foreign Affairs of the Republic of Philippines. The formalities of the evidence are complete. However, the *Zamboanga Star* itself is an incomplete newspaper, with only the 3rd, 4th, 5th, and 6th pages, but not the 1st and 2nd pages. The mastheads of the four pages are obviously inconsistent, where the mastheads of the 4th and 5th pages are similar, but the mastheads of the 3rd and 6th pages are significantly different from those of the other two pages. The font of serial numbers in the 6th page is obviously different from that in the other three pages, and the commas in the logo and the publication date of the 3rd, 4th, 5th and 6th pages are significantly different. The front and back of the same page of the paper are different in font, and also different in clarity. The publisher of *Zamboanga Star*, Amelia C. Erasga, has successively issued sworn proof materials to Chen Limin and Deyi, but there are inconsistencies in the statements for the authenticity of *Zamboanga Star* on February 20, 2004 in Evidence 1, and the authenticity of the newspaper cannot be determined." "Chen Limin raised many reasonable doubts about the authenticity of the newspaper, and Deyi did not provide other supplementary evidence to prove the authenticity of the newspaper. By comprehensive judgment based on logical reasoning and life experience, this court cannot confirm the authenticity of the *Zamboanga Star* on February 20, 2004 in Evidence 1, so this court does not recognize its authenticity."

In the case *(2012) Xing Ti Zi No. 19*,[20] the SPC pointed out: "For a document cited for judging the novelty or inventive step of an invention or utility model, that is, for a publication serving as a reference document, the petitioner making the request for invalidation must prove its time of release or publication. Only publications whose publication date is before the filing date of the patent at issue can be used as a reference document. In general, the date of printing of a publication is considered the date of publication, unless there is other evidence of the date of publication. In this case, Nuojin did not submit the original copy of the Compilation. In order to prove

---

[20] Invention patent No. 200410050135.5. The invalidation decision (No. WX14008) declared the patent right invalid in whole. The first instance judgment (*(2010) Yi Zhong Xing Chu Zi No. 767*) upheld the invalidation decision. The second instance judgment (*(2011) Gao Xing Zhong Zi No. 267*) upheld the first instance judgment and the invalidation decision. The patentee filed for a retrial. The SPC brought the case up for trial, and ruled to overturn the invalidation decision, and the first and second instance judgments.

12.8 Determination of the Authenticity of Evidence

the authenticity of the Compilation and the time of its publication, Nuojin submitted notarial certificates No. 40365 and No. 38246. Judged from the information on the copyright page of the Compilation attached to the notarial certificate No. 40365, the ISBN displayed on it is 957-414-366-1, but the publication corresponding to this ISBN has been proved to be the book International Cooperation Finance submitted by Yulin, which is not published by Dafu Bookstore. At the same time, with the denial statement made by the lawyer Yan Yuqin entrusted by Dafu Bookstore to the publisher's information displayed on the copyright page of the Compilation, it can be determined that the ISBN and publisher information displayed on the copyright page of the Compilation are not authentic. Under such circumstance, it cannot be determined whether the information, including the edition, editor, etc., displayed on the copyright page of the Compilation is authentic, that is, the time of publication cannot be determined from the edition on the copyright page." In addition, the SPC also examined the relevant notarial documents. "The notarial certificate No. 38246 states that the staff of Juzhou Library operated the 'LibMis Library Management Integrated System' to consult the management information of the Compilation in front of the notary staff, and the management system showed that the warehousing time of the Compilation was January 8, 2004, which was earlier than the filing date of the patent at issue. This court believes that the notarial certificate can prove the information displayed in the computer management system of Juzhou Library that the notary staff saw on the day of notarization, but it cannot prove the formation process of the information loaded in the management system and whether the contents of the information are authentic. First of all, electronic materials, subject to their own particularity, are easy to be modified and forged with no traces, so there are strict conditions on the use of electronic materials as evidence. According to the Article 64 of the Provisions of the SPC on Several Issues Concerning Evidence in Administrative Litigation, an electronic material, only if its production and authenticity have been confirmed by the opposite party or have been proved by other effective means such as notarization, can obtain the probative force of the original. In this case, Yulin did not recognize the authenticity of the warehousing time of the Compilation notarized by the notarial certificate No. 38246, and Nuojin did not corroborate the authenticity of the information in other effective ways. The authenticity of the information cannot be determined. Secondly, in the 'Borrowing History' of the Compilation displayed in the notarial certificate No. 38246, the borrowing information notarized by the notarial certificate No. 40365 was not recorded, which is contradictory as the borrowing information should have been recorded in the electronic borrowing system. Thirdly, the barcode and call number of the Compilation recorded in the notarial certificate No. 38246 cannot be found in the Compilation notarized by the notarial certificate No. 40365, which is also contradictory. Lastly, Yulin submitted in the proceedings a record made by the Intermediate People's Court of Nanning City, Guangxi Zhuang Autonomous Region earlier than the notarial certificate No. 38246, which proved that the Compilation was not warehoused in the Juzhou Library for management, and the use of the computer borrowing system did not exist, which is obviously contrary to the content recorded in the notarial certificate No. 38246. Thus, the notarial certificate No. 38246 cannot prove that the warehousing time of the Compilation in the Juzhou Library is authentic, that is, the time of publication of the Compilation cannot be determined accordingly."

In the case *(2015) Zhi Xing Zi No. 61*,[21] the determination of the authenticity and probative force of web page evidence fixed in the form of a notarial certificate was involved. The SPC clarified that, "In examination of the authenticity and probative force of the publishing time of a web page of an Internet website fixed in the form of a notarial certificate, all the related factors, such as the process of making the corresponding notarial certificate, the process of forming the web page and its publishing time, and the qualifications and credit status, the operation and management status of, and the technical means used by the website managing the web page, shall be taken into consideration comprehensively, and combined with other evidence of the case so as to make a clear judgment on the authenticity and probative force of the notarial certificate and the publishing of the attached web page. On the basis of examination of evidence, if it is believed that the existing evidence can prove a high probability of the existence of a fact to be proved, and the other party's challenge to the corresponding evidence or counter-evidence provided by the other party is insufficient to weaken the probative force of the evidence to reach the standard of high probability of proof, it shall be deemed that the fact to be proved exists." The notarial certificate evidence involved in this case showed that when a non-registered common user visited the "Worldwide Factories" website, it could be seen that the publishing time of a hotfix mold picture displayed on page 7 was August 16, 2010, and the publishing time of a hotfix mold picture displayed on page 10 was March 8, 2010, both earlier than the filling date of the application at issue (September 7, 2010). The SPC held that "The 'Worldwide Factories' website is a large-scale and well-known e-commerce platform with good credit and efficient management. Under this condition, unless there is a case of manual deletion, the publishing time of a picture displayed on the web page of the website is generally consistent with its real time of publication. Dong Jianfei submitted a notarial certificate No. 15901 as counter-evidence, in order to prove that the publisher of the "Worldwide Factories" website was allowed to replace a picture with the publishing time unchanged on the modified web page. However, the notarial certificate No. 15901 shows that if a registered user of the 'Worldwide Factories' website had replaced a picture, the status of the picture indicates 'Repost,' but in Annex 1, i.e., the notarial certificate No. 2461, the pictures on page 7 and page 10 show no sign of repost. At the same time, at the time when the notarized act shown in the notarial certificate No. 15901 occurred, the "Worldwide Factories" website had been revised, and could hardly reflect the actual condition of the "Worldwide Factories" website when the notarized act shown in the notarial certificate No. 2461 occurred in Annex 1. Therefore, the notarial certificate No. 15901 submitted by Dong Jianfei did not substantially weaken the probative force of Annex 1. Where the authenticity and probative force of the

---

[21] Design patent No. 201030506103.8. The invalidation decision (No. WX20444) upheld the validity of the patent. The first instance judgment (*(2013) Yi Zhong Xing Chu Zi No. 2307*) overturned the invalidation decision. The second instance judgment (*(2014) Gao Xing Zhong Zi No. 1408*) upheld the first instance judgment. The patentee filed for a retrial, and was rejected by the SPC.

notarial certificate of Annex 1 and the publishing time of the attached web page could be confirmed, and the notarial certificate No. 15901 submitted by Dong Jianfei did not substantially weaken the probative force of Annex 1, the determination of the courts of first and second instance that the pictures of the Internet website fixed in the form of the notarial certificate of Annex 1 had been published before the filing date of the application at issue, was not inappropriate."

12.9 Determination of the Openness of Evidence

Where the reference document for determining the novelty or inventive step of an invention is a publication, the party concerned with the burden of proof shall prove that it is a publication. Publications come in many forms, such as books, journals, etc.

The three cases *(2012) Zhi Xing Zi No. 54, 55 and 56*[22] all have a dispute on whether the "Compilation of National Standards for Chinese Patent Medicines - Part of National Standards Raising from Local Standards of Chinese Patent Medicines - Branches of Meridian Limbs and Brains" (hereinafter referred to as "the Compilation") submitted by Puzheng is a publication. Regarding the issue whether the Compilation had been made public, the SPC held in its judgment that "Publications in the context of the *Patent Law* mean the independently existing disseminating carriers of technical or designing contents, which shall indicate or have other evidence to prove the date of release or publication. According to the 'Foreword' and other relevant contents of the Compilation, the purpose of the Compilation is to strengthen the management of national standards for Chinese patent medicines, and the purpose of formulating the standards for Chinese patent medicines is to unify the production process and quality standards of medicines nationwide, so as to ensure the quality and safety of Chinese patent medicines in the production and manufacturing process. In order to achieve the above purposes, the standards must be promoted in the related field, and the producers in the field must be guided to follow the standards. For this

---

[22] The case *(2012) Zhi Xing Zi No. 54* involved the invention patent No. 200510096351.8. The invalidation decision (No. WX16187) declared the patent right invalid in whole. The first instance judgment (*(2011) Yi Zhong Xing Chu Zi No. 2150*) upheld the invalidation decision. The second instance judgment (*(2011) Gao Xing Zhong Zi No. 1692*) upheld the first instance judgment and the invalidation decision. The patentee filed for a retrial, and was rejected by the SPC. The case *(2012) Zhi Xing Zi No. 55* involved the invention patent No. 200510096361.1. The invalidation decision (No. WX15312) declared the patent right invalid in whole. The first instance judgment (*(2011) Yi Zhong Xing Chu Zi No. 576*) upheld the invalidation decision. The second instance judgment (*(2011) Gao Xing Zhong Zi No. 1691*) upheld the first instance judgment and the invalidation decision. The patentee filed for a retrial, and was rejected by the SPC. The case *(2012) Zhi Xing Zi No. 56* involved the invention patent No. 200510096361.1. The invalidation decision (No. WX15314) declared the patent right invalid in whole. The first instance judgment (*(2011) Yi Zhong Xing Chu Zi No. 573*) upheld the invalidation decision. The second instance judgment (*(2011) Gao Xing Zhong Zi No. 1695*) upheld the first instance judgment and the invalidation decision. The patentee filed for a retrial, and was rejected by the SPC.

reason, the standards must be disclosed at least among the producers in the field, and it must be available to anyone who wants to obtain it. The fact that the Compilation had been published was further supported by the fact that Puzheng obtained the evidence from the public inquiry agency of the State Intellectual Property Office, i.e., the standards for Chinese patent medicine contained in the Compilation were available to anyone who wants to obtain them. Qianhe submitted the Notification of Information Disclosure issued by the China Food and Drug Administration on June 5, 2012 to prove that the Compilation had not been publicly issued, and was in a state of non-disclosure. However, the notification clearly indicated that the public was allowed to access information in the Compilation that could be disclosed according to law by means of applying for the disclosure of government information, which also proved that the standards for Chinese patent medicine contained in the Compilation were available to anyone who wants to obtain them." Therefore, Qianhe's belief that the Compilation was not a publication, and it was distributed within a limited scope and contained tentative standards, and thus was presumably not closed, as the ground for the request for reexamination, was not tenable.

In the case *(2015) Zhi Xing Zi No. 27*,[23] the dispute lied in the determination of openness of the notarized installation manual, brochure, etc., of the model VSS7 lift from Rotary, U.S. In the invalidation procedure, in order to prove the existence of the prior design, the petitioner for invalidation submitted Evidence 1: a notarized installation manual of the Rotary VSS7 lift and its Chinese translation; Evidence 2: a brochure of the Rotary VSS7 lift downloaded from the website of Rotary and its Chinese translation; Evidence 3: four advertisements of the Rotary VSS7 lift and their Chinese translations, which were placed in the magazine *Parking Today*. The invalidation decision held that Evidence 1 was a product installation manual made by the enterprise and could be very arbitrary, and it was insufficient to prove that the publication date was October 2003 only based on the text in the lower left corner of the first page; Evidence 2 was a content from an enterprise website with interest to the petitioner, and it was insufficient to prove that the publishing date was in 2005 only based on the characters "?2005" on the last page of Evidence 2; Evidence 3 was published earlier than the filing date of the patent at issue, so it was an foreign publication before the filing date, and could be taken as evidence to assess whether the patent at issue is in conformity with the Article 23 of the *Patent Law*. However, in general, prints or publications similar to the product installation manual of Evidence 1 are not known to the public as a separate publication but to the consumers or public along with the products being sold. The publication of the advertisements does not prove the actual sale of the product. Therefore, the petitioner for invalidation's allegation based on Evidence 3 that the products of Evidence 1 and Evidence 2 had been sold in China before May 2005 was not tenable. As it could not draw the conclusion that the patent did not comply with Article 23 of the *Patent Law* based on

---

[23] Design patent No. 200730147567.2. The invalidation decision (No. WX20983) upheld the validity of the patent. The first instance judgment (*(2013) Yi Zhong Xing Chu Zi No. 3557*) upheld the invalidation decision. The second instance judgment (*(2014) Gao Xing Zhong Zi No. 1221*) upheld the first instance judgment and the invalidation decision. The invalidation petitioner filed for a retrial, and was rejected by the SPC.

Evidence 3 alone, the validity of the patent right was upheld. In the ruling, the SPC held that "The product installation manual is different from common publications, and whether it has been published by market circulation with the product cannot be determined only based on this evidence. However, with other existing evidence of the case, in particular, Evidence 3, which is a published magazine carrying the advertisements of the Rotary VSS7 lift, it is proved that at least in May 2005, VSS7 lift related products had emerged. Therefore, from this evidence, it can be concluded that before May 2005, the product installation manual as Evidence 1 was deemed to have been published. In the invalidation decision and the first and second instance judgments, the determination that the product manual was not put into circulation by itself, but with the product, and the logo 'October2003' of Evidence 1 alone was insufficient to prove that it was published in October 2003, is inappropriate and shall be corrected. As the invalidation decision and the first and second instance judgments are correct in determining whether Evidence 3 constitutes a prior design of the patent at issue, the request for a retrial is rejected."

12.10 New Evidence Submitted During Administrative Litigation

Patent administrative litigation is an administrative litigation in which the Patent Reexamination Board is the defendant. In principle, the people's court shall examine the legitimacy of reexamination and invalidation decisions made by the Patent Reexamination Board on the basis of the grounds and evidence on which the reexamination or invalidation decisions are based.

New evidence submitted by the party concerned in the administrative litigation, if used to prove the grounds not involved in the administrative review procedure or to prove new facts of the case, shall not be taken into account by the people's court. In the case *(2013) Zhi Xing Zi No. 68*,[24] the SPC made it clear that "The people's court hears administrative cases for post-grant review of patents and examines whether the accused decision is legal. In the invalidation administrative procedure, the Microchip did not allege that the relevant distinct technical feature falls into the common knowledge, but it submitted new evidence to prove that the distinct technical feature belonged to common knowledge, which was beyond the scope of the grounds for invalidation it proposed and beyond the scope of examination of the invalidation decision No. 13812. Microchip may, based on relevant evidence, file another request for invalidation."

---

[24] Utility model patent No. 200620046589.X. The invalidation decision (No. WX13812) upheld the validity of claims 1, 2, and 5, and declared claims 3–4 invalid. The first instance judgment (*(2010) Yi Zhong Xing Chu Zi No. 1936*), and the second instance judgment (*(2011) Gao Xing Zhong Zi No. 839*) both upheld the invalidation decision. The petitioner for invalidation filed for a retrial, and was rejected by the SPC.

However, if the new evidence submitted in the administrative litigation is used to explain the level of knowledge and cognitive ability that those skilled in the art should have before the filing date or the priority date and falls into common knowledge evidence, it shall be accepted and adopted directly, while for non-common knowledge evidence, it may be adopted as a reference after cross-examination. The SPC has expressed this view in several judgments. For example, in the case *(2011) Zhi Xing Zi No. 54*,[25] the petitioner for retrial Zeng Guansheng submitted in the request for retrial the *Decree of the State Council of the People's Republic of China Concerning the Use of Uniform Legal Metrology In the Country*, the *Circular of the State Council Concerning the Approval and Transmission of the National Bureau of Standards and Metrology and Other Units on the Reform of the Measures of Chinese Medicine Prescription Drugs*, as well as textbooks and technical manuals such as *Chinese Pharmacology, Mineral Materia Medica, Pharmacy of Chinese Materia Medica*, etc. The SPC held that "said evidence is used for further explanation of the conversion relationship between 'liang' and 'g' which are commonly used in the field of traditional Chinese medicine formulations on the date of filing of the patent at issue, but not for proof of new facts of the case. On the basis of the evidence, it is possible to further reasonably determine the level of knowledge that those skilled in the art should have on the date of filing of the patent at issue, which is conducive to correct and objective examination and judgment of relevant legal issues. Therefore, this court does not support the allegation of the Patent Reexamination Board that the evidence should be inadmissible as it has not been submitted in the administrative procedure." For another example, in the case *(2014) Zhi Xing Zi No. 17*,[26] regarding the Evidence 1-7 submitted by Li Xiaodong during the retrial, the SPC held that although "Evidence 1-7 was not the basis on which the Patent Reexamination Board made the decision No. 14794. However, with its contents, it is possible to more objectively and accurately determine the level of knowledge and cognitive ability that those skilled in the art should have before the date of filing of the patent at issue, and to accurately define the meaning of relevant technical terms involved in this case. Therefore, this court accepts Evidence 1-7." As for the three articles published in the academic journals submitted in the procedure of first instance, the SPC held that "said documents are not evidence of common knowledge, and shall not be directly used to prove the level of knowledge and cognitive ability that those skilled in the art should have before the date of filing of the patent at issue, but they provide reference to enable accurate determination of the technical facts involved in

---

[25] Invention patent application No. 00113917.7. The reexamination decision (No. FS20574) upheld the decision of rejection in accordance to the Article 33 of *the Patent Law*. The first instance judgment (*(2010) Yi Zhong Xing Chu Zi No. 1329*), and the second instance judgment (*(2010) Gao Xing Zhong Zi No. 1117*) both upheld the invalidation decision. The petitioner for reexamination filed for a retrial, and the SPC ruled that the court of second instance brought the case up for retrial.

[26] Invention patent No. 03123304.X. The invalidation decision (No. WX14794) upheld the validity of the patent. The first instance judgment (*(2010) Yi Zhong Zhi Xing Chu Zi No. 3093*), and the second instance judgment (*(2011) Gao Xing Zhong Zi No. 1106*) both upheld the invalidation decision. The invalidation petitioner filed for a retrial. The SPC brought the case up for trial, and vacated the invalidation decision, and the first and second instance judgments.

this patent, thus being related to the case. After cross-examination and verification, the court of first instance identified the aforementioned documents as reference for attestation of relevant technical facts of this case, but it adopted above documents as the basis of verdict without cross-examination, this was obviously inappropriate and should be corrected."

12.11 Options for the Court to Overturn the Decision of the Patent Reexamination Board

According to the Article 54(2) of the *Administrative Procedure Law*, where the people's court makes a judgment to overturn or partially overturn a specific administrative act being sued, the respondent may be ordered to perform another administrative act, but whether the respondent is actually ordered to perform another administrative act depends on circumstances. In the case *(2012) Xing Ti Zi No. 7*,[27] the SPC pointed out that "When the people's court examines an invalidation decision made by the Patent Reexamination Board, where the Patent Reexamination Board holds the patent right valid, but the people's court holds invalid, the people's court shall make a judgment to overturn the decision being sued, and also order the Patent Reexamination Board to make another decision. Where the Patent Reexamination Board holds the patent right invalid, the people's court shall make a judgment to overturn the decision being sued, and decide whether to order the Patent Reexamination Board to make another decision depending on the following two circumstances: where the Patent Reexamination Board has given comments on all the grounds and evidence proposed by the petitioner for invalidation, and the people's court holds the patent right valid, the judgment shall not order the Patent Reexamination Board to make another decision; where the Patent Reexamination Board has not given comments on the grounds and evidence proposed by the petitioner for invalidation, and the invalidation decision made based on a part of the grounds and corresponding evidence is untenable, the people's court shall rule to order the Patent Reexamination Board to make another decision based on other grounds and evidence proposed by the petitioner for invalidation."

In this case, the petitioner for invalidation, Jingkai, proposed the following grounds for invalidating the patent at issue: Claims 1, 2, and 3 of the patent concerned did not comply with the provisions of the Article 22(2) and 22(3), and the Article 26(3) and 26(4) of the *Patent Law*, and the Rule 20(1) of the *Implementing Regulations of the*

---

[27] Utility model patent No. 200520014575.5. The invalidation decision (No. WX13216) declared the patent right invalid in whole. The first instance judgment (*(2009) Yi Zhong Zhi Xing Chu Zi No. 1326*), and the second instance judgment (*(2010) Gao Xing Zhong Zi No. 634*) both upheld the invalidation decision. The patentee filed for a retrial. The SPC brought the case up for trial, and vacated the invalidation decision, and the first and second instance judgments.

Patent Law. Claim 3 did not comply with the Rule 21(3) of the *Implementing Regulations of the Patent Law*. Multiple reference documents were submitted, including Annex 5–1. The Patent Reexamination Board made the decision No. 13216, holding that according to Annex 5–1, all the claims of the patent at issue did not involve any inventive step, and accordingly the patent right was declared invalid in whole. In the invalidation decision, the Patent Reexamination Board "on account of the fact that claims 1-3 of this patent are already not in conformity with the provisions of the Article 22(3) of the *Patent Law*, (therefore) shall make no more comments on other grounds for invalidation submitted by the petitioner." Regarding this, the SPC held that "As this court has ruled to vacate the decision No. 13216 made by the Patent Reexamination Board, the Patent Reexamination Board should make another decision on other invalidation grounds and evidence proposed by Jingkai."

Chapter 13
Issues Related to Designs

Article 23 of the *Patent Law* provides that any design for which patent right may be granted, first, shall not be a prior design, nor has any entity or individual filed before the date of filing with the patent office an application relating to the identical design and disclosed in patent documents announced after the date of filing; second, shall significantly differ from a prior design or the combination of prior design features; third, must not be in conflict with the legitimate right obtained before the date of filing by any other person.

13.1 A Normal Consumer

Just as the examination of patents for inventions and utility models requires the virtual subject of "a person skilled in the art", the *Guidelines for Patent Examination* introduces the concept of "a normal consumer" in order to make the judgment of the patentability of designs more objective.

In the case *(2011) Xing Ti Zi No. 1*,[1] the SPC clarified that "a normal consumer is an abstract judgment subject with specific knowledge and cognitive capability to make judgment conclusions more objective and accurate. In terms of knowledge, a normal consumer has a common-sense understanding of the products that are identical to or similar to the design patent product, a good knowledge of the designs of relevant products before the filing date, and familiarity with the usual designs on relevant products. In terms of cognitive capability, a normal consumer only has average

---

[1] Design patent No. 200630067850.X. The invalidation decision (No. WX13585) declared that all patent rights were invalid. The first instance judgment *((2009) Yi Zhong Xing Chu Zi No. 1797)* vacated the invalidation decision. The second instance judgment *((2010) Gao Xing Zhong Zi No. 124)* affirmed the first instance judgment. The invalidation decision petitioner filed for a retrial. The SPC ruled to review the case, and reversed the first and second instance judgments and upheld the invalidation decision.

attention and discernment for the changes in design elements such as shape, color, pattern, etc. A normal consumer notices the overall visual effect of the design instead of partial subtle differences between the design patent and comparative designs.

The so-called overall observation and comprehensive judgment refers to a normal consumer determining whether there are distinctive differences between a design patent and a comparative design in terms of visual effects from the overall design rather than changes in part of the design. When making a judgment, a normal consumer notices both the similarities and differences between the visible part of the design patent and the comparative design and comprehensively considers the impact of the similarities and differences on the overall visual effect."

In the case *(2010) Xing Ti Zi No. 3*,[2] the SPC further emphasized, "a basic method of determining whether designs are identical or similar provided in the *Guidelines for Patent Examination* is to make a comprehensive judgment of whether the differences between the design concerned and the prior design have a significant impact on the visual effect of the product through an overall observation of the design concerned and the prior design and based on the knowledge and cognitive capability of a normal consumer of the product incorporating the design concerned.

Under the provisions of the *Guidelines for Patent Examination*, a normal consumer shall have the following characteristics: common knowledge of the designs in products identical with or similar to the product incorporating the design concerned; certain capability of distinguishing the differences in shape, pattern, and color between design patent products, but without notice to the minor differences in shape, pattern or color of products. 'Common knowledge' refers to knowing the designs of relevant products without the ability to design, but the knowledge is not limited to a basic and simple understanding. 'Overall' includes all the design features of the visible part of the product, rather than a specific part thereof. 'Comprehensive' means the synthesis of all the factors that can affect the overall visual effect of the product design."

---

[2] Design patent No. 01319523.9. The invalidation decision (No. WX8105) declared that all patent rights were invalid. The first instance judgment (*(2006) Yi Zhong Xing Chu Zi No. 779*) and the second instance judgment (*(2007) Gao Xing Zhong Zi No. 274*) both upheld the invalidation decision. The patentee filed for a retrial. The SPC ruled to review the case and reversed the first and second instance judgments and the invalidation decision.

13.1 A Normal Consumer

In the cases *(2010) Xing Ti Zi No. 5 and (2010) Xing Ti Zi No. 6*,[3] the SPC's understanding of "a normal consumer" was somewhat different from the previous two cases. In the judgments of the two cases, the SPC held that "the above-mentioned provisions in the *Guidelines for Patent Examination (2006)* on the subject of a judgment of the identical or similar design patents were reasonable and feasible, and the People's Courts might refer to and apply them. As the subject of judging identical or similar designs, a normal consumer is an abstract concept with the above-mentioned knowledge and cognitive capability, rather than a specific person engaged in a specific job. However, it has little practical significance for the judgment of identical or similar designs if a normal consumer is only recognized as an abstract person. What matters most is to specifically define the knowledge and cognitive capability of a normal consumer. For a specific design product, it necessarily requires that purchasers and users of products of identical or similar categories as the design product be considered to make a specific determination of the knowledge and cognitive capability of a normal consumer of this design product.

As for the design of a motorcycle wheel product, since motorcycle wheels are the main external visible parts of a motorcycle, the determination of the knowledge and cognitive capability of a normal consumer shall consider not only the knowledge and cognitive capability of assemblers and maintenance providers of motorcycles but also that of ordinary purchasers and users."

On this basis, the SPC rejected the Patent Reexamination Board's argument against the second instance judgment. Specifically, the Patent Reexamination Board argued that "although the second instance judgment reversed the specific definition of a normal consumer in the first instance judgment, yet "a normal consumer" was defined as specific categories of people, i.e., 'maintenance providers, assemblers and ordinary purchasers and users in the second instance judgment. It is erroneous to define normal consumers as corresponding to specific groups of people in the examination of different types of cases."

The SPC was not convinced of this argument on the grounds that: "first, the second instance judgment while correcting the error of a much too narrow definition of a normal consumer in the first instance judgment, made it clear that the judgment subject should be a normal consumer who had common knowledge of motorcycle wheel products. It was only when summarizing the scope of normal consumers that the second instance judgment mentioned that normal consumers included not only

---

[3] The case *(2010) Xing Ti Zi No. 5* related to a design patent No. 200630110998.7. The invalidation decision (No. WX13657) declared that all patent rights were invalid. The first instance judgment (*(2009) Yi Zhong Xing Chu Zi No. 2719*) vacated the invalidation decision. The second instance judgment (*(2010) Gao Xing Zhong Zi No. 467*) affirmed the first instance judgment. The Patent Reexamination Board filed for a retrial. The SPC ruled to review the case, reversed the first and second instance judgments and upheld the invalidation decision. The case *(2010) Xing Ti Zi No. 6* related to a design patent No. 200730112575.3. The invalidation decision (No. WX13658) declared that all patent rights were invalid. The first instance judgment (*(2009) Yi Zhong Xing Chu Zi No. 2556*) vacated the invalidation decision. The second instance judgment (*(2010) Gao Xing Zhong Zi No. 448*) affirmed the first instance judgment. The Patent Reexamination Board filed for a retrial. The SPC ruled to review the case, reversed the first and second instance judgments and upheld the invalidation decision.

assemblers and maintenance providers but also ordinary purchasers and users. Moreover, the second instance judgment showed that normal consumers of the patented product at issue not only included assemblers and maintenance providers but also ordinary purchasers and users, which is actually a summary and approval of the basis for the appeal by the Patent Reexamination Board.

Second, although the *Guidelines for Patent Examination (2006)* provides that a normal consumer is an abstract person, in the judgment of whether a specific design is identical or similar, the abstract concept of a normal consumer shall be personified as groups of people related to the product incorporating the design to be determined, rather than an abstract concept as claimed by the Patent Reexamination Board in the retrial. Therefore, the second instance judgment is not obviously improper regarding the judgment subject of determining identical or similar designs of the patent at issue."

13.2 Determination of Identical or Similar Categories

Under the provisions of Part IV, Chapter 5 of the *Guidelines for Patent Examination (2006)*, similar designs may exist only among products of identical or similar categories. In the case *(2013) Zhi Xing Zi No. 56*,[4] the SPC clarified that "when determining the category of a product, reference may be made to the name of the product, the *International Classification for Industrial Designs*, and the classification of product shelves, but the use of the product shall be taken as the basis."

The design product in this case relates to a push blade. The SPC held that "first, from the use and name of the product, the patent at issue and the prior design are of the same category of products. The "use" refers to the aspect or scope of application. The patent at issue is a push blade and the prior design is a multi-function double-blade art knife, both of which are cutting tools functioning to carve. This granted patent document does not define the specific application scope of this patent. Second, according to the *International Classification for Industrial Designs*, the patent at issue and the prior design are of the same category of products. The granted patent document specifies that the classification number of the patent at issue is 08-03. Under the *International Classification for Industrial Designs* (8th Edition) when the patent was granted, the products of class 08-03 refer to Cutting Tools and Implements. The notes to this product classification are: '(a) including tools and instruments (for sawing). (b) not including table knives (Cl. 07-03), cutting tools and implements for kitchen use (Cl. 31), or knives used in surgery (Cl. 24-02). A product category in this classification that is also related to cutting tools is 'razors' of Class 28-03 'Toilet Articles and Beauty Parlor Equipment'. Apart from the above product categories

---

[4] Design patent No. 200630130035.3. The invalidation decision (No. WX18221) declared that all patent rights were invalid. The first instance judgment (*(2012) Yi Zhong Xing Chu Zi No. 2014*) and the second instance judgment (*(2013) Gao Xing Zhong Zi No. 99*) both upheld the invalidation decision. The patentee filed for a retrial and was rejected by the SPC.

related to cutting tools, there are no other product categories for 'cutting tools' in this classification. The prior design 'multi-function double-blade art knife' is a cutting tool and shall also be classified into category 08-03, which means the prior design and the patent at issue clearly are of the same category of products."

13.3 Comparison Basis for Identical or Similar Categories

Paragraph 2, Article 59 of the *Patent Law* provides that the extent of protection of the patent right for design shall be determined by the design of the product as shown in the drawings or photographs. When making a judgment of (whether a design is) identical or similar (or identical and substantially identical), only the appearance of the product shall be used as the judgment object; for a combination product with only one assembly option, the overall design in the assembled state shall be the comparison object; for a combination product with more than one assembly options, the appearance of all individual components shall be compared.

The case *(2013) Zhi Xing Zi No. 56*[5] relates to an art blade. The patentee Zhang Zhiguo stated during the oral hearing of the invalidation procedure that the assembly figure of the patent at issue was the pattern of the patented product for sale, the front view was the pattern of the patented product in use and the assembly pattern figure was the main pattern. Based on this statement, the SPC held that "the patented product is objectively a strip blade set composed of multiple isosceles trapezoidal blades when it is for sale, and after purchasing, a normal consumer breaks off the isosceles trapezoidal blade for use; the front view of the patent at issue is actually the unit design in the assembly pattern, which is helpful to understand the assembly pattern. Both the assembly pattern figure and the front view shall be considered in the determination of the protection scope of the design patent at issue… In this case, Zhang Zhiguo's Observations submitted on November 3, 2011, in the invalidation procedure stated that the patent at issue was a combination product with only one assembly option, and the overall design in the assembled state should be the object to make the judgment of being identical or similar… Zhang Zhiguo also claimed in the retrial petition that the assembly pattern figure of the patent at issue was completely different from the combination products prescribed by the *Patent Law*, and should not be used as a comparison object. Under the provisions of combination products under Part IV, Chapter 5, Section 5.4.1 of the *Guidelines for Patent Examination (2006)*, each component of the combination product in the *Patent Law* exists independently, and one component only cannot achieve the purpose of use as the complete combination product. Therefore, the patented product at issue is not a combination product in the sense of the *Patent Law*."

---

[5] Design patent No. 200630130035.3. The invalidation decision (No. WX18221) declared that all patent rights were invalid. The first instance judgment (*(2012) Yi Zhong Xing Chu Zi No. 2014*) and the second instance judgment (*(2013) Gao Xing Zhong Zi No. 99*) both upheld the invalidation decision. The patentee filed for a retrial and was rejected by the SPC.

13.4 Design Space

Design space is a concept introduced in the amendment of the *Guidelines for Patent Examination* in 2010, which is used for the determination of identical or similar designs. In the cases *(2010) Xing Ti Zi No. 5* and *(2010) Xing Ti Zi No. 6*,[6] the SPC discussed the concept of design space and its influence on the judgment of identical or similar designs. The cases related to the design of a motorcycle wheel. Regarding whether the patent at issue was identical with or similar to the prior design, the first and second instance judgments both concluded that the difference between the patent at issue and the prior design was sufficient to have a significant impact on the overall visual effect on the premise that the design space of a motorcycle wheel was limited.

The SPC explained in its judgment: "Design space refers to the degree of freedom a designer has when creating the design of a specific product. The degree of freedom of the designer's design in a specific product field is usually subject to the restriction and influence of prior designs, technologies, laws, and concepts. The size of the design space of a specific product is closely related to the knowledge and cognitive capability of a normal consumer of the design product regarding the designs of identical or similar products. For a product field with an extremely large design space, due to the high degree of creative freedom of the designer, the designs in this product field are bound to have various forms, styles, and colors, and a normal consumer of the design product is even less likely to notice relatively minor design differences. On the contrary, in the field where the design space is greatly restricted, due to the low degree of freedom of creation, there must be many identical or similar designs in the field of the product, and a normal consumer of the design product usually notices minor differences among different designs. It can be seen that design space is of great significance to determine the knowledge and cognitive capability of a normal consumer of the relevant design products. In the judgment of whether the design patent is identical with or similar to a prior design, design space, or a designer's creative freedom may be considered in order to accurately determine the knowledge and cognitive capability of a normal consumer."

In addition, "When design space is considered as a factor, it shall be noticed that the size of the design space is a relative concept. There is a spectrum between the two extreme cases i.e., the design space is extremely large in the field of the product

---

[6] The case *(2010) Xing Ti Zi No. 5* related to a design patent No. 200630110998.7. The invalidation decision (No. WX13657) declared that all patent rights were invalid. The first instance judgment (*(2009) Yi Zhong Xing Chu Zi No. 2719*) vacated the invalidation decision. The second instance judgment (*(2010) Gao Xing Zhong Zi No. 467*) affirmed the first instance judgment. The Patent Reexamination Board filed for a retrial. The SPC ruled to review the case, reversed the first and second instance judgments and upheld the invalidation decision. The case *(2010) Xing Ti Zi No. 6* related to a design patent No. 200730112575.3. The invalidation decision (No. WX13658) declared that all patent rights were invalid. The first instance judgment (*(2009) Yi Zhong Xing Chu Zi No. 2556*) vacated the invalidation decision. The second instance judgment (*(2010) Gao Xing Zhong Zi No. 448*) affirmed the first instance judgment. The Patent Reexamination Board filed for a retrial. The SPC ruled to review the case, reversed the first and second instance judgments and upheld the invalidation decision.

versus the design space is extremely limited in the field of the product. Moreover, the size of the design space of the same product may also vary from large to small, or from small to large according to increased prior designs, technological advances, legal reformation, changes in ideas, etc. Therefore, the design space of a design product examined in a patent invalidation procedure shall be based on the filing date.

In this case, the evidence *Motorcycle Technology* (Issue 8, 2003) submitted by the Patent Reexamination Board (i.e., Annex 3 in the invalidation decision No. WX13657) shows that, even though motorcycle wheels are composed of rims, spokes, and hubs, and are subject to default functional limitations, there is still adequate design space for the design of spokes to have various shapes as long as the design meets the requirements of force balance.

The first and second instance judgments' determination that the design space of motorcycle wheels was small lacked evidence. Therefore, the conclusion of the first and second instance judgments of this case that the difference between the patent at issue and the prior design makes them neither identical nor similar on the premise of the limited design space of motorcycle wheels lacks factual basis and shall be corrected."

13.5 The Right to Apply for a Trademark as a Prior Legitimate Right Afforded by Article 23 of the *Patent Law*

"The legitimate right obtained before the date of filling by any other person" provided in Article 23 of the *Patent Law* mainly refers to the trademark right, copyright, portrait right, etc. If any other person has previously acquired the above-mentioned legal rights, a patent applicant shall not be granted with a design patent right based on these trademarks, works of art, etc.

The issue in the case *(2014) Zhi Xing Zi No. 4*[7] was whether a right to apply for a trademark was the legitimate right obtained before the date of filing under Article 23 of the *Patent Law*. In this case, the invalidation petitioner did not expressly claim the right to apply for a trademark in the request for invalidation. The Patent Reexamination Board determined that there was no conflict of rights due to the exclusive right to use the right to apply for a trademark as a prior right. The invalidation petitioner expressly claimed that the right to apply for a trademark was a prior right in the second instance and the second instance judgment held that the right to apply for a trademark was a prior right. Regarding this issue, the Patent Reexamination Board argued in the retrial petition that a prior right should be a legitimate right and have a

---

[7] Design patent No. 00333252.7. The invalidation decision was No. WX14261. The Patent Reexamination Board lost in both the first instance judgment *((2010) Yi Zhong Xing Chu Zi No. 1242)* and the second instance judgment *((2011) Gao Xing Zhong Zi No. 1733)*. The Patent Reexamination Board filed for a retrial and was rejected by the SPC.

legal basis; otherwise, the exploitation of a patent would not constitute an infringement, nor would a conflict of rights arise. There was no such thing as a right to apply for a trademark in the *Trademark Law*, nor was the right to apply for a trademark a right "related to trademark review and adjudication" set forth in the *Trademark Review and Adjudication Rules*. Even if the right to apply for a trademark is a legitimate right, it will not conflict with the design patent right because the exploitation of a design patent will not hinder the exercise of the right to apply for a trademark, including the applicant's disposition of the trademark application, nor will it hinder the trademark applicant's subsequent acquisition of the exclusive right to use the registered trademark. In other words, a trademark applicant's exclusive right to use the trademark has not been damaged, thus not constituting an infringement.

The SPC was not convinced by the above-mentioned arguments of the Patent Reexamination Board. In its ruling, the SPC pointed out: "The exclusive right to use a registered trademark is a legitimate right that is previously obtained as provided in Article 23 of the *Patent Law (2000)*. If a symbol identical with or similar to another's registered trademark is used in the design of identical or similar products, the exploitation of the design patent right may mislead the relevant public into believing that the product comes from the trademark owner, thereby damaging the legitimate rights of the trademark owner, causing a conflict between the design patent right and the registered trademark patent right. The criterion for determining this conflict is in essence to examine whether the exploitation of the design patent right will infringe on the exclusive right to use the registered trademark.

In this case, the date of registration of the trademark No. 1506193 was after the date of filing of the patent at issue, and the exclusive right to use the registered trademark was not obtained earlier, only that the date of application for the trademark was earlier than the date of filing of the patent at issue. The prior right claimed by Baixiang Company was also based on the right to apply for a trademark that was filed earlier. Regarding this, this court holds that if the date of application for a trademark is earlier than the filing date of a design patent application, the design patent does not constitute a conflict of rights with the right to apply for a trademark, and the right to apply for a trademark cannot be regarded as a prior legitimate right under Article 23 of the *Patent Law (2000)*. However, based on the nature and function of the right to apply for a trademark and the principle of protecting prior rights, as long as the trademark application date is earlier than the patent filing date, and the trademark has been registered and remains valid before the filing of the invalidation request, the earlier application for the exclusive right to use the registered trademark is effective against the latter application for the design patent right, and can be used to determine whether the design patent right conflicts with it."

The SPC came to this conclusion based on the following three reasons: First, the legal nature of the right to apply for a trademark. The SPC held that "first, under the relevant provisions of the *Trademark Law* on the first-to-file principle of trademark applications, when two or more applicants apply for the registration of identical or similar trademarks for the same or similar products, the Trademark Office hears the trademark application that is filed first. In other words, once an applicant files for trademark registration, he or she will enjoy the right to exclude others from applying to register an identical or similar trademark on the same or similar products from the date of application. Second, under relevant provisions of the *Implementing Regulations of the Trademark Law*, an applicant can assign his or her trademark application, i.e., the applicant can dispose of the right to apply for a trademark as a civil right interest at will. Finally, the ultimate goal of a trademark application, i.e., the realization of the right to apply for a trademark is to have the trademark registered. In this sense, the right to apply for a trademark is an inchoate right, which is an expectation for obtaining the exclusive right to use a registered trademark in the future, starting from the date of application of a trademark, and finally realized when the trademark is registered. In conclusion, the right to apply for a trademark is a legitimate interest that exists in reality. It is an inchoate right of the exclusive use of a registered trademark and shall be protected by law."

Second, the role of the right to apply for a trademark in determining a conflict of rights. The SPC held that "the right to apply for a trademark is a legitimate interest. If the date of application of a trademark is earlier than the filing date of a design patent, the exploitation of the design patent by the patentee will not affect whether the trademark will be finally approved for registration, and there will be no conflict between the design patent right and the right to apply for a trademark. Therefore, the right to apply for a trademark shall not be relied on to determine whether a design patent conflicts with it…as a legitimate right obtained previously under Article 23 of the *Patent Law (2000)*.

However, the right to apply for a trademark is of great significance for determining whether a design patent conflicts with the exclusive right to use a registered trademark, mainly represented as following: as an inchoate right, the ultimately expected complete right of the right to apply for a trademark is the exclusive right to use the registered trademark. Only when the trademark is registered can the ultimate right and interest of the trademark application be realized. Here, the right to apply for a trademark shall be protected retrospectively to confirm the legal significance of the application date of a trademark on the exclusive right to use a registered trademark. As long as the trademark application date is earlier than the filing date of the design patent, the exclusive right to use a registered trademark applied for earlier can be effective against the design patent right applied for later."

Third, the principle of protecting prior rights. The SPC held that "in this case, after the trademark No. 1506193 has been registered, the exploitation of the patent at issue objectively may conflict with this trademark. As the trademark was applied for earlier, the patent at issue is not a prior right of this trademark. The conflict may be resolved only by determining that Baixiang Company's registered trademark that was applied for earlier was effective against the design patent right of Chen Zhaohui under the principle of protecting prior rights. Moreover, the announcement date of the preliminary examination and approval of trademark No. 1506193 was also earlier than the filing date of the patent at issue. For a trademark that has been preliminarily approved and announced, the Trademark Office has conducted a preliminary examination of the trademark application and believes that it conforms to the relevant provisions of the *Trademark Law*. The announcement of a trademark aims to solicit the opinions of relevant operators and the public, during which period relevant persons may protest to the Trademark Office. As the filing date of the patent at issue is later than the date on which the trademark No. 1506193 was preliminarily approved and announced, it is objectively possible that a design patent applicant may imitate or copy this trademark, a situation which falls well within the regulation under Article 23 of the *Patent Law*."

Based on these three reasons, the SPC concluded that: "the application date of Baixiang Company's trademark No. 1506193 was earlier than the filing date of the patent at issue, and the trademark No. 1506193 remains valid after registration and when the invalidation request was filed by Baixiang Company. The exclusive right to use the trademark No. 1506193 can be effective against the patent at issue and can be relied on to determine whether the patent at issue conflicts with it."

Chapter 14
Conclusion

Based on the summary of previous cases, it can be seen that the Intellectual Property Court of the SPC of China has formulated and put forward its own opinions and views on the examination rules of patent granting and patent confirmation cases through a large number of retrial applications and cases brought up for trial in recent years. A majority of such views confirmed the *Guidelines for Patent Examination*, but there were also questions about the *Guidelines for Patent Examination* and the examination rules of the Patent Reexamination Board. Meanwhile, there are also inconsistencies in the understanding of some issues between the first and second instance courts and the SPC or within the Intellectual Property Court of the SPC. The reason why the author chose to summarize the cases in the way of legal restatement is to present the original state of authentic cases, so that readers can make their own objective judgment through first-hand information.

In practice, readers should pay attention not only to the cases in which the views of the four trial levels differ in the examination/judicial processes, but also to the cases where the four trial levels share the same views, and the latter may be even more important than the former because if the four trial levels share the same opinion, it is an indication that there is a consensus among the examination/judiciary authorities on the relevant issues. If the issue of a disputed case happens to be such an issue, it means that even if the litigation commences, the chance of changing the review conclusion through argument is relatively slim. Among the 130 cases cited in this book, more than 50% are cases in which the four trial levels agreed with each other.

In addition, it is also necessary to pay attention to the cases in which the Patent Reexamination Board and the SPC share the same opinions because these cases show the Intellectual Property Court of the SPC shares the same understanding of the disputed issues with the Patent Reexamination Board, so even if the examination conclusion may change during the first and second instances, at the petition stage, the examination conclusion of the reexamination or invalidation decision is very likely to be sustained by the SPC. Of the 130 cases cited in the book, such cases account for about two-thirds (of the uncited cases, the Patent Reexamination Board won the vast majority of them. Therefore, in fact, the likelihood that the Patent Reexamination Board wins is much higher than two-thirds).

Part II
Comments

In this part, drawing from a comprehensive analysis of relevant cases adjudicated by the SPC between 2009 and 2015, the author discusses the similarities and discrepancies in claim construction across patent granting, patent confirmation, and patent infringement procedures, the examination of patentable subject matter, the sufficiency of disclosure, the definiteness of claims, the amendment beyond scope, the nature of the reexamination and invalidation procedures and the *ex officio* examination.

Chapter 15
Similarities and Differences of Claim Construction in Patent Granting, Patent Confirmation, and Patent Infringement Procedures

Claim construction is an eternal topic in the field of patent law. Over the years, controversies regarding claim construction have primarily focused on specific construction rules, particularly how to correctly handle the relationship between interpreting claims based on the description and its drawings and improperly introducing the contents of the description and its drawings into the claims. However, one problem that must be addressed is whether the rules of claim construction should be the same in patent granting, patent confirmation, and patent infringement procedures or if there is any difference, where do these differences manifest?

15.1 The Meaning of Claim Construction

There are currently two different views regarding what "claim construction" means. One is that "claim construction" is the process of determining the true meaning and delineating the literal meaning of the claims,[1] a concept that exists at all stages of patent prosecution. The U.S. Court of Appeals for the Federal Circuit (CAFC) wrote in the case *Scripps Clinic & Research Foundation v. Genentech, Inc.*,[2] "the construction of claims is simply a way of elaborating the normally terse claim language: in order to understand and explain, but not to change, the scope of the claims."[3] The other point of view is that claim construction is a unique concept in patent infringement procedures, the process of determining the scope of patent protection. Currently, most countries and regions adopt the "doctrine of equivalents" to extend the scope of patent protection beyond the literal meaning of the claims to protect the

---

[1] Yan, W. (2007). *Scope of Patent Rights* (1st ed., p.30). Law Press.
[2] Translator's note: There is a spelling mistake in the book. "Scipps" should be "Scripps".
[3] Scripps Clinic & Research Foundation v. Genentech, Inc. 927 F. 2d 1565, 18 U.S. P. Q. 2d 1001 (Fed. Cir. 1991).

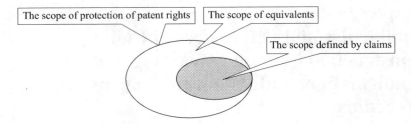

Fig. 15.1 The scope of protection of patent rights, the scope of equivalents, and the scope defined by claims

interests of patentees adequately. Therefore, determining the scope of equivalents is also claim construction.[4]

The following figure (Fig. 15.1) illustrates these two views: The former view of claim construction refers to the process of determining the scope defined by the claims. In contrast, the latter refers to the process of determining the actual scope of protection of the patent rights (that is, the scope defined by the claims and the scope of equivalents).

The author advocates the first point of view. First, claim construction is a concept that exists not only in the process of handling infringement disputes but also in patent granting and patent invalidation (hereinafter referred to as patent confirmation) procedures. In theory, claim construction shall be utterly consistent in these three procedures to respect the public notice function of claims. Defining claim construction as "determining the true meaning of the claims" is conducive to maintaining consistency of claim construction in these three procedures. Second, although determining the scope of equivalents depends on the claims and the description, the determination of equivalents distinguishes from the determination of the true meaning of claims in terms of both methods and purposes.

Moreover, the scope of equivalents may vary slightly depending on the date of the infringement; however, the true meaning of the claim is determined at the filing date and does not change with the date of the infringement. Therefore, it is more reasonable to define claim construction as a process of determining the true meaning of claims. In patent infringement procedures, claim construction is a process of restoring the scope defined by the claims and determined in the patent granting or patent confirmation procedures.

"The scope of protection of patent rights" is the broadest scope of protection that the right holder can obtain, based on the scope defined by the claims and extended by applying the doctrine of equivalents. The patent granting procedure clarifies the scope defined by the claims through the examination of the application documents and the communication and interaction between the examiner and the applicant. In a patent confirmation procedure, the Patent Reexamination Board determines whether the scope defined by the already granted claims is proper upon the request of the

---

[4] Xie, W. (2008). *Claim Construction* [Master's thesis, Southwest University of Political Science & Law].

invalidation petitioner according to the arguments and evidence submitted. In a patent infringement procedure, the judicial authority clarifies the scope of protection that the right holder can obtain based on the interpretation of the scope defined by the claims and by determining the applicability of the doctrine of equivalents and the scope of equivalents.

15.2 Possible Differences Among the Claim Construction Rules in Patent Granting, Patent Confirmation, and Patent Infringement Procedures

In theory, the construction standards for the scope of protection of the claims shall be consistent in patent granting, patent confirmation, and patent infringement procedures to "help the patentee and the public hold a unified expectation of the scope of protection of the patent, guarantee the expected interests of the public and also help encourage patentees to disclose their inventions and creations" to achieve the purpose of encouraging inventions and creations.[5] However, in practice, the rules of claim construction may and are allowed to be slightly different due to the different nature and tasks of the three procedures and the extent to which the patent holder may amend the application documents or patent documents. Generally, to overcome the same defect, the extent to which the applicant may amend the application documents shall be inversely proportional to the extent of the allowable interpretation or description. The greater the extent of the allowable amendment is, the smaller the allowable interpretation range; conversely, the smaller the extent of the allowable amendment is, the greater the allowable interpretation range.

1. Patent Granting Procedures

An examiner deals with a patent application yet to be granted in a patent granting procedure. The examiner's task is to examine the patent application documents submitted by the patent applicant to ensure that the scope of protection of the would-be patent is definite and that the patent rights are valid enough to avoid granting flawed patent rights. Therefore, the examiner shall focus on the claims in a patent granting procedure. In some circumstances, the examiner may find that a particular feature of the claim if understood according to its plain meaning, covers a wider range to include some disclosed technology in the prior art and causes the claim to lack novelty as a whole. However, such a feature is not covered by prior art under the restrictive definition of the description. If interpreted according to this restrictive definition of the description the claim shall be novel. Then, in order to grant a stable and definite patent right, it is proper to adopt the plain meaning of this feature rather than the restrictive definition of the description to avoid issuing a Notification of an Office Action for lack of novelty.

---

[5] Zhang, P. (2011). Rediscussing the timing of interpreting the scope of protection of claims. *Examination Practice Report*, 17(4).

The reasons are: on the one hand, only in this way may the patent applicant be allowed to clarify or amend the feature at the patent granting phase to avoid future disputes concerning this issue in subsequent procedures; on the other hand, in the patent granting procedure, the patent applicant may amend the claims in almost any way to overcome the defects pointed out by the examiner as long as the amendment is within the scope of the original application document. Amendment of claims helps to make patent applicants disclose in the claims the technical solutions that genuinely contribute to the society to perform the public notice function of claims better.

2. Patent Infringement Procedures

In contrast, in patent infringement procedures, the judge deals with patents that have been granted and published. His or her job is to determine whether the alleged infringing technical solutions fall within the scope of patent protection. According to the "binary system" of Chinese patent law, the Patent Reexamination Board determines the validity of patent rights. A patent is presumed to be valid until the Patent Reexamination Board issues the invalidation decision, unless of course, as explained by the SPC in the case of *(2012) Min Shen Zi No. 1544*, the patent rights are so "insolubly ambiguous" that it is impossible to determine whether the alleged infringing technical solution falls within the scope of protection of the patent right. Based on this basic principle, in the aforementioned situation, a judge shall and must use the restrictive definition in the description rather than the plain meaning to interpret the features in the claims because, in a patent infringement procedure, the patentee does not have the opportunity to amend the patent documents. If the description is not relied on to construe claims, the scope of protection that the patentee receives will be obviously disproportionate to his or her contribution to society, which is apparently unreasonable.

3. Patent Confirmation Procedures

What is troublesome is patent confirmation procedures. The Patent Reexamination Board deals with granted and published patents in this procedure. Its job is to reexamine whether the patent granting is appropriate based on the reasons and evidence submitted by the invalidation petitioner. If the granting of patent rights does not meet the statutory granting conditions, the Patent Reexamination Board is responsible for correcting improper granting by declaring that the patent rights are invalid or partially invalid. As the granting decision is examined for its correctness in a patent confirmation procedure, in theory, the rules for claim construction shall be the same in both patent confirmation procedures and patent granting procedures. However, under current laws and regulations, the extent to which a patentee is allowed to amend his or her claims in a patent confirmation procedure is greatly restricted compared to a patent granting procedure. In particular, an amendment may not be made by extracting features from the description and adding them to claims, which means that many defects that can be overcome by amending claims in a patent granting procedure cannot be overcome in a patent confirmation procedure. In this circumstance, if the claim construction standards and rules are the same as in a patent

15.2 Possible Differences Among the Claim Construction Rules in Patent ...

granting procedure, the claim at issue may be declared invalid. As a result, some errors caused by drafting flaws and other reasons may not be remedied, which may seem overly harsh for minor errors, contrary to the aim of encouraging invention and creation.

In the above-mentioned circumstances, if the plain meaning is adopted to interpret the features without introducing relevant information from the description, as the description may not be added to the claim through amendment, the only conclusion that could be made is that the claim lacks novelty and shall be declared invalid. However, such a conclusion is apparently inadequate to reflect the contribution made by the patentee to society. Therefore, the author believes that claim construction in patent confirmation procedures shall not be the same as in patent granting procedures in which claims are the focus and the broadest reasonable interpretation principle is strictly followed for claim construction.

Even so, it is undeniable that in a patent confirmation procedure, a patentee may still perfect his or her patent rights by amending the patent documents to redefine the scope of protection of the patent rights, a right that the patentee does not enjoy in a patent infringement procedure. In addition, a patent confirmation procedure will be meaningless if the methods and rules for claim construction in a patent infringement procedure are completely followed. Therefore, the interpretation standards of the claims in a patent confirmation procedure may not be the same as in a patent infringement procedure which relies heavily on claim construction to reconcile the interests of the right holder and the public, rather, such standards shall be somewhere between a patent granting procedure and a patent infringement procedure.

The SPC expressed the same view in the case of *(2010) Zhi Xing Zi No. 53-1*.[6] In this case, the SPC held that as the respective positioning and functions of the patent granting, patent confirmation, and patent infringement procedures differed, the claim construction methods in these three procedures were "largely consistent and slightly different." The difference was "particularly prominent regarding the function of the parties' statement of opinions...In patent granting and patent confirmation procedures, the applicant's statement of opinions in the examination documents is generally a reference rather than a decisive basis to understand the meaning of the description and the claims. While in a patent infringement procedure, as long as the patent applicant waives a specific technical solution through a statement of opinions, generally the scope of protection of the claims shall be interpreted restrictively based on this statement of opinions."

There have been heated discussions in the United States recently regarding the standards and rules for interpreting claims in patent granting, patent confirmation, and patent infringement procedures. Since the adoption of the new inter partes review (IPR) on September 16, 2013, the Patent Trial and Appeal Board (PTAB) has been construing claims during IPRs by applying the Broadest Reasonable Interpretation

---

[6] Invention patent No. 00131800.4. The invalidation decision (No. WX11291) declared that all patent rights were invalid. The first instance judgment (*(2008) Yi Zhong Xing Chu Zi No. 1030*) maintained the invalidation decision. The second instance judgment (*(2009) Gao Xing Zhong Zi No. 327*) vacated the first instance judgment and the invalidation decision. The invalidation petitioner filed for a retrial and was rejected by the SPC.

(BRI) standard instead of the Pillips standard adopted in patent infringement procedures. In June 2015, the U.S. Patent and Trademark Office (USPTO) published data which showed that in IPRs, claims that were declared invalid accounted for 84% of the total number of claims involved. It was suspected within the intellectual property industry that such a high percentage of invalidity was related to the PTAB's adoption of the BRI standard. According to a report on the website of Intellectual Property Protection in China on January 20, 2016, the U.S. Supreme Court granted Cuozzo Speed Technologies' writ of *certiorari* challenging the PTAB's decision to invalidate its patent covering technology used in a speedometer based on the BRI standard.[7] Cuozzo argued in its writ, "A primary reason for the high cancellation rate is that, although IPR was expressly designed to be a surrogate for litigation, the PTAB does not use the same claim construction standard as federal courts… Of course, the broader the interpretation, the more extensive the array of relevant prior art—and the more likely the claim will be held invalid in light of that prior art." The decision of this case will significantly impact the U.S. patent practice community and have some implications for the standards of claim construction in the patent confirmation and patent infringement procedures in China.

15.3 Similarities and Differences of Claim Construction in Patent Granting, Patent Confirmation, and Patent Infringement Procedures

Regarding the similarities and differences of claim construction in patent granting, patent confirmation, and patent infringement procedures, the author partly agrees with the SPC's opinion in the case of *(2010) Zhi Xing Zi No. 53-1*[8]: claim construction in the three procedures is all about textual interpretation and shall follow the general rules of it. The differences in the interpretation rules are prominently reflected in the role of the parties' statement of opinions. However, in this case, the SPC referred to the patent granting and patent confirmation procedures collectively as the "patent granting and review procedure" and compared it with the patent infringement procedure without further distinguishing and discussing whether the claim construction rules in a patent granting procedure and a patent confirmation procedure should be the same or in what way they would be different.

---

[7] Intellectual Property Protection in China. *U.S. Supreme Court Will Review PTAB Claim Construction Standard*. http://ipr.mofcom.gov.cn/article/gjkx/201604/1889137.html

[8] Invention patent No. 00131800.4. The invalidation decision (No. WX11291) declared that all patent rights were invalid. The first instance judgment (*(2008) Yi Zhong Xing Chu Zi No. 1030*) maintained the invalidation decision. The second instance judgment (*(2009) Gao Xing Zhong Zi No. 327*) vacated the first instance judgment and the invalidation decision. The invalidation petitioner filed for a retrial and was rejected by the SPC.

15.3 Similarities and Differences of Claim Construction in Patent Granting ...

To further highlight the differences in claim construction rules in the three procedures, the author sorted out the common situations that need to be interpreted in practice and suggested the interpretation methods in various situations, as shown in Table 15.1.

Table 15.1 Comparison of claim construction rules in patent granting, patent confirmation, and patent infringement procedures

No.	Situations	Patent granting	Patent confirmation	Patent infringement	Comparison
1	Coined words with specific meanings in the description	Specific meanings in the description	Specific meanings in the description	Specific meanings in the description	Patent granting = patent confirmation = patent infringement
2	Known terms or superordinate concepts with specific meanings in the description	General meanings	Specific meanings in the description	Specific meanings in the description	Patent confirmation = patent infringement
3	Functional features	All methods that can realize this function	All methods that can realize this function	Embodiments + equivalents	Patent granting = patent confirmation
4	Obvious mistakes in claims	Office Action for obvious mistakes	The only correct answer	The only correct answer	Patent confirmation = patent infringement
5	Indefinite claims, impossible for a definite construction	Office Action for indefiniteness	Declaration of invalidity for lack of definiteness	Uncomparable Non-infringement	Patent granting = patent confirmation = patent infringement
6	Indefinite claims, impossible for a definite construction	Office Action for indefiniteness	Make a definite construction	Make a definite construction	Patent confirmation = patent infringement
7	Definite claims with a scope too wide to be supported by the description	Claim-based, interpreted according to the plain meaning	Claim-based, interpreted according to the plain meaning	Claim-based, interpreted according to the plain meaning	Patent granting = patent confirmation = patent infringement
8	Product claims limited by methods, uses, and administrative features	No limitation if there is no effect on the structure and composition of the product	No limitation if there is no effect on the structure and composition of the product	All features shall be considered (the entirety principle)	Patent granting = patent confirmation

1. When Claim Construction Rules Are Completely Consistent in the Three Procedures

In Situations 1, 5, and 7, the construction rules in the three procedures shall be completely consistent. Situations 1 and 5 are relatively easy to understand. For Situation 7, the scope of the claims is too wide to be supported by the description. On the one hand, the current "binary system" dictates that the court hearing infringement disputes does not have the authority to determine the validity of patents. As a result, even if the court hearing the infringement disputes thinks that the scope of the claim is too wide to be supported by the description, as long as the accused infringer has not requested for invalidation or the Patent Reexamination Board has not declared the patent right invalid, it still shall focus on the claims instead of construing the claims restrictively based on the description to effectively amending the claims. On the other hand, the determination of whether the claims are supported by the description relies heavily on the knowledge of prior art from the perspective of a person of ordinary skill in the art appertaining to the field, unlike an interpretation of rectification of obvious mistakes which relies only on the description to make an accurate judgment. When the claims are definite, allowing the description to be interpreted restrictively into the claims will render the patent confirmation procedure meaningless and seriously damage the public notice function of claims.

2. When Claim Construction Rules Are the Same in Patent Confirmation and Patent Infringement Procedures but Different in Patent Granting Procedures

In Situations 2, 4, and 6, claim construction rules in a post-grant procedure shall be the same as in a patent infringement procedure but different from those in a patent granting procedure.

The claim construction methods in the patent granting and patent infringement procedures are relatively easy to understand. For example, in Situation 2, when the known features or superordinate concepts in the claims are defined explicitly in the description, in the patent granting procedure, the claims shall be the focus for claim construction to grant valid patent rights with clear boundaries. Application of the plain meanings to the corresponding features, etc., may encourage the patent applicant to amend the claims to include the specific definition or correct content in the description, which is helpful to avoid possible disputes in the subsequent patent confirmation and patent infringement procedures. Applying the specific meaning in the description to the known terms and superordinate concepts in a patent infringement procedure is more beneficial to balance the interests of the right holder and the public. For example, in Situation 4, where there is an obvious mistake in the patent granting procedure, an office action for indefiniteness may make the patent applicant aware of the mistake as soon as possible and submit the only correct answer, which helps grant patent rights with clear boundaries. On the contrary, in the patent infringement procedure, when the only correct answer can be obtained according to the description, correction of the apparent mistake through claim construction contributes to the adequate protection of patent rights and the balance of interests between right holders and the public.

Claim construction in the patent confirmation procedure is a headache. The author believes that the description shall be used to clarify or rectify claims because in these three situations, the claims' defects are mostly drafting mistakes and honest mistakes. Under the provisions of the current *Guidelines for Patent Examination*, what can be used to remedy the mistakes shall be included in the description and cannot be added or supplemented to the claims by amending the patent documents. Therefore, it is reasonable to correct these mistakes through claim construction to protect real inventions and creations. More importantly, claim construction in these three situations is to rectify the flawed content and does not constitute a substantive amendment to the scope of the claim.

Some readers may compare Situations 2, 4, and 6 with Situation 7 and wonder why in patent confirmation procedures, the description is allowed to be used to interpret claims in Situations 2, 4, and 6, whereas, in Situation 7, claim construction is strictly based on the claims rather than covers what is supported by the description. For this matter, the author believes that, first, as the SPC has emphasized in many cases, claim construction shall be based on the technical features defined in the claims to avoid construing into claims what is stated in the description only but not defined in the claims, resulting in improper limitation on the scope of the claims. In Situations 2, 4, and 6, claim construction is to clarify the claims rather than restrict the scope of the claims. In Situation 7, if what is supported by the description is allowed to be interpreted into the claims even if the description does not support the claims, it would constitute a substantive amendment to the scope of the claims.

Second, the first thing to deal with when filing a patent application is to summarize the technical solutions to be protected in clear and concise language, indicate the claimed scope of protection and form a three-dimensional protection system through the progressive restriction of dependent claims. Even for the sake of protection strategies, a broader scope is summarized beyond the scope supported by the description. Therefore, the scope supported by the description shall be stated in the claims as dependent claims, "just in case." It is, at most, "negligence with undue assumption" rather than an honest mistake by only stating a broad scope of protection without further precautions through dependent claims. Moreover, the patent applicant should also bear the risks corresponding to the broad scope of protection. Therefore, the author believes it is unreasonable to construe the claims restrictively by relying on what is supported by the description in Situation 7.

3. When Claim Construction Rules Are Consistent in Patent Confirmation and Patent Granting Procedures but Different in Patent Infringement Procedures

In Situations 3 and 8, claim construction rules in a patent confirmation procedure shall be the same as in a patent granting procedure but different from a patent infringement procedure.

Functional features are the most typical. In patent confirmation procedures, under relevant provisions of the *Guidelines for Patent Examination*, functional features shall be interpreted as all the embodiments that can realize the function. Under relevant judicial interpretations, functional features shall be construed in patent infringement procedures as the specifically described embodiments and their equivalents. Although the inconsistency in the construction rules in patent confirmation and patent infringement procedures is often criticized in the industry, the author thinks this inconsistency is acceptable.

First, in most cases, the difference between the two rules only exists in words, while the actual determination results are the same. During the substantive examination process, for the claims containing functional features, the examiner needs to examine whether the functional limitation is supported by the description, which may result in two possible outcomes: one is that the function is realized in the specific way described in the embodiment of the description; the other is that the realization of the function does not depend on the particular way explained in the embodiments of the description, instead, any component or structure can be used in the relevant technical solution as long as the function is real. For the first circumstance, the examiner shall examine whether a person of ordinary skill in the relevant art recognizes that this function can also be realized by alternative methods not mentioned in the description or whether it is reasonable to suspect that one or more of the methods contained in the functional feature cannot solve the technical problem to be solved by the invention and achieve the same technical effect. This determination process is consistent with determining whether there is any equivalent or what equivalents are available based on the specifically described embodiments in the description in patent infringement procedures. Therefore, if the examiner allows the functional feature, it means that the meaning of the functional feature is the enablement of the embodiments in the description and alternative ways to realize the function; if the examiner does not allow the functional feature, it means that the patent applicant will inevitably be required to limit it to the enablement of the embodiments in the description and alternative ways to realize this function, which is completely consistent with the results of a patent infringement procedure, as shown in Fig. 15.2.

Secondly, even if the determination results of the two rules may differ in some circumstances, such differences are acceptable in encouraging patent applicants to use structural features instead of functional features as much as possible to define claims.

For example, in the second circumstance above, in patent granting procedures, if the examiner believes that the realization of the function does not depend on the

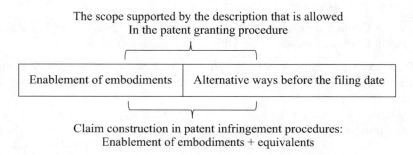

Fig. 15.2 Relevant functions can only be realized by enabling the embodiments in the description

enablement of the embodiments in the description, and any component or structure with the function can be used in the relevant technical solution, functional features are allowed to be included in the claims. In this circumstance, the meaning of the functional features includes the enablement of the embodiment and equivalent alternatives of the enablement and alternatives not equivalent to the enablement of embodiments but able to achieve the function. Accordingly, such a functional feature that appears in a patent granting procedure is interpreted as including only the former two categories in patent infringement procedures (as shown in Fig. 15.3).

In this circumstance, the difference in the rules will cause inadequate protection of some of the patentee's rights, a result essentially caused by the fact that the patentee adopted the less preferred functional feature to limit the claimed invention. Although less preferred, it does not mean that functional features will necessarily damage the patentee's interests. If the patentee believes that the realization of the relevant functions does not depend on the enablement of the embodiments, functional features are more suitable than structural features. In addition to reciting the enablement of the embodiments, alternative ways to achieve this function (if not equivalents, but alternative ways to accomplish the function) can also be listed and explained in the description. In this case, there should not be a situation where some solutions cannot be protected, as shown in Fig. 15.3. Therefore, the different claim construction rules regarding functional features in patent granting and patent infringement procedures help to encourage patent applicants to draft better application documents.

As for why claim construction rules in a patent confirmation procedure shall be the same as in a patent granting procedure but different from a patent infringement procedure, the author believes the reason is the same as in Situation 7 and will not ramble on this matter.

To sum up, as the upstream and downstream of the patent system, the administrative and judicial agencies need to cooperate with each other to jointly regulate the balance of interests between the right holders and the public. Administrative policies and judicial policies are like two nails with an elastic band in between representing patentees' rights. Loose administrative policies entail tight judicial policies; otherwise, the right holders will get excessive benefits disproportionate to their contributions to society. On the contrary, tight administrative policies require loose

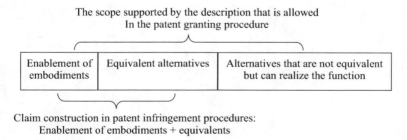

Fig. 15.3 The realization of relevant functions does not depend on the enablement of the embodiments in the description

judicial policies; otherwise, the right holders' interests will be damaged, inconsistent with their contributions to society. The same applies to claim construction in patent granting, patent confirmation, and patent infringement procedures. The rules of claim construction may and are allowed to be slightly different due to the different nature and tasks of the three procedures and the extent to which the patent holder amends the application documents and patent documents. This difference manifests not only in the role of the party's statement of opinions but also in the specific construction rules in particular circumstances.

Chapter 16
Patentable Subject Matter

The administrative organs and the three levels of courts generally agree on what inventions-creations are patentable and whether the claimed invention-creation meets the practical applicability requirements. The Patent Reexamination Board seldom loses such cases, and the courts of different levels rarely have divided opinions regarding these two issues.

With the implementation of the "Internet Plus" Action Plan,[1] in the next 30–40 years, numerous new inventions-creations integrating hardware and software will emerge in the five dimensions of product intelligence, equipment intelligence, production mode intelligence, management intelligence, and service intelligence with a focus on "intelligent manufacturing," characterized by interconnection, data, integration, innovation, and transformation, such as the integration of industrial Internet of things, industrial network security, industrial big data, cloud computing platforms, manufacturing execution systems (MES), virtual reality, artificial intelligence, knowledge work automation with industrial robots (including high-end components), sensors, Radio Frequency Identification (RFID),[2] 3D printing, machine vision, automatic guided vehicles (AGV), programmable logic controllers (PLC), data collectors and industrial switches, etc. Are these invention-creations patentable? Or assuming that the answer is no, are these invention-creations worthy of protection, and how can they be protected? Issues such as these will become the focus of debates in the industry for some time in the future. They will certainly trigger extensive discussion on the scope of protection of traditional industrial property rights.

In this general context, it will be worthy of discussion in the future on the appropriateness of determining whether the claimed invention-creation is a technical solution based on the elements of "technical problems, technical means, and technical effects"

---

[1] Similar concepts have been introduced abroad, such as "Industry 4.0" proposed in Germany and the "Industrial Internet" advanced in the United States. The core of these concepts is the same, i.e., "smart manufacturing."

[2] Translator's Note. In the original book, the term was PFID, which in fact should be RFID.

© Intellectual Property Publishing House 2024
R. Xiaolan, *Patent Administrative Litigation*, Understanding China,
https://doi.org/10.1007/978-981-97-1131-4_16

or denying protection by applying the criterion of "only artificially setting rules on existing commonly-known equipment."

Chapter 17
Sufficiency of Disclosure

Current cases show that the Patent Reexamination Board holds almost the same view with the SPC on the determination of sufficiency of disclosure but differs significantly from the Beijing Higher People's Court. For example, in the case *(2014) Xing Ti Zi No. 8*, the SPC fully supported the Patent Reexamination Board regarding the steps and order to determine sufficiency of disclosure.

As for how to determine whether the description sufficiently discloses the claimed technical solution, the disputes in practice focus on the following aspects: (1) the intendment of Article 26(3) of the *Patent Law* and its relationship with other relevant provisions, such as Article 22 of the *Patent Law*; (2) the determination elements and methods under Article 26(3) of the *Patent Law*; (3) the elements to determine whether inventions in the field of chemistry (especially chemical product inventions) are sufficiently disclosed.

17.1 The Intendment of Article 26(3) of the *Patent Law*

Article 26(3) of the *Patent Law* specifies the requirement for the vehicles to express the claimed technical solution. This provision is not only the requirement for the applicant on how to draft an application, but also a necessary condition for an invention-creation to be granted a patent right, and an inevitable requirement of "disclosure in exchange for protection."

First, from the factual logic of how an invention-creation is generated, sufficiency of disclosure of the claimed invention-creation is the most basic requirement for the applicant to draft an application. An invention-creation goes through three stages, from being created to being granted a patent (or being rejected). The inventor first generates a technical concept, validates it through experiments, and then refines it to form an invention-creation; next, the applicant expresses the invention-creation in words and formulates an application document to be submitted to the Patent Office for examination, including a description, claims and an abstract; then, an examiner examines the patent document to determine whether the claimed invention-creation meets the requirements for granting a patent. In the process of putting the invention-creation into an application document, the applicant needs to expound clearly on the technical solution of this invention-creation and the technical information required by a person skilled in the art to carry out the invention-creation, i.e., explain what the claimed technical solution is (what), how to carry it out (how to make), and how to use it (how to use). Concretely speaking, when a product is claimed, the applicant needs to explain the structural composition, manufacturing method, and use of the product; when a method is claimed, the applicant needs to explain the steps and the sequence of these steps to carry out the method, the application conditions of each step, and other information. The disclosure of such information is essentially the process of sufficiently disclosing the invention-creation. If it is difficult or impossible for a person skilled in the art to carry out the claimed invention-creation due to the lack of all or part of the information, the applicant has not disclosed the invention-creation sufficiently and does not meet the primary requirement for obtaining patent protection. Therefore, sufficiency of disclosure of the claimed invention-creation is the most fundamental obligation of an applicant to draft an application.

Second, the structure and legal logic of the *Patent Law* indicate that sufficiency of disclosure is a substantive requirement for invention-creations to be granted patent rights. According to the relevance of the content, the *Patent Law* divides all provisions into eight chapters, including "General Provisions" (Articles 1–21), "Requirements for Grant of Patent Rights" (Articles 22–25), "Application for Patent" (Articles 26–33), "Examination and Approval of Application for Patent" (Articles 34–41), "Duration, Cessation and Invalidation of Patent Right" (Articles 42–47), "Compulsory License for Exploitation of Patent" (Articles 48–58), "Protection of Patent Right" (Articles 59–74) and "Supplementary Provisions" (Articles 75–76). Structurally, Article 26(3) of the *Patent Law* is in the chapter of "Application for Patent", which means that the legislators had realized at the beginning of the making of the *Patent Law* that the sufficiency of disclosure of claimed invention-creations is mainly a fundamental obligation imposed on applicants. In theory, it is conclusive whether the disclosure of the invention-creation in the application document meets the requirement that a person skilled in the art could have been able to carry it out by the moment the applicant submits the application document to the Patent Office, an objective fact unaffected regardless of the wish of a person skilled in the art. This is because that if the application document is defective due to insufficient disclosure, it means that the application document lacks at least part of elements indispensable for carrying out the invention, and because that adding such elements after the filing date is not allowed for violation of the first-to-file rule under the provisions of Article 33 of the *Patent Law*. Therefore, the applicant is strictly bound to sufficiently disclose the claimed invention-creation when drafting the application.

However, although Article 26(3) of the *Patent Law* is in the chapter of "Application for Patent" rather than in the chapter of "Requirements for Grant of Patent Rights", it means neither that this provision binds only the applicants, nor that this provision is not a substantive requirement for granting patent rights, which can be

17.1 The Intendment of Article 26(3) of the *Patent Law*

viewed from two perspectives. On the one hand, the structure of the *Patent Law* is not strictly logical.[1] Although there are only four articles (novelty, inventive step, practical applicability, and unpatentable subject matters) in the chapter "Requirements for Grant of Patent Rights", it only indicates that an invention-creation must have novelty, inventive step, and practical applicability and must not be excluded under Article 25 of the *Patent Law* in order to obtain patent protection. It does not mean that only these four requirements need to be met for an invention-creation to obtain a patent. For example, a patentable subject matter must be an invention-creation in the sense of the *Patent Law*. A subject matter that is not an invention-creation in the sense of the *Patent Law* will not be granted a patent right for incompliance with Article 2 of the *Patent Law* (e.g., the application of a preparation method for a utility model patent does not comply with Article 2(3) of the *Patent Law*).

On the other hand, from the perspective of legal logic, the most essential prerequisite for determining whether the claimed invention-creation is novel and involves an inventive step is that a person skilled in the art can understand the technical solution of the claims and the recitation of the technical solution in the description meets the requirements of "disclosure in exchange for protection"; otherwise even if the technical concept proposed by the applicant is unprecedentedly brilliant, its contribution to society is not worthy enough for the applicant to enjoy the exclusive protection for a period of ten or twenty years in that no one can benefit in any way from the technical concept proposed by the applicant when certain key technical know-how is kept secret. Therefore, although sufficiency of disclosure is not in the chapter of "*Requirements for Grant of Patent Rights*", it shall be a substantive requirement for invention-creations to obtain patent protection. If Article 26(3) is not complied with, the examiner may reject the application under Article 38 of the *Patent Law*, which means that Article 26(3) of the *Patent Law* is not only a requirement for the applicant to draft the application documents, but also a substantive article that the examiner must consider in patent examination.

Third, the relationship between Article 26(3) and Article 22 of the *Patent Law* indicates that Article 22 is a requirement for the claimed technical solution; in contrast, Article 26(3) is a requirement for the vehicles for expressing the claimed technical solution. Under Article 22 of the *Patent Law*, if a claimed technical solution does not meet the requirements of novelty, inventive step, and practical applicability, it will not be granted a patent right. However, patent protection cannot be based on abstract technical solutions. Abstract technical solutions must be expressed in vehicles which are the claims and the description. The claims express the claimed technical solution through words, and the description explains and illustrates the claimed technical solution. As the vehicles for the literal expression of the technical solution, if the claims fail to clearly describe the technical solution and the description fails to clearly explain and illustrate the technical solution to cause a person those skilled in the art unable to know what technical solution the patent applicant intends to protect, the patent right cannot be granted even if the technical solution in the mind of the patent

---

[1] Yin, X. (2011). *Introduction to the Patent Law of China* (1st ed., p. 242). Intellectual Property Publishing House.

applicant meets the requirements of Article 22 of the *Patent Law*, which shows precisely the role of Article 26(3) of the *Patent Law: i.e.,* the requirement for the vehicles to express the claimed technical solution.

17.2 Determination Elements and Methods Under Article 26(3) of the *Patent Law*

Under the current *Guidelines for Patent Examination,* the standard to determine sufficiency of disclosure is whether a person skilled in the art can "carry out the technical solution of the invention or utility model, solve its technical problems, and produce the expected technical effects" based on what is recited in the description. However, in practice, an extreme tendency is that so much emphasis is put on the determination of the technical problems and whether the technical effects can be achieved that the definiteness of the technical solution is ignored. For example, in the case *(2014) Xing Ti Zi No. 8,* the court of second instance held that "the Patent Reexamination Board did not determine the technical problem to be solved by the invention... It is obviously improper to determine that the patent disclosure is insufficient without considering the technical problem to be solved by the invention as a whole."

This tendency has an ideal basis, i.e., the patent applicant should know all prior art, accurately define in the description the technical problem to be solved and all the essential technical features of the technical solution to solve this technical problem, as well as to recite them completely in the claims. However, it means that, on the one hand, very stringent requirements are imposed on patent applicants, including patent attorneys, for application document drafting, and on the other hand, an examiner should be able to accurately define the technical problems to be solved by the invention at the beginning of the examination or before the patent search, otherwise the examination opinion under Article 26(3) of the *Patent Law* will lack a legal basis.

The patent system aims to promote the development of science and technology and encourage innovation. The government grants patent applicants a monopoly period of 10–20 years in exchange for the disclosure of the claimed technical solutions. The disclosure should be to such an extent that those skilled in the art can conduct further research and development based on this technical solution. From this perspective and considering the factual logic of generating invention-creations, the vehicle for expressing the claimed technical solution is required first to make those skilled in the art knows what is claimed after reading it, and second, to enable them to reproduce or carry out the claimed technical solution, including how to make or use the claimed technical solution, and to understand the uses of the technical solution. As the function of the claims is to express the scope of the invention or utility model the patent applicant intends to protect, it is not realistic to rely solely on the claims to define clearly and comprehensively all the details, such as what is claimed, how to make or use the technical solution, and what uses the technical solution has. Therefore, the description must cover the three details mentioned above so that those skilled in the art can carry out the technical solution without extra creative work, avoiding repetitive work on the one hand and also the disproportion between the benefits that a patent applicant obtains and his or her contributions to society on the other hand.

Therefore, considering the essential requirements of the patent system and the feasibility of practical operations, it is more practical to determine whether the claimed technical solution complies with Article 26(3) of the *Patent Law* by following the order of whether a person skilled in the art knows what the claimed technical solution is, how to make or use this technical solution and what uses the technical solution has. There is a logical sequence in the above three elements: i.e., first determine what the claimed technical solution is, then determine how to make or use the technical solution, and finally determine what uses the technical solution has. This approach coincides with the assessment approach proposed by the SPC in the case *(2014) Xing Ti Zi No. 8* and is also identical to the view of the United States Court of Appeals for the Federal Circuit on sufficiency of disclosure.

17.3 Disclosure of the Uses of Product Inventions in Chemical and Pharmaceutical Fields

The above approach of examination, when applied in product inventions in the chemical field, requires that the structure, confirmation, preparation method and use of the product be disclosed in the description, which is in fact also the requirement of the *Guidelines for Patent Examination*.

However, some scholars argued that "for new compound products, the technical problem to be solved by those skilled in the art is to discover and characterize a new compound, and to make sure that it really exists… Whether certain therapeutic effect or specific use can be achieved is not the technical problem to be solved or the effects to be achieved by this new compound and its preparation method."[2] This is the view held by the Beijing Higher People's Court in the judgment of the case *(2014) Gao Xing Zhong Zi No. 79*.

In this case, claim 1 claims a compound represented by a general formula and a salt thereof. The description recites the general synthesis method of the compound. Examples 1–478 provide the preparation processes and confirmation data of many compounds but with no effect experiments or data of specific compounds listed in Table 1. The reexamination decision held that the description recited an assay protocol for compound activity but failed to provide the effect experiments and data obtained by applying the specific compounds in Table 1. In the absence of prior technical

---

[2] The case relates to an invention patent (No. 200680037279.4) with an internal number 1F115089 at the Patent Reexamination Board. The reexamination decision was No. FS47537. The first instance judgment (*(2013) Yi Zhong Zhi Xing Chu Zi No. 1454* maintained the reexamination decision, and the second instance judgment (*(2014) Gao Xing Zhong Zi No. 79*) affirmed the first instance judgment.

evidence, it would have been impossible to determine through theoretical analysis or explanation whether the compound had PI3K inhibitory activity or efficacy in treating cancer. Therefore, the description lacked sufficiency of disclosure. The court of second instance upheld the reexamination decision on the grounds that although the compound was sufficiently disclosed in the description, the disclosure of the salt of the compound was insufficient. However, the second instance court's conclusion that the compound was sufficiently disclosed triggered a range of discussions.

In essence, the above two views on the sufficiency of disclosure of the compound reflect the matter of examination policies, rather than of examination standards, i.e., for chemical and pharmaceutical industries, does China aim to protect upstream industries which focus on theoretical explorations and research and development or downstream industries that can quickly produce practical applications? The court of second instance was apparently inclined to protect scientific research results which were at the upstream of research and development, by holding that it was not necessary to disclose the uses of the new compound products and relevant experimental evidence, while the standards implemented by the *Guidelines for Patent Examination* emphasized on protecting practical applications what were at the downstream of research and development.

The patent system aims ultimately at promoting the development of related industries and enhancing the overall economic strength of the country through the protection of innovation. In the operation of China's patent system, the formulation of both patent examination policies and patent protection policies should be based on and serve for the development of the national economy. The author believes that the following issues shall be considered for adopting particular policies for the patent protection of new compounds.

1. The Overall Situation of China's National Economy

At present, China is in the stage of transforming from a large manufacturing country to a country of mass entrepreneurship and innovation. Promoting the rapid transformation and upgrading of industries is the general context facing the operation of the patent system at this stage. Each year, the number of patent applications approaches one million or above, but the majority of the basic patents of technologies are still monopolized by large foreign companies. It is unrealistic for Chinese innovators to surpass large foreign counterparts in terms of theoretical research and discoveries in the short run, especially in the chemical and pharmaceutical fields. Therefore, the fundamental issues to be considered in the making of current examination policies are to accelerate the transformation and application of technology, promote downstream industries that can produce practical applications as soon as possible, diversify market supply, and boost market vitality. From this perspective, patent rights should be granted to those who have not only prepared new compound products but also have conducted corresponding scientific research on the practical applications of the products. If the patent applicant does not disclose the use and related experimental evidence in the patent description, it is difficult for new compound products to be quickly transformed into practical applications and launched into the market rapidly and effectively.

2. The Characteristics of the Research and Development of Chemical and Pharmaceutical Products

In pharmaceutical research and development, it is just one of the many links in the chain to synthesize compounds and form a compound library. The activity screening and application are the bottlenecks in research and development. At present, the synthesis and separation of chemical products are theoretically very mature. If the view of the court of second instance in the case *(2014) Gao Xing Zhong Zi No. 79* is adopted, on the one hand, compound patents will lead to multiple and chaotic patent applications, just like trademark squatting, resulting in patent rights more likely held in the hands of scientific research institutes engaged in fundamental research. If the application and production capacity of such institutes are limited, and subsequent development is subject to the control of prior rights holders, technology will be dormant, and subsequent applications will be significantly affected. On the other hand, this policy orientation will not benefit domestic patent holders more because large foreign companies will seize more opportunities with their research and development abilities and patent portfolio capabilities. Ultimately more patent rights will concentrated in the hands of large foreign companies, which is harmful to the development of domestic enterprises and affects the overall environment for innovation.

3. Impact on Foreign and Domestic Innovative Enterprises

The theory of chemical product synthesis is mature, and it is relatively easy to design structures and conduct synthesis but relatively complex to form a creative invention. If, as advocated by the present *Guidelines for Patent Examination*, the structure design of compounds is combined with target discovery and compound applications in the criteria for determining sufficiency of disclosure and inventive step, the patented invention-creations will be closer to the industry than to fundamental theory, which is more helpful to protect downstream industries, shortening the distance between patents and actual production. On the one hand, although on the surface, such practice equally increases the difficulty of obtaining patents for both domestic and foreign companies, but because it takes longer and costs more to apply compounds than to synthesize compounds, it becomes less difficult for Chinese companies to obtain patents compared with foreign companies than before, leaving more room for domestic companies to grow. On the other hand, this practice is more beneficial to the structural adjustment of China's overall national economy.

Based on the above analysis, the author thinks that even if a patent application claims a new compound and its preparation method, it is still necessary to disclose the use of the compound and the experimental evidence to prove its use in the description. The new approach put forward by the court of second instance in the case *(2014) Gao Xing Zhong Zi No. 79* not only departed from the actual research and development in the chemical and pharmaceutical fields but also deviated from the empirical analysis of China's national conditions and the development of the industry. Although the case is still in the examination stage of the retrial by the SPC, it can be expected that this approach of the court of second instance may not be upheld by the SPC in light of the views held by the SPC in the cases *(2015) Zhi Xing Zi No. 340* and *(2015) Zhi Xing Zi No. 342*.

17.4 Extent of Disclosure of the Uses of Product Inventions in the Chemical and Pharmaceutical Fields

Since it is necessary to disclose the uses of the chemical and pharmaceutical product inventions in the description, a problem to be addressed inevitably is to what extent the disclosure of the use can be considered to have met the requirement of sufficiency of disclosure. This issue has been debated a lot in the industry, especially in the past five years. Foreign pharmaceutical companies have put forward many different opinions, and even directly triggered discussions and statements on this issue in Sino-US business negotiations.

There may be four circumstances in the disclosure of the use of chemical and pharmaceutical products in the description: first, only the general use of the compound is mentioned, and no experimental methods nor any data are disclosed; second, only experimental methods are recited without mentioning any experimental data of verification with specific samples; third, the range of partial experimental data is disclosed without reciting any specific samples, such as expressing the effect of the product in such a way: "the IC_{50} value of the compound of the present invention is within the range of ..."; fourth, the experimental data is complete with detailed descriptions of the samples used in the experiments. In the above four circumstances, the description in the first and the second situations is considered as not disclosing the use of the product, and the fourth is considered to meet the requirements of sufficiency of disclosure. Disputes mainly concentrate on the description in the third circumstance: can the expression of the product's effect such as "the IC_{50} value of the compound of the present invention is within the range of ..." be considered as having disclosed the use of the product?

The SPC answered this question unequivocally in the two cases *(2015) Zhi Xing Zi No. 340* and *(2015) Zhi Xing Zi No. 342*, and the author entirely agrees to the arguments and opinions contained therein. The author believes that the correct judgment on this issue requires the consideration of the relationship between the research and development and patent applications of pharmaceutical products, the overall research and development status of the product at issue, and the bottom line that the invention has been completed by the filing date or the priority date.

1. The Relationship Between the Research and Development of Pharmaceutical Products and Patent Applications

First, the timing of the patent application. There are usually two stages in contemporary pharmaceutical research and development: the drug discovery stage and the drug

17.4 Extent of Disclosure of the Uses of Product Inventions in the Chemical ...

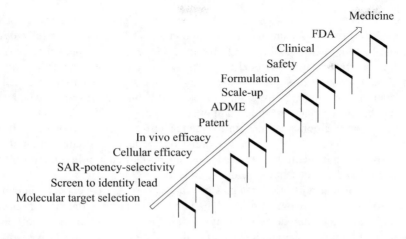

Fig. 17.1 Timeline of the drug research and development and patent application of brand name pharmaceutical companies

development stage. Most of the research and development of drugs originates from the discovery of targets, and with the identification and confirmation of the targets, the method of testing the efficacy of drugs will be improved. At the same time, many compounds are synthesized to enter the screening and evaluation phase, which lays a good foundation for the discovery of lead compounds. After that, drug candidate compounds are obtained through the structural optimization of the lead compounds. Drugs with promising development prospects obtained through a series of pre-clinical optimization screenings enter the market after clinical trials and approval by the drug regulatory authority. During the above research and development process, there are the two most important issues that need to be considered: when to file a patent application and how to generalize the scope of protection of the claims when filing a patent application.

Usually, brand name pharmaceutical companies choose to file a patent application in the drug discovery stage (see Fig. 17.1[3]). These companies will generally consider the following three factors when determining the precise timing to file a patent application for the first time: first, the novelty of the selected target; second, the fierceness of the competition of the selected target or chemical substance; and third, make sure that a patent can be obtained. If the selected target is new and the company is still making a series of improvements, a brand name pharmaceutical company will usually consider obtaining the priority date by first filing an application, and then submitting the supplementary application documents within 12 months afterward, thereby minimizing the risk of the patent application not being granted.

---

[3] Liu, G. *Drug Patent Strategies* [Lecture Notes for the 2014 Master's Program in International Pharmaceutial Engineering and Management].

Second, the strategies for patent application. When applying for a patent, on the one hand, in order to ensure that the compounds that have not been fully developed by the filing date can at least be protected by the original application to some extent, brand name pharmaceutical companies usually choose to generalize a relatively broad scope of protection in the claims of the first application and then, in subsequent patent applications, claim compounds within a narrower scope than the first application or claim specific compounds; on the other hand, while ensuring that the first application is granted, brand name pharmaceutical companies will also deliberately select certain key groups in order to prevent the first application, due to its disclosure, from becoming a reference document that undermines the novelty or inventive step of the subsequent patent applications.

Third, the patent portfolio strategies of brand name pharmaceutical companies. In the process of technological research and development, brand name pharmaceutical companies generally develop two types of patent portfolio strategies: offensive strategies and defensive strategies. Among them, the most basic offensive strategy is to apply patents for their core research results to form their patent protection network. When forming a patent network, brand name pharmaceutical companies usually build a mixed portfolio of patents, including basic patents, dependent patents, and Paper patents that play a defensive role.

Fourth, the characteristics of patent document drafting. Generally, when applying for a basic patent, brand name pharmaceutical companies will express a claimed product with a general chemical formula and include many compound preparation examples in the patent application. Meanwhile, these companies generally choose to disclose partial experimental data that meets the minimum requirements for granting a patent, rather than voluntarily disclose all experimental data. Moreover, the sample used in the activity test is usually expressed in the data as the "compound of the present invention" or, at most, the "compound of the example of the present invention", because, at this stage, if the activity data of the lead compound discovered by the company is included in the description, the publication of the patent application in the early stage will enable the competitors to discover its target lead compound earlier, costing its competitive advantage. When applying for dependent patents, as the product research and development has entered a relatively mature stage, brand name pharmaceutical companies are less cautious about disclosing data than when applying for basic patents, and more likely to provide more detailed data in patent documents. However, if brand name pharmaceutical companies apply for a surrounding patent, more commonly referred to as a Paper patent in the industry as a defensive strategy, they usually only provide numerous compound preparation examples in the patent application documents and at most a broad range of activity data of the "compounds of the present invention."

2. The Overall Status of the Technological Research and Development of the Product at Issue

The sufficiency of disclosure of the description for a claimed product should not be judged solely on the basis of the patent application document itself. It is also necessary to examine the overall status of the technological research and development

17.4 Extent of Disclosure of the Uses of Product Inventions in the Chemical …

related to the claimed product and how product uses are expressed in related patent applications, to make a comprehensive judgment on what stage the technology related to the patent application is at in this field based on the experimental methods and verification means generally recognized by those skilled in the art on the filing date.

In a specific determination process, factors that need to be considered comprehensively include the correlation between the experimental design and experimental result and the operability of the technical solution, the technological development level in related fields, the customary experimental methods, the limitation of objective conditions, etc. It should be avoided that the requirements for experimental data are so unrealistically stringent that the ideal experimental data proof standard is inconsistent with common practices in the relevant field, or even exceeds the current technological development level, or is impossible to achieve under objective conditions. However, it should also be avoided that the requirements are so lax that the contribution of the patent applicant to society is not proportional to the rights he or she may obtain. Under this fundamental principle, pioneering inventions shall be appropriately encouraged, and dependent patents shall be subjected to strict requirements. The requirements for the experimental data of a dependent patent of the use of a chemical compound should not be relaxed just because a product patent of the compound has been granted.

3. Sticking to the Bottom Line that the Invention Has Been Completed by the Filing Date or Priority Date

The first-to-file rule is one of the primary rules adopted by China's *Patent Law*. Article 26(3) of the *Patent Law* provides the obligations that the patent applicant must undertake in order to obtain the exclusive patent right, that is, the description shall set forth the invention in a manner sufficiently clear and complete so as to enable those skilled in art to carry it out. This provision ensures that the public can obtain new and useful information from the patent application documents, and that patent rights are granted to inventions that have been completed by the filing date to prevent some patent applicants from preempting the filing date and obtaining a filing date earlier than the date that should have been designated for their subsequent invention-creations, which is contrary to the original intention of the first-to-file system. In addition, the patent right protects tangible technical solutions rather than technical concepts, imaginations, or guesses. In the patent application documents submitted on the filing date, there must be at least preliminary evidence to show that it is not just a guess, but an invention-creation on a scientific basis.

This requirement is not unique to China's *Patent Law*. In fact, there are similar requirements in U.S. patent practice. For instance, the CAFC held that "the applicant must provide substantiating evidence unless a person with ordinary skill in the art can determine that the claims are clearly correct." Where a valid correlation between the technical solution and the use has not been established in prior art, the applicant should provide data in the description to prove the corresponding use. "If mere plausibility were the test for enablement under § 112, applicants could obtain patent rights to 'inventions' consisting of little more than respectable guesses as to the likelihood of their success." "When one of the guesses later proved true, the title of 'inventor' would be awarded to those who were 'predators' rather than to those who had proved that the method actually worked." "That scenario is not consistent with the statutory requirement that the inventor enable an invention rather than merely proposing an unproved hypothesis."[4]

In short, the experimental data requirements for the relevant uses of chemical and pharmaceutical products is not one-size-fits-all. Instead, it should be assessed based on the characteristics of the product to which the patent application relates and the product's status in prior art. The experimental data provided in the description only function to enable a person skilled in the art to determine preliminarily that the technical solution has been completed and is feasible based on the application documents submitted on the filing date, avoiding granting patent rights to technical solutions that cannot be carried out and granting patentees rights that are disproportionate to their contributions to the prior art.

17.5 Experimental Evidence Submitted After the Filing Date to Prove Sufficiency of Disclosure

Regarding whether the additional evidence submitted after the filing date can be used to prove whether the description sufficiently discloses the claimed technical solution, the *Guidelines for Patent Examination* provides in Part Two, Chapter 10, §3.4 that whether or not the description is sufficiently disclosed is judged on the basis of the disclosure contained in the initial description and claims, and that any embodiments and experimental data submitted after the date of filing shall not be taken into consideration. This provision was added when the *Guidelines for Patent Examination* was amended in 2006. In practice, examiners' refusal to consider any supplemented embodiments and experimental data across the board has triggered extensive discussions in the industry in recent years.

The SPC reinterpreted this provision in the case *(2014) Xing Ti Zi No. 8* and classified such experimental evidence into two types according to the subject of proof and purpose of proof: one is the experimental evidence that proves the knowledge level and cognitive ability of those skilled in the art before the filing date; the other is the experimental evidence that proves the rest of items other than the knowledge

---

[4] Rasmusson v. Smith Kline Beecham Corp., 413 F.3d 1318, 75 U.S.P.Q. 2d (BNA) 1297(Fed. Cir. 2005). In this case, the Board of Patent Appeals and Interferences held that Rasmusson was not entitled to the benefit of a priority date based on certain previous applications because a person having ordinary skill in the art would not have believed that the chemical compound finasteride claimed by Rasmusson would be effective in treating prostate cancer without undue experimentation. And, it was impossible to predict that finasteride could be used to treat prostate cancer in light of the state of the art and in light of Rasmusson's failure to provide any data to demonstrate the effects of finasteride in treating prostate cancer. Therefore, Rasmusson could not defeat the priority date accorded to Smith Kline's patents and reissue applications. The CAFC upheld the decision of the Board of Patent Appeals and Interferences because that decision was supported by substantial evidence and was not contrary to law.

17.5 Experimental Evidence Submitted After the Filing Date to Prove …

level and cognitive ability of those skilled in the art before the filing date. The SPC expressly stated that the first type of experimental evidence may be considered. As for the second type of experimental evidence, although the SPC did not specify clearly in its judgment, it can be inferred that such experimental evidence should not be considered from the context of the judgment and previous cases regarding whether it is allowed to consider experimental evidence submitted after the filing date in the assessment of inventive step. The reason is that most of this type of experimental evidence is to prove that the technical solution claimed by the patent application can be carried out, a task that the patent applicant should have completed by the filing date.

Of course, where the experimental evidence submitted after the filing date is to prove that by the filling date the patent applicant has accomplished the task for demonstrating that the technical solution can be carried out, but only failed to recite it in the patent description, it is reasonable to accept such evidence if its qualification is admissible.

Chapter 18
Definiteness of Claims

Claims are a critical part of the patent application documents, indicating the scope of protection that the applicant wants to obtain for the patent. Claims shall define clearly the claimed scope of protection, which is expressly provided both in the *Patent Law* of China[1] and the U.S. *Consolidated Patent Laws*.[2] The *America Invents Act,* para. 2 of 35 U.S.C. §112 provides: "The specification shall conclude with one or more claims particularly pointing out and distinctly claiming the subject matter which the applicant regards as his invention." It is a provision that not only can be invoked by the examiner during the patent examination process for a rejection decision but also can be relied on by the court or the PTO to determine a claim as invalid in patent confirmation.

In practice, the definiteness of a claim is often disputable. Most disputes concern factual issues. Disputes of legal significance are rare or have yet to appear. After studying all the cases involving the definiteness of claims in the U.S. Court of Appeals for the Federal Circuit (hereinafter referred to as the CAFC) from 2001 to 2013, the author concluded that the issue the worthiest of the discussion focused on whether an identical standard of the definiteness of claims should be followed in the patent granting, patent confirmation, and patent infringement procedures. The following will discuss this issue in conjunction with the study of the U.S. CAFC cases.

---

[1] Article 26(4) of the *Patent Law* provides: the claims shall be supported by the description shall define the extent of the patent protection sought for in a clear and concise manner.

[2] Paragraph 2 of 35 U.S.C. §112 provides: The specifications shall conclude with one or more claims particularly pointing out and distinctly claiming the subject matter which the applicant regards as his invention.

18.1 Legislative Intent

The U.S. Supreme Court explained the legislative intent of this provision in the case of *Permutit v. Graver Corp.*[3] in 1931: "The statute requires the patentee not only to explain the principle of his apparatus and to describe it in such terms that any person skilled in the art to which it appertains may construct and use it after the expiration of the patent, but also to inform the public during the life of the patent of the limits of the monopoly asserted, so that it may be known which features may be safely used or manufactured without a license and which may not." That is to say, indefinite claims will not be able to delineate the boundaries of the patentee's rights for the public, nor will they inform the public whether their conduct constitutes infringements. Moreover, if patentees are allowed to write ambiguous claims, this practice will encourage more patentees to follow suit because ambiguous claims will force competitors to expand their safety distance from the patentees' scope of rights, enlarging the scope of protection of patent rights,[4] which is not conducive to promoting innovation and scientific development.

Therefore, the statutory requirement that "claims be definite" mainly serves two purposes: first, ensuring that a person skilled in the art can understand and practice the teaching of the invention; second, encouraging enterprises to engage in invention and creation by requiring the certainty of the scope of patent protection,[5] in order to avoid the patentee being granted a scope so unreasonably large that the interests of the public are harmed, other inventors' interest in further experimentation and invention being dampened due to their inability to demarcate the boundaries of the patent rights accurately, and the possibility and risk of litigation being increased because competitors interpret the boundaries of unclear protection scope inappropriately.[6]

---

[3] 284 U.S. 52, 60 (1931).

[4] General Elec. Co. v. Wabash Appliance Corp., 304 U.S. 364, 369 (1938).

[5] 317 U.S. 228, 55 U.S.P.Q. (BNA) 381, (1942). "The statutory requirement of particularity and distinctness in claims is met only when they clearly distinguish what is claimed from what went before in the art and clearly circumscribe what is foreclosed from future enterprise. A zone of uncertainty which enterprise and experimentation may enter only at the risk of infringement claims would discourage invention only a little less than unequivocal foreclosure of the field. Moreover, the claims must be reasonably [clear-cut] to enable courts to determine whether novelty and invention are genuine."

[6] Athletic Alts, Inc. v. Prince Mfg., Inc., 73 F.3d 1573, 1581 (Fed. Cir. 1996).

18.2 The Standard for Determining the Definiteness of Claims

The CAFC is currently adopting the mainstream "insolubly ambiguous" standard to assess whether a claim is definite. As explained by the CAFC in the case of *Exxon Research and Engineering Co. v. United States*,[7] "we have not insisted that claims be plain on their face in order to avoid condemnation for indefiniteness; rather, what we have asked is that the claims be amenable to construction, however difficult that task may be." A claim is found indefinite only when "a claim is insolubly ambiguous, and no narrowing construction can properly be adopted" Difficulty in claim construction does not warrant the determination of indefinite claims.

One of the reasons why the CAFC upholds this view is that it believes that a claim shall be presumed valid under 35 U.S.C. §282 of the *America Invents Act*. Another reason is, as the CAFC explained in *Funai Electric Co. v. Daewoo Electronics Corp.*[8]: due to the strict rules imposed on patent applications, the terminology of claims cannot always be expressed in the most pleasant and direct language. More specifically, first, the law specifically requires a claim to be restricted to a single sentence, no matter how complex the invention is. This can lead to awkward phrasing. Second, claim content is burdened by tradition. Third, although patents are written for persons knowledgeable in the field of the invention, the draftsman knows that, ultimately, the patent must survive the legal scrutiny of lay judges and juries. Therefore, an "awkward" claim is not indefinite if a person skilled in the art to which the invention pertains can understand it, according to the patent documents.

Applying the "insolubly ambiguous" standard means it is difficult for the court to agree with the reasons for indefinite claims. According to statistics, the CAFC heard 48 cases involving indefinite claims from 1998 to 2008, among which 32 cases were found definite by the court, and only 16 cases were found indefinite. Most of the indefiniteness cases centered around "means-plus-function" claims.[9] From 2009 to 2013, 15 cases involved whether the claims were definite, and only one was held to be indefinite. None of the remaining cases were considered "difficult to explain."

18.3 Determining the Definiteness of Claims

Since the CAFC has always been adhering to the "insolubly ambiguous" standard to determine the definiteness of claims, the specific rules that the CAFC applies exhibit the following characteristics: (1) definiteness of claims is determined based on the knowledge and ability of a person skilled in the art as of the filing date; (2) the

---

[7] 265 F. 3d 1371, 1375 (Fed. Cir. 2001).
[8] 616 F. 3d 1357, 96 U.S.P.Q. 2d (BNA) 1329 (Fed. Cir. 2010).
[9] "A Definite Claim on Claim Indefiniteness: An Empirical Study of Definiteness Cases of the Past Decade with a Focus on the Federal Circuit and the Insolubly Ambiguous Standard," 10-CHI.-Kent J. Intell. Prop., 25 (2010).

method to determine the definiteness of claims is essentially the same as the method for claim construction; (3) the methods to determine the definiteness of claims are not distinguished regardless of whether the patent is granted or not.

1. As of the Filing Date

The definiteness of claims is determined from the perspective of a person skilled in the art as of the filing date. However, patents and publications after the filing date can be used to construe claims.[10]

2. Adoption of the Claim Construction Method

The definiteness of claims is determined from the perspective of a person skilled in the art in the context of the specification and the knowledge of the relevant art.

Proof of indefiniteness must meet "an exacting standard." "A patent claim is not indefinite merely because parties disagree concerning its construction; an accused infringer must thus demonstrate by clear and convincing evidence that one of ordinary skill in the relevant art could not discern the boundaries of the claim based on the claim language, the specification, the prosecution history, and the knowledge in the relevant art."[11] This shows that the CAFC's method for determining the definiteness of claims is essentially the same as the method of claim construction.

(1) Claim Language

A claim is a technical solution composed of some technical features. Examining whether a particular technical feature is clear shall consider the entire claim. The other features in the claim related to this technical feature shall be examined first. For instance, in *Marley Mouldings Ltd. v. Mikron Industries, Inc.*,[12] the CAFC construed the meaning of the disputed term based on other features of the claim. The disputed term in the claims of the patent at issue is "in parts (volume)." The District Court held that the term referred to the proportional volumetric quantity of one material component to all other components within a given formulation. The means to calculate the percent volume of wood flour, a critical determination to discern whether the final product had been produced by the claimed process and necessary to the practice of the invention, was not specified in the patent and could not be discerned by the specification. This signifies that the claims were indefinite. The CAFC reversed this finding of the District Court and held that the definiteness requirement for patentability was satisfied if a person skilled in the field of the invention would reasonably understand the claim when read in the context of specification. In this case, in accordance with the recitation in claim 1, the minimum amount of wood flour in the first stage of the claimed process was 11.1% by volume (15 parts of 135 total parts). They

---

[10] U.S. Steel Corp. v. Phillips Petroleum Co., 865 F.2d 1247, 1251, 9 U.S.P.Q. 2d (BNA) 1461, 1464 (Fed. Cir. 1989); In re Glass, 492 F. 2d 1228, 1232, 181 U.S.P.Q. (BNA) 31, 34 (C. C. P. A. 1974).

[11] Haemonetis Corp. v. Baxter Healthcare Corp., 607 F.3d 776, 783.

[12] 417 F. 3d 1356, 75 U.S.P.Q.2d (BNA) 1954 (Fed. Cir. 2005).

agreed that the minimum amount of wood flour for the second stage was 10.7% by volume (15 parts of 140 total parts). It can be seen that the meaning of the term "in parts (volume)" can be ascertained. The District Court erred in this fact. It was not impossible to construe the term "in parts (volume)" in the claim.

(2) Specification

As a part of the patent application documents, the specification is the thesaurus for the patentee. It is an essential basis not only for claim construction but also for determining the definiteness of claims. A claim is not indefinite simply because it is hard to understand when viewed without benefit of the specification.[13] In contrast, a claim is indefinite if it is impossible to determine the scope of this claim because the content of the specification conflicts with the subject matter of the claim.[14] Furthermore, to make the claims meet the definiteness requirements, how specific the specification should be depends on the specific circumstance of the invention and the state of the prior art.[15]

In the case of *Wellman, Inc. v. Eastman, Chemical Co.*,[16] Wellman holds two patents, both of which relate to slow-crystallizing polyethylene terephthalate (PET) resins for use in plastic beverage containers. The slow-crystallizing PET possesses a significantly higher heating crystallization exotherm peak temperature (T_{CH}) than conventional PET resins, making it have exceptional clarity and reduce haze. T_{CH} is measured by a differential scanning calorimetry (DSC) machine. In order to ensure the consistency of the measurement results, the instrument requires accurate sample conditions and test parameters. The District Court declared the Wellman patent invalid for indefiniteness on the grounds that the patent at issue did not provide sufficient guidance for construing the T_{CH} claim term. The CAFC first examined the specification and found there was sufficient information in the claims to interpret the term T_{CH} in the claims as the test required for amorphous raw materials. Wellman's expert also testified that "less than four percent crystallinity" would typically be referred to as an amorphous PET material by people in the PET industry. Moreover, although the terms of the claims do not clearly recite the humidity conditions determined by DSC, a person skilled in the art will be aware and will also use well-known industrial standards for the measurement of DSC, i.e., use the specified humidity and thermal history conditions. Since a person skilled in the art will be able to interpret the claims following the specifications and well-known international standards, the CAFC concluded that the District Court's determination that the claims were indefinite was incorrect.

---

[13] S3, Inc. v. Nvidia Corp., 259 F.3d 1364, 1369 (2001).

[14] In re Cohn, 438 F.2d 989, 993, 169 U.S.P.Q. (BNA) 95, 98 (C.C.P.A. 1971) (rejecting claims as indefinite upon a finding of an inconsistency between the claims).

[15] Polymer Indus. Prods Co. v. Bridgestone/Firestone, Inc., 10 F. App'x 812, 817 (Fed. Cir. 2001) (quoting Shatterproof Glass Corp. v. Libbey-Owens Ford. Co., 758 F.2d 613, 225 U.S.P.Q. (BNA) 634, 641 (Fed. Cir. 1985).

[16] 642 F.3d 1355, 98 U.S.P.Q.2d (BNA) 1505 (Fed. Cir. 2011), cert. Denied, No. 11-584, 2012 WL 538344 (U.S. Feb. 21, 2012).

(3) Prosecution History

Prosecution history refers to all the documents with which the applicant and the examiner communicate on the patent application during the patent examination process, including the Office Action, the patent applicant's response, the evidence submitted, etc. The discussion between the examiner and the patent applicant on a particular technical feature, especially the observations provided by the patent applicant on the meaning of the technical feature and its difference from the prior art, constitutes the basis for the interpretation of the technical feature as well as the determination of the definiteness of it.

The case of *All Dental Prodx v. Advantage Dental Products*[17] relates to a method for making a custom dental impression tray, the disputed phrase in the claim being "original unidentified mass." The CAFC believed that although the contested language was not a model of clarity, it was capable of being understood by a person skilled in the art in the context of the patent specification. In addition, the prosecution history could be relied upon to clarify the meaning of this phrase. The patentee had made it clear twice in the examination process that his invention was distinguishable over the prior art on the basis of the limitation of this phrase. Therefore, according to the prosecution history, the phrase "original unidentified mass" should be construed as a mass that did not have specific preformed size and shape, and the claims should be considered definite.

In another case, *Howmedica Osteonics Corp. v. Tranquil Prospects, Ltd.*,[18] the CAFC also discussed the clarification of the prosecution history on the meaning of claim language. This case involved two patents relating to an intramedullary prosthesis apparatus used for the replacement of a ball of the hip joint and surgical orthopedic implantation of an intramedullary prosthesis. The two patents have identical written descriptions. The claims require that the "transverse sectional dimensions" of the apparatus constitute specific percentages of the "transverse sectional dimensions" of the medullary canal. The District Court found that although a "transverse section" was a slice taken perpendicular to the vertical axis of the bone, it was unclear whether the word "dimensions" referred to the diameter of this transverse section and thus, the term "transverse sectional dimensions" rendered the claim indefinite.

The CAFC reversed this judgment. The reasons are: (1) One of ordinary skill in the art would readily ascertain from the written description of the patents that the "transverse sectional dimension" called for a two-dimensional measurement; given the choice between a construction of "transverse sectional dimensions" that would require a relatively loose fit and a construction that would require a much tighter fit, and a snug fit of the prosthesis is needed in the medullary canal, sufficient information in the specification shows that one of skill in the art would readily understand and adopt the latter construction. (2) A two-dimensional measurement provided the snug fit that was the centerpiece of this invention. Therefore, it was self-evident that the "transverse-sectional dimensions" meant cross-sectional areas. (3) This construction

---

[17] 309 F.3d 774, 776-77 64 U.S.P.Q.2d (BNA) 1945, 1946-47 (Fed. Cir. 2002).
[18] 401 F.3d 1367, 74 U.S.P.Q. 2d (BNA) 1680 (Fed. Cir. 2005).

18.3 Determining the Definiteness of Claims

also found support in numerous references in the prosecution history. These references occurred during a reexamination proceeding. Thus, these references did not directly address the definiteness requirement of claims—an assessment relevant to the time of filing. Nonetheless, a person skilled in the art would know that these references were relevant to the meaning of the claims on the filing date of the patent application and could be relied on to construe the meaning of the terms on the filing date of the patent application. For the preceding reasons, the CAFC reversed the District Court's judgment that the claims were indefinite.

However, claim language and the specification generally carry greater weight than the prosecution history in claim construction. In the case of *HTC Corp. v. IPCom GmbH & Co., KG*,[19] the CAFC mentioned that "the prosecution history represents an ongoing negotiation between the U.S. Patent and Trademark Office (hereinafter referred to as USPTO) and the applicant. It often lacks the clarity of the specification." Therefore, if the content mentioned by the applicant in the prosecution process is inconsistent with the claims and specification, the content of the claims and specification shall prevail. The applicant's statement in the prosecution history should not be overemphasized.

(4) Knowledge and Ability of a Person Skilled in the Art

A person skilled in the art is a fundamental concept in patent law, running through the patent examination and infringement judgment processes. When determining whether a claim is definite, it is also necessary to view it from the perspective of a person skilled in the art.

In the case of *Star Scientific, Inc. v. R. J. Reynolds Tobacco Co.*,[20] the CAFC reversed the District Court's decision that the claims were indefinite. The patent of Star relates to a method of treating tobacco to maximumly reduce the content of, or prevent the formation of, nitrosamines (TSNAs, a known carcinogen) which are normally found in tobacco. Tobacco curing is generally performed using diesel gas or propane gas heaters. The combustion gases can create an anaerobic environment which can lead to the formation of TSNAs.

The Star's patents disclose a "controlled environment" that controls at least one of the following factors: humidity, temperature, rate of temperature change, airflow, arrangement of the tobacco leaves, and CO level and/or CO_2 level and/or O_2 level, to prevent the creation of an anaerobic condition and to reduce or prevent the formation of TSNAs. The accused infringer R.J. Reynolds Tobacco Co. (RJR) argued the Star's patents were indefinite because one of ordinary skill would be unable to determine the difference between conventional processes and the "controlled environment" required by the patents at issue. The jury agreed with RJR's conclusion that the "controlled environment" was indefinite but for a different reason. The jury believed the term "controlled environment" was indefinite because the patents did not give exact numbers measuring humidity, temperature, and airflow.

---

[19] 667 F.3d 1270 (Fed. Cir. 2012).
[20] 655 F.3d 1364, 99 U.S.P.Q.2d (BNA) 1924 (Fed. Cir. 2011).

The CAFC believed that the issue of this case was "whether a person of ordinary skill would know how to establish a controlled environment to perform the claimed method." The CAFC noticed that the "controlled environment" described herein referred to "conventional methods commonly and commercially used in the U.S." In that context, the term "controlled environment" in the Star's patents fell well within the bounds of ordinary skill in the art. Although specific measuring numbers or numerical range were not disclosed in the patent, the term "controlled environment" was not insolubly ambiguous and was not indefinite.[21]

(5) Consideration of Both Intrinsic and Extrinsic Evidence

Both intrinsic evidence (claim language, description, and prosecution history) and extrinsic evidence (technical dictionaries, textbooks, etc.) shall be considered in claim construction. Similarly, both shall also be considered in the determination of the definiteness of claims, and neither shall be ignored.

The case of *Datamize, LLC v. Plumtree Software, Inc.*[22] is a good case in point. The issue in this case was whether the term "aesthetically pleasing" in the claims was indefinite. The CAFC addressed this issue as follows: first, under para. 2 of 35 U.S.C. §112, a claim is definite if the claim delineates the scope of the invention using language that adequately notifies the public of the patentee's right to exclude. Then, (the CAFC) defined the plain meaning of "aesthetically pleasing" to include "having beauty that gives pleasure or enjoyment" and "beautiful." Next, the CAFC pointed out that the term should be construed in light of the intrinsic evidence:

① Language of Claim 1: "Claim 1 does not suggest or provide any meaningful definition for the phrase 'aesthetically pleasing' itself. Merely understanding that this term relates to the look and feel of interface screens fails to provide one of ordinary skill in the art with any way to determine whether the aggregate layout of elements on interface screens is 'aesthetically pleasing' or whether an interface screen is 'aesthetically pleasing.' The patentee had not identified any objective standard for determining whether or not the interface screen was "aesthetically pleasing." Such an objective standard was important to ensure that the claims delineated the scope of protection that adequately notified the public. Without an objective standard, the phrase "aesthetically pleasing" was entirely subjective.

② Specification: The written description indicated that there were "good standards of aesthetics" but did not set forth an objective way to determine whether an interface screen was "aesthetically pleasing." There was no indication, however,

---

[21] Judge Dyk dissented. He believed that Star's patents did not equate the "controlled environment" to conventional curing methods; thus, one of skill in the art would not be able to determine the "controlled environment" by relying on the knowledge of conventional curing processes. Star's patents described the claimed "controlled environment" as something different from conventional curing methods, but failed to explain those differences in a way that would permit a skilled artisan to determine the bounds of the claims.

[22] 655 F.3d 1364, 99 U.S.P.Q.2d (BNA) 1924 (Fed. Cir. 2011).

18.3 Determining the Definiteness of Claims

other than by referring to the considered opinions of aesthetic design specialists, database specialists, and academic studies on public access systems and user preferences and problems, how to determine what button styles, sizes, and placements, for example, were "aesthetically pleasing."

The CAFC next consulted the extrinsic evidence in the record. "Even the expert could not determine whether the look and feel of particular interface screens are 'aesthetically pleasing' using the parameters he specified. Instead, this evidently testified that whether an interface screen is 'aesthetically pleasing' is a multidimensional question that is not amenable to a single-word answer. That is to say, 'aesthetically pleasing' could not precisely delineate the boundaries of the claim and is indefinite."

3. Being Granted is not Required

The CAFC determines the definiteness of claims using the claim construction method without considering whether the patent is granted or not, i.e., the definiteness of claims is determined by the claim construction method regardless of whether the patent is in examination or is granted. For example, in the case of *Standard Oil Co. v. American Cyanamid Co.*[23] the CAFC believed that "the descriptive part of the specification aids in ascertaining the scope and meaning of the claims inasmuch as the words of the claims must be based upon the description. The specification is, thus, the primary basis for construing the claims." Similarly, in the case of *In re Marosi*,[24] the CAFC believed that "general guidelines are disclosed in the specification for determining the meaning of the term in the claim, i.e., a method for synthesizing zeolites 'essentially free of alkali metal.'".

4. Notes for Determining the Definiteness of Claims

Through the research on all the cases concerning the definiteness of claims reviewed by the CAFC from 2001 to 2013, the author found that it depended on the technical field and the specific circumstance of the case whether the same term in different claims would cause indefiniteness. Moreover, a broad scope of a claim does not necessarily mean it is indefinite; similarly, multiple meanings of a claim do not necessarily render it indefinite.

(1) The Definiteness of Claims Varies in Different Fields

Claim language should describe the invention clearly. The criterion for determining the definiteness of claims is whether a person skilled in the art can perceive the clear meaning from the seemingly vague language. Some seemingly vague terms, such as "substantially equal to," "close proximity," etc. may be definite if they can be interpreted as an operable or distinguishable difference by a person skilled in the art.[25]

---

[23] 774 F.2d 452, 227 U.S.P.Q.2d 293 (1985).

[24] 710 F.2d 799, 228 U.S.P.Q.2d 289 (1983).

[25] Rosemount, Inc. v. Beckman Indus., 727 F.2d 1540, 1546-47 (1984). Translator's note: The correct title of the case should be: Rosemount, Inc. v. Beckman Instruments, Inc.

Whether a term in a claim is definite may depend on the case's technical field or specific circumstances. For example, in the case of *Exxon Eng'g & Res. Corp. v U.S.*,[26] the CAFC believed that the term "to increase substantially" in the claim was definite, whereas in *Verve, LLC v. Crane Cams, Inc.*,[27] the CAFC held that while the term "substantially" may notice a person skilled in the art of how to satisfy a patent claim in some cases, in this case, judging from the intrinsic record as a whole, the term was indefinite.

(2) A Broad Scope Does not Equate to an Indefinite Scope

The breadth of the scope of claims is a concept completely different from the definiteness of claims. The former examines the scope of protection that the claims can cover, while the latter relates to the literal expression of the claims. A broad scope of the claimed invention does not mean the indefiniteness of claims.

In the case of *Ultimax Cement Mfg. Corp. v. CTS Cement Mfg. Corp.*,[28] the patent relates to a high-strength cement containing a special crystalline compound (referred to as "crystal X" in the specification) and a compound with both fluorine and chlorine needed to be present, which does not exist in nature. The claim defines crystal X with a complex formula encompassing over 5000 possible combinations. The District Court found the claim to be indefinite because (1) the formula for crystal X was too broad; (2) the other recited compound lacked a comma between "f" and "cl" ("F Cl"), indicating that both fluorine and chlorine needed to be present in the claimed compound.

The CAFC did not agree with the District Court on these two reasons. It explained that "merely claiming broadly does not render a patent claim insolubly ambiguous, nor does it prevent the public from understanding the scope of the patent." In this case, first, although the crystalline compound had a complex structure and covered a broad scope, it was not insolubly ambiguous because a person of ordinary skill in the art could determine whether his or her conduct fell within the scope defined by this formula. Second, for the comma between "f" and "cl," although courts could not rewrite claims to correct material errors, a court could correct an obvious, undisputed typographical error based on the understanding of a person of ordinary skill in the art after reading the claims, specification, and prosecution history. The District Court had determined that the claimed formula with both fluorine and chlorine needed to be present corresponded to no known mineral and that one of ordinary skill in the

---

[26] 265 F.3d 1371 (2001). This case relates to a method for converting natural gas into liquid hydrocarbon products, which includes the term "for a period sufficient to increase substantially the initial catalyst productivity." The CAFC believed that the specification defined "substantially increased" as an increase of at least about 30% and illustrated properly how to calculate the increase in catalyst productivity through examples. And the specification also disclosed how long was a sufficient period. Besides, both parties agreed that the "period sufficient" could be measured by conducting activity checks. Therefore, the CAFC concluded that "when a word of degree is used, (the District Court) must determine whether the patent's specification provides some standard for measuring that degree."

[27] 60 U.S.P.Q.2d 1219, 1221 (2001).

[28] 587 F.3d 1339, 1352 92 U.S.P.Q.2d (BNA) 1865, 1873 (Fed. Cir. 2009).

art would know that the formula should contain a comma. In such a circumstance, the claimed formula was not indefinite.

The CAFC reached a similar conclusion in the case of *Smith Kline Beecham Corp. v. Apotex Corp.*,[29] i.e., "the test for indefiniteness does not depend on a potential infringer's ability to ascertain the nature of its own accused product to determine infringement, but instead on whether the claim delineates to a skilled artisan the bounds of the invention." Breadth is not indefiniteness. Therefore, even if a claim is broad enough to embrace undetectable trace amounts of the claimed invention, it cannot be determined that the claim is indefinite.

(3) A Claim with Multiple Meanings is not Necessarily Indefinite

The requirement that claims be definite aims to notify the public of the boundaries of the patent rights. In this sense, the public may not know what activity constitutes an infringement of the patent if a claim has multiple meanings, and therefore, the claim may not be definite. However, multiple meanings of a claim do not necessarily mean that a claim is indefinite. It all boils down to whether a person skilled in the art can determine the term's appropriate meaning.

Microprocessor Enhancement Corp. v. Texas Instruments, Inc.[30] is a good case in point to illustrate this issue. The patent in this case is directed to computer processor architecture and methods for increasing microprocessor efficiency. Claim 1 claims a method for executing instructions in a pipelined processor, and claim 7 claims a pipelined processor for executing instructions. The District Court held that these two claims were insolubly ambiguous on the grounds that (1) the claims required that a single word be interpreted differently in different portions of a single claim; (2) both claims impermissibly mixed two distinct classes of patentable subject matter (e.g., claim a method and a product simultaneously).

The CAFC disagreed with neither of the above two reasons. For the first reason, although the disputed term could have had one of two meanings, the appropriate meaning was readily apparent from each occurrence in context. Meanwhile, although generally, a single claim term should be construed consistently in all the claims of this patent, the patentee's mere use of the term "said" with an antecedent did not require that both terms have the same meaning. As for the second reason, although claim 1 purported to describe a method and an apparatus for executing said instructions, the description of the apparatus actually described a component in a preamble rather than claiming this component independently. Therefore, claim 1 was definite and had a clear scope of protection covering a method in a pipelined processor possessing the requisite structure. Similarly, claim 7 only covered an apparatus using functional language. On the one hand, functional language in a means-plus-function format was authorized by statute. On the other hand, claim 7 was clearly limited to an apparatus possessing a specific structure capable of performing specific functions and thus was not indefinite. Therefore, the CAFC reversed the District Court's finding of the indefiniteness of the claim.

---

[29] 403 F.3d 1331, 74 U.S.P.Q.2d (BNA) 1398 (Fed. Cir. 2005).
[30] 520 F.3d 1367, 86 U.S.P.Q.2d (BNA) 1225 (Fed. Cir. 2008).

18.4 Circumstances in Which the Issue of Indefinite Claims Arises

A panoramic view of all the cases concluded by the CAFC from 2001 to 2013 relating to the definiteness of claims shows that the disputes over the definiteness of claims mostly center on, for example, whether the subject matter of the claim was definite, whether the means-plus-function claims were definite, whether using words of degree in the claims would cause an indefinite protection scope of the claims and whether errors occurred in the granting process at the patent office would cause the indefiniteness of claims.

1. The Subject Matter of Claims

A claim shall distinctly point out the subject matter, either a product or a process. A single claim that claims both a product and the process of using the apparatus is indefinite because it fails to provide the public with an accurate determination of the metes and bounds of protection involved.

In the case of *IPXL Holdings, L.L.C. v. Amazon.com, Inc.*,[31] the patent relates to an electronic financial transaction system. Claim 25 recites: "the system of claim 2…wherein the predicted transaction information comprises both a transaction type and transaction parameters associated with that transaction type, and the user uses the input means to either change the predicted transaction information or accept the displayed transaction type and transaction parameters." The CAFC found that claim 25 was indefinite as it attempted to claim both a system and a method for using that system. The reason was "it is unclear whether infringement of claim 25 occurs when one creates a system that allows the user to change the predicted transaction information or accept the displayed transaction, or whether infringement occurs when the user actually uses the input means to change transaction information or uses the input means to accept a displayed transaction. Because claim 25 recites both a system and the method for using that system, it does not apprise a person of ordinary skill in the art of its scope, and it is invalid under §112, paragraph 2."

To determine whether the subject matter of a claim is to protect an apparatus or method steps, or both, one should not just look at the words in the claim but rather consider the claim, the specification, and the prosecution history as a whole.

In the case of *HTC Corp. v. IPCom GmbH & Co., KG*,[32] the IPCom patent covers a handover in a cellular telephone network. A handover occurs when a cellular telephone—called a "mobile station"—switches from one tower—called a "base station"—to another. The claims recited the functions to achieve the "handover." The District Court concluded that IPCom's claims were indefinite because they claimed both an apparatus and method steps. The CAFC reversed this judgment because the District Court misconstrued the claims. The reasons were: (1) The District Court did not adequately examine the claims. The claim recited six enumerated functions as

---

[31] 430 F.3d 1377 (Fed. Cir. 2005).
[32] 667 F.3d 1270 (Fed. Cir. 2012).

the functional structures for the network in the independent claim, meaning that they were not method steps. (2) The District Court should have referred to the specification to understand the claims. The specification confirmed that the network performed the six enumerated functions rather than the base station. (3) Although the applicant referred to the word "process" in the prosecution history, the District Court placed too much weight on the applicant's use of the word "process" when the claim language and the specification indicated that the applicant did not claim a process. Since the prosecution history represented an ongoing negotiation between the USPTO and the applicant, it often lacked the clarity of the specification and thus carried less weight in claim construction.

2. Means-Plus-Function Claims

Means-plus-function claims are the type of claims that are most likely to give rise to the issue of the definiteness of claims in practice and the most probable to be found by the CAFC as indefinite in such cases.

(1) Development of Means-Plus-Function Claims

Claims usually include two types of features: structural features and functional features. Structural features indicate "what it is," and functional features indicate "what it does." Compared with structural features, the scope of functional features is much broader, including any structure that can achieve this function.

In the early U.S. patent system, functional language was prohibited in claims. In 1946, in the case of *Halliburton Oil Well Cementing Co. v. Walker*,[33] the U.S. Supreme Court considered functional language as a technique for drafting broad claims and declared that the claim expressed as "means ...for ...to ..." invalid. Partly influenced by this case, the amendment of the *America Invents Act* in 1952 added the current §112 (f): An element in a claim for a combination may be expressed as a means or step for performing a specified function without the recital of structure, material, or acts in support thereof, and such claim shall be construed to cover the corresponding structure, material, or acts described in the specification and equivalents thereof.

The clause is very broad in appearance. However, judging from the mainstream interpretation of this clause in practice, since the "combination" feature is mentioned here, a single means claim that covers every conceivable means for achieving the stated result is not allowed. For example, in the case of *In re Hyatt*,[34] the CAFC believed that a claim which included "an apparatus to retain one element on another including a means of attaching the first element to the second" was purely functional and should be rendered invalid.

(2) The Definiteness Requirement of Means-Plus-Function Claims

For a means-plus-function claim to satisfy the definiteness requirement, the specification must disclose sufficient information to indicate what the limitation means,

---

[33] 329 U.S. 1 (1946).
[34] 708 F.2d 712-713 (Fed. Cir. 1985).

i.e., to disclose the corresponding structure fully. Whether the written description adequately sets forth the structure corresponding to the claimed function must be considered from the perspective that "the written description must clearly link or associate structure to the claimed function."[35] Moreover, how much structure shall be disclosed to make the means-plus-function claims definite is determined based on the specific circumstance of the field of art.[36]

The case of *Aristocrat Technologies Australia PTY Ltd. v. International Game Technology*[37] that the CAFC concluded in 2008 relates to the definiteness of means-plus-function claims. The patent in this case is directed to an electronic slot machine that allows a player to select winning combinations of symbol positions. The disputed claim includes the terms: "control means" and "game control means." The patentee acknowledged that the only portion of the specification that described the structure corresponding to the functions performed by the "control means" was the statement that it was within the capability of a worker in the art "to introduce the methodology on any standard microprocessor basic gaming machine by means of appropriate programming."

The CAFC believed such a description was insufficient disclosure of the necessary structure and did not meet the requirement of 35 U.S.C. §112. The reasons were as follows: The specification should disclose a structure rather than merely a general-purpose computer or microprocessor for means-plus-function claims. For a patentee to claim a means for performing a particular function and then to disclose only a general-purpose computer as the structure designed to perform that function amounted to pure functional claiming. The so-called corresponding structure to perform the function was not "the general-purpose computer or microprocessor, but rather the special-purpose computer programmed to perform the disclosed algorithm."

The patent at issue recited a "standard microprocessor" and "appropriate programming," which is insufficient disclosure of structure for means-plus-function purposes. The specification disclosed merely a general-purpose computer. Although "the patentee was not required to produce a listing of source code or a highly detailed description of the algorithm to be used," it was required, however, the patentee at least disclose the algorithm that "transforms the general-purpose microprocessor to a special-purpose computer" to satisfy the structural requirement of means-plus-function claims. The patent at issue did not disclose that, and the District Court held correctly that the claim was indefinite.

Two other cases reached similar conclusions in 2008. One is *Finisar Corp. v. The DirecTV Group, Inc.*[38] and the other is *Net MoneyIN, Inc. v. Versign, Inc.*[39] In both

---

[35] Telcordia Technologies., Inc. v. Cisco Systems, Inc., 612 F.3d 1365, 95 U.S.P.Q.2d (BNA) 1673 (Fed. Cir. 2010).

[36] Intel Corp. v. VIA Technologies, Inc., 319 F.3d 1357, 65 U.S.P.Q.2d (BNA) 1934 (Fed. Cir. 2003).

[37] 521 F.3d 1328, 86 U.S.P.Q.2d (BNA) 1235 (Fed. Cir. 2008).

[38] 523 F.3d 1323, 86 U.S.P.Q.2d (BNA) 1609 (Fed. Cir. 2008).

[39] 545 F.3d 1359, 88 U.S.P.Q.2d (BNA) 1751 (Fed. Cir. 2008).

cases, the CAFC believed that the patents at issue failed to disclose the corresponding structures of the claimed functions.

3. Functional Language Other Than Means-Plus-Functions

In addition to the means-plus-function claims under 35 U.S.C. §112, in practice, some other functional language, such as "what it does" rather than "what it is," is also likely to cause the claims to be indefinite.

For example, in the case of *Halliburton Energy Services, Inc. v. M-I LLC*,[40] the CAFC affirmed the District Court's holding that the claims were indefinite. The patent in this case relates to a method for conducting a drilling operation. The claims include the term "fragile gel." Halliburton asserted that this term referred to a gel that (1) quickly transitioned to a liquid state upon the introduction of force (e.g. when drilling started) and returned to a gel when the force was removed (e.g. when drilling stopped); and was capable of suspending drill cuttings and weighting materials.

Regarding this, the CAFC believed that (1) The fact that there was a definition of "fragile gel" in the specification did not end the inquiry. What mattered most was that a person of ordinary skill in the art could translate it into a meaningfully precise claim scope. Even if a claim term's definition could be reduced to words, the claim was still indefinite if a person of ordinary skill in the art could not translate the definition into a meaningfully precise claim scope. (2) The patent at issue did not adequately distinguish the fragileness of the invention from disclosed prior art, i.e., how quickly the gel must transition to a liquid when force was applied and how quickly it must return to a gel when the force was removed. Neither did the patent at issue recite how strong the gel must be (i.e., gel strength). (3) In a specific well, various factors could affect liquid-gel transition or gel strength (formation geology, wellbore size, depth, angle, etc.). An artisan would not know from one well to the next whether a particular drilling fluid was within the scope of the claims. (4) When a construction proposed by the patentee required that an artisan make a separate infringement determination for every set of circumstances in which the composition might be used, and when such determinations were likely to result in differing outcomes (sometimes infringing and sometimes not), that construction was likely to be indefinite. (5) The definition of "fragile gel" in the patent at issue was functional, i.e., the fluid was defined by "what it does" rather than "what it is." It was risky to use only functional claim limitations to distinguish the claimed invention from the prior art. Although a claim was not necessarily indefinite using functional language, the use of functional language could fail to provide a clear-cut indication of the scope of the subject matter embraced by the claim and thus could be indefinite. It was for these reasons that the definition of "fragile gel" in this patent at issue could not be adequately construed to render the claims definite. The CAFC affirmed the District Court's holding that the claims were indefinite.

In contrast, in the case of *Hearing Components, Inc. v. Shure Inc.*,[41] the CAFC believed that the term "readily" was definite. The patent at issue relates to an ear

---

[40] 514 F.3d 1244, 85 U.S.P.Q.2d (BNA) 1654 (Fed. Cir. 2008).
[41] 600 F.3d 1357, 94 U.S.P.Q.2d (BNA) 1385 (Fed. Cir. 2010).

piece component that requires a device having a structure "being readily installed and replaced by a user." The District Court found the "readily installed" phrase indefinite. The CAFC reversed this holding, explaining that not all functional terms were indefinite. What mattered most was determining "whether the patent's specification supplies some standard for measuring the scope of the phrase." The written description of the patent at issue states that one of the advantages of the patent is that it "requires no tools for installation or removal." Meanwhile, persons wearing hearing aids were often advanced in years and unable either to see clearly enough or to perform fine physical actions well enough to replace the filters. These facts showed that the patent at issue could be distinguished from the prior art which was relatively difficult to remove or replace, and thus, the claim was definite.

4. Terms of Degree in Claims

Generally speaking, terms of degree, such as "near," "far," "more," "less," "about," etc. tend to be vague because there is no fixed benchmark for comparison. However, it does not mean that using such degree terms is absolutely prohibited in claims. Instead, the key is whether a person skilled in the art can distinguish the scope of the claims from the prior art and whether the public knows what activity constitutes infringement.

In the case of *Young v. Lumenis, Inc.*,[42] the patent at issue is directed to a surgical method for removing a claw from a domesticated cat. The claim includes a step that begins "by making a circumferential incision in the epidermis of the ungual crest." The District Court held that the term "near" was indefinite because it failed to distinguish the invention from the prior art and did not permit a person of ordinary skill to know what activity constituted an infringement. The CAFC reversed this finding on the ground that from the illustration and the references of measurement, a person of ordinary skill in the art could understand the meaning of "near" and define the term reasonably and meaningfully.

In another case *Enzo Biochem, Inc. v. Applera Corp.*,[43] the CAFC once again was confronted with the definiteness of words of degree. The patents at issue are directed to techniques for labeling and detecting nucleic acids, such as DNA and RNA. The claims include the term "not interfering substantially." The CAFC believed that even though there was no reference to "precise numerical measurement" in the patent, the description and prosecution history "provide(d) at least some" guidance as to the scope of the claim. Therefore, the use of this term did not render the claims indefinite.

5. Product-by-Process Claims

Product claims are usually defined by the structure and composition features of the product. When a product is defined by the preparation method or parameters, the indefiniteness of claims is likely to arise regarding whether the claims can distinguish the invention from the prior art, whether the public knows the boundaries of the patent right, etc.

---

[42] 492 F.3d 1336, 83 U.S.P.Q.2d (BNA) 1191 (Fed. Cir. 2007).
[43] 599 F.3d 1325, 94 U.S.P.Q.2d (BNA) 1321 (Fed. Cir. 2010).

In the case of *Amgen Inc. v. F. Hoffmann-La Roche, Ltd.*,[44] Roche contended that no skilled artisan knew the amino acid sequence of human EPO at the time of the invention. Moreover, the claims appeared to fail to distinguish the (claimed product) from the (product) of the prior art in terms of properties and structures, and thus, the source limitation in the claims at issue was indefinite.

The CAFC did not support this contention of Roche. It believed that in those situations in which the differences between the claimed product and the product of the prior art were not particularly susceptible to the definition by the recitation of structures, the product-by-process format allowed the patentee to obtain a patent on the product even though the patentee could not adequately describe the features that distinguished it from prior art products. Thus, to call the process limitation indefinite in this situation would defeat the purpose of product-by-process claims.

6. Errors Made by the Patent Office in Patent Granting

During the patent examination and granting process, due to the reasons attributable to the patent applicant or the examiner, there may be specific problems in the printed patent documents, resulting in the indefinite protection scope of the claims. Will these problems cause the claims to be declared invalid for indefiniteness? The CAFC seems to delineate a boundary in the following three cases.

The first case is *Group One Ltd. v. Hallmark Cards, Inc.*[45] The patent at issue claims a device of curling ribbon. During the prosecution of the patent, the applicant made an amendment to add a limitation. However, a printing error by the PTO resulted in the omission of the emphasized language from the claims. The District Court held that it lacked the authority to correct the error. The CAFC agreed. It believed that while the PTO could correct the error under 35 U.S.C. §254, Group One had failed to seek correction from the PTO. The District Court could correct errors retroactively, but it could correct an error only if the error was evident from the face of the patent. The error in this case was not as described above because even if the missing language was required to be added by the examiner as a condition for issuance, one could not discern what language was missing simply by reading the patent. The missing language was essential to the validity of the patent, and the patentee had made no claim that the omitted language was not essential to validity. Thus, the CAFC affirmed the District Court's determination that the patent was invalid for the indefiniteness of claims.

Hoffer v. Microsoft Corp.[46] is a similar case. The issue of this case was whether an error in dependency of a claim would result in the indefiniteness of this claim. The disputed claim 22 should have been dependent from claim 21, but as written, it was dependent from claim 38. The District Court found that in preparation for printing, the examiner renumbered the claim but did not make the corresponding change in the text of the claim. The patentee never contended that "the PTO was responsible for the error." In this circumstance, the District Court stated that it was powerless to correct

---

[44] 580 F.3d 1340, 92 U.S.P.Q.2d (BNA) 1289 (Fed. Cir. 2009).
[45] 407 F.3d 1297, 74 U.S.P.Q.2d (BNA) 1759 (Fed. Cir. 2005).
[46] 405 F.3d 1326, 74 U.S.P.Q.2d (BNA) 1481 (Fed. Cir. 2005).

the error of claim 22. It is worth noticing that the patentee obtained a certificate of correction in accordance with 35 U.S.C. §254 after this action was filed. The CAFC believed that absent evidence of culpability or intent to deceive by delaying formal correction, a patent should not be invalidated based on an obvious administrative error. When a harmless error in a patent was not subject to reasonable debate by both parties could be corrected by the court. Based on this ground, the CAFC reversed the District Court's holding of indefiniteness of claim 22.

As can be seen from the above two cases, the CAFC's view on the errors in the PTO's examination process seems to be: on the one hand, examine whether the error is apparent from the face of the patent and on the other hand, examine the party's subjective attitude, i.e., whether the patentee actively seeks corrective relief from the PTO.

As to whether a court can correct an error in a patent by interpretation without the patentee seeking or obtaining a certificate of correction, the CAFC explained this issue in the case of *Novo Indus. Inc. v. Micro Molds Corp.*,[47] which it concluded in 2003. The patent is directed to a carrier structure for a vertical blind assembly. The claim includes a feature: "stop means formed on a rotatable with said support finger and extending outwardly therefrom into engaging relation with one of two spaced apart stop members formed on said frame." The term "a rotatable with" did not appear in the original application. Novo argued that this was an obvious typographical error that could be corrected. The District Court construed the word "a" to mean "and" rather than "one" and found the claim indefinite.

The CAFC found that Novo never sought or obtained a certificate of correction pursuant to 35 U.S.C. §254 from the Patent and Trademark Office ("PTO"). Thus, the issue in this case lay in whether a District Court could act to correct an error in a patent by interpretation of the patent where no certificate of correction had been issued.

The CAFC analyzed as follows: first, nothing in the enactment of either §254 and §255 of 35 U.S.C. suggested that Congress intended to deny limited correction authority to the District Courts. However, "before the correction becomes effective, the patent must be considered without the benefit of the certificate of correction." Second, the District Court had no authority to "correct any and all errors that the PTO would be authorized to correct under §254 and §255." To allow the District Court to correct such errors under §254 and §255, it always would apply its own corrections retroactively in the action before it, unlike certificates of correction issued by the PTO, which applied only in actions brought after the certificate of correction was issued. Therefore, a District Court could correct a patent only if "(1) the correction was not subject to reasonable debate based on consideration of the claim language and the specification and (2) the prosecution history did not suggest a different interpretation of the claims." Finally, in this case, Novo had suggested two different corrections, i.e., deletion of the words "a rotatable with" or deletion of the words "with said." Moreover, the interpretation by the District Court, which changed the word "a" to "and," raised still a third possibility. For the preceding reasons, the CAFC believed

---

[47] 350. F.3d 1348,1353, 69 U.S.P.Q.2d (BNA) 1128, 1131 (Fed. Cir. 2003).

that "since we cannot know what correction is necessarily appropriate or how the claim should be interpreted, we must hold the claim invalid for indefiniteness in its present form."

18.5 Lessons from the American Rules for Determining the Definiteness of Claims for the State Intellectual Property Office of the People's Republic of China

In a nutshell, for the determination of the definiteness of claims, the mainstream opinion reflected in the CAFC cases demonstrates the following characteristics: (1) adoption of the "insolubly ambiguous" standard; (2) The definiteness of claims is determined by the same method as in claim construction; (3) The same rules and standards are adopted for both patent applications and granted patents.

There are certain advantages of adopting such a rule to determine the definiteness of claims in practice. For example, claim drafting defects can be cured to a certain extent, avoiding failure of a patent grant of an invention due to merely drafting errors, which is beneficial to those inventions to be protected that genuinely contribute to society. In addition, adopting a unified standard for the understanding of claims in the patent granting, patent confirmation, and patent infringement procedures is also conducive to the stability of patent rights to a certain extent and to respecting the notice function of the entire patent document.

However, this rule will lead to some problems if it is applied in China because, under this rule, the same rule and standard are adopted in the determination of the definiteness of claims regardless of whether the patent is in a patent granting procedure, patent confirmation procedure or patent infringement procedure. For example, a patent applicant/patentee may put so much weight on the specification to construe claims that he/she may ignore the accuracy and precision of generalizing and expressing the claims, which will, to a certain extent, shift claim construction further toward the principle of central limitation. In addition, the rule may further increase the circumstances in which claim construction is required in actual cases, as well as the likelihood that different explanations regarding the same issue may occur due to different courts or different judges, or even worsening the problem of different judgments of similar cases, proliferating litigation and making it hard for upper-level courts to unify the standard of judgment.

The author believes that, currently in China, the standards for determining the definiteness of claims should vary between the patent granting procedure and patent confirmation and patent infringement procedures. In a patent granting procedure, more focus should be placed on the expression of the claim to avoid applying the "insolubly ambiguous" rule, whereas in patent confirmation and patent infringement procedures, the so-called "insolubly ambiguous" rule in the U.S. may be used for reference. A claim is indefinite only when it is difficult to resolve ambiguities based on the specification and/or the prosecution history.

Firstly, this view is based on the essential difference between the patent granting procedure and patent confirmation and patent infringement procedures in terms of nature and responsibilities. In a patent granting procedure, the examiner examines whether the invention-creation in the claims is qualified to be granted a patent based on the patent application documents submitted by the applicant. In a patent confirmation procedure, the Patent Reexamination Board reexamines whether the patent was properly granted at the request of the invalidation petitioner. In a patent infringement procedure, the People's Court determines whether the alleged infringing technical solution falls into the protection scope of the patent.

In a patent granting procedure, the examiner faces an unauthorized patent application. The examiner's task is to examine the patent application documents submitted by the applicant to ensure that the scope of protection to be granted is clear, and patent rights are as stable as possible to avoid granting defective patents. Therefore, the examiner's examination should focus on claims in a patent granting procedure. If the examiner finds that the claims do not clearly delineate the boundaries of the scope of rights to properly notify the public of the scope of protection of the claims, an Office Action should be issued to notify the applicant to amend or clarify the claims. If the applicant amends the claims or clarifies the ambiguities to answer the examiner's questions and overcome the defect of indefiniteness, then indefiniteness is no longer an issue.

On the contrary, if the applicant refuses to amend the claims or the clarification fails to dispel the examiner's doubts, the examiner may refuse to grant the patent right on the grounds of indefiniteness. Even if the examiner believes that the claim can be clarified relying on the specification, however, if the applicant does not clarify or amend the claims or the applicant's interpretation of the claims is inconsistent with the examiner's understanding, it is also reasonable for the examiner to refuse to grant the patent for indefiniteness in order to grant stable rights with clear boundaries.

In a patent confirmation procedure, the examiner faces the rights that have been granted and solidified. The examiner's task is to reexamine whether the patent granting is appropriate based on the arguments and evidence provided by the invalidation petitioner. Therefore, on the one hand, if the claim does not meet the definiteness requirements and the patent rights should not have been granted, the Patent Reexamination Board may declare it invalid under Article 26(4) of the *Patent Law*. On the other hand, if the claim has minor drafting defects and can be defined clearly relying on the specification or common knowledge in the art, and if the public can clearly discern the scope of protection of patent rights based on their understanding of the overall content of patent documents, the claim is definite because it can be construed definitely. Compared with declaring invalidation of the claims, this result is more beneficial for balancing the interests between the patentee and the public and more conducive to maintaining the stability of the granted patent.

In a patent infringement procedure, the judge faces a patent that has been granted and published. The judge's task is to determine whether the alleged infringing technical solution falls within the scope of protection of the patent right. Under the "dual" patent system in China, the validity of the patent right shall be determined by

18.5 Lessons from the American Rules for Determining the Definiteness ...

the Patent Reexamination Board, and a patent is presumed valid before the Patent Reexamination Board decides to declare the patent right invalid.

Based on this basic principle, a judge shall employ every method and means to construe a claim, even if it is determined indefinite in the infringement determination process, to avoid declaring the patent invalid for indefiniteness of claims. In principle, if the "dual" system is strictly followed, if a judge considers that a claim is indefinite, he shall suspend the adjudication on a patent infringement case until the invalidation decision of the Patent Reexamination Board is made. If the alleged infringer does not file an invalidation petition or before the Patent Reexamination Board makes an invalidation decision, the judge shall construe the claim no matter how indefinite it is. The "insolubly ambiguous" standard adopted in the American "unitary" system shall not be applied here.

In practice, although strictly following the "dual" system has certain legal rationality, it is not very reasonable to reach a conclusion of infringement based on an indefinite claim that should not have been granted. Therefore, the author agrees with the view of the SPC in the case of *Min Shen Zi No. 1544 (2012)* that "defining the protection scope of a patent right accurately is a prerequisite for determining whether the alleged infringing technical solution constitutes infringement. For patent rights whose scope of protection is obviously unclear, the accused infringing technical solution should not be determined as constituting an infringement." In fact, the rule adopted in this case was the "insolubly ambiguous" rule.

Secondly, this view is based on the requirement for different amendment standards of patent application documents/patent documents in patent granting, patent confirmation, and patent infringement procedures. The extent to which a patent applicant/patentee is allowed to amend the application documents/patent documents is gradually limited from the patent granting procedure the patent confirmation procedure and to the patent infringement procedure.

In a patent granting procedure, a patent applicant can amend claims to overcome the indefiniteness defect pointed out by the examiner or discovered by the patent applicant in almost any way as long as the amendment does not go beyond the scope of the original application documents. In contrast, in a patent confirmation procedure, the extent to which the patentee is allowed to amend claims is minimal. In particular, the claims cannot be amended by extracting features from the specification and adding them to the claims. Indefiniteness defects cannot be overcome by amending the claims even if the recitation in the specification is definite. The patentee has no right to amend the claims in a patent infringement procedure. To overcome the same defect, the extent to which a patentee is allowed to amend the patent application documents shall be inversely proportional to the extent to which the claim is allowed to be construed or explained. The greater the extent of allowable amendments, the smaller the extent of allowable construction; on the contrary, the smaller the extent of allowable amendments, the greater the extent of allowable construction.

In sum, for the definiteness of claims, only by adopting different standards in different procedures can the interests of the patentee and the public be genuinely balanced to promote the healthy development of the patent system.

Chapter 19
Amendments Beyond Scope

Article 33 of the *Patent Law* has been very controversial in the industry in recent years. The SPC alone has expressed its opinion in a number of cases on the legislative intent, meaning and interpretation of Article 33 of the *Patent Law*. The relevant judgments demonstrate that even within the SPC, the criteria applied to determine whether the amendment is beyond the scope are not exactly the same. For example, in the cases *(2011) Zhi Xing Zi No. 17*, *(2011) Zhi Xing Zi No. 62*, *(2011) Zhi Xing Zi No. 85* and *(2011) Zhi Xing Zi No. 54*, the SPC endorsed the criterion of "direct and undoubted determination" in the *Guidelines for Patent Examination*, but in the case *(2010) Zhi Xing Zi No. 53*, the SPC advocated the criterion of "direct and explicit deduction that is also obvious"; in 2013, in the case *(2013) Xing Ti Zi No. 21*, though the SPC returned to the "direct and ascertainable" criterion, it also advanced the theory that the amendment to the "point of novelty" should be distinguished from that of the "contents other than point of novelty."

In the light of these judgments and the highlighted relevant views, the author believes that the following issues need to be resolved with respect to the criteria for determining amendments beyond scope: (1) the legislative intent or purpose of Article 33 of the *Patent Law*; (2) the understanding of "the scope of the original description and claims", i.e., the feasibility of "the theory of determination" and "the theory of support" in legal theory and practice on the basis of the criteria for determining amendments beyond scope; (3) the feasibility or possible problems to distinguish the amendment to the "point of novelty" from that to the "contents other than point of novelty" on the basis of the criteria for determining amendments beyond scope; (4) the necessity to set up a special "response procedure" for the amendments to post-grant "contents other than point of novelty" to remedy the loss of rights caused by drafting or response errors.

19.1 The Legislative Intent of Article 33 of the *Patent Law*

Regarding the legislative intent of Article 33 of the *Patent Law*, the SPC expounded explicitly in both the case *(2010) Zhi Xing Zi No. 53* and the case *(2013) Xing Ti Zi No. 21* that "the legislative intent of Article 33 of the *Patent Law* is to strike a balance between the rights and interests of the patent applicant and those of the public, so that on the one hand, the applicant has the opportunity to amend and correct the patent application documents, ensuring as much as possible that truly inventive invention-creations can be granted a patent and protected; on the other hand, it prevents the applicant from obtaining illegitimate rights and interests from the content of the invention that was not disclosed at the date of filing, which will undermine the public's reliance on the original patent application documents."[1]

There is no controversy in the industry as to the legislative intent. What is controversial concerns the understanding of "the amendment shall not exceed the scope of the original description and claims" in Article 33 of the *Patent Law*.

---

[1] In the case *(2010) Zhi Xing Zi No. 53*, the SPC held that "Article 33 of the Patent Law contains two meanings, one is to allow the applicant to amend the patent application documents, and the other is to limit the amendments of the patent application documents. The reasons why the applicant is allowed to amend the patent application documents are that, first, limitations on the applicant's expression and cognitive ability. In the process of expressing abstract inventive contemplation in words, and generalizing them into specific technical solutions, due to the limitation of language, there are inevitably defects of sloppy wording or inaccurate expression. Moreover, when drafting the patent application documents, the applicant may misunderstand the invention-creation because of his or her limited knowledge of prior art and the invention-creation. In the process of patent application, as the understanding of prior art and invention-creation improves, especially after the examiner issues the Notification of an Office Action, the applicant often needs to amend the claims and the description based on his or her new understanding of the invention-creation and prior art. Second, the amendments are required in order to improve the quality of patent application documents. Since patent application documents are important vehicles for delivering patent information to the public, in order to facilitate the public's understanding and use of invention-creation and to promote the application and spreading of invention-creation, it is objectively necessary to improve the accuracy of patent application documents through amendments. While allowing the applicant to amend the patent application documents, Article 33 of the Patent Law also limits the amendments of patent application documents, i.e., the amendments of patent application documents for inventions and utility models shall not exceed the scope recited in the original description and claims. Reasons for this limitation are that, firstly, by limiting the amendments to the scope of the original description and claims, it can encourage the applicant to disclose the invention sufficiently at the application stage so that the granting procedures can be carried out smoothly. Secondly, it is to prevent the applicant from subsequently adding to the patent application documents the invention that was not completed at the date of filing and from which the applicant may improperly obtain the rights and interests of first-to-file, so as to ensure the implementation of the first-to-file principle. Thirdly, it is to safeguard the public's confidence in patent information and avoid unnecessary damage to third parties who rely on the original application documents to take actions accordingly."

19.2 How to Understand "The Scope of the Original Description and Claims"

The two different judgments of the SPC represent different understandings of "the scope of the original description and claims." The SPC held in the case *(2010) Zhi Xing Zi No. 53* that "the scope of the original description and claims should include the following: first, the contents clearly expressed in words or figures in the original description, drawings and claims; second, the contents that can be directly and undoubtedly deduced by a person having ordinary skill in the art by combining the original description, drawings and claims. The contents are within the scope of the original description and claims as long as the deduced contents are obvious to a person having ordinary skill in the art." However, in the case *(2013) Xing Ti Zi No. 21*, the SPC held that "'the scope of the original description and claims' shall be interpreted as all the information of the invention-creation disclosed in the original description and claims, a fixture of all the information of this invention-creation, which is not only the cornerstone of the first-to-file system, but also the objective basis for the subsequent stages of the patent application." Concretely speaking, "the scope of the original description and claims" can be the contents directly recited in words and figures in the original description, drawings and claims, as well as the contents that can be determined by a person having ordinary skill in the art based on the original description, drawings and claims.

1. The Differences and Similarities of "The Theory of Support" and "The Theory of Determination with Technical Information"

The two expressions above, although only different in wording, reflect two completely different views and values in the context of the two cases. The case *(2012) Zhi Xing Zi No. 53* maintains "the theory of support" (hereinafter referred to as Viewpoint 1), which allows the amendment to extend to what obviously can be "directly and undoubtedly deduced" by a person having ordinary skill in the art on the basis of the original application documents; the case *(2013) Xing Ti Zi No. 21*, adheres to the "the theory of determination with technical information" (hereinafter referred to as Viewpoint 2), which allows the amendment to extend to what can be "determined" by a person skilled in the art on the basis of the original application documents. The similarities and differences between the two points of view can be briefly illustrated by the following case.

Assuming that for a technical feature, the original application document recites three options a1, a2 and a3. During the examination, the examiner points out that feature a3 is not clear, and for this reason the patent applicant only amends feature a3, and leaves the other features unamended, as shown in Table 19.1.

Table 19.1 shows that Viewpoint 1 and Viewpoint 2 are identical as far as the amendment to what is impliedly disclosed in the original application document is concerned. They differ in that Viewpoint 1 allows the amendment to include the obvious equivalent at the filing date, while Viewpoint 2 does not. The essence of this difference lies in the following two aspects: (1) Can the obvious equivalent before

Table 19.1 Comparison of the allowed amendment between "the theory of support" and "the theory of determination with technical information"

The original description	The original claims	The amendments (only to the claims)	Viewpoint 1	Viewpoint 2
a1, a2, a3	a1, a2, a3	Amendment 1: A	✓	×
		Amendment 2: a1, a2, a4	✓	×
		Amendment 3: a1, a2, a3′	✓	✓

Note The amendments to A and a4 in Amendment 1 and Amendment 2 can be deduced directly and undoubtedly from the original application documents, and it is obvious that, all the subordinate methods (including a4) in superordinate concept A can solve the corresponding technical problem; a3′ in Amendment 3 is implied in the original application documents

the filing date be included in the scope of protection by applying the doctrine of equivalents in the process of determining a patent infringement? (2) Who should bear the adverse consequences of the applicant's drafting errors?

2. Analysis of "The Theory of Support" and "The Theory of Determination with Technical Information" Under the Doctrine of Equivalents

In theory, the doctrine of equivalents is relied on to solve the problem that the emergence of obvious equivalents brought by technological development after the filing date may cause the technical solutions of the patent proposed at the filing date many years ago failing to be protected properly, rather than remedying the applicant's drafting errors. In principle, the applicant should have sufficient knowledge of the obvious equivalents before the filing date when drafting the application documents, and should include these obvious equivalents in the scope of patent protection by listing them in the application documents, especially in an overview manner. If the applicant knew or should have known of the existence of these obvious equivalents before the filing date, but did not explicitly recite them in the application documents, it seems to imply that the applicant does not subjectively want to protect them, in this case, the dedication rule shall be applied in the same way as the applicant reciting certain technical solutions in the description but not in the claims, rendering these obvious equivalents dedicated by the applicant to all mankind. This is a mainstream view in the industry for applying the doctrine of equivalents, i.e., the obvious equivalents before the filing date cannot be included in the scope of protection by applying the doctrine of equivalents when determining the patent infringement. This also means that the applicant should bear the adverse consequences resulted from his or her drafting errors which cannot be remedied by applying the doctrine of equivalents after the patent is granted.

Under this theory, it is clear that under the rule of Viewpoint 1, the technical solutions that should not have been protected due to drafting errors will be included in the scope of protection by amending the patent document, while under the rule of

19.2 How to Understand "The Scope of the Original Description and Claims"

Viewpoint 2, it is the applicant who should bear the risk and adverse consequences caused by drafting errors.

Of course, it should be taken into account that this theory imposes very high requirements on the drafting of application documents. It has only been thirty years since the *Patent Law* was enacted in China, and although in recent years, with the promotion of the *Outline of the National Intellectual Property Strategy*, the public's awareness of patent protection has been improved to a certain extent, the contradiction between the rapid improvement of protection awareness and the relative lack of protection ability has become more and more intensified, in particular, the ability and skills of applicants or agents to draft application documents still have great room for improvement, leading to many cases in which invention-creation are not properly protected due to drafting. In this context, the strict application of the above theory may affect the realization of the purpose of the *Patent Law* which is to "encourage invention-creation", thus a reasonable compromise and adaptation by the administrative organs and judicial organs without violating the basic legal principles may be the primary issue to be considered at this stage.

Viewpoint 1 is indeed a way to solve this problem by giving the applicant an opportunity to include obvious equivalents not recited in the application documents before the filing date into the protection scope during the patent examination. However, two problems ensue: first, technical solutions that were originally infringements under the doctrine of equivalents may become literal infringements after the amendments of the patent application documents; second, the patent rights may be unduly protected if the doctrine of equivalents is allowed to be applied to this technical feature in the determination of an infringement.

To adopt Viewpoint 2 does not necessarily mean that excessive penalties will be imposed on the patent applicant for drafting errors, as some people fear. On the contrary, the biggest advantage of adopting Viewpoint 2 is that it ensures the technical information in the amended application document is consistent with that in the original application document; on this basis, if the application of the doctrine of equivalents is extended from the obvious equivalents brought about by technological development after the filing date to the equivalents both before and after the filing date, the loss of rights brought about by improper drafting can be saved. In addition, such adaption will neither interfere with the basic legal principles, turning technical solutions from infringements under the doctrine of equivalents into literal infringements; nor is it necessary in practice to distinguish the equivalents before the filing date from new ones after the filing date, making it more brief and clearer for both the patentee and the judge to determine this matter.

In conclusion, the author believes that the scope of "the original description and claims" in Viewpoint 2 is understood as all the information of the invention-creation presented in the original description and claims, which is more reasonable both in theory and in practice.

19.3 Distinction Between "Point of Novelty" Amendments and "Contents Other Than Point of Novelty" Amendments

As stated by the SPC in the case *(2013) Xing Ti Zi No. 21*, "Generally speaking, a technical solution contains several technical features, among which the technical feature that embodies the invention-creation's contribution to the prior art is usually referred to as the "point of novelty." The "point of novelty" endows the invention-creation novelty and inventive step in relation to the prior art and is the basis and fundamental reason for an invention-creation to be granted patent rights. In practice, it is true that the applicant may make amendments both to the "point of novelty" and the "contents other than point of novelty." It seems that if the same criteria are applied to both of them, it may be difficult for the entire invention-creation to be patented because the amendment to the "contents other than point of novelty" in the patent application document exceeds the scope of the original application document, which seems to make the benefits obtained by the patent applicant incommensurate with his or her contribution to society and is also contrary to substantive fairness. However, the author believes that both in legal theory and in practice, there are huge obstacles and difficulties in distinguishing the "point of novelty" from "contents other than point of novelty" based on the criteria of determining amendments beyond scope, and the end result of a deliberate distinction will only lead to a greater degree of unfairness.

First of all, the so-called "point of novelty" and "contents other than point of novelty" are relative to the closest prior art, the changes of which will lead to the changes or transitions between the "point of novelty" and "contents other than point of novelty." On the one hand, the starting point of prior art based on which the applicant made the invention may not be the real closest prior art, which will cause the "point of novelty" the applicant believed may not be the real "point of novelty"; on the other hand, the search of prior art documents cannot be exhausted, and the closest prior art retrieved by the examiner in the substantive examination process may probably be overturned in the invalidation process, resulting in great changes in the "point of novelty" at different stages. In such a circumstance, adopting different criteria to determine the amendments beyond scope regarding "point of novelty" and "contents other than point of novelty" will possibly make a once-permitted amendment disallowed due to a change in the closest prior art, or make a once-not-permitted amendment subsequently overruled due to a new closest prior art. Such fluctuations will complicate the "fact-finding" issue of amendments beyond scope.

Second, as discussed previously, "the scope of the original description and claims" should be understood as all the information of the invention-creation presented in the original description and claims, and a person having ordinary skill in the art will make the judgment in conjunction with his or her common knowledge in the art to determine the full picture of the information rather than simply relying on the amount of information that are recited in the original application documents. Moreover, by adjusting the application rules of the doctrine of equivalents, it is fully possible to make up for the drafting errors of "contents other than point of novelty", and the obvious equivalents that are not recited in the application documents can be remedied by the application of the doctrine of equivalents.

Therefore, it is meaningless to distinguish between features of "point of novelty" and "contents other than point of novelty" in the criteria of the determination of the amendments beyond scope, which will only make the practice more complicated and the end result more subjective.

19.4 Post-grant Remedial Procedures for "Contents Other Than Point of Novelty" Amendments Errors

As to the remedial procedures for "contents other than point of novelty" amendments, the SPC suggested in the case *(2013) Xing Ti Zi No. 21* that "a corresponding response procedure may be considered to be set up in the administrative review process of patent granting and patent confirmation, which allows the patent applicant and the patentee to renounce the amendment that does not comply with Article 33 of the *Patent Law* and to restore the documents of patent application and grant of patent right to the original status at the date of filing", so as to "prevent truly inventive invention-creation from losing the patent rights that should have been granted and that are commensurate with the contribution to the prior art due to amendments of 'contents other than point of novelty' beyond the scope of the original description and claims, promoting scientific and technological progress and innovation, and maximizing the capability of science and technology to support and lead economic and social development."

The above suggestion is reasonable to some extent, however, a variety of factors need to be considered in the design of the procedure, such as the purpose of setting up the procedure, details about how the procedure works, how the procedure works with other related procedures, and the impact on the overall effectiveness of the examination and granting process. In addition, it is also necessary to consider the differences between pre-grant and post-grant reliefs in terms of the nature.

1. The Feasibility of Setting up a Pre-grant "Response Procedure"

A patent application undergoes preliminary and/or substantive examination, and even reexamination before it is granted. If the applicant's amendment to the application document is deemed to be beyond the scope of the original application document, whether it is an "point of novelty" or a "contents other than point of novelty" amendment, the examiner will issue a Notification of an Office Action. Under the current *Guidelines for Patent Examination*, the applicant has at least two opportunities to state opinions or resubmit an amendment to the same amendment in the preliminary and/or substantive examination procedures; even if the application is rejected and proceeds to the reexamination procedure, the applicant has at least two opportunities to amend the application again to overcome the defect of the amendment beyond scope when filing a request for reexamination and responding to the Notification of Reexamination issued by the panel.

Patent examination and granting is a procedure for the administrative organ empowered by the state to exercise administrative functions. Striking a balance between fairness and efficiency is a factor that must be considered when the administrative organ conducts specific administrative actions. Neither efficiency can be sacrificed for fairness without limitation, nor fairness can be sacrificed for efficiency. The *Guidelines for Patent Examination* provides that before a rejection decision is made, the patent applicant is generally given at least two opportunities to defend against the same defect, which reflects the consideration of both fairness and efficiency.

In the case where the Notification of an Office Action has clearly informed the applicant that the amendment of a certain feature cannot be determined from the original application document with specific and sufficient reasons, if in addition to the above four opportunities for amendments, a "response procedure" is set up for the amendments to "contents other than point of novelty" that are beyond the scope, on the one hand, the function of the procedure would overlap with that of the preliminary examination and/or substantive examination, leading to lengthy procedures; on the other hand, it would also mislead the applicant into paying inadequate attention to the response to the Notification of an Office Action or the Notification of Reexamination, which will objectively prolong the whole examination and granting process and reduce the efficiency of the examination and granting. In addition, if the application has a real prospect of being granted, the problem can be solved by adding one more Notification of an Office Action or accepting the amendment to the "contents other than point of novelty" initiated by the applicant, rather than having to set up the so-called "response procedure."

Therefore, it is not necessary to set up a "response procedure" for pre-grant patent applications to remedy the defect of amendments to "contents other than point of novelty" that are beyond the scope. In practice, the examination policy can guide examiners to make a case-by-case analysis to strike a balance between "promotion of scientific and technological progress and innovation" and administrative efficiency.

2. The Feasibility of Setting up a Post-grant "Response Procedure"

China implements a substantive examination system for invention patents and a preliminary examination system for utility model and design patents. After a patent is granted, anyone (including the patentee) who believes that the grant of the patent right does not comply with the relevant provisions of the *Patent Law* may correct this improper granting only through initiating the invalidation procedure. Therefore, if the granted patent has the defect of amendment beyond scope, whether it is an amendment to "point of novelty" or to "contents other than point of novelty", only the invalidation procedure can be initiated, and there is only one result, i.e., the patent right is declared invalid.

In fact, this problem exists not only in amendments to "contents other than point of novelty", but also in other substantive granting conditions, including claims that are too broad, claims that are unclear, and even novelty and inventive step. For example,

19.4 Post-grant Remedial Procedures for "Contents Other Than Point ...

for the case of utility models, since only a preliminary examination is conducted, the applicant generally does not receive doubt about novelty and inventive step during the examination. However, when a patent is granted, assuming that the patentee submits a request to the Patent Office for a patent right evaluation report and receives an evaluation conclusion that some of the claims lack novelty or inventive step, or have defects such as amendment beyond the scope, the patentee can only resolve the problem of improper granting by initiating the invalidation procedure on his/her own or passively waiting for others to initiate the invalidation procedure so as to amend the claims; even so, the scope of relief for drafting errors is very limited due to the many restrictions on post-grant patent document amendments, and the results are basically unfavorable to the patentee. Therefore, how to remedy the patentee's mistakes in a diversified manner through procedural design is one of the key points to be considered in planning the system.

The post-grant procedures have been diversified in many countries. For example, in order to relieve judicial pressure, the U.S. is constantly adjusting the post-grant procedures, and the main procedures currently in force include: correction procedure, reissue procedure, ex parte reexamination procedure, inter partes reexamination procedure, and covered business method review,[2] etc. These different procedures have different tasks and provide different types of parties with diverse options for administrative rights. Among them, when a mistake of a clerical or typographical nature, or of minor character is discovered in a granted patent, the patentee or patent assignee may request, or the USPTO may initiate on its own, the correction procedure to correct a non-substantive error in the patent[3]; when a claim that may be invalidated or a partially substantive error is discovered in a granted patent, the patentee may initiate the disclaimer procedure[4] or reissue procedure[5]; any person (including the patentee) may initiate the ex parte reexamination procedure[6] to challenge the novelty or inventive step by reference to the patent or prior art in the public publication category, or the public (excluding the patentee) may initiate the patent confirmation[7] or inter partes reexamination procedure[8] to challenge the validity of the patent right in its entirety, depending on the specific time period after the grant.

There are also various post-grant procedures in Japan, mainly including the trial for correction procedure,[9] the patent opposition procedure,[10] and the patent invalidation

---

[2] Translator's note: Covered business method review was replaced by The Transitional Program Covered Business Method (TPCMB) patents on September 16, 2012. The program will sunset for new TPCBM petitions on September 16, 2020.
[3] Articles 254–256 of the current *U.S. Patent Law*.
[4] Articles 253 of the current *U.S. Patent Law*.
[5] Articles 251–252 of the current *U.S. Patent Law*.
[6] Articles 301–307 of the current *U.S. Patent Law*.
[7] Chapter 30 Articles 301–307 of the current *U.S. Patent Law*.
[8] Chapter 31 Articles 311–318 of the current *U.S. Patent Law*.
[9] Article 126 of the *Patent Act of Japan*.
[10] Articles 113, 118, 120–125 of the *Patent Act of Japan*.

trial procedure.[11] Among them, the trial for correction procedure is a procedure that allows the patentee to remedy the granting errors on his own initiative, and is initiated by the patentee to limit the scope of the claims, correct errors or incorrect translations in the granted text, clarify ambiguities in the claims, and explain the relationship between the claims by reference; the opposition procedure is a procedure for the public to challenge a patent right that does not meet the granting conditions to ascertain the stability of the patent rights as soon as possible, and anyone who believes that a patent should not have been granted may file a request with the Appeals Department of the JPO within six months after the publication of the patent; in contrast, the patent invalidation trial procedure is initiated by interested parties to resolve disputes over the validity of a patent, and is tried by the Appeals Department of the JPO following a "quasi-judicial" procedure.

The invalidation procedure in China, which simultaneously undertakes the multiple tasks of correcting improper granting, amending claims, and resolving disputes between the parties over the validity of patent rights, has been subject to many undeserved controversies in recent years. In this context, especially under the system of preliminary examination for utility model and design patents, a specially designed procedure to correct improper granting (see Chap. 21 of this book), and to improve the stability of patent rights by giving the patentee the opportunity to initiate a simple and effective self-correction procedure to motivate the patentee, may not only solve the imbalance of rights caused by amendments to "contents other than point of novelty" that are beyond scope, but also play a positive role in reducing the pressure of the invalidation procedure and satisfying the needs of different types of parties.

---

[11] The trial for correction procedure and the patent invalidation trial procedure are two types of patent trial procedures in Japan. The Japanese patent trial system also includes other procedures such as the appeals against a rejection (equivalent to the patent reexamination procedure in China). Since the appeals against a rejection is not a post-grant procedure, it will not be discussed further more here. In addition, the patent trial system can also be classified into "ex parte appeals" and "inter partes trials." "Ex parte appeals" refer to trials initiated by a petitioner against the JPO, such as "the trial for correction." "Inter partes trials" refer to trials initiated by the petitioner against the patentee, rather than the JPO, such as the "patent invalidation trial."

Chapter 20
Ex Officio Examination in the Reexamination Procedure

Under the current *Guidelines for Patent Examination*, the reexamination procedure is a relief procedure initiated by the patent applicant who is dissatisfied with the decision of rejection of the application by the Patent Office; meanwhile, it is a continuation of the examination and granting procedure for a patent application. This dual nature determines that the Patent Reexamination Board normally restricts its examination to the grounds and evidence on which the decision of rejection is based, and is not obliged to undertake a comprehensive examination on the patent application. However, the Patent Reexamination Board may conduct *ex officio* examination on other obvious substantive defects than those mentioned in the decision of rejection, so as to improve the quality of the patent granted and avoid unreasonable prolongation of the examination and granting procedure.

20.1 Consensus and Conflicts Between the Patent Reexamination Board and the People's Court

Overall, multiple patent administrative litigation cases show that there is no disagreement between the People's Court and the Patent Reexamination Board regarding the dual nature of the reexamination procedure. The People's Court allows the Patent Reexamination Board to introduce *ex officio* some defects not mentioned in the decision of rejection and perform examination in certain circumstances. For example, in the following circumstances the *ex officio* examinations have been sustained by the People's Court.

(1) After the defects pointed out in the decision of rejection are overcome, the panel introduces *ex officio* previously examined grounds. For example, in the case *(2013) Gao Xing Zhong Zi No. 358*,[1] after the defect that the amendment went beyond the scope pointed out in the decision of rejection was overcome, the panel introduced *ex officio* the grounds for inventive step examined before and upheld the decision of rejection on this ground.

(2) When the patent applicant amends the application document during the reexamination procedure, the panel conducts *ex officio* examination whether the amendment goes beyond the scope, such as in the cases *(2011) Gao Xing Zhong Zi No. 823*[2] and *(2013) Gao Xing Zhong Zi No. 368*.[3]

(3) The panel introduces *ex officio* the grounds closely related to the defect pointed out in the decision of rejection. For example, in the case *(2012) Gao Xing Zhong Zi No. 1573*[4] the panel introduced *ex officio* the grounds for insufficient disclosure to examine the defect that the claims were not supported by the description pointed out in the decision of rejection.

---

[1] In this case, the examiner once issued an office action on inventive step in the substantive examination procedure. The patent applicant amended the application document to overcome this defect. The examiner made a decision of rejection on the ground that the amendment went beyond the scope. In the reexamination procedure, the patent applicant amended the patent application document again and overcame the defect that the amendment went beyond the scope pointed out in the decision of rejection. However, compared with the references cited by the examiner in the substantive examination procedure, the patent application at issue still did not involve an inventive step. Therefore, the panel introduced *ex officio* the grounds for inventive step in the examination and upheld the decision of rejection on this ground. The reexamination decision was upheld by the courts of first and second instance. Both courts believed that the ground examined before the rejection could be introduced in the reexamination procedure.

[2] In this case, the ground for rejection was that the claims lacked of practical applicability. During the reexamination procedure, the panel believed that the amendments of relevant claims went beyond the scope and upheld the decision of rejection by introducing Article 33 of the *Patent Law*. Both the courts of first and second instance upheld the reexamination decision.

[3] In this case, the ground for rejection was that the claims lacked of an inventive step. During the reexamination procedure, the panel believed that the amended patent application document submitted by the patent applicant during the reexamination procedure went beyond the scope, introduced this ground for conducting examination and upheld the decision of rejection for incompliance with Article 33 of the *Patent Law*. Both the courts of first and second instance upheld the reexamination decision. The two courts believed that Article 33 of the *Patent Law* provided for the examination of document in the reexamination procedure and could be introduced by the Patent Reexamination Board *ex officio*.

[4] In this case, the ground for rejection was that the claims were not supported by the description. The lack of sufficient disclosure defect was introduced in the reexamination procedure and the decision of rejection was upheld on this ground. The courts of first and second instance both upheld the reexamination decision on the ground that Article 26(3) of the *Patent Law* was the precondition for determining the compliance with Article 26(4) of the *Patent Law*. The defect under Article 26(3) of the *Patent Law* was an obvious substantive defect.

(4) It will be meaningless or unreasonable to examine the defect pointed out in the decision of rejection if certain defects are not introduced *ex officio* for examination. For example, in the four cases *(2010) Gao Xing Zhong Zi No. 1034*,[5] *(2010) Gao Xing Zhong Zi No. 1129*,[6] *(2011) Gao Xing Zhong Zi No. 473* and *(2011) Zhi Xing Zi No. 68*,[7] the panel conducted examination whether the patent application at issue was patentable subject matter by introducing *ex officio* Article 2(1) and (2) of the *Implementing Regulations of the Patent Law*. In the case *(2011) Gao Xing Zhong Zi No. 625*, the decision of rejection pointed out that the patent application at issue did not involve an inventive step. The collegial panel conducted *ex officio* examination whether the relevant claims were clear.

In practice, the disagreements between the Patent Reexamination Board and the People's Court are mainly reflected in two aspects: first, how much discretion does the Patent Reexamination Board have in conducting *ex officio* examination? Second, are there any prerequisites for the Patent Reexamination Board to perform the *ex officio* examination function?

For the first aspect, the author notices that the biggest difference between the Patent Reexamination Board and the People's Court lies in that the People's Court generally does not agree with the leap from novelty to inventive step examination by the panel in the reexamination procedure, i.e., the examination on inventive step has never been performed before the decision of rejection but the ground for inventive step is introduced *ex officio* in the reexamination procedure. For example, in the case *(2014) Gao Xing Zhong Zi No. 1101*,[8] in the substantive examination procedure, the examiner made the decision of rejection on the grounds that claims 1–3 and 5 lacked novelty and claim 4 lacked an inventive step. During the reexamination

---

[5] In this case, the grounds for rejection were that claims 1 and 3 lacked novelty, and claims 2 and 4 lacked an inventive step. During the reexamination procedure, the panel introduced *ex officio* Article 2(1) of the *Implementing Regulations of the Patent Law* to conduct examination and upheld the decision of rejection accordingly. Both the courts of first and second instance upheld the reexamination decision.

[6] In this case, the ground for rejection was that claims 1–5 were not patentable subject matter under Article 25 of the *Patent Law*. During the reexamination procedure, the panel introduced *ex officio* Article 2(2) of the *Implementing Regulations of the Patent Law* to conduct examination and upheld the decision of rejection accordingly. Both the courts of first and second instance upheld the reexamination decision.

[7] This case and the *case (2011) Gao Xing Zhong Zi No. 473* were related to the same reexamination decision. The ground for rejection was that claims 1–10 were not clear enough to comply with the provisions of Article 20(1) of the *Implementing Regulations of the Patent Law*. During the reexamination procedure, the panel introduced *ex officio* Article 2(2) of the *Implementing Regulations of the Patent Law* to conduct examination and upheld the decision of rejection accordingly. The courts of first and second instance and the SPC all upheld the reexamination decision.

[8] This case related to an invention patent application, application No. 200580019074.9. The grounds for rejection were that claims 1–3 and 5 lacked novelty and that claim 4 lacked an inventive step. During the reexamination procedure, the collegiate panel upheld the decision of rejection on the grounds that claims 1–5 all lacked an inventive step. The court of second instance vacated the reexamination decision and held that the examination order should be followed to determine which grounds were examined before and that claim 5 could never have been examined in any case on the inventive step in previous examinations.

procedure, the petitioner for reexamination deleted claim 2 and amended claims 1–5 to claims 1–4. The Patent Reexamination Board made a reexamination decision (No. FS48402) to uphold the decision of rejection on the grounds that the amended claims 1–4 lacked an inventive step. The first instance judgment *(2013) Yi Zhong Zhi Xing Chu Zi No. 1569* upheld the reexamination decision. The second instance judgment *(2014) Gao Xing Zhong Zi No. 1101* vacated the first instance judgment and the reexamination decision.

The reasons given by the courts are: under the provisions of the *Guidelines for Patent Examination (2001)*, particularly the principle of avoiding the examination level loss and the provisions on the examination order, "in the patent reexamination procedure, in principle, only the grounds and evidence on which the decision of rejection was based shall be reviewed. However, if there are other grounds for a decision of rejection than the grounds that the rejection decision was based on or before the rejection decision was made, the Patent Reexamination Board may introduce *ex officio* the previous grounds for rejection to perform examination, and issue a decision of rejection of the request for reexamination". As inventive step is examined after novelty, the Patent Reexamination Board violated the provisions of the *Guidelines for Patent Examination (2001)* by introducing *ex officio* the causes for inventive step examination, causing an examination level loss to the administrative counterparts and constituting a procedural violation.

Another example is the case *(2014) Zhi Xing Zi No. 2*.[9] During the substantive examination, the examiner issued the First Office Action pointing out that claims 1–11 lacked novelty. After the patent application document was amended, the examiner finally made a decision of rejection on the grounds that claims 1–31 did not comply with Article 33 of the *Patent Law*. During the reexamination procedure, the petitioner for reexamination amended the claims. The panel believed that the amended claims 1–11 lacked novelty and an inventive step, and finally made the reexamination decision No. FS30895 to uphold the decision of rejection on the grounds that the claims 1–11 lacked an inventive step. The first instance judgment *(2011) Yi Zhong Xing Chu Zi No. 2876* and the second instance judgment *(2012) Gao Xing Zhong Zi No. 1486* both vacated the reexamination decision. The Patent Reexamination Board petitioned for a retrial and was rejected by the SPC.

The issue of this case was whether the evaluation of inventive step was an "obvious substantive defect" that the Patent Reexamination Board could introduce *ex officio*. Regarding this, the Patent Reexamination Board argued that in the reexamination procedure, the panel normally examined only the grounds and evidence on which the decision of rejection was based. However, the *Guidelines for Patent Examination* did not prohibit the examination of grounds other than the grounds for the decision of rejection. In this case, a person skilled in the art could determine whether the patent application at issue involves the inventive step without any in-depth investigations. Therefore, this defect was an "obvious substantive defect" that could be introduced *ex officio*.

---

[9] This case related to an invention patent application, application No. 200410047791.X.

20.1 Consensus and Conflicts Between the Patent Reexamination Board ...

The court of first instance held that the "examination of obvious substantive defects" listed in Part I, Chapter 1, Sections 1 and 7 of the *Guidelines for Patent Examination (2001)* did not explicitly include inventive step. Although these provisions were about the preliminary examination of invention patent applications, under Article 53 of the *Implementing Regulations of the Patent Law*, the relevant provisions on "examination of obvious substantive defects" did not include the examination of inventive step. Therefore, the examination of inventive step of the patent application at issue initiated by the Patent Reexamination Board was not the examination of "obvious substantive defects."

The court of second instance held that the preliminary examination and the substantive examination differed in terms of the examination scope, method, and content, which meant the corresponding reexamination procedures must also be different, causing the difference in the scope of the "examination of obvious substantive defects" in the reexamination procedures regarding a decision of rejection in preliminary examination and a decision of rejection in substantive examination. The first instance judgment was without merit in which the scope of the "examination with obvious substantive defects" was delineated in the preliminary examination the same as in the substantive examination of an invention patent. Moreover, the ground for inventive step was not a necessary issue that the Patent Reexamination Board must deal with when examining a decision of rejection. And inventive step could not be determined based on the knowledge and level of a person skilled in the art without in-depth investigations and verifications. Therefore, the inventive step issue introduced by the Patent Reexamination Board was not an "obvious substantive defect." And the Patent Reexamination Board's assertion in the appeal that introducing inventive step could save the time of the patent applicant, and avoid the back-and-forth oscillation of the application between the substantive examination procedure and the reexamination procedure was not sustained and could not be relied on to determine the legality of the reexamination decision.

The SPC held that, first, the "preliminary examination" section of the *Guidelines for Patent Examination* listed various circumstances of "obvious substantive defects", and the evaluation of inventive step was not included. The "substantive examination" section did not provide "obvious substantive defects" specifically. Although the examination scopes in preliminary examination, substantive examination and the examination for reexamination and invalidation should not be exactly the same, the natures of the three types of examination should be the same and the examination scope should be determined on a case-by-case basis in accordance with the natures listed in the "preliminary examination" section. Second, for a person skilled in the art, to evaluate the inventive step of an invention-creation, not only the technical solution of an invention-creation should be considered, but also the technical field to which the invention-creation belongs, the technical problems it solves, and the technical effect it produces should be taken into account. Therefore, it is not appropriate to interpret broadly the "obvious substantive defects" listed in the *Guidelines for Patent Examination* to include inventive step.

For the second aspect, the most representative case was the case *(2013) Gao Xing Zhong Zi No. 902*.[10] In this case, the court of second instance pointed out that although the Patent Reexamination Board's *ex officio* examination in the reexamination procedure "to a certain extent, sacrifices the procedural justice of the applicant's request for reexamination, yet given that the Patent Reexamination Board examines the 'obvious substantive defects,' and keeping in mind the goal of substantive resolution of disputes and taking into account fairness and efficiency, the Patent Reexamination Board's *ex officio* examination of 'obvious substantive defects not mentioned in the rejection decision' can be tolerated in certain procedures… However, the Patent Reexamination Board's *ex officio* examination should be tolerated only to the extent of 'obvious substantive defects not mentioned in the decision of rejection'. As for what 'an obvious substantive defects not mentioned in the decision of rejection' is, there is no explicit provision in the *Guidelines for Patent Examination*.[11]

In the invention patent application examination practice, although it is somewhat reasonable that the Patent Reexamination Board reviews the 'obvious substantive defects not mentioned in the rejection decision,' yet the Patent Reexamination Board indeed is also susceptible to abusing the 'obvious substantive defects not mentioned in the rejection decision'. This is mainly reflected in the increasing number of cases in which the Patent Reexamination Board directly upholds the rejection decision on the basis of the reason not mentioned in the rejection decision without reviewing the request for reexamination first. Moreover, the Patent Reexamination Board tends to interpret 'obvious substantive defects not mentioned in the rejection decision' more and more arbitrarily. Almost all the reasons for the Patent Reexamination Board to arbitrarily modify the rejection decision have been interpreted as 'obvious substantive defects not mentioned in the rejection decision'.

In this circumstance, the 'obvious substantive defects not mentioned in the decision of rejection should be interpreted narrowly, and the Patent Reexamination Board should generally review the 'obvious substantive defects not mentioned in the decision of rejection' only after examining the request for reexamination and determining that the petitioner's request for reexamination is not allowed." This is in fact a new requirement for the Patent Reexamination Board to introduce *ex officio* new grounds in the reexamination procedure.

In addition, in the analysis of patent administrative litigation cases, the author found that the court of second instance might also be inconsistent in the understanding

---

[10] This case related to the invention patent application, application No. 200480043469.8. The ground for rejection was that claims 1–8 did not comply with Article 25 of the Patent Law, and claims 9 and 11 lacked novelty, and claims 10 and 12–17 lacked an inventive step. During the reexamination procedure, the collegial panel upheld the invalidation decision on the ground that claim 1 did not comply with Article 26(4) of the Patent Law. The court of second instance held that the obvious substantive defects should be interpreted restrictively, and that the obvious substantive defects which are introduced *ex officio* should be conducted only after the Patent Reexamination Board examined the request for reexamination and determined that it could not be granted.

[11] Here, in accordance with the views of the SPC in other cases, the *Guidelines for Patent Examination* shall refer to the *Guidelines for Patent Examination* applicable on the filing date of patent application at issue, i.e., the *Guidelines for Patent Examination (2001)*.

and handling of the same or similar issues. For example, regarding the same issue of introducing the unexamined defect of "a claim not supported by the description" in the reexamination procedure, the court of second instance of the case *(2011) Gao Xing Zhong Zi No. 654*[12] held that "incompliance with the provisions of Article 26(4) of the *Patent Law* is an obvious substantial defect under the provisions of the *Guidelines for Patent Examination*[13]... It was not inappropriate for the Patent Reexamination Board to review whether the claims of the patent application at issue complied with the provisions of Article 26(4) of the *Patent Law* in the reexamination decision No. 17592." However, in the case *(2013) Gao Xing Zhong Zi No. 902*,[14] the court of second instance held that "the examination of novelty cites the reference documents correspondingly, whereas the examination under the provisions of Article 26(4) of the *Patent Law* only requires examination of the patent documents. There is no evidence to show that the examination under the provisions of Article 26(4) of the *Patent Law* must precede the examination of novelty, or in other words, there is no evidence to show if an invention patent application has been examined for novelty in the prosecution, it necessarily means that the invention patent application complies with the provisions of Article 26(4) of the *Patent Law* after examination. Therefore, the Patent Reexamination Board's determination of changing the ground for the decision of rejection which was lack of novelty, to the ground for the rejection of reexamination, which was that the patent application at issue did not comply with Article 26(4) of the *Patent Law* as it was an 'obvious substantive defect not mentioned in the rejection decision,' was without merit."

The above cases show that regarding the Patent Reexamination Board's *ex officio* examination standard in the reexamination procedure, there is a difference of understanding not just between the administrative organ and the judicial organ, but also within the judicial organ. To solve this problem, the author believes that a discussion can be conducted in the following four aspects: (1) the purpose of setting up the reexamination procedure and the necessity for the Patent Reexamination Board to introduce *ex officio* other grounds than the grounds for the decision of rejection in the reexamination procedure; (2) factors to be considered in the determination of the *ex officio* examination standard; (3) whether the grounds of inventive step can

---

[12] In this case, the ground for rejection was that claims 1–7 did not involve an inventive step. The collegial panel upheld the decision of rejection on the grounds that claims 1–7 were not supported by the description. In this case, although the court of second instance held that the reexamination decision erred in finding that the claims were not supported by the description and thus did not prevail, it sustained the collegiate panel's *ex officio* introduction of this ground.

[13] Here, the *Guidelines for Patent Examination* should be the *Guidelines for Patent Examination (1993)*.

[14] In this case, the grounds for rejection were that claims 1–8 did not comply with Article 25 of the *Patent Law*, claims 9 and 11 lacked novelty, and claims 10 and 12–17 did not involve an inventive step. During the reexamination procedure, the collegial panel upheld the decision of rejection on the grounds that that claim 1 did not comply with Article 26(4) of the *Patent Law*. The court of second instance held that the obvious substantive defects should be interpreted narrowly, and that the *ex officio* examination of obvious substantive defects should be conducted only after the Patent Reexamination Board examined the request for reexamination and determined that it could not be granted.

be included in the *ex officio* examination; and (4) whether the Patent Reexamination Board performs the *ex officio* examination function only on the premise that the request for reexamination is not allowed.

20.2 The Purpose of the Reexamination Procedure and the Necessity of the *Ex Officio* Examination in This Procedure

The provision on the dual nature of the reexamination procedure was added in the current *Guidelines for Patent Examination* in 2006 when it was amended. According to the *Introduction to the Amended Guidelines for Patent Examination*, the reexamination procedure was set up, on the one hand, to correct mistakes in the patent examination and granting procedure, safeguard the legitimate rights and interests of the applicant, and also provide the applicant with the opportunity to finally obtain the grant through submitting additional statements of opinions and supplementary evidence and amending the application documents; on the other hand, to improve the quality of granted patents and the stability of rights, and to avoid unreasonably prolonging the examination and granting procedure[15] by empowering the Patent Reexamination Board to review the obvious substantive defects not mentioned in the decision of rejection.

Viewing retrospectively, the reexamination procedure was set up because it was difficult to ensure that all decisions of rejection were reasonable and correct in practice. In order to fully protect the legitimate rights and interests of patent applicants from being infringed, China set up a reexamination procedure in the patent law system in the early days of the enactment of the patent law, which allowed the applicant to file an appeal against the decision of rejection.[16] As the first stage in the patent appeal system, the review by the Patent Reexamination Board upon the request of the petitioner for reexamination is similar in nature to an administrative review, and provides a relief to the patent applicant when the decision of rejection is improper. However, since patent examination is different from general administrative examination and approval, in particular under the current patent law, the patent applicant has the right to amend the patent application documents in the reexamination procedure, the factual situation in the reexamination procedure often changes. It is for this reason that the reexamination procedure cannot be equated with a pure administrative review procedure. If the reexamination procedure is treated as a pure administrative review procedure, then either the patent applicant is not allowed to amend the application document in the reexamination procedure so that the examination will be focused on

---

[15] Examination Management Department of the State Intellectual Property Office. (2006) *Introduction to the Amended Guidelines for Patent Examination (2006)* (1st ed., p.254). Intellectual Property Publishing House.

[16] Yin, X. (2001) *Guide to the Newly Amended Patent Law* (1st ed., p.452). Intellectual Property Publishing House.

the legality of the decision of rejection; or the patent applicant is allowed to amend the application document, then as long as the fact based on which the decision of rejection has been made changes, the decision of rejection should be vacated, and the previous examination department continues the examination and granting procedure. As a result, the almost inexhaustible factual changes in the examination procedure will cause the entire examination and granting procedure to delay indefinitely, and the patent applicant will have to oscillate back and forth between the substantive examination and the reexamination procedure, which will not only waste administrative resources, but also is not conducive to the protection of the interests of the patent applicant. In this sense, the "relief" in the reexamination procedure should be understood broadly, including both the relief granted to the patent applicants when they believe that there are errors in the previous examination, and the relief granted to the patent applicants when they believe that there are errors due to themselves.

The reexamination procedure, as a stage in the patent examination and granting procedure, is an administrative procedure in which the Patent Reexamination Board exercises the statutory function of administrative examination and approval. It is the most basic requirement on an administrative law to exercise its functions and powers quickly and efficiently on the basis of ensuring fairness and justice. Nowadays, the number of patent applications is growing rapidly, with the average annual invention patent applications approaching one million, and the average annual reexamination cases exceeding 20,000. Since patent disputes are increasing rapidly, and both the administrative examination and granting procedure and the judicial protection procedure are facing the dilemma of rising caseload and severe personnel shortage, on the premise of basic protection of the procedural interests of patent applicants, it is beneficial from the perspective of the overall operation efficiency of the society, and it is also the requirement of the current status of intellectual property protection, to solve the problems of whether the patent right can be granted and whether it is worth the state protection with a monopoly period of 10–20 years, and try to avoid those patent applications that obviously cannot be granted oscillating back and forth between the substantive examination and the reexamination procedure for various reasons to cause waste of administrative resources in vain. In this sense, the nature of the reexamination procedure as the "continuation of the examination and granting procedure" should not be weakened.

20.3 Factors to Be Considered in the Determination of the Scope of the *Ex Officio* Examination in the Reexamination Procedure

Since the administrative efficiency cannot be improved at the expense of unreasonably sacrificing fairness and justice and the interests of the patent applicants, to strike a balance in the reexamination procedure both as a relief and a continuation of the examination and granting procedure, a basic approach is that the reexamination procedure as a relief should be the focus while it as a continuation of the examination and granting procedure should be a supplement. Correspondingly, the principle of request corresponding to the relief attribute should be regarded as a basic principle, and the principle of conducting *ex officio* examination corresponding to the continuation of the examination and granting procedure attribute can only be an exception and supplement to the principle of request. Since the principle of conducting *ex officio* examination is an expedient in special circumstances to balance fairness and efficiency, on the one hand, the scope of the *ex officio* examination should be kept appropriate; and on the other hand, the scope of the *ex officio* examination should be determined by following these principles: "providing relief as the purpose, not substituting substantive examination as the principle, not confusing the legal logic as the limit, and striking a balance between fairness and efficiency." The author believes that these are the factors that need to be particularly considered when determining the scope of the *ex officio* examination.

"Providing relief as the purpose" is the most basic requirement to define the scope of the *ex officio* examination. One of the most basic functions of the reexamination procedure is to provide relief for the patent applicants who disagree with the decision of rejection. Therefore, even if the examination is conducted beyond the grounds and evidence on which the decision of rejection has been based, it should also revolve around the basic purpose of providing "relief." For example, when examining the grounds for inventive step on which the decision of rejection has been based, a ground for novelty may be introduced *ex officio*. This is because it is a necessary stage for evaluating inventive step to identify distinguishing features through feature comparison. In the stage of feature comparison, if it is found that all the features in the claims are disclosed, it is to grant a relief for the grounds of inventive step to introduce the ground for novelty, which is reasonable; in contrast, if the rejection has been made for lack of novelty, and in the reexamination procedure, the panel finds that the claims have distinctive features compared with the reference documents, which means that the ground for rejection is no longer valid. Here, if the panel introduces *ex officio* the grounds for inventive step, on the one hand, it will be contrary to the petitioner's request for reexamination; on the other hand, it does not solve the problem of "providing relief."

"Not substituting substantive examination as the principle" is the second requirement to define the scope of the *ex officio* examination. In the patent system, different procedures have different goals and values. Although these procedures are related to each other, they cannot substitute for each other; otherwise a certain procedure may become meaningless.

During the granting procedure, an invention patent application may undergo preliminary examination, substantive examination, reexamination and administrative litigation, among which the substantive examination is the most comprehensive examination in the granting procedure, the administrative litigation is the judicial supervision of administrative review, and the reexamination is in the middle these two procedures which determines that it cannot fully perform all the functions of the substantive examination. If a matter that has not been mentioned in the substantive examination is reviewed (for example, leaping from novelty to inventive step), the examination essentially determines the direction of the patent application in lieu of the substantive examination.

"No confusing the legal logic as the limit" is the third requirement to define the scope of *ex officio* examination. For an invention-creation to be granted a patent, in addition to the requirements for the technical solution itself (novelty, inventive step, practical applicability, and patentable subject matter, etc.), and there are also requirements for the text expressing the technical solution (for example, compliance with the provisions of Article 26(3) and (4) of the *Patent Law*). In the examination process, there is a natural though not absolutely strict logical sequence between these legal provisions. For example, it is meaningless to evaluate the novelty and inventive step of a technical solution that is not a patentable subject matter; if the claimed technical solution is not fully disclosed in the description, it will not be granted a patent even if it possesses novelty and possesses an inventive step, etc. If the grounds for the decision of rejection are in a relatively posterior position according to legal logic, it means that the examiner should have examined the preceding laws in the substantive examination; on the contrary, if the grounds for the decision of rejection are in an anterior position, the *ex officio* introduce of a rule in a relatively posterior position in the reexamination procedure may confuse the basic legal logic.

"Striking a balance between fairness and efficiency" is the fourth requirement to define the scope of *ex officio* examination. The administrative actions of administrative organs pursue both fairness and efficiency. In the reexamination procedure, the amendment of the application documents by the petitioner for reexamination may cause the reexamination procedure to face the facts different from those in the decision of rejection. In this circumstance, a pure pursuit for fairness will delay the whole examination; on the contrary, a pure pursuit for efficiency will deviate from the relief purpose of the reexamination procedure. Therefore, the determination of the *ex officio* examination scope of the Patent Reexamination Board should not deviate from the requirement of "striking a balance between fairness and efficiency" while following the previous three principles. Currently what has been generally accepted in practice are the situations (1) and (3) provided in the *Guidelines for Patent Examination* that may be examined *ex officio*, which is the representation of striking a balance between fairness and efficiency.

20.4 How to Determine Obvious Substantive Defects Triggering an *Ex Officio* Examination

What has caused the most controversy in the industry is situation (2) provided in the *Guidelines for Patent Examination* in which an *ex officio* examination may be conducted, i.e., which defects are the obvious substantive defects that the Patent Reexamination Board may *ex officio* introduce. As reflected in the case *(2014) Zhi Xing Zi No. 2*, there are many different views on this issue. The author believes that there are two issues that are most worthy of discussion: one is whether the scope of the *ex officio* examination can be determined according to whether an in-depth investigation is needed? The other is whether it is reasonable to judge which defects are the obvious substantive defects that the Patent Reexamination Board may *ex officio* introduce according to the nature of the obvious substantive defects mentioned in the preliminary examination.

1. Whether an In-Depth Investigation Can Be Relied on to Determine the Scale of *Ex Officio* Examination

In the case *(2014) Zhi Xing Zi No. 2*, the reason why the panel introduced the ground of inventive step in the reexamination procedure was that, in order to overcome the novelty defect pointed out in the decision of rejection, the petitioner for reexamination amended the claims in the request for reexamination with newly added technical features which were determined by the panel as common knowledge. If the rejection decision of rejection was vacated on the grounds that the defect of the decision of rejection had been overcome, the original examination department would definitely make another decision of rejection for lack of inventive step on the basis of following the hearing principle, which would cause the application that obviously did not have the prospect of being granted occupying too many administrative resources. The panel introduced *ex officio* the ground for inventive step without any in-depth investigations of the newly added technical feature because it wanted to resolve the substantive dispute over patentability.

The author believes that it is understandable that this method was adopted to resolve substantive disputes. However, it is practically unfeasible to delineate the scope and scale of *ex officio* according to whether it is necessary to conduct an in-depth investigation of technical features.

Firstly, the dual nature of the reexamination procedure is not defined by the simplicity or complexity of the technical solutions or features. Even for simple technical solutions, if the decision of rejection made in the preliminary examination applied laws wrong, lacked necessary evidence, or violated legal procedures, the panel should also vacate the decision of rejection to provide relief for the rights and interests of the patent applicant.

Secondly, whether it is necessary to conduct in-depth investigations is a matter open to discussion, and there is considerable uncertainty about it. Although the law requires every examiner train himself to be a person skilled in the art during the patent examination process, it is always an ideal state which the examiner can only approach infinitely and never completely reach. Different examiners, based on the amount of knowledge they have, how capable and how prepared they are during the examination process, may come to completely different conclusions regarding what matters need in-depth investigations, and what matters can be determined without further investigation. Delineating the scope and scale of *ex officio* based on whether any in-depth investigations are needed will lead to different judgments in the same case and affect the consistency of the implementation of the examination guidelines.

In addition, using whether any in-depth investigations are needed as a yardstick to define the scope of *ex officio* that the Patent Reexamination Board can conduct will

20.4 How to Determine Obvious Substantive Defects Triggering an *Ex* ...

increase the unpredictability of the petitioner for reexamination. The administrative law basically requires that the scope of authority of the administrative organ should be clear and be expected by the administrative counterpart particularly when the exercise of its functions may be disadvantageous to the administrative counterpart.

Although in some cases, the panel performs *ex officio* functions in the reexamination procedure in order to enable the patent applicant to obtain more stable patent rights (for example, when the defect mentioned in the decision of rejection has been overcome, but there are still defects in the patent application of the same nature as the defect for which the application was rejected, the panel introduces *ex officio* the defect of the same nature, to avoid the patent application being rejected again due to the defect or the patent being invalidated after it has been granted due to this defect), in most cases where the panel introduces *ex officio* the defects not mentioned in the decision of rejection will lead to an unfavorable conclusion for the petitioner for reexamination. Therefore, the scope of the *ex officio* examination by the panel must be clear and predictable. If the necessity of an in-depth investigation is relied on to determine whether the *ex officio* examination is required, the subjectivity and uncertainty of in-depth investigations would render the scope of conducting *ex officio* examination completely unpredictable.

Although in the case *(2014) Zhi Xing Zi No. 2*, for the newly added technical features, the panel could conclude without an in-depth investigation that it was common knowledge, and thus introduced the ground for inventive step, which seemed to help resolve the substantive dispute over patentability, yet the citation of the ground for inventive step far exceeded the expectations of the petitioner for reexamination. The petitioner for reexamination initiated the reexamination procedure to seek a remedy for the decision of rejection for lack of novelty. Adding new technical features to overcome the defect of novelty was the most common way in the industry, and this way did indeed achieve the purpose of overcoming the defect of the decision of rejection. What the petitioner for reexamination could expect was that the reexamination request would be denied on the grounds that the defect of the decision of rejection had been overcome. However, the petitioner for reexamination could never predict that the panel introduced the grounds for lack of an inventive step and upheld the decision of rejection accordingly. This approach of the panel cannot be understood as an examination for the purpose of providing relief, and can also easily confuse the boundary between substantive examination and reexamination. Even if this approach has certain rationality in individual cases, it does not mean that it is reasonable to upgrade it to a general rule.

2. Determining Which Defects Can Be Introduced Reasonably by Referring to the Nature of the Obvious Substantive Defects Enumerated in the "Preliminary Examination"

Although in terms of legislative techniques, if the same phrase is used in different chapters of a regulation, then in principle the phrase should be understood as having the same meaning. However, in practice, the true meaning of the phrase needs to be understood in the context and according to the relevant content.

As held by the court of second instance in the case *(2014) Zhi Xing Zi No. 2*, before the patent application for invention is granted, the Patent Office shall conduct preliminary examination and substantive examination on the invention patent application, wherein the preliminary examination mainly focuses on whether the formality of the patent application documents complies with the relevant provisions of the *Patent Law* and the *Implementing Regulations of the Patent Law* and does not involve substantive issues related to patent granting. In particular, in the preliminary examination, the examiner does not search, and basically does not issue an office action on inventive step by comparing reference documents. This is also the reason why the *Guidelines for Patent Examination* does not include inventive step in the category of "obvious substantive defects" in Part I. In contrast, in the substantive examination, the examiner should examine the invention-creation more in depth and more comprehensively. In particular, the examiner should determine whether the invention-creation meets the "three elements" criteria on the basis of the prior art search. Therefore, the scope of the preliminary examination is totally different than that of the substantive examination. After entering the reexamination procedure due to the decision of rejection in the preliminary examination or the substantive examination, the scope of examination by the panel on the "obvious substantive defects" will inevitably differ. The author finds it unpersuasive that the first instance judgment follows and the retrial judgment refers to the nature of the obvious substantive defects listed in the preliminary examination part to determine which defects are "obvious substantive defects" that may be introduced *ex officio* in the reexamination procedure.

3. Reasonableness and Practicality to Determine Which Defects Are Obvious Substantive Defects According to the Logical Order of Examination

In addition to clarifying the nature of the reexamination procedure, the *Guidelines for Patent Examination* amended in 2006 deleted the "principle of avoiding the examination level" and the "principle of procedural economy" in the 2001 version of the *Guidelines for Patent Examination* as well as the provisions on the examination order. According to the *Introduction to the Amended Guidelines for Patent Examination*, the amendment was made because the examination order of the reexamination procedure in Part IV of the *Guidelines for Patent Examination (2001)* differed from that in the substantive examination in Part II. It may be inaccurate if the panel presumes that the grounds and evidence "should be examined" in the substantive examination according to the examination order of the reexamination. These grounds and evidence may not have been examined in the substantive examination, and may not even be grounds and evidence that "should be examined." Moreover, the logical relationship among different reasons in different cases is not static, which affects the accuracy of the presumption. It may lead to the actual examination level loss by presuming that the "grounds and evidence should be examined" by the previous examination department in accordance with the examination order.[17]

---

[17] Examination Management Department of the State Intellectual Property Office. (2006) *Introduction to the Amended Guidelines for Patent Examination(2006)* (1st ed., p.254). Intellectual Property Publishing House.

The above reasons are reasonable to a certain extent. However, the author believes that in recent years, the State Intellectual Property Office has been implementing the concept of comprehensive examination and examination based on the "three elements" evaluation, which means it has become less and less likely that for a patent application, a decision of rejection is made after mere examination of some of the conditions for granting a patent right, and there are fewer and fewer opportunities for the Patent Reexamination Board to exercise the *ex officio* examination function. Under this background, on the basis of following the above four factors, to determine which defects are obvious substantive defects that can be introduced *ex officio* by following the logical examination order, on the one hand, it can improve the prediction of the petitioner for reexamination of the scope of *ex officio* examination; and on the other hand, it is helpful for consistency of the examination standard among different panels.

20.5 Is the Request for Reexamination Being Denied a Prerequisite for the *Ex Officio* Examination

In the case *(2013) Gao Xing Zhong Zi No. 902*, the court of second instance put forward the viewpoint that "the Patent Reexamination Board should generally review 'the obvious substantive defects not mentioned in the decision of rejection' only after it performs examination of the request for reexamination and determines that it cannot be allowed." Although this viewpoint is innovative and seems reasonable in theory, it lacks the understanding of the examination practice and practicality.

First, in the examination practice, regardless of whether the panel finally introduces *ex officio* the grounds other than the grounds for the decision of rejection, when facing a reexamination case, the panel, on the basis of combing through the examination process, should first examine whether any amendments are submitted in the reexamination procedure, and if yes whether these amendments are allowable; next it examines whether the defects mentioned out in the decision of rejection have been overcome; then it examines whether it is necessary to conduct *ex officio* examination by the panel in this case. It is impossible for the panel to examine the grounds other than those for the decision of rejection before it examines the grounds for the decision of rejection first.

Second, the examination in the reexamination procedure also follows the general rules of patent examination—"negative" examination, i.e., the panel only mentions the unacceptable grounds in the notification of reexamination or reexamination decision, and it generally does not comment affirmatively as for which grounds are acceptable, or whether there are multiple unacceptable grounds for the same claim. Therefore, in the circumstance in which the panel has introduced *ex officio* the grounds other than those for the decision of rejection, it cannot be summarily presumed that the grounds for the examination are sustained and that no affirmative comments in the notification of reexamination or the reexamination decision does not mean that the panel has "examined" the matters.

Third, in the examination practice, there are three circumstances in which the Patent Reexamination Board conducts an *ex officio* examination, generally as follows:

(1) If the panel introduces *ex officio* the ground examined before (situation (1) provided in the *Guidelines for Patent Examination*), it generally means that the defect mentioned in the decision of rejection has been overcome and the request for reexamination is sustained. The reason for exercising the *ex officio* examination function is that if the previously examined grounds are not introduced *ex officio*, after the rejection decision is vacated, the previous examination department may issue a second rejection without hearing, causing unnecessary oscillations in the procedure.

(2) If the panel introduces *ex officio* a defect of the same nature as the defect mentioned in the decision of rejection, (situation (3) provided in the *Guidelines for Patent Examination*), it may be that the defect mentioned in the rejection defect has been overcome through amendments or other means, or that it has not been overcome. In this circumstance, the panel performs the *ex officio* function mainly to improve the quality of patent granting. For example, the same wording in both claims 1 and 5 causes the claims indefinite. The decision of rejection points out that claim 1 is indefinite, omitting claim 5. If the indefiniteness of claim 1 is overcome, the panel points out in the reexamination procedure that claim 5 is indefinite to avoid that after the decision of rejection is vacated, the previous examination department may grant the patent directly, which may finally lead to the patent invalidated for this defect in the granted patent document. If the indefiniteness of claim 1 has not been overcome, the panel points out in the reexamination procedure that claim 5 is indefinite to remind the patent applicant to amend them together, so as to obtain higher quality and stable patent rights. In the latter case, the *ex officio* examination will not be allowed according to the court of second instance, and the final consequence will be to watch in vain the defective patent right be granted or the notices of examination be split twice, which is obviously unreasonable.

(3) If the panel introduces *ex officio* obvious substantive defects, it is most likely that the panel finds that an accurate opinion on the reexamination request cannot be produced after examination (for example, it is impossible to determine the inventive step if the claims are indefinite.) or it is meaningless to express an opinion on whether the request for reexamination is sustained (for example, it is meaningless to comment on whether the claimed technical solution involves an inventive step if it is not a patentable subject matter.). Here, it is unreasonable and unpractical to require rigidly that other grounds other than the grounds for the decision of rejection be introduced *ex officio* only when the request for reexamination is not sustained.

To sum up, the author believes that currently the dual nature of the reexamination procedure should be kept. The Patent Reexamination Board should be allowed to introduce *ex officio* the grounds other than the grounds for the decision of rejection under certain circumstances. In the exercise of the *ex officio* function, it should not be a prerequisite that "the request for reexamination is not sustained", rather, the following four factors should be considered comprehensively—"providing relief as the purpose, not substituting substantive examination as the principle, not confusing the legal logic as the limit, and striking a balance between fairness and efficiency", to reasonably determine the scope of the Patent Reexamination Board's *ex officio* examination.

Chapter 21
Ex Officio Examination in the Invalidation Procedure

Under the current *Guidelines for Patent Examination*, in the invalidation procedure, the Patent Reexamination Board follows two basic principles—the principle of examination upon request and the principle of conducting examinations *ex officio*—to determine the scope of examination of a case, i.e., to generally perform examination only on the causes and evidence of the request for invalidation submitted by the invalidation petitioner. But the causes and evidence not mentioned by the invalidation petitioner may be introduced *ex officio* in specific circumstances.

The fourth amendment of the *Patent Law* brought about extensive discussion in the industry regarding the function and scope of the Patent Reexamination Board's *ex officio* examination in the invalidation procedure. There have been both approvals and disapprovals. The author sorted out and analyzed the patent litigation cases regarding the *ex officio* examination in the invalidation procedure in recent years and found that the controversy revolved around the following three issues: (1) What is the legal nature of the invalidation procedure? Is it an administrative procedure that corrects improper granting or a civil procedure that resolves the disputes between the invalidation petitioner and the patentee over the validity of the patent impartially? (2) Should the *ex officio* examination be a basic principle in the invalidation procedure? Should the Patent Reexamination Board's *ex officio* examination be strictly limited to the several circumstances listed in the *Guidelines for Patent Examination* or may be extended to other circumstances? (3) When the invalidation petitioner withdraws part of the request or renounces some of the causes and evidence of the request for invalidation (hereinafter the invalidation request), may the Patent Reexamination Board conduct the *ex officio* examination under Rule 72 of the *Implementing Regulations of the Patent Law*?

The author will discuss the above three issues on the basis of some cases.

21.1 The Legal Nature of the Invalidation Procedure

The patent invalidation procedure is one of the most important procedures in the *Patent Law*. There has always been debate in the industry on whether this procedure is an administrative procedure to correct improper patent granting or a civil procedure to resolve the disputes over the validity of patent rights impartially. The author believes that under the current legal framework, it is inaccurate to define the patent invalidation procedure either as a pure civil procedure for impartial adjudication, or as a pure administrative procedure for correcting improper patent granting. The invalidation procedure under the current legal framework has the dual functions of correcting improper patent granting and resolving disputes over the validity of patent rights, which determines that it also has dual legal nature.

1. The Invalidation Procedure Should not be Defined as a Pure Civil Procedure for Impartial Adjudication

It is impossible to define the invalidation procedure as a pure civil procedure for impartial adjudication for reasons in the following aspects: the nature of disputes resolved by the invalidation procedure, the legislative evolution of the invalidation system, the purpose of the invalidation procedure, and the comparison with similar procedures in other countries or regions.

(1) The nature of disputes resolved by the invalidation procedure

There are two views on whether a patent invalidation dispute is a civil dispute or an administrative dispute currently. The main reason put forward by the scholars who believe that a patent invalidation dispute is a civil dispute is that the patent right is a private right, and the declaration of the invalidity of the patent right is a declaratory judgment between the invalidation petitioner and the patentee regarding the existence of this private right, in which the Patent Reexamination Board is actually exercising the judicial power on behalf of the People's Court. The author thinks that this point of view is debatable.

First of all, although under the provisions of the TRIPS Agreement, the patent right is a private right, yet this private right is different from the real property right in the traditional sense and is not a natural right. Rather, it is statutorily granted by the nation, the existence and exercise of which is inseparable from the intervention of administrative organs representing state power. Therefore, patent rights are private rights intervened by administrative power. Secondly, limited by administrative costs and examination efficiency, it is impossible for the Patent Office to examine patent applications absolutely thoroughly. Within a reasonable range allowed by administrative costs, if "no grounds for a rejection are found", the patent right is granted for the patent application. Such a grant is only "temporary" and does not imply that the patent right has no defects for which the patent right should not be granted. The patent right that should not have been granted but has been improperly granted should be revoked. The design of the patent granting procedure in the current *Patent Law* makes it only through the initiation of the invalidation procedure can the granted

21.1 The Legal Nature of the Invalidation Procedure

patent be declared non-existent from the date of filing. Under the current *Patent Law*, although "anyone" has the right to initiate an invalidation procedure, in essence, it is a request made to the Patent Reexamination Board to revoke the decision to grant the patent right, because the decision to grant the patent right is the direct basis on which the patent right is created. Therefore, the invalidation dispute is essentially a dispute over the validity of the act by the Patent Office to grant a patent right. In theory, the two parties to this dispute should be the invalidation petitioner and the Patent Office, with the patentee as the third party. However, since the patentee can better safeguard the patent right and the legitimacy of the decision to grant the patent right, making it not very necessary for the Patent Office to participate in the procedure, the law provides that the invalidation petitioner and the patentee participate in the invalidation procedure.

The patent invalidation disputes share the same nature with the disputes over the rejection of patent applications if a comparison is made between them. For example, for a dispute over the rejection of a patent application, the Patent Reexamination Board reviews whether there is an error in the decision of rejection; while in a patent invalidation dispute, the Patent Reexamination Board examines whether there is an error in the decision to grant the patent right. The mere difference between these two types of disputes is that the former happens before the patent granting and the latter happens after. If the disputes over the rejection of patent applications arising from the patent applicant's dissatisfaction with the decision of rejection are defined as administrative disputes, it is unreasonable to define the disputes arising from the invalidation petitioner's dissatisfaction with the decision to grant the patent right with the very similar nature as civil disputes only because the disputes occur after the patent granting.

Therefore, from the perspective of the nature of disputes to be resolved in the invalidation procedure, it is not proper to define it as a pure civil procedure.

(2) The legislative evolution of the patent invalidation system

The patent confirmation procedures have undergone many changes during the previous amendments of the *Patent Law*. The *Patent Law* promulgated in 1984 provided the opposition procedure wherein any entity or individual might file an opposition with the Patent Office within a specified time limit for opposition before the granting of the patent right. When the *Patent Law* was first amended in 1992, the pre-granting opposition procedure was amended to a post-grant revocation procedure, for the purpose of providing the public with an opportunity to evaluate whether the patent rights granted by the Patent Office were in compliance with the provisions of the *Patent Law*, and to assist the Patent Office in correcting errors of patent granting in order to protect the interests of the public. Under relevant provisions, once the revocation procedure was initiated, the examination team not only should consider the causes put forward by the revocation petitioner, but also might cite various causes for revocation on its own. When the *Patent Law* was amended for the second time in 2001, given that the objective of the revocation procedure could be substantially achieved through the invalidation procedure, the revocation procedure was cancelled, and only the invalidation procedure was retained for the public to assist the patent administrative department to correct errors in patent granting through the invalidation procedure. This system has continued to this day.

It can be seen from this historical change that the current invalidation procedure has inherited the administrative function of the previous opposition procedure and revocation procedure to prevent and correct improper patent granting, and it would be contrary to the objective historical development to define the invalidation procedure as a pure civil procedure.

(3) The purpose of the invalidation procedure

It is almost inevitable in any country to grant patent rights to patent applications that should not have been granted, which will harm the legitimate rights and interests of the public. Therefore, it is necessary to establish a mechanism to provide a relief when a granting error is discovered. To invalidate a patent right that should not have been granted is actually a process of introducing public supervision after the patent is granted by mobilizing the public, especially the power of stakeholders, to examine the patent right and strike out those patents that do not meet the granting conditions to protect the interests of the public. This is the purpose of the invalidation procedure. In addition, the invalidation procedure does not aim to declare the invalidity of the patent rights. As part of the patent system, the fundamental purpose of the invalidation procedure is to protect inventions that should obtain or deserve protection, and to stimulate technological innovation. Therefore, in the invalidation procedure the patentee also has the opportunity to amend patent documents and redefine the protection scope of patent rights, so as to obtain more stable rights.

The above two purposes show that in the invalidation procedure, considering the causes and evidence submitted by both parties and combining with the amended document of the patentee, the Patent Reexamination Board actually reviews whether the decision to grant the patent right will be made anyways rather than just resolves the dispute between the patentee and the invalidation petitioner over whether the patent right meets the granting conditions. The invalidation procedure should not be defined only to resolve the civil dispute between the two parties over the validity of the patent right.

(4) The comparison with corresponding systems in other countries and regions

Through the examination of the patent invalidation procedures in other countries and regions, it is not difficult to find that in most countries and regions, neither patent validity disputes are simply characterized as civil disputes nor is the invalidation procedure simply defined as a civil procedure.

For example, in Japan, after the patent is granted, the validity of the patent right can be challenged through the opposition procedure and the invalidation procedure. The opposition procedure is to determine the stability of the patent right as early as possible so that the public can challenge the patent right that does not meet the granting conditions. Anyone that believes that the patent should not have been granted may file a request with the Appeals Department of the Japan Patent Office (JPO) within 6 months after the patent is published. Correspondingly, the patent invalidation procedure resolves disputes between the parties regarding the validity of the patent and is initiated by stakeholders and shall be adjudicated by the Appeals Department of the JPO following the "quasi-judicial" procedure. The former is a typical administrative procedure, while the latter is a "quasi-judicial" procedure.

Nonetheless, if the parties are not satisfied with the invalidation decision and appeals to the Tokyo High Court, although the petitioner and the patentee are the original plaintiff and defendant in the lawsuit, and the Appeals Department of the JPO does not appear in the court as the defendant, this lawsuit is still characterized as an administrative lawsuit rather than a civil one. This means that the invalidation procedure of the Appeals Department of the JPO is not a pure civil procedure.

In Germany, although patent invalidation cases are heard by the Federal Patent Court of Germany in which only the invalidation petitioner and the patentee participate, and the German Patent Office does not participate in the proceedings as the defendant, the patent invalidation procedure of the Federal Patent Court of Germany is also similar to the procedure of the administrative court, and only borrows part of the provisions of the *Civil Procedure Law*.

In Taiwan, China, anyone who believes that a patent right violates Article 71 of the "*Intellectual Property Law*" may file a request with the patent examination authority. The "Intellectual Property Office" appoints persons that did not participate in the previous examination of this application to reexamine and makes a decision. If a party is dissatisfied with the reexamination decision of the "Intellectual Property Office", he may file an "appeal" with the "Petitions and Appeals Committee M. O. E. A." under the "*Administrative Appeal Act*." If the party still believes that his rights haven't been fully remedied after the "appeal", he may bring an administrative action against the "Intellectual Property Office" or the "Petitions and Appeals Committee M. O. E. A." to seek a vacation of the reexamination decision and the original administrative decision. Therefore, the invalidation procedure in Taiwan is also not a typical civil procedure.

(5) The provisions of current laws and regulations and the examination practice

In practice, although the review of invalidation cases follows the principle of disposal by the party concerned, under Rule 72 of the *Implementing Regulations of the Patent Law*, if the Patent Reexamination Board can declare the patent right invalid or partially invalid based on the review already carried out, even if the petitioner withdraws the invalidation request, it may not terminate the examination, instead, it may make a decision to declare the patent right invalid or partially invalid. If the invalidation procedure is defined as a pure civil procedure, the principle of disposal by the party concerned should be the most basic principle of this procedure, i.e., if the petitioner withdraws his request for invalidation, the Patent Reexamination Board shall terminate the review, which is inconsistent with the provisions of Rule 72 of the current *Implementing Regulations of the Patent Law*. Moreover, if the invalidation procedure is regarded as a pure civil procedure, the end result of the dispute should be only valid for both parties rather than *erga omnes*, which is not the case under the current law. In addition, the invalidation procedure is the only procedure after a patent is granted. If it is defined as a pure civil procedure, there will be no longer any supervision and correction procedures for the improper granting of the Patent Office, which does not meet the basic requirements of administrative law. From these three aspects, the current invalidation procedure has the nature of resolving disputes between the parties, yet it cannot be defined as a pure civil procedure for resolving disputes over the validity of patent rights.

2. The Invalidation Procedure Should not be Defined as a Procedure Purely for Correcting Improper Granting

Judging from the current laws and practical implementation, the invalid procedure cannot be defined as a procedure purely for correcting improper granting. If it is a typical procedure for correcting improper granting, the procedure should be initiated not only upon the request of the invalidation petitioner but also in a variety of ways. For example, if the administrative organ finds that the granted patent does not meet the granting conditions, it can initiate the procedure to correct the improper granting. The invalidation request made by the invalidation petitioner shall serve as a clue based on which the administrative organ shall actively review whether the granting of the patent right is appropriate. The termination of the procedure shall not depend on whether the invalidation petitioner withdraws the request. However, under the current *Guidelines for Patent Examination*, the present invalidation procedure is initiated upon the request of the invalidation petitioner. If the invalidation petitioner withdraws his request before the Patent Reexamination Board makes an invalidation decision, the invalidation procedure shall generally terminate unless the provision of Rule 72 of *Implementing Regulations of the Patent Law* applies. In this sense, the current invalidation procedure has the nature of correcting improper granting, yet it cannot be defined as a procedure purely for correcting improper granting.

21.2 The Relationship Between the Principle of Examination Upon Request and the Principle of *Ex Officio* Examination Under Dual Nature and the Application of the Principle of *Ex Officio* Examination

In view of the dual nature of the invalidation procedure under the current legal framework, the principle of examination upon request and the principle of conducting *ex officio* examination, which correspond to the two aspects of the dual nature, have become two basic principles that are both contradictory and interdependent in the invalidation procedure.

China has adopted a dual mechanism for resolving the disputes over patent confirmation and patent infringement. In practice, the initiation of an invalidation procedure is mostly due to actual or potential infringement disputes. Meanwhile, with the advancement of the national intellectual property development strategy and the

21.2 The Relationship Between the Principle of Examination Upon Request ...

increased awareness of intellectual property protection in the whole society, patent infringement disputes have spiked with the increase in the number of patent applications. The conflict between the limited personnel in the courts at all levels and the growing caseload has become increasingly intensified, and the prolonged litigation process has caused strong public dissatisfaction. In this situation, quickly resolving disputes between the parties on the validity of the patent right should become the most basic task of the invalidation procedure. Therefore, under the current institutional framework, the principle of examination upon request should be the general rule, and the principle of *ex officio* examination should be an exception and supplement to it.

The Patent Reexamination Board exercises the *ex officio* examination function, and in most cases it finds that the patent right has more serious defects than the causes claimed by the invalidation petitioner. Meanwhile, from the perspective of the administrative law, the scope of exceptions within the authority of the administrative organ which may produce adverse effects on the parties must be clear, otherwise the public will be unable to predict the result of the administrative organ's decision. Therefore, the *Guidelines for Patent Examination* should explicitly provide the scope of the Patent Reexamination Board's *ex officio* examination, and the relevant provisions on the scope of the *ex officio* examination should also be understood as "anything not mandated by the law is unpermitted," to avoid applying analogical interpretation to arbitrarily expand the scope of the Patent Reexamination Board's *ex officio* examination. In this sense, the seven circumstances listed in Part IV, Chapter 3 of the *Guidelines for Patent Examination* in which the Patent Reexamination Board may conduct an *ex officio* examination in the invalidation procedure should be understood as an exhaustive and "closed" list. The Patent Reexamination Board shall not examine *ex officio* beyond this scope.

For example, in the case *(2014) Gao Xing Zhong Zi No. 1135*,[1] the patent at issue has 7 claims, where claims 2–6 refer to claim 1. The causes for invalidation asserted by the invalidation petitioner were: claims 1, 2 and 4–6 lacked novelty; and claims 3, 4, and 7 lacked an inventive step. The Patent Reexamination Board declared the patent right invalid in whole on the ground that claims 1–7 lacked an inventive step. The courts of the first and second instance both vacated the invalidation decision on the ground that the Patent Reexamination Board exceeded the scope by introducing *ex officio* the ground for inventive step of claims 2 and 5.

In this case, the invalidation petitioner asserted that claim 3 did not involve an inventive step. The *ex officio* examination on the inventive step of claim 3 following the principle of examination upon request would inevitably involve the independent claim 1. When the collegial panel determined that claim 3 lacked an inventive step, if the ground for inventive step of claim 1 was not introduced accordingly, a conclusion will be reached that claim 1 novelty and should be maintained whereas claim 3 lacked

---

[1] Utility model patent No. 201120242508.4. The invalidation decision (No. WX21059) declared the patent right invalid in whole. The first instance judgment (*(2013) Yi Zhong Zhi Xing Chu Zi No. 2888*) vacated the invalidation decision. The second instance judgment (*(2014) Gao Xing Zhong Zi No. 1135*) upheld the first instance judgment.

an inventive step and should be invalidated, which is absurd. Therefore, the Patent Reexamination Board conducted *ex officio* examination the grounds for an inventive step of claim 1. The courts of first and second instance also sustained the rationality of this *ex officio* action out of the same consideration.

However, for claims 2 and 5, the invalidation petitioner only asserted that they lacked novelty. In the examination of the inventive step of claims 3, 4 and 7, the issue of the inventive step of claims 2 and 5 would not be dealt with in any way. Even if the collegial panel introduced the grounds of inventive step by applying the basic logic of "no novelty, no inventive step", the citation is based on the fact that all the technical features of claims 2 and 5 were disclosed in the reference document, rather than the fact that the technical features of claims 2 and 5 had distinguishing features compared with the reference documents and these distinguishing features were common knowledge. Therefore, whether claims 2 and 5 involved an inventive step was not what must be examined in the reexamination of the causes of the invalidation asserted by the invalidation petitioner. The citation of such causes by the Patent Reexamination Board was beyond the scope of conducting *ex officio* examination provided in the seven circumstances in the *Guidelines for Patent Examination*.

Although under the current institutional framework, regarding the application the principle of *ex officio examination* in this case, the author is more in favor of the views of the courts of first and second instance, there are indeed many cases in practice, such as demonstrated by the case *(2014) Gao Xing Zhong Zi No. 1135* in which the conclusion can be drawn that the patent right should not have been granted based on the evidence in the case and the common knowledge in the art, yet the patent right which obviously should not be granted was maintained valid simply because of the negligence or lack of experience of the invalidation petitioner. If the seven circumstances in which the *ex officio* examination may be conducted in the *Guidelines for Patent Examination* remain unchanged, and a view similar to that the courts of first and second instance in the case *(2014) Gao Xing Zhong Zi No. 1135* is adopted, the review scope of the Patent Reexamination Board will be strictly limited to the specific causes and evidence put forward by the invalidation petitioner, which will cause the review results of the Patent Reexamination Board extremely dependent on the technical level and patent law literacy of the invalidation petitioner. Then an unreasonable result as described above may happen. For example, even though the causes and evidence of invalidation raised by the invalidation petitioner may undermine the inventive step of the patent in question, if the invalidation petitioner only asserts the invalidity for lack of novelty due to his serious lack of experience and skills, the Patent Reexamination Board can only determine that the invalidation request is not allowed and continue to maintain the patent rights that are obviously lack of inventive step. This is undoubtedly contrary to the responsibilities of the Patent Reexamination Board to correct improper granting and safeguard the interests of the public, and it will also increase social costs.

An overview of the invalidation systems in other countries and regions shows that the *ex officio* examination is adopted as a basic principle in many countries and regions, not just an exception and supplement to the principle of examination upon request. For example, Article 153 of the *Patent Act* of Japan provides: in an invalidation procedure, the Appeals Department may also examine the grounds not pleaded by a party or intervenor, but it must give them an opportunity to present their opinions. Article 159 of the *Patent Act* of South Korea provides that grounds which have not been pleaded by a party or intervenor in a trial may be examined, but no examination may be made on the purpose of a claim not requested by the petitioner. Article 87 of the *Patent Act* of Germany explicitly provides that the Federal Patent Court examines the facts *ex officio*. It is not bound by the pleadings and the motions to take evidence filed by the parties. The patent law in Taiwan, China is particularly representative in this aspect. Article 75 of the *"Intellectual Property Law"*[2] provides, "When conducting invalidation proceedings, the Specific Patent Agency may, by *ex officio*, examine the reason(s) and evidence not provided by the requester of invalidation action but within the scope of the invalidation statement, and notify the patentee to respond within a specified time period. The invalidation proceedings shall be conducted accordingly if the patentee fails to respond within the time period." The "Intellectual Property Office of the Ministry of Economic Affairs" further stipulates in the *"Guidelines for Patent Examination"* that "although the invalidation proceedings may be initiated by anyone, considering that the patent system also protects the interests of the public, this regulation stipulates that the invalidation proceedings shall follow the principle of conducting *ex officio* examination in order to reduce the waste of judicial and administrative resources."

Taking these factors into consideration, the author believes that it is just expedient to amend the *Guidelines for Patent Examination* to extend the scope of the *ex officio* examination of the Patent Reexamination Board and adjust the ratio of the two aspects of the dual nature of the invalidation procedure. In contrast, a top-level system design of diverse post-granting procedures will solve this problem more outrightly.

21.3 Application of Rule 72 of the *Implementing Regulations of the Patent Law*

Under Rule 72 of the *Implementing Regulations of the Patent Law*, before the Patent Reexamination Board makes a reexamination decision on the request for invalidation, the invalidation petitioner may withdraw his request and the invalidation procedure shall be terminated. However, if the Patent Reexamination Board determines that a decision to declare the patent right invalid or partially invalid may be made based on the already performed review work, the invalidation procedure shall not be terminated.

The dispute over this Rule in practice is what "withdraw his request" exactly means. Does it include the circumstance of renouncing part of the causes and evidence for the invalidation? For example, in the case *(2013) Zhi Xing Zi No. 92*, the Patent Reexamination Board argued that renouncing part of the invalidation causes was

---

[2] Translator's note: The author referred to this article as Article 75 of the *"Intellectual Property Law"*, but in fact this article is Article 75 of the *"Patent Act."*

equivalent to withdrawing part of the invalidation request. If the *Implementing Regulations of the Patent Law* was not understood as covering the renouncement of part of the invalidation request, it would lead to unreasonable results that when all the invalidation causes and evidence of invalidation were renounced, the Patent Reexamination Board might conduct *ex officio* examination whereas when part of the causes and evidence of invalidation were renounced, the Patent Reexamination Board might not. The SPC did not sustain this argument and held this understanding was without merits. This dispute in essence was a matter of legal interpretation.

According to the subject of interpretation, legal interpretation can usually be divided into statutory interpretation and academic interpretation. Statutory interpretation refers to a legally binding interpretation of the law made by a specific state organ or other persons with the power to interpret. According to the extent of interpretation, statutory interpretation can usually be divided into literal interpretation, restrictive interpretation and extensive interpretation. Literal interpretation refers to interpreting the law strictly in accordance with the plain meaning of legal provisions, neither narrowly nor extensively; restrictive interpretation refers to interpreting the legal provisions more narrowly than the literal meaning when the literal meaning of the legal provisions is obviously broader than the original legislative intent; extensive interpretation means that when the literal meaning of the legal provisions is obviously narrower than the legislative intent, the legal provision is interpreted more broadly than the literal meaning. Generally, statutory interpretation by the legislature should take precedence and if there is no statutory interpretation, the literal interpretation of the statute should take precedence.

According to the description in the Introduction to the Third Amendment of the *Implementing Regulations of the Patent Law* regarding Rule 72 of the *Implementing Regulations of the Patent Law*, the reason why the Patent Reexamination Board's *ex officio* examination was added in this Rule was that "in a case where the patentee and the invalidation petitioner have reached a settlement and a request has been made to withdraw the invalidation request, if after reexamination, a decision to declare the patent right invalid or partially invalid can be made, and the patent right remains valid only because the invalidation petitioner has withdrawn the invalidation request, such a defective patent right will become an obstacle to restricting the public's use of the technology."[3]

This wording shows that when Rule 72 of the *Implementing Regulations of the Patent Law* was amended, the original intent was to regulate only the circumstance in which the invalidation petitioner withdrew the entire invalidation request, not including the circumstance of the petitioner renouncing part of the causes and evidence for the invalidation request. In this Rule, the literal meaning of "withdraws the request" in "where the invalidation petitioner withdraws the request or …the review procedure for the request for invalidation shall be terminated", should also refer to the withdrawal of the entire invalidation request, otherwise, if the "withdrawal of partial request" is included, the review procedure of the invalidation request

---

[3] Department of Treaty and Law (CNIPA). (2010). *Introduction to the Third Amendment of the Implementing Regulations of the Patent Law* (1st ed., p. 83). Intellectual Property Publishing House.

should not be terminated. Therefore, from the perspectives of legislative interpretation and literal interpretation, Rule 72 of the *Implementing Regulations of the Patent Law* only provides the circumstance where the invalidation petitioner withdraws the entire invalidation request, not the circumstance where part of the causes and evidence for the invalidation are renounced.

In the case of renouncing part of the causes and evidence for invalidation, the author thinks that it is necessary to examine whether there are any explicit provisions on this in the *Implementing Regulations of the Patent Law*. In the circumstance as provided explicitly by Part IV, Chapter 3 of the *Implementing Regulations of the Patent Law* that "the Patent Reexamination Board generally does not review the scope, causes and evidence that the invalidation petitioner renounced in the invalidation procedure",[4] the relevant provisions of the *Implementing Regulations of the Patent Law* should be applied, rather than adopting an extensive interpretation based on Rule 72 of the *Implementing Regulations of the Patent Law*.

Of course, as explained by the Patent Reexamination Board in this case, the reason why the Patent Reexamination Board can conduct *ex officio* examination if all the causes for invalidation and evidence are renounced as provided in Rule 72 of the *Implementing Regulations of the Patent Law* is that the Patent Reexamination Board has the function of correcting improper granting. Then, if the invalidation petitioner renounces part of the causes and evidence for invalidation, the Patent Reexamination Board also needs to exercise the function of correcting improper granting, then why cannot the Patent Reexamination Board introduce *ex officio* the causes and evidence renounced by the invalidation petitioner? This is indeed a problem of the pot calling the kettle black. The author believes that the solution to this problem can only depend on procedure design and law amendment rather than on misinterpretation and extensive interpretation of the legislative intent of the law.

21.4 How to Better Exercise the Administrative Function of Correcting Improper Patent Granting Without Causing Social Dissatisfaction

As analyzed above, the invalidation procedure simultaneously undertakes the two tasks of correcting improper granting and resolving disputes arising from the validity of the patent right between the parties. These two tasks impose different requirements for the Patent Reexamination Board, especially regarding the extent of the *ex officio* examination. The former requires the Patent Reexamination Board to focus on the authority principle, while the latter requires the Patent Reexamination Board to focus on the parties and make impartial adjudication. These two completely different values are difficult to reconcile to some extent. The result of a compromise may be that neither party is satisfied.

---

[4] Part IV, Chapter 3, Section 2.2 of the *Guidelines for Patent Examination*.

The reason lies in the system design. In China's patent system, after the patent is granted, the only way to solve the problem of defective granting is to initiate the invalidation procedure, regardless of whether the patentee wants to amend the patent document, or the accused infringer wants to make a non-infringement defense from the foundation, or the public (including the Patent Office) discovers that the granted patent is flawed. The problem can only be resolved by initiating an invalidation procedure. As the nature of the issues to be resolved is different, the requirements for the Patent Reexamination Board to exercise its powers and determine the scope of examination will also vary. It is difficult to meet different individual needs with a single invalidation procedure.

The author believes that setting different individual procedures to solve different problems may be the best solution. However, as these procedures are designed for granted patents, the procedure design needs to take into consideration the overlapping among different procedures and tries to avoid it. The same problem is addressed in this way in the U.S. and Japan.[5] In light of China's specific circumstance, Japan's mature experience may be borrowed and two post-grant procedures may be set up: one is a typical procedure to correct improper granting (hereinafter referred to as special invalidation procedure), and the other is a typical procedure for impartial adjudication (hereinafter referred to as the general invalidation procedure) to resolve disputes between the parties over the validity of the patent right.

1. Special invalidation procedure

The subject that can initiate the procedure is the Patent Office or the public (including the patentee himself) who are not involved in infringement disputes. If the Patent Office identifies defects in the granted patent during the quality inspection and other processes, it can initiate the procedure on its own. If a patent is found to have defects that should be examined *ex officio* during the examination in a general invalidation procedure, the relevant causes and evidence may be submitted to the Patent Office to initiate a special invalidation procedure.

In the special invalidation procedure, the Patent Reexamination Board has a relatively large scope of authority, including the ability to search, introduce new evidence and new causes, etc. After the special invalidation procedure is initiated, if there is a general invalidation procedure case for the same patent right, the two cases may be consolidated.

In order to avoid the indefinite entanglement between the special invalidation procedure and the general invalidation procedure, and to solve the stability of the patent as soon as possible, the time limit for initiation of the special invalidation procedure can be set forth, for example, within a certain period of time (such as 2 years, and the specific time period requires further empirical research) after the patent is granted.

---

[5] See Section 6 of this chapter. (Translator's note: This is an error by the author. There is no Section 6 in this Chapter.)

2. General invalidation procedure

The initiation of the general invalidation procedure is limited to the parties to the infringement dispute (the interested parties in the infringement dispute). When a member of the public makes a request for invalidation, he needs to choose whether to initiate the special invalidation procedure or the general invalidation procedure. If the general invalidation procedure is initiated, the petitioner needs to show that the infringement dispute has been heard in a local Patent Office or a People's Court, otherwise the special invalidation procedure is initiated.

In the general invalidation procedure, the Patent Reexamination Board examines only the causes and evidence for invalidation and the conclusion is not whether the patent is declared valid or invalid, rather, it is whether the cause for the invalidation request is sustained.

The exact steps are illustrated in Table 21.1.

In a word, under the current institutional framework, the patent invalidation procedure has the dual nature of correcting improper granting and resolving disputes over the validity of patent rights. With the constraints of this dual nature, the principle of examination upon request should be the basis, and the principle of conducting *ex officio* examination should be the exception and supplement to it. Regarding the current regulations on *ex officio* examination, there are two points worth clarifying. First, the seven circumstances listed in the *Guidelines for Patent Examination* should be an exhaustive enumeration of the scope of conducting *ex officio* examination. The Patent Reexamination Board shall not perform the *ex officio* examination function beyond this scope. Second, Rule 72 of the *Implementing Regulations of the Patent Law* only provides the circumstance where the invalidation petitioner withdraws the entire invalidation request, and does not include the circumstance where part of the invalidation causes and evidence are renounced. If the invalidation petitioner

Table 21.1 Comparison of the exact steps between a special invalidation procedure and a general invalidation procedure

	Special invalidation procedure	General invalidation procedure
Purpose	To correct improper granting	To resolve disputes between parties over the validity of the patent
Petitioner	The Patent Office, any member of the public	Interested parties in the infringement dispute
When to make the request	Within a period of time after the patent is granted, for example, 2 years	Any time after the patent is granted
Cause of the request	Any cause for invalidation	Any cause for invalidation
Manner of Examination	Written proceedings and oral proceedings	Oral proceedings
Administrative Litigation	The Patent Reexamination Board as the defendant	The opposing party as the defendant

renounces part of the causes and evidence of the invalidation, the relevant provisions of the *Guidelines for Patent Examination* should be applied, rather than making an extensive interpretation of Rule 72 of the *Implementing Regulations of the Patent Law*. Such understanding and application will indeed lead to many unreasonable results, which can only be avoided through top-level procedural changes. For example, an alternative might be to learn from Japan's mature experience and set up two post-grant procedures: one is a typical procedure to correct improper granting, i.e., a special invalidation procedure, and the other is a typical impartial adjudication procedure for resolving the disputes between the parties on the validity of the patent right, i.e., the general invalidation procedure.

Appendix

Chapter	Supreme People's Court Judgment / Ruling No.	Application/ Patent No.	Reexamination/ Invalidation Decision No.	First Instance Judgment No.	Second Instance Judgment No.
1.1	(2014) Xing Ti Zi No. 17	03123304.X	WX14794	(2010) Yi Zhong Zhi Xing Chu Zi No. 3093	(2011) Gao Xing Zhong Zi No. 1106
1.2	(2012) Zhi Xing Zi No. 59	03112761.4	WX14220	(2010) Yi Zhong Xing Chu Zi No. 2023	(2011) Gao Xing Zhong Zi No. 911
	(2011) Zhi Xing Zi No. 29	01107559.7	WX13794	(2010) Yi Zhong Xing Chu Zi No.485	(2010) Gao Xing Zhong Zi No. 1234
	(2011) Zhi Xing Zi No. 91	200620154970.8	WX13991	(2010) Yi Zhong Xing Chu Zi No.483	(2010) Gao Xing Zhong Zi No. 918
	(2011) Xing Ti Zi No. 8	97108942.6	WX8113	(2006) Yi Zhong Xing Chu Zi No.786	(2007) Gao Xing Zhong Zi No. 146
1.3	(2012) Xing Ti Zi No. 29	01234722.1	WX13560	(2009) Yi Zhong Xing Chu Zi No.2300	(2011) Gao Xing Zhong Zi No. 676
	(2013) Zhi Xing Zi No. 103	2006200477030	WX13862	(2010) Yi Zhong Xing Chu Zi No.1837	(2011) Gao Xing Zhong Zi No. 842

(continued)

(continued)

Chapter	Supreme People's Court Judgment / Ruling No.	Application/ Patent No.	Reexamination/ Invalidation Decision No.	First Instance Judgment No.	Second Instance Judgment No.
	(2013) Zhi Xing Zi No.104	2006200477045	WX13861	(2010) Yi Zhong Xing Chu Zi No.1936	(2011) Gao Xing Zi No. 840
	(2012) Zhi Xing Zi No. 57	200510102984.5	WX12819	(2009) Yi Zhong Xing Chu Zi No.1138	(2010) Gao Xing Zhong Zi No. 364
	(2012) Zhi Xing Zi No. 23	200320102652.3	WX14276	(2010) Yi Zhong Xing Chu Zi No.1168	(2010) Gao Xing Zhong Zi No. 1422
	(2015) Zhi Xing Zi No. 7	200820139377.5	WX20200	(2013) Yi Zhong Zhi Xing Chu Zi No.2289	(2014) Gao Xing Zhong Zi No. 1126
	(2013) Zhi Xing Zi No. 109	99110929.5	WX16929	(2012) Yi Zhong Zhi Xing Chu Zi No.272	(2012) Gao Xing Zhong Zi No. 1076
	(2013) Zhi Xing Zi No. 110	99110929.5	WX13733	(2009) Yi Zhong Zhi Xing Chu Zi No.2684	(2010) Gao Xing Zhong Zi No. 383
	(2013) Xing Ti Zi No. 17	01106125.1	WX13610	(2009) Yi Zhong Xing Chu Zi No.2215	(2012) Gao Xing Zhong Zi No. 293
1.4	(2010) Zhi Xing Zi No. 9	200420015152.0	WX12310	(2009) Yi Zhong Xing Chu Zi No.487	(2009) Gao Xing Zhong Zi No. 1114
1.5	(2012) Xing Ti Zi No. 24	02800004.8	WX14134	(2010) Yi Zhong Zhi Xing Chu Zi No.1283	(2011) Gao Xing Zhong Zi No. 784
1.6	(2013) Zhi Xing Zi No. 31	99811707.2	FS11964	(2008) Yi Zhong Xing Chu Zi No.628	(2009) Gao Xing Zhong Zi No. 719
1.7	(2012) Zhi Xing Zi No. 75	99812498.2	WX13188	(2009) Yi Zhong Xing Chu Zi No.1847	(2010) Gao Xing Zhong Zi No. 547
1.8	(2010) Zhi Xing Zi No. 53-1	00131800.4	WX11291	(2008) Yi Zhong Xing Chu Zi No.1030	(2009) Gao Xing Zhong Zi No. 327
2.1	(2013) Zhi Xing Zi No. 67	200610061959.1	FS40583	(2012) Yi Zhong Zhi Xing Chu Zi No.3315	(2013) Gao Xing Zhong Zi No. 998

(continued)

Appendix

(continued)

Chapter	Supreme People's Court Judgment / Ruling No.	Application/ Patent No.	Reexamination/ Invalidation Decision No.	First Instance Judgment No.	Second Instance Judgment No.
	(2011) Zhi Xing Zi No. 68	200710120845.4	FS22835	(2010) Yi Zhong Xing Chu Zi No.2703	(2011) Gao Xing Zhong Zi No. 473
	(2014) Zhi Xing Zi No. 73	200410027344.8	FS40616	(2012) Yi Zhong Zhi Xing Chu Zi No.2341	(2013) Gao Xing Zhong Zi No. 671
2.2	(2015) Zhi Xing Zi No. 21	201110024602.7	FS58291	(2014) Yi Zhong Zhi Xing Chu Zi No.450	(2014) Gao Xing Zhong Zi No. 1227
3.1	(2010) Zhi Xing Zi No. 10	02100209.6	FS10155	(2007) Yi Zhong Xing Chu Zi No.705	(2007) Gao Xing Zhong Zi No. 519
	(2015) Zhi Xing Zi No. 48	200910147641.9	FS42529	(2012) Yi Zhong Zhi Xing Chu Zi No.3061	(2013) Gao Xing Zhong Zi No. 53
	(2015) Zhi Xing Zi No. 53	201110056234.4	FS66342	(2014) Yi Zhong Zhi Xing Chu Zi No.6105	(2014) Gao Xing Zhi Zhong Zi No. 3328
	(2010) Zhi Xing Zi No. 11	97118378.3	FS10945	(2007) Yi Zhong Xing Chu Zi No.1371	(2008) Gao Xing Zhong Zi No. 140
	(2015) Zhi Xing Zi No. 90	200610137229.5	FS36836	(2012) Yi Zhong Zhi Xing Chu Zi No.1300	(2013) Gao Xing Zhong Zi No. 271
	(2013) Zhi Xing Zi No. 44	200510064778.X	FS21594	(2010) Yi Zhong Xing Chu Zi No.1425	(2011) Gao Xing Zhong Zi No. 67
3.2	(2009) Xing Ti Zi No. 4	99219875.5	WX3974	(2001) Yi Zhong Zhi Chu Zi No.309	(2002) Gao Min Zhong Zi No. 202
4.1	(2014) Zhi Xing Zi No.119	200510100795.4	WX19287	(2013) Yi Zhong Zhi Xing Chu Zi No.2209	(2013) Gao Xing Zhong Zi No. 2257
4.2	(2014) Xing Ti Zi No. 8	96195564.3	WX13582	(2009) Yi Zhong Xing Chu Zi No.2710	(2010) Gao Xing Zhong Zi No. 1489
4.3	(2011) Zhi Xing Zi No. 71	00126685.3	WX12482	(2009) Yi Zhong Xing Chu Zi No.687	(2010) Gao Xing Zhong Zi No. 785

(continued)

(continued)

Chapter	Supreme People's Court Judgment / Ruling No.	Application/ Patent No.	Reexamination/ Invalidation Decision No.	First Instance Judgment No.	Second Instance Judgment No.
4.4	(2011) Zhi Xing Zi No. 23	02149132.1	FS15379	(2009) Yi Zhong Zhi Xing Chu Zi No.1096	(2010) Gao Xing Zhong Zi No. 857
4.5	(2014) Zhi Xing Zi No. 123	200610075959.7	FS57456	(2013) Yi Zhong Zhi Xing Chu Zi No.3711	(2014) Gao Xing Zhong Zi No. 1112
	(2015) Zhi Xing Zi No. 340	200480026458.9	FS45152	(2013) Yi Zhong Zhi Xing Chu Zi No.751	(2013) Gao Xing Zhong Zi No. 1602
	(2015) Zhi Xing Zi No. 342	200580043628.9	FS45016	(2013) Yi Zhong Zhi Xing Chu Zi No.604	(2013) Gao Xing Zhong Zi No. 1604
4.6	(2014) Xing Ti Zi No. 8	96195564.3	WX13582	(2009) Yi Zhong Xing Chu Zi No.2710	(2010) Gao Xing Zhong Zi No. 1489
5	(2012) Zhi Xing Zi No. 81	98802322.9	WX13177	(2009) Yi Zhong Xing Chu Zi No.2001	(2010) Gao Xing Zhong Zi No. 642
	(2015) Zhi Xing Zi No. 223	03103421.7	WX20220	(2013) Yi Zhong Zhi Xing Chu Zi No.2268	(2014) Gao Xing Zhong Zi No. 1584
6.1	(2012) Zhi Xing Zi No. 13	02122558.3	WX14143	(2010) Yi Zhong Xing Chu Zi No.1404	(2010) Gao Xing Zhong Zi No. 1172
	(2012) Zhi Xing Zi No. 15	200720033902.0	WX13158	(2009) Yi Zhong Xing Chu Zi No.1681	(2010) Gao Xing Zhong Zi No. 407
6.2	(2013) Zhi Xing Zi No. 57	95194418.5	WX16325	(2011) Yi Zhong Zhi Xing Chu Zi No.2028	(2012) Gao Xing Zhong Zi No.1215
	(2015) Zhi Xing Zi No. 67	200920059107.8	WX19614	(2013) Yi Zhong Xing Chu Zi No.1702	(2014) Gao Xing Zhong Zi No. 2243
6.3	(2012) Zhi Xing Zi No. 3	01274761.0	WX14603	(2010) Yi Zhong Xing Chu Zi No.2005	(2011) Gao Xing Zhong Zi No. 213
	(2014) Zhi Xing Zi No. 89	200420090400.8	WX18323	(2012) Yi Zhong Zhi Xing Chu Zi No.2252	(2013) Gao Xing Zhong Zi No. 1744

(continued)

Appendix

(continued)

Chapter	Supreme People's Court Judgment / Ruling No.	Application/ Patent No.	Reexamination/ Invalidation Decision No.	First Instance Judgment No.	Second Instance Judgment No.
	(2011) Zhi Xing Zi No. 29	01107559.7	WX13794	(2010) Yi Zhong Xing Chu Zi No.485	(2010) Gao Xing Zhong Zi No. 1234
6.4	(2015) Zhi Xing Zi No. 75	200710112701.4	FS44817	(2012) Yi Zhong Zhi Xing Chu Zi No.3654	(2013) Gao Xing Zhong Zi No. 1557
7	(2015) Zhi Xing Zi No. 158	200720142844.5	WX21304	(2013) Yi Zhong Zhi Xing Chu Zi No.3305	(2014) Gao Xing Zhong Zi No. 1198
8.1	(2012) Xing Ti Zi No. 7	200520014575.5	WX13216	(2009) Yi Zhong Xing Chu Zi No.1326	(2010) Gao Xing Zhong Zi No. 634
	(2011) Zhi Xing Zi No. 19	97216613.0	WX12613	(2009) Yi Zhong Xing Chu Zi No.466	(2010) Gao Xing Zhong Zi No. 811
	(2014) Zhi Xing Zi No. 84	99800339.5	WX15158	(2011) Yi Zhong Zhi Xing Chu Zi No.1113	(2012) Gao Xing Zhong Zi No. 528
8.2	(2010) Zhi Xing Zi No. 13	99214371.3	WX8034	(Unavailable)	(2007) Gao Xing Zhong Zi No. 183
	(2014) Zhi Xing Zi No. 43	96194851.5	WX16394	(2011) Yi Zhong Zhi Xing Chu Zi No.2961	(2013) Gao Xing Zhong Zi No. 1759
	(2015) Xing Ti Zi No.12	200720183183.0	WX17922	(2012) Yi Zhong Zhi Xing Chu Zi No.1191	(2012) Gao Xing Zhong Zi No. 1455
8.3	(2014) Zhi Xing Zi No. 8	931000162.5	WX17265	(2012) Yi Zhong Zhi Xing Chu Zi No.1171	(2013) Gao Xing Zhong Zi No. 1465
	(2013) Zhi Xing Zi No. 77	200510000429.1	WX15409	(2011) Yi Zhong Zhi Xing Chu Zi No.675	(2011) Gao Xing Zhong Zi No. 1704
	(2012) Zhi Xing Zi No. 41	96111063.5	WX12712	(2009) Yi Zhong Xing Chu Zi No.1371	(2010) Gao Xing Zhong Zi No. 566
	(2011) Zhi Xing Zi No. 86	01817143.5	WX12206	(2009) Yi Zhong Xing Chu Zi No.83	(2010) Gao Xing Zhong Zi No. 751

(continued)

(continued)

Chapter	Supreme People's Court Judgment / Ruling No.	Application/ Patent No.	Reexamination/ Invalidation Decision No.	First Instance Judgment No.	Second Instance Judgment No.
8.4	(2011) Xing Ti Zi No. 8	97108942.6	WX8113	(2006) Yi Zhong Xing Chu Zi No.786	(2007) Gao Xing Zhong Zi No. 146
	(2015) Zhi Xing Zi No. 156	200710006408.X	FS41041	(2012) Yi Zhong Zhi Xing Chu Zi No. 2947	(2013) Gao Xing Zhong Zi No. 37
	(2014) Zhi Xing Zi No. 29	200710151989.6	WX18566	(2012) Yi Zhong Zhi Xing Chu Zi No. 3190	(2013) Gao Xing Zhong Zi No. 640
	(2015) Zhi Xing Zi No. 362	201010167896.4	FS72420	(2015) Jing Zhi Xing Chu Zi No. 7	(2015) Gao Xing Zhi Zhong Zi No. 1989
8.5	(2013) Zhi Xing Zi No. 31	99811707.2	FS11964	(2008) Yi Zhong Xing Chu Zi No.628	(2009) Gao Xing Zhong Zi No. 719
	(2012) Zhi Xing Zi No. 41	96111063.5	WX12712	(2009) Yi Zhong Xing Chu Zi No.1371	(2010) Gao Xing Zhong Zi No. 566
	(2012) Xing Ti Zi No. 8	200420012332.3	WX12728	(2009) Yi Zhong Xing Chu Zi No.911	(2011) Gao Xing Zhong Zi No. 1441
8.6	(2011) Zhi Xing Zi No. 19	97216613.0	WX12613	(2009) Yi Zhong Xing Chu Zi No.466	(2010) Gao Xing Zhong Zi No. 811
	(2012) Zhi Xing Zi No. 15	200720033902.0	WX13158	(2009) Yi Zhong Xing Chu Zi No.1681	(2010) Gao Xing Zhong Zi No. 407
8.7	(2013) Zhi Xing Zi No. 115	03112085.7	WX16411	(2011) Yi Zhong Zhi Xing Chu Zi No. 2552	(2012) Gao Xing Zhong Zi No. 744
	(2011) Zhi Xing Zi No. 86	01817143.5	WX12206	(2009) Yi Zhong Xing Chu Zi No.83	(2010) Gao Xing Zhong Zi No. 751
	(2015) Zhi Xing Zi No. 353	03805473.6	WX20640	(2014) Yi Zhong Zhi Xing Chu Zi No. 885	(2014) Gao Xing Zhong Zi No. 1661
	(2015) Zhi Xing Zi No. 261	200610000601.8	WX19578	(2013) Yi Zhong Zhi Xing Chu Zi No. 989	(2014) Gao Xing Zhong Zi No. 1454

(continued)

Appendix 251

(continued)

Chapter	Supreme People's Court Judgment / Ruling No.	Application/ Patent No.	Reexamination/ Invalidation Decision No.	First Instance Judgment No.	Second Instance Judgment No.
	(2015) Zhi Xing Zi No.262	200610000200.2	WX17576	(2012) Yi Zhong Zhi Xing Chu Zi No. 1327	(2013) Gao Xing Zhong Zi No. 191
9.1	(2013) Zhi Xing Zi No. 102	200620046588.5	WX13813	(2010) Yi Zhong Xing Chu Zi No.1933	(2011) Gao Xing Zhong Zi No. 833
9.2	(2013) Zhi Xing Zi No. 3	94194707.6	WX13841	(2010) Yi Zhong Xing Chu Zi No.535	(2010) Gao Xing Zhong Zi No. 1506
9.3	(2012) Zhi Xing Zi No. 4	93100008.4	WX11016	(2008) Yi Zhong Xing Chu Zi No.440	(2009) Gao Xing Zhong Zi No. 647
9.4	(2009) Zhi Xing Zi No. 3	93109045.8	WX9525	(2007) Yi Zhong Xing Chu Zi No.922	(2008) Gao Xing Zhong Zi No. 451
9.5	(2014) Xing Ti Zi No. 32	03112809.2	WX15243	(2010) Yi Zhong Zhi Xing Zi No. 5	(2012) Gao Xing Zhong Zi No. 1836
	(2010) Zhi Xing Zi No. 23	91100026.7	WX8713	(2007) Yi Zhong Xing Chu Zi No.190	(2009) Gao Xing Zhong Zi No. 623
9.6	(2011) Xing Ti Zi No. 13	200720128801.1	WX13091	(2009) Yi Zhong Xing Chu Zi No.1356	(2010) Gao Xing Zhong Zi No. 500
	(2015) Zhi Xing Zi No. 171	200780001269.X	WX17492	(2012) Yi Zhong Zhi Xing Chu Zi No. 953	(2013) Gao Xing Zhong Zi No. 123
9.7	(2014) Xing Ti Zi No. 32	03112809.2	WX15243	(2010) Yi Zhong Zhi Xing Zi No. 5	(2012) Gao Xing Zhong Zi No. 1836
9.8	(2014) Zhi Xing Zi No. 34	02812609.2	WX18680	(2012) Yi Zhong Zhi Xing Chu Zi No. 3286	(2013) Gao Xing Zhong Zi No. 577
10	(2014) Xing Ti Zi No. 11	02803734.0	WX14538	(2010) Yi Zhong Zhi Xing Chu Zi No. 2636	(2011) Gao Xing Zhong Zi No. 522
	(2014) Xing Ti Zi No. 12	02803734.0	WX14542	(2010) Yi Zhong Zhi Xing Chu Zi No. 2637	(2011) Gao Xing Zhong Zi No. 401

(continued)

(continued)

Chapter	Supreme People's Court Judgment / Ruling No.	Application/ Patent No.	Reexamination/ Invalidation Decision No.	First Instance Judgment No.	Second Instance Judgment No.
	(2014) Xing Ti Zi No. 13	02803734.0	WX14543	(2010) Yi Zhong Zhi Xing Chu Zi No. 2635	(2011) Gao Xing Zhong Zi No. 531
	(2015) Zhi Xing Zi No. 56	200720120561.0	WX20022	(2013) Yi Zhong Zhi Xing Chu Zi No. 1442	(2013) Gao Xing Zhong Zi No. 2041
11.1	(2010) Zhi Xing Zi No. 53	00131800.4	WX11291	(2008) Yi Zhong Xing Chu Zi No.1030	(2009) Gao Xing Zhong Zi No. 327
11.2	(2013) Xing Ti Zi No. 21	02127848.2	WX15307	(2011) Yi Zhong Zhi Xing Chu Zi No. 1139	(2011) Gao Xing Zhong Zi No. 1577
	(2010) Zhi Xing Zi No. 53	00131800.4	WX11291	(2008) Yi Zhong Xing Chu Zi No.1030	(2009) Gao Xing Zhong Zi No. 327
11.3	(2013) Xing Ti Zi No. 21	02127848.2	WX15307	(2011) Yi Zhong Zhi Xing Chu Zi No. 1139	(2011) Gao Xing Zhong Zi No. 1577
11.4	(2012) Zhi Xing Zi No. 94	200610145533.4	FS31558	(2011) Yi Zhong Zhi Xing Chu Zi No. 2304	(2012) Gao Xing Zhong Zi No. 117
11.5	(2011) Zhi Xing Zi No. 54	00113917.7	FS20574	(2010) Yi Zhong Xing Chu Zi No.1329	(2010) Gao Xing Zhong Zi No. 1117
11.6	(2010) Zhi Xing Zi No. 18	96117491.9	WX9600	(unavailable)	(2008) Gao Xing Zhong Zi No. 308
11.7	(2013) Xing Ti Zi No. 21	02127848.2	WX15307	(2011) Yi Zhong Zhi Xing Chu Zi No. 1139	(2011) Gao Xing Zhong Zi No. 1577
11.8	(2010) Zhi Xing Zi No. 53	00131800.4	WX11291	(2008) Yi Zhong Xing Chu Zi No.1030	(2009) Gao Xing Zhong Zi No. 327
11.9	(2010) Zhi Xing Zi No. 53	00131800.4	WX11291	(2008) Yi Zhong Xing Chu Zi No.1030	(2009) Gao Xing Zhong Zi No. 327
12.1	(2012) Xing Ti Zi No. 20	02123866.9	WX13327	(2010) Yi Zhong Xing Chu Zi No.1729	(2011) Gao Xing Zhong Zi No. 76

(continued)

Appendix 253

(continued)

Chapter	Supreme People's Court Judgment / Ruling No.	Application/ Patent No.	Reexamination/ Invalidation Decision No.	First Instance Judgment No.	Second Instance Judgment No.
	(2012) Zhi Xing Zi No. 59	03112761.4	WX14220	(2010) Yi Zhong Xing Chu Zi No.2023	(2011) Gao Xing Zhong Zi No. 911
12.2	(2014) Zhi Xing Zi No. 2	200410047791.X	FS30895	(2011) Yi Zhong Zhi Xing Chu Zi No. 2876	(2012) Gao Xing Zhong Zi No.1486
	(2014) Zhi Xing Zi No. 123	200610075959.7	FS57456	(2013) Yi Zhong Xing Chu Zi No.3711	(2014) Gao Xing Zhong Zi No. 1112
12.3	(2014) Zhi Xing Zi No. 1	200610006562.2	FS31646	(2012) Yi Zhong Zhi Xing Chu Zi No. 868	(2012) Gao Xing Zhong Zi No.1316
	(2015) Zhi Xing Zi No. 173	200710148482.5	FS47456	(2013) Yi Zhong Zhi Xing Chu Zi No. 610	(2013) Gao Xing Zhong Zi No. 1756
12.4	(2014) Zhi Xing Zi No. 52	200610069781.5	WX17452	(2012) Yi Zhong Zhi Xing Chu Zi No. 761	(2012) Gao Xing Zhong Zi No. 1377
	(2013) Zhi Xing Zi No. 92	200620074801.3	WX18967	(2012) Yi Zhong Zhi Xing Chu Zi No. 3616	(2013) Gao Xing Zhong Zi No. 530
	(2012) Zhi Xing Zi No. 50	200610035815.9	WX14933	(2010) Yi Zhong Xing Chu Zi No.3027	(2011) Gao Xing Zhong Zi No. 667
	(2014) Zhi Xing Zi No. 82	98800051.2	WX14219	(2010) Yi Zhong Zhi Xing Chu Zi No. 1885	(2011) Gao Xing Zhong Zi No. 1505
12.5	(2009) Xing Ti Zi No. 4	92106401.2	WX3974	(2001) Yi Zhong Zhi Chu Zi No.309	(2008) Gao Min Zhong Zi No. 202
12.6	(2011) Zhi Xing Zi No. 17	03150996.7	WX14275	(2010) Yi Zhong Xing Chu Zi No.1364	(2010) Gao Xing Zhong Zi No. 1022
12.7	(2013) Xing Ti Zi No. 20	03123169.1	FS15603	(2009) Yi Zhong Xing Chu Zi No.937	(2009) Gao Xing Zhong Zi No. 1395
12.8	(2013) Xing Ti Zi No. 18	200430067996.5	WX15790	(2011) Yi Zhong Zhi Chu Zi No. 831	(2011) Gao Xing Zhong Zi No. 1624

(continued)

(continued)

Chapter	Supreme People's Court Judgment / Ruling No.	Application/ Patent No.	Reexamination/ Invalidation Decision No.	First Instance Judgment No.	Second Instance Judgment No.
	(2012) Xing Ti Zi No. 19	200410050135.5	WX14008	(2010) Yi Zhong Xing Chu Zi No.767	(2011) Gao Xing Zhong Zi No. 267
	(2015) Zhi Xing Zi No. 61	201030506103.8	WX20444	(2013) Yi Zhong Zhi Xing Chu Zi No. 2307	(2014) Gao Xing Zhong Zi No. 1408
12.9	(2012) Zhi Xing Zi No. 54	200510096351.8	WX16187	(2011) Yi Zhong Zhi Xing Chu Zi No. 2150	(2011) Gao Xing Zhong Zi No. 1692
	(2012) Zhi Xing Zi No. 55	200510096361.1	WX15312	(2011) Yi Zhong Zhi Xing Chu Zi No. 576	(2011) Gao Xing Zhong Zi No. 1691
	(2012) Zhi Xing Zi No. 56	200510096361.1	WX15314	(2011) Yi Zhong Zhi Xing Chu Zi No. 573	(2011) Gao Xing Zhong Zi No. 1695
	(2015) Zhi Xing Zi No. 27	200730147567.2	WX20983	(2011) Yi Zhong Zhi Xing Chu Zi No. 3557	(2014) Gao Xing Zhong Zi No. 1221
12.10	(2013) Zhi Xing Zi No. 68	200620046589.X	WX13812	(2010) Yi Zhong Xing Chu Zi No.1936	(2011) Gao Xing Zhong Zi No. 839
	(2011) Zhi Xing Zi No. 54	00113917.7	FS20574	(2010) Yi Zhong Xing Chu Zi No.1329	(2010) Gao Xing Zhong Zi No. 1117
	(2014) Xing Ti Zi No. 17	03123304.X	WX14794	(2010) Yi Zhong Zhi Xing Chu Zi No. 3093	(2011) Gao Xing Zhong Zi No. 1106
12.11	(2012) Xing Ti Zi No. 7	200520014575.5	WX13216	(2009) Yi Zhong Xing Chu Zi No.1326	(2010) Gao Xing Zhong Zi No. 634
13.1	(2011) Xing Ti Zi No. 1	200630067850.X	WX13585	(2009) Yi Zhong Xing Chu Zi No.1797	(2010) Gao Xing Zhong Zi No. 124
	(2010) Xing Ti Zi No. 3	01319523.9	WX8105	(2006) Yi Zhong Xing Chu Zi No.779	(2007) Gao Xing Zhong Zi No. 274
	(2010) Xing Ti Zi No. 5	200630110998.7	WX13657	(2009) Yi Zhong Zhi Xing Chu Zi No. 2719	(2010) Gao Xing Zhong Zi No. 467

(continued)

Appendix

(continued)

Chapter	Supreme People's Court Judgment / Ruling No.	Application/ Patent No.	Reexamination/ Invalidation Decision No.	First Instance Judgment No.	Second Instance Judgment No.
	(2010) Xing Ti Zi No. 6	200730112575.3	WX13658	(2009) Yi Zhong Zhi Xing Chu Zi No. 2256	(2010) Gao Xing Zhong Zi No. 448
13.2	(2013) Zhi Xing Zi No. 56	200630130035.3	WX18221	(2012) Yi Zhong Zhi Xing Chu Zi No. 2014	(2013) Gao Xing Zhong Zi No. 99
13.3	(2013) Zhi Xing Zi No. 56	200630130035.3	WX18221	(2012) Yi Zhong Zhi Xing Chu Zi No. 2014	(2013) Gao Xing Zhong Zi No. 99
13.4	(2010) Xing Ti Zi No. 5	200630110998.7	WX13657	(2009) Yi Zhong Zhi Xing Chu Zi No. 2719	(2010) Gao Xing Zhong Zi No. 467
	(2010) Xing Ti Zi No. 6	200730112575.3	WX13658	(2009) Yi Zhong Zhi Xing Chu Zi No. 2556	(2010) Gao Xing Zhong Zi No. 448
13.5	(2014) Zhi Xing Zi No. 4	00333252.7	WX14261	(2010) Yi Zhong Zhi Xing Chu Zi No. 1242	(2011) Gao Xing Zhong Zi No. 1733
Total	130				

Printed in the United States
by Baker & Taylor Publisher Services